PUBLIC ENTERPRISE ECONOMICS

ADVANCED TEXTBOOKS IN ECONOMICS

VOLUME 23

Editors:

C. J. BLISS

M. D. INTRILIGATOR

Advisory Editors:

W. A. BROCK

D. W. JORGENSON

M. C. KEMP

J.-J. LAFONT

J.-F. RICHARD

NORTH-HOLLAND
AMSTERDAM · NEW YORK · OXFORD

PUBLIC ENTERPRISE ECONOMICS
Theory and Application

DIETER BÖS

*Institut für Gesellschafts- und
Wirtschaftswissenschaften
der Universität Bonn*

1986

NORTH-HOLLAND
AMSTERDAM · NEW YORK · OXFORD

ISBN: 0 444 87899 8

Publishers:
ELSEVIER SCIENCE PUBLISHERS B.V.
P.O. BOX 1991
1000 BZ AMSTERDAM
THE NETHERLANDS

Sole distributors for the U.S.A. and Canada:
ELSEVIER SCIENCE PUBLISHING COMPANY, INC.
52 VANDERBILT AVENUE
NEW YORK, N.Y. 10017
U.S.A.

Library of Congress Cataloging-in-Publication Data

Bös, Dieter.
   Public enterprise economics.

   (Advanced textbooks in economics ; v. 23)
   Bibliography: p.
   Includes index.
   1. Government business enterprises. 2. Industry
and state. 3. Price regulation. I. Title.
II. Series.
HD3845.6.B67 1986   338.5'26   85-24602
ISBN 0-444-87899-8

PRINTED IN THE NETHERLANDS

INTRODUCTION TO THE SERIES

The aim of the series is to cover topics in economics, mathematical economics and econometrics, at a level suitable for graduate students or final year undergraduates specializing in economics. There is at any time much material that has become well established in journal papers and discussion series which still awaits a clear, self-contained treatment that can easily be mastered by students without considerable preparation or extra reading. Leading specialists will be invited to contribute volumes to fill such gaps. Primary emphasis will be placed on clarity, comprehensive coverage of sensibly defined areas, and insight into fundamentals, but original ideas will not be excluded. Certain volumes will therefore add to existing knowledge, while others will serve as a means of communicating both known and new ideas in a way that will inspire and attract students not already familiar with the subject matter concerned.

The Editors

PREFACE

When I started to write this book, I thought it would be a comparatively
easy task, given my previous work on public enterprise economics *, coupled
with the permission of both Springer and North-Holland to reproduce parts
of my previous publications. Today, after finishing the last chapter, I know
how wrong I was. Writing the chapters on nationalization and privatization,
on piecemeal policy, and on optimal quality, turned out to be as as difficult as
compiling all the empirical material for the applied chapters, and computing
normative and positive fares for the London bus and underground services.
Moreover, not only did I revise all the chapters, I had published before, but
rewrote parts of them completely.

I am indebted to many colleagues and students for comments on earlier
drafts of this book. It is impossible to list here all those who have helped
me. But I should like to thank particularly: Patricia Apps, Heinz-Jürgen
Büchner, Wolfgang Peters, Ray Rees, Hans-Dieter Stolper, Georg Tillmann
and Ruth Watzke for having read carefully and criticized incisively successive drafts of this book; Alexander Löser and Hans-Georg Zimmermann for
doing all the computations of the empirical chapters and for commenting
meticulously on earlier drafts of them; Kurt Klappholz for cross-examining
me on the exact meaning of so many of my statements and for carefully
correcting my English; Maurice Garner for improving my knowledge of nationalization and privatization; Malcolm Fairhurst, Stephen Glaister and
Hugh Gravelle for many discussions of London (Regional) Transport; Mrs.
Lydia Danner and Barbara Zimmermann for their faultless typing of the
manuscript which had to be camera-ready.

---

* Economic theory of public enterprise, Lecture notes in economics and mathematical
systems, vol. 188, Springer, Berlin, Heidelberg, New York 1981; Public sector pricing,
in: A. Auerbach and M. Feldstein, eds., Handbook of public economics, vol. I, North-
Holland, Amsterdam, New York 1985, pp. 129 - 211.

I also must thank the London School of Economics for inviting me to lecture on public enterprise economics every year for over ten years, and the Special Research Units 21 and 303 at the University of Bonn for financial and moral support which they have given to this book.

Bonn, August 1985 Dieter Bös

TECHNICAL NOTE

Formulas are indicated by a number which refers to the order in which they occur within one chapter. When reference is made, say to equation (25), it is always the equation of the same chapter. References to formulas of other chapters are made by using two numbers, the first referring to the chapter and the second to the order within the chapter. Thus, equation (8-2) is the second equation of chapter 8.

CONTENTS

CHAPTER 1   INTRODUCTION

1.1   NORMATIVE AND POSITIVE THEORY

This is a book about prices. The reader may be astonished that pricing can be seen as the central problem of public enterprises. But why should prices of railways, of postal services, of local public utilities, or of nationalized enterprises be of less importance than prices of private enterprises? Pricing of publicly supplied goods is the primary vehicle for embedding public enterprises adequately into a market economy.

We concentrate on publicly supplied private goods, i.e. goods which individuals consume in different quantities and where people who do not pay are excluded from consumption. The reader may be aware that most public enterprises, in fact, supply such private goods. Rail, mail, communal electricity or gas supply, nationalized steel or car producers provide good examples. Therefore, in our context, free riding causes no greater problems than in the case of private enterprises.

If there is such a far-reaching similarity between public and private enterprises, why is a separate theory of public enterprises necessary? The simple fact that the owner of an enterprise is either a public authority or a private authority does not justify the development of such a special theory from the point of view of ordinary microeconomic theory. Theorists who adhere to the "property rights"-school will, of course, dissent.

Thus, from our point of view, the main difference is not ownership. The main difference is the multitude of political and economic determinants of public enterprises' activities as compared to the mainly commercial determinants of the activities of private enterprises. The consequences, and not the genesis, of government objectives and constraints for an enterprise that tries to "make the best of it" are the center of an economic theory of public enterprises. Prices are the best indicator of the consequences of combining such political and economic determinants of public enterprises.

We do not deny that some public enterprises are allowed to behave in much the same way as private enterprises do [1]. However, a theory of public enterprises must not concentrate primarily on those few enterprises which behave like private ones, but on the many which behave differently. The major aspects of such a theory of public enterprises in Western-type economies are as follows:

First, public enterprises usually do not aim to maximize profits. This negative proposition allows for different positive statements regarding public enterprises' objectives:

a) Public enterprises ought to maximize welfare. This statement is the basis of a *normative economic theory of public enterprises.* "Normative" means that the application of the respective pricing rules can be justified by some higher-order value judgements as formally expressed by social welfare functions. As "ought" implies "can", normative pricing rules are empirically applicable. There are many examples where marginal-cost pricing or Ramsey pricing have actually been applied. (See, for example, Quoilin (1976) on Electricité de France.) On the other hand, it must be admitted that there are many examples where prescriptions of the welfare kind failed in practice. (See, for instance, the NEDO-report (1976) on British nationalized enterprises.) After presenting the basic features of a fairly general model of an economy with public enterprises in part I of the book, we will turn to a detailed treatment of pricing policies for welfare maximization, deriving the most important normative pricing rules in part II. The empirical applicability of normative theory will be illustrated in part IV using London Transport data as an example.

---

[1] Volkswagen in Germany, or Elf Aquitaine in France provide good examples.

b) Public enterprises maximize particular managerial or political objectives. Such objectives are the basis of a *positive economic theory of public enterprises.* "Positive" means that the respective objective functions are meant as an actual description of economic reality. Pricing rules of this positive type cannot be justified by means of higher-order value judgements. But they are, of course, a good basis for an analytical investigation of actual public pricing policy. The theory of positive pricing rules will be presented in part III of the book, the empirical applicability, once again, in part IV.

The above proposition that public enterprises do not maximize profits constitutes the main difference between public enterprise pricing and regulatory pricing of a private enterprise. Starting from Averch and Johnson (1962) the typical regulatory pricing model is based on the assumption of a profit maximizing enterprise which is constrained by a limit on the rate of return. Needless to mention, both normative and positive public enterprise theories could also be applied to regulated enterprises. However, models of this type do not constitute the core of the theory of regulated private enterprises. Therefore we do not deal with such extensions.

Second, like private enterprises, public enterprises are constrained by having to cope with other economic agents in the markets and by the pressure to produce efficiently, created not least by the need to finance production costs. Despite this basic similarity there are distinctive features of public enterprises' constraints as will be shown in what follows.

a) *Constraints I: markets*

When selling its output, a public enterprise will be "constrained by the market" as it has to consider the demand side of the market and has to cope with actual or potential competitors on the supply side.

Public monopolies are often obliged to cover all *demand* at a given price, even if a deficit results. Such a strict constraint will, of course, never be imposed on private enterprises which are usually assumed to stop production if losses occur in the long run. On the other hand we should not forget the many cases of consumers left unserved by public monopolies (as they were in the past by the telephone administrations in Britain, Germany, and France through capital restrictions imposed by governments; in Italy and Britain the quality of postal services is being impaired by similar restrictions). The acceptance of excess peak demand in electricity, transportation or telephone services may even be welfare optimal [2].

Competition on the *supply* side is often eliminated if a public monopoly is sheltered against potential market entrants. Such sheltering may be justified on welfare grounds if the monopoly behaves appropriately. Otherwise barriers to entry should be abolished to force the monopoly into entry resistent policies which can be shown to be welfare optimal under particular assumptions (Baumol-Bailey-Willig (1977)). On the other hand, there are many public enterprises in oligopolistic competition with private ones or even in nearly perfect competition. Examples are nationalized and private automobile companies or the small communal breweries in Germany which compete with the many private ones. In these cases, constraints by the market forces must be considered explicitly by the public enterprise and, therefore, by any model of public enterprise theory.

When buying their inputs, on the other hand, public enterprises typically have to compete for blue and white collar staff with private firms whereas they may be monopsonistic with respect to capital inputs, e.g. if state railways buy locomotives.

b)   *Constraints II: production*

In private enterprises inefficient production will always be considered to result from mismanagement. In public enterprises there are kinds of inefficiency which are accepted by government as the cost of

---

[2] See chapter 14.

achieving particular objectives of economic or social policy. In our theoretical approaches we will postulate efficient production by public enterprises, and by private enterprises as far as they are explicitly considered.

c)   *Constraints III: finance*

Today's Western governments usually do not reckon on public enterprises' profits as a means of financing their budgets. Many public enterprises are even allowed to run permanent deficits which are financed from general tax revenue or public debt. The trade-off between public prices and taxes as instruments for financing public supply is the reason the determination of profits or deficits is not left to the discretion of public enterprises but is constrained by government.

Generally, public enterprises are not expected to exploit fully their monopoly power. Public prices that exactly cover costs are taken as an indicator of public-spirited motives. A usual element of public enterprise theory, therefore, is the explicit consideration of a revenue-cost constraint which allows us to model different economic phenomena, such as the acceptance of permanent deficits, the break-even enterprise and the prescription of an arbitrary, but positive, profit target.

Private firms, to draw a comparison, are typically expected to maximize profits with the exception of regulated ones where profit restrictions are applied. Only in exceptional cases, as a temporary relief, does government intervene in the case of private enterprises' deficits. Chrysler in the United States and AEG in Germany are good examples from the early eighties.

d)   *Constraints IV: political environment*

There may exist many further constraints on public enterprise policy, for instance the obligation not to dismiss as many workers as

economically optimal or not to increase prices until after the next
election. Such constraints seem to be typical for public enterprises.
Sometimes private firms have to cope with similar troubles. Maintaining employment levels in public enterprises, however, will usually
result from a more explicit government direction whereas in private
enterprises indirect instruments of subsidization, public purchasing,
and moral suasion will prevail.

1.2   THE PUBLIC ENTERPRISE

1.2.1   RANGE OF ACTIVITY

Public enterprises can be found in almost every sphere of economic
activity. However, looking across countries, there are particular areas where
public enterprises are more likely to be found than in others. These areas
are closely associated with supplying *essential goods and services*, either to
industries or directly to consumers. "Essential" means that they cannot be
cut off without danger of total or partial collapse of an economy. Starting
from an allocative point of view, we stress the importance of these goods and
services as part of the *infrastructure* for producers and consumers. Starting
from a distributional point of view, we would have to stress their importance
for providing consumers with *necessities of life*.

Essential goods and services are almost the same in all industrialized
countries. Hence, it is possible to present a fairly general basic catalogue
of candidates for public enterprises. How many of these become public
enterprises in any country depends on the prevailing degree of confidence in
the efficiency of the private sector, which differs from country to country.
The institutional arrangements which are used to attain the aims mentioned

above vary widely and range from the establishment of public enterprises to the regulation of private enterprises.

The basic catalogue is as follows:

a) *Public utilities*, i.e. energy, communication and transportation.

Examples include:

– electricity, gas, water,

– telephone, postal services,

– radio, TV,

– airlines, railroads, urban traffic, toll bridges,

– stockyards, refuse collection.

These industries are publicly priced in most Western countries. In the United States they are either regulated private or public enterprises. In Europe they tend to be public enterprises.

b) *Basic goods industries*, producing coal, oil, atomic energy and steel. Nationalized enterprises in these branches can be found in any Western European country. The percentages of nationalized enterprises in these branches do, however, vary from country to country, Austria, France, Great Britain, Italy and Spain being the countries with the highest percentages.

c) *Finance*. Savings-banks are often established as local public enterprises, whence their interest rates are public prices. In most European countries there are at least some publicly owned banks, and in some countries – Austria, Italy, France – more extensive nationalization has taken place. Public insurance companies are extensively regulated in most countries, from rates to terms of policies and the calculation of risks and reserves.

d) *Education and health*. Here we may refer to fees at publicly owned schools and universities and pricing of publicly owned hospitals.

After presenting this basic catalogue we must again stress that it is impossible to explain all prevailing instances of public enterprises by reference to such an expository scheme. There is almost no good or service which has not been offered by a public enterprise at some time in some country. The following are examples, presented in alphabetic order: ale (State Hofbräuhaus in Munich), automobiles (British Leyland, Renault), books (government printing offices), china (Royal Prussian china manufacture in Berlin), cigarettes (public monopolies in France and in Austria) etc.

1.2.2   MORE PRECISE DEFINITIONS [3]

The responsibility for public pricing is shared between the public enterprise and the government. Acting for the public enterprise is its management which in this book will be called the "board" of the enterprise. Acting for the government are appropriate government agencies, appointed by federal, state or local governments, or other appropriate public authorities [4].

Because of the sharing of responsibility, the position of any public enterprise can only be described adequately by

- characterizing the enterprise itself,
- characterizing the relevant government agency, and
- characterizing the means and ways government influences the enterprise.

a)   *Characterization of the enterprise*

---

[3] For a good survey of the literature on the institutional aspects of European public enterprises see CEEP (1984) and Keyser-Windle (1978), on Japan see Yoshitake (1973). For a similar institutional overview on US regulated industries see Kahn (1970, 1971).

[4] For example social insurance institutions: if such an institution owns a hospital or an outpatients department, the relevant "government agency" of our public pricing models is appointed by this institution.

The enterprise, typically, is characterized as some entity which produces or distributes goods or services, and sells them to either producers or consumers at a price which may or may not cover costs. Such an entity may have diverse legal or corporate forms, such as departmental agencies, public corporations, or state companies (for details see Hanson (1965), Garner (1983)).

Departmental agencies do not have a separate legal personality. A substantial proportion of their total staff are civil servants and their revenue account is incorporated into the government's budget, albeit, usually, in highly summarized form. They are, however, typically relieved of some elements of the normal system of governmental control and accountability. (The PTT in France, the Bundesbahn in West Germany, the Vattenfallsverket in Sweden offer examples.)

Public corporations are institutions of public law with a separate legal personality, usually created by a specific law or decree which defines the corporation's powers and duties (and also the powers and duties of the government and of any other institutions, such as consumers' consultative councils, concerned with the oversight of the corporation). Their characteristic mode of financing is by loans or allotments of capital (such as "public dividend capital" in Great Britain and "dotations" in France) and not by the issue of shares or stock. Such corporations are numerous in France, in Great Britain (where all the "nationalized industries" are public corporations), in Italy (where the enti di gestioni belong to this type of public enterprise) and in the USA. In West Germany, this type of public enterprise is unusual.

State companies are private law institutions, established under the ordinary company law, which are controlled by government by virtue of its ownership of the shares, whether wholly or in part. What minimum proportion of the total share issue is regarded as conferring sufficient control for the company to be deemed a state company varies from country to country and across international classifications. In the eyes of the European Economic Commission, over 50 per cent would normally be considered necessary. This type of public enterprise is found almost worldwide and abundantly - for example, Rolls Royce and British Leyland in Great Britain, Air France and Elf Aquitaine in France, Lufthansa in West Germany, and the "nationalized industries" in Austria.

b) *Characterization of the relevant government agencies*

The government institutions which control public enterprises vary widely: parliament, courts, ministries, special bodies or particular courts of auditing being solely or jointly responsible according to the law of the country concerned. One may query the merits of parliament and of the courts as controlling agencies of public enterprises, because parliamentary control might accentuate political aspects too much, and the courts' control might accentuate political aspects too little [5].

Whether national banks are part of government or public enterprises has often been disputed. Whatever the merits of the dispute, it remains the case that they perform typical governmental functions of monetary policy and in this context they should be considered as a part of government. Their control of the borrowing and lending rates of other monetary institutions has the same character as other controls over prices by government agencies. Yet they may also be acting on commercial motives. The Bank of England, for example, was founded as a shareholding company by private entrepreneurs. The German Bundesbank often made a profit from its interventions in the foreign exchange markets, in the exceptional years 1981 and 1982 more than 10 billion DM p.a.

---

[5] Garner (1983) poses the problem of who should decide whether an airport should be located here or there. In Germany such a decision, on the third runway of the Frankfurt airport, was actually taken by a court.

c) *Characterization of the means and ways government influences the enterprise*

The appropriate government authorities may exercise their influence on public enterprises

-   directly, by taking entrepreneurial decisions, for instance on prices, on investment programs, on financing deficits;

-   indirectly, ex ante, by appointing the enterprise's board (in the case of partial ownership by appointing enough members of the board to ensure effective control);

-   indirectly, ex post, by financial and managerial auditing; or

-   indirectly, ex post, by criticisms and inquiry as well as by adjudication on disputes with third parties, e.g. consumers.

This book concentrates on particular problems of direct control. We do not intend to give any theoretical explanations of appointments to public enterprises' staffs or of auditing.

1.2.3   INSTITUTIONAL DIVERSITY VERSUS THEORETICAL ABSTRACTION

Various institutions may engage in the operation of the above controls, and the kinds of controls used may differ from country to country. To present a general theory we must abstract from institutional detail. We will therefore characterize the institutional background by one "board" and one "government", ignoring specific details. The board may be thought of as the management of a single public enterprise or group of related public enterprises, or as the composite management of the total public enterprise sector. Typically, our economic models fit all these interpretations. For convenience, however, we will always speak of *the* public enterprise, public production or public supply. The government will be interpreted accordingly as the sponsor department of a single public enterprise or group of public enterprises, or as the representative government agency of the public sector. Again for convenience, we will speak of *the* government only.

Even in this stylized world there is no unique institutional structure for setting public prices. Consider the principal-agent relationship between the government as principal and the board of a public enterprise as agent. Government and board should agree upon guidelines which encourage the board to optimize government objectives whenever the board wants to optimize its own interests. The main problem of drafting such regulatory rules may be illustrated with the example of social welfare maximization. One could think of concentrating the rules for maximizing social welfare in the public enterprise itself. The board then has to achieve optimal prices, input and output quantities in the light of social welfare considerations. But will the board have the necessary incentive to act along these lines? There will be the appropriate incentive in the case of a competitive, profit-maximizing nationalized enterprise working under decreasing or constant returns to scale where marginal-cost pricing is identical to welfare maximization. However, this is only a very special type of public enterprise!

Therefore the aim of maximizing social welfare is often entrusted to the government, which in turn will try to implement "incentive- compatible" regulatory rules to induce the board to act according to managerial targets under constraints formulated by government. Special incentive schemes can be introduced if necessary, e.g. linking managerial incomes negatively with the deviation from welfare-optimal prices [5a].

The above approach shows that the institutional distribution of responsibility for public pricing is a complex phenomenon of decision sharing between government and public enterprise. In the following chapters of the book it will be a convenient basic hypothesis that the board of the enterprise decides on public pricing, and that the government fixes adequate

---

[a] For a discussion of different incentive schemes see Gravelle (1982a).

constraints. Wherever the above hypothesis does not apply this will be indicated explicitly.

1.3 NATIONALIZATION OF ENTERPRISES

Nationalization of an enterprise involves the compulsory transfer of the enterprise from private to public ownership, generally with full compensation [6]. As for the reasons for nationalization measures, Reid and Allen (1970) point out that "most of the nationalized industries were not taken into public ownership primarily for economic reasons, though there has often been an attempt to include an economic rationale in the decision to nationalize a particular industry". Let us therefore begin with the most important non-economic reasons, namely the ideological ones.

1.3.1 IDEOLOGY

Large-scale nationalization changes the distribution of power within a society. Decisions on prices, investment and technology are taken out of the domain of private entrepreneurs and shifted to people who should be responsible to the public. Thus large-scale nationalization leads to a new balance between private and public economic power; according to some socialist ideologists to a "shift in power away from private capital in favour of labour" (Holland (1978)).

Recently the international distribution of power has been stressed, favoring nationalization as a means of countering large-scale private enterprise, most of which is multinational in operation (Attali (1978), Holland

---

[6] We skip the intricate problems of computing the corporate value as a basis of full (or partial) compensation.

(1975, 1978)). Re-gaining national control over the economy has been an influential argument for the French nationalization activities in 1982 (Charzat (1981)). This argument restores the literal meaning of nationalization as an instrument of making the economy "national".

Socialist authors, moreover, sometimes regard nationalization as an instrument for achieving "genuine" industrial democracy. The keyword is "self-government"; and, as J. Delors (1978) puts it, "at the base of the pyramid, in the enterprise, the essential self-government function should be assigned to workers and management to extend the idea of community life". The basis of such ideas seems to be a sort of mystical belief that nationalization might substitute co-operation for conflict and competition, a belief which has an old tradition in the socialist discussions of nationalization [7]. However, even proponents of these ideas know the difficulties in actually bringing about such fundamental changes in the functioning of enterprises and stress the danger of enterprises becoming politically oriented and bureaucratically dominated [8].

The above outline of the mainstream of socialist discussions indicate that they belong to "revisionist" approaches, using the traditional socialist terminology. Nationalization is not primarily regarded as a way to achieve an ideologically desired public ownership of the means of production in a step-by-step process. "... public enterprise might itself appear socialist in character, but is not. For the French Left today, a formula of nationalization and state intervention not only is not socialist but could be a trap for socialists. Public ownership and state intervention may be necessary means for socialist ends, but are not socialist in themselves" (Attali (1978, 36-37)).

---

[7] See for instance the survey of the history of the discussion of nationalization in the British Labour Party in Tivey (1966).

[8] Moreover, there are many alternative means of democratization within privately owned enterprises as the recent discussions on codetermination of employees and shareholders show. For further references see Backhaus (1979) and McCain (1980).

1.3.2   ECONOMIC REASONING

In contemporary Western-type economies both the existence and the establishment of nationalized enterprises have been justified by attempts to show their particular allocational, distributional and stabilization superiority over private enterprises.

a)   The best-known *allocational* argument justifies public utilities by their being natural monopolies. Such monopolies are characterized by a subadditive cost function and by sustainability (Baumol (1977)): it is cheaper to produce goods by a monopoly than by many firms and potential market entrants can be held off without predatory measures. In such cases unregulated private enterprises would exploit the market. Establishing public enterprises should ensure economically or politically desired prices and at the same time guarantee the reliability of supply.

Another allocational argument favors the entrance of public enterprises into competitive markets to maintain or restore decentralization of political and economic control. The public enterprises are conceived as centers of largely independent decision making authorities oriented towards welfare optimization instead of profit maximization. Such ideas influenced the French nationalization activities in 1982 and the Labour Party Green Paper (1973) [9].

b)   The basic *distributional* argument in favor of nationalization stresses the more equal distribution of incomes or wealth which may be brought about by switching from private to public ownership. Most proponents of such an argument overlook the distinction between nationalization, which implies "full compensation" of the former private

---

[9]   The Green Paper proposed the nationalization of 20 to 25 of the 100 leading manufacturing enterprises, in order to give the government an established position in the market using capitalistic market mechanisms to fight capitalistic (and foreign) market exploitation.

owners, and confiscation, which implies no compensation. In case of "full compensation", ideally the act of nationalization itself would have no influence whatever on the distribution of incomes or wealth. Only in the long run could the replacement of private entrepreneurs with salaried managers and of shareholders with rentiers at fixed interest have definite effects on income distribution, arguments which can be traced back to Pigou (1937, 26-27).

The Pigovian arguments hold if all private enterprises are nationalized in a complete transition from capitalism to socialism. If only part of the economy is nationalized, the arguments are only valid if the entrepreneurs are compensated by bonds, the sale of which explicitly is forbidden. Otherwise, the compensated entrepreneurs may even be happy to get rid of their stagnating enterprises [10], gaining the chance to invest in growing industries by use of the compensation payments.

Any discussion on distributional effects of nationalization is, moreover, blurred by differing concepts concerning the computation of "full" compensation. During the recent French nationalization, for example, the first bill of the government (1981) chose a form of computing compensation payments which afterwards was declared nonconstitutional by the Constitutional Council. A second and final nationalization bill (1982) had to choose a new formula [11]. The fairness of the 1982-formula has since been challenged by a study which estimated the compensation of former shareholders to include a premium of 46 % (!) over the compensation that would have made the former owners indifferent, at the margin, to nationalization (Langohr-Viallet (1982)).

---

[10] In Germany after World War II Herr Flick was forced to sell his steel industry and coal mining shares whereafter he successfully entered Mercedes and other growing corporations.

[11] For details see Langohr-Viallet (1982, 3-4).

Distributional effects of nationalization are not restricted to the shift in ownership and the compensation. Contrary to private firms, public enterprises are often instructed to reduce prices of goods which are mainly demanded by lower income earners, thereby influencing the personal distribution of real incomes.

It should be noted, finally, that the overall distributional impact of nationalized industries needs more explicit study. As Littlechild (1979) observes, "the pattern and cost of income redistribution consequent upon nationalisation is neither well known to, or explicitly approved by, society as a whole".

c) Let us now turn to the *stabilizational* objectives of nationalization. The long-standing planning tradition in some European market economies, first of all France and the Netherlands, leads to a heavy accentuation of public enterprises' role in the planning procedure. The French socialist author Attali (1978) concludes that planning can only be performed successfully in case of "... control by the state of at least 50 percent of investment. That is the reason why in our Common Programme in France, we propose to nationalize nine of the main private enterprise groups, ... ". In 1967, Tinbergen, in his textbook on economic policy, argued that "the existence of a public sector of some size is a favourable basis for anti-cyclic policies in the field of investment".

Moreover, anti-cyclic variation of public labor inputs, and of public prices, have often been postulated. In long recessions, however, these policies can be highly disadvantageous, maintaining economic structures instead of allowing the necessary changes – in the European steel industry there have been many situations where these problems have arisen since 1970.

With respect to *monetary policy*, it has been argued that the money supply can be controlled better if a larger part of the financial sector is nationalized. Proponents of the nationalization of banks usually

stress the international financial connections which impede control of
the national money supply and, thereby, of national economic policy.

1.3.3   OTHER REASONS

History cannot be treated exhaustively by reasoning in terms of two
categories only. Hence, it should be mentioned that nationalization may be
enacted for many other reasons, which are neither ideological nor economic.

Consider, for example, the historical explanation of the great 1946/47
Austrian nationalization [12]. At the end of World War II, a great part of
the Austrian industry was owned by Germans. The German management
of those enterprises left Austria during the chaotic weeks of mid-1945 and
the provisional Austrian government appointed administrations to keep the
enterprises running (or to start them running again). However, the subsequent nationalization acts were not only based on this actual occupation
of property which was derelict, at least economically. In Potsdam, 1945,
Austria's occupying powers had claimed ownership of the German property. Fearing that the occupying powers would confiscate the enterprises,
the Austrian parliament unanimously decided to nationalize them. It must
be noted that the Austrian parliament, when taking that decision, was a
parliament *with an absolute conservative majority* [13].

---

[12] For details see Smekal (1963), Koren (1964).

[13] The reader may be interested to learn the rest of the (hi)story. The Western occupying powers accepted the Austrian decision. The Russians did not accept it, but
executed the Potsdam treaty by establishing USIA and SMV as two particular groups
of enterprises under Russian leadership. The affected enterprises in the Russian zone
of occupation were not given to Austria until the state treaty of 1955. At that time
they employed some 50.000 employees, nearly half as many as the other nationalized
enterprises.

1.4 PRIVATIZATION: A SWELLING TIDE?

1.4.1 ON THE IDEOLOGICAL, ECONOMIC AND FINANCIAL BACKGROUND

In recent years there has been considerable controversy over the privatization of public enterprises in countries [14] with emphatically conservative governments. The development in Great Britain is well-known [15]; the United States is undergoing a similar experience in its deregulation debates. In both countries the debate has led to political consequences. In Great Britain, the privatization of telecommunications (commencing 1985) constitutes a decisive break with the principle and practice of public provision of vital services and even paves the way for a possible privatization of electricity and gas.

Privatization means the transfer of an enterprise from public to private ownership, either totally or partially. The actual carrying-out of privatization turns out to be rather complicated, first because many of the affected enterprises are unprofitable and second because the ability of the private capital markets to absorb the relevant share issues is restricted in the short run (Heald and Steel (1981)). In practice, therefore, privatization is usually carried out in a series of steps.

The theoretical arguments in favor of privatization look impressive [16]:

---

[14] In other countries, at the same time, the contrary is valid, as shown in France by recent acts of nationalization, and in Sweden by a political climate which is much in favor of nationalization.

[15] For a summary of the recent British privatization program see Prest-Coppock (1984, 205-212).

[16] For some literature on this topic see Beesley (1981), Garner (1983), Hayek (1960, 253-58), Heald-Steel (1981), LeGrand-Robinson (1984), Olsen (1974, 327-31), Walsh (1978), and the special issue of Fiscal Studies on Privatisation and after (1984).

a) Ideologically, socialist ways of thinking are replaced with capitalist ones, as for instance stressed by Howell (1981). Conservatives, moreover, regard privatization as a means of democratization because of more wide-spread ownership of shares. This argument is in striking opposition to the socialist view that nationalization is the best means of democratization.

b) Economically, greater efficiency is predicted because private sector discipline will receive priority in all planning and actions. Internal cross-subsidization will be abolished, at least in the long run. The consideration of income redistribution or of stabilization will no longer interfere with the achievement of microefficiency [17].

c) Financially, the government receives money from those who buy the shares of the enterprises and expects relief from its obligation to finance public enterprises' deficits.

d) Last but not least, a privatized enterprise might be less inclined to give in to trade union pressure to increase wages. The possibility of collusion of a socialist government, a trade union and a public enterprise in favor of the workers, but at the expense of the consumers or the taxpayers, is restricted.

On closer investigation, some of the above arguments look less impressive. Counter-arguments derive partly from theoretical considerations and partly from observing privatization in practice:

ad a) The first argument is unsound on theoretical grounds. Does democracy actually increase if, say, 49 % of the shares of a public airport are sold to the public? Mostly the shares remain with a few new owners (banks, insurance companies), reducing the idea of more wide-spread ownership to a political illusion.

---

[17] The achievement of microefficiency excludes not only any production below the possibility frontier, but also production along the frontier at allocatively non optimal points.

ad b) As many empirical studies do indeed show public enterprises to be less efficient than comparable private ones [18], one should expect privatization to increase efficiency. Yet, if a government is unable to achieve its social objectives without public ownership of some enterprises, it should oppose the privatization of those enterprises [19]. Accepting the latter argument implies accepting the micro-inefficiencies which result from the optimal achievement of macro-objectives like income redistribution or stabilization. Cost-benefit analysis will reveal when the achievement of macro- objectives is too costly in terms of increased micro-inefficiency and when it is desirable to reduce the macro-objectives which the public enterprise should pursue.

ad c) Given the usual practice, government's expectations of financial gains from privatization should not be too high. It is just the deficit enterprises which tend to remain public. And the potential revenue from selling shares is often reduced because the shares are sold at too low a price. The reasons for such behavior differ among countries. In Austria and Germany the so-called "people's shares" were underpriced to enable lower-income earners to buy shares, so as to immunize them against communist ideology. Again, the selling price may be fixed at too low a level for fear of losing political support for the privatization campaign if too many shares remain unsold. Moreover, financial gains or losses from privatization do not only include the short-run effects of privatization. The government may also lose future dividends and capital gains which may well offset the non-recurring revenue from privatization (Heald and Steel (1981, 359)).

ad d) One should not overestimate the results of changing ownership on trade unions influence because of the long-standing tradition of a

---

[18] See subsection 2.4.2 below.

[19] Cfr. Garner (1983) and Young and Lowe (1974, 204-10.).

well-organized labor-force in these enterprises. Such influence of trade unions need not necessarily be negative when a conservative government is in power. The trade unions might constitute a countervailing force against possible collusion between a conservative government and the capitalist management of the privatized firm.

1.4.2   TRANSITION TO PUBLIC REGULATION?

If government privatizes some enterprise, it wants to rely on the market for the achievement of a welfare optimum, and therefore does not want to engage in further regulation.

This aim can be achieved if competitive firms are privatized. A hotel, formerly owned by a nationalized railway company, and now sold to a private owner, competes with other hotels and the market mechanism fully replaces regulatory activities.

A totally different situation arises if a natural monopoly is privatized. Market forces will not prevent the monopoly from using all allowed means to keep its monopolistic position and to exploit it in order to maximize profit. If the government is not willing to accept such a result it can *either* refuse to privatize the monopoly, *or* regulate the privatized monopoly in respect of prices, quantities, rate of return etc.

Most nationalized enterprises, however, are neither pure natural monopolies in the theoretical sense, nor pure competitive enterprises. Typically they exhibit a high degree of market power, caused by legal measures, by technology, capital requirements, innovations, product differentiation (goodwill) etc. If such enterprises are to be privatized for the sake of allocative efficiency, the government has to abolish all legal measures preventing market entry. But even then, technology, capital requirements etc., might work as barriers to entry, making further interventions necessary. "Like it or not, we have here the beginning of a public regulatory process" (Beesley (1981)).

1.5   SOCIALIZATION OF COMMODITIES

A commodity is defined as socialized if every consumer is given the opportunity of equal access to the consumption of the good or service regardless of his income or wealth. Such a socialization has been suggested, and often applied, for medical treatment, for primary and secondary education, in European countries also for universities and opera houses. The means by which socialization is performed vary widely. Their common features are low price or zero price policy and a sufficiency of quantities supplied. Institutionally, government may establish public enterprises and oblige them to meet demand at very low or zero prices. Examples are museums, schools, and universities in Europe.

Alternatively, production may remain in private hands, but government purchases the goods and reallocates the supply to consumers. It is equally possible that consumers themselves purchase the commodities, government paying subsidies either to the private producers or to the consumers. The financial means for the necessary subsidization come from general or special taxation [20].

Socialization gives an opportunity of equal access. However, the actual consumption will typically vary among consumers (Wilson-Katz (1983)). Therefore, socialized commodities should not be treated as public goods in the Samuelson sense (as in Usher (1977)). In any model it is sufficient to allow the public enterprise to be run at a high deficit [21] in order to achieve prices which are low enough to allow the poor to buy the same quantity as the rich if they ever want to. In limiting cases, therefore, the prices must be zero. The obligation to meet all demand at these prices is part of the

---

[20]   In many European countries there exists a system of governmental health insurance: every income earner has to pay a special tax, the "health insurance contribution" and the total tax yield is devoted to the subsidization of health care. Purchasing particular health care services costs nothing or a small lump-sum fee only.

[21]   In our model the revenue-cost constraint Π must be chosen as sufficiently low.

market clearing conditions of our model.

We should, however, understand the rationale of Usher's (1977) treatment of socialized commodities as public goods in the Samuelson sense. There is a public good component included in the provision of health care or education, supplied at zero or low prices. Such commodities have been socialized following an egalitarian objective: equal education, equal medical care for everybody are postulates which imply

- a public good component, as a normative concern [22];

- a redistributional objective, so as to avoid worse medical treatment or worse education for the poor;

- a merit want [23] component, so as to achieve certain consumed quantities notwithstanding differing individual preferences.

However, we should not confuse the above ethical concept with the reality of public enterprises. In practice people are given the right to buy different quantities of higher education or health care at particular prices. Hence any realistic model must treat these socialized commodities as private goods [24]. Such an analysis does not make any difference to our definition of socialization as long as everybody is given the opportunity of equal access.

There is yet another way of allowing for variation in the consumption of goods which are characterized by some public good properties: we can treat the "public good" components as particular quality properties which are equal for everybody and influence the quantity demanded by each individual. (See below section 1.6.)

The distinction between the consumption of different quantities and the consumption of equal quality allows us to avoid the analysis of "public goods pricing" in this book. We do not consider models which introduce the

---

[22] Cfr. Klappholz (1972, 262-264) who also gives further references.

[23] This term is due to Musgrave (1959) and characterizes cases where the decision of the politician intentionally deviates from the preferences of the consumers.

[24] Drèze and Marchand (1976) take a different view.

consumption of equal quantities as a constraint. The most typical examples of pure public goods in the Samuelson sense, namely national defense and jurisdiction, are not supplied by public *enterprises*. Socialized goods which are supplied by public enterprises can be treated adequately by expressing the public good component by a quality parameter, giving any consumer the possibility to consume any quantity he wants to.

1.6 OPTIMAL QUALITIES

1.6.1 ON THE EXPLICIT INTRODUCTION OF QUALITY INDICATORS

In the analysis of public supply the usual approach has been to define goods of different quality as different goods. This approch may be appropriate in many instances such as first and second class railways, or hospitals. However, there are many cases of public production where the above approach fails to deal with essential features of publicly supplied private goods. Consider, for example, a transport enterprise deciding whether the deficit should be reduced by increasing fares or by decreasing the frequence of bus or train services. It is not very sensible to assume different goods in such a case, x_1 being "bus with 4 minutes waiting time", x_2 being "bus with 4.5 minutes waiting time" etc., under the explicit constraint that one and only one of the above goods can actually be supplied. In such cases, the straightforward approach is to introduce explicitly quality indicators into the analysis. Bus demand, x, depends on price and on a quality indicator measuring waiting time which is treated as continuously variable by the transport enterprise. Quality indicators enter the individual utility and demand functions, and public enterprises' production functions.

Assuming differentiability of these functions with respect to the quality indicators, such a procedure allows the explicit modelling of the optimal quality choice, and of the quality-price trade-off, in a way which is easily tractable by calculus.

1.6.2   QUALITY STANDARDIZATION FOR PUBLICLY SUPPLIED PRIVATE GOODS[25)]

Nationalized automobile enterprises or communal breweries provide good examples of cases where qualities are determined by actual or potential competition between public and private enterprises. Mostly, however, public supply of private goods occurs in politically determined or natural monopolies, without free market entry.

Thus, political and technological constraints determine the quality pattern of many publicly supplied private goods: for instance, equity considerations against too intensive quality differentiation, regulation-induced biases (e.g. safety prescriptions, obligation to cover a particular basic supply), bureaucratic constraints, technological constraints (reducing quality differentiation to exploit increasing returns to scale) and too restrictive or insufficiently restrictive financial constraints.

The quality pattern that results from these constraints will mostly imply the production of only one or a few standard levels of quality, which may, but need not, match private tastes. Problems of this kind are well-known in the case of natural monopolies (railway, telephone, motorways, airlines), urban transport, public utilities (electricity, water, refuse collection), health care and hospitals.

[25)] Subsections 1.6.2 and 1.6.3 are taken from Bös-Genser-Holzmann (1982).

1.6.3   EX ANTE AND EX POST QUALITY

Consider a board of a public enterprise which has to decide how to build a new motorway or a new hospital. It can choose the quality of a motorway in terms of the number of lanes, the width of the lanes, the material to be used; or, in the case of a hospital, the installation of modern medical instruments. These choices at the planning stage determine the overall quality of the output. Once the public investment is made, the general quality level is fixed, although the manager or the politician may introduce minor quality variations around this given level.

Let us concentrate on the determination of the overall quality level, since variations around this level are of minor importance in the case of public supply. For instance, quality differentiation within a given hospital (e.g., first-versus second-class) is marginal in comparison with the quality difference between technologically highly equipped clinics and a provincial hospital. Local public transport offers another good example in which the ex ante decision for a particular technology establishes a particular quality level, whereas further changes in comfort, travelling time, etc., are possible only within a limited range.

In these examples the technology fixes the quality level which, once selected, has the characteristic of a public good in that the same level of quality is available to all consumers and does not decrease if the number of consumers increases. (We disregard congestion effects.) Given the fixed quality level of the good, each consumer can make a quantity choice, for instance the number of trips using local transport, the number of telephone calls and, within certain limits, even the length of hospital treatment. The above situation can be described most easily by using a one-dimensional quality indicator for each of the goods of our model (Spence (1975), Sheshinski (1976)). Concentrating on one dimension of quality implies no loss of generality if we regard the chosen indicator as the parameter of a technologically feasible quality path in an n-dimensional quality space. For practical purposes, it is often sufficient to interpret the chosen indicator as the facet of quality that is dominant with respect to individual evaluations, for instance the travelling time of public transport (Glaister and Collings (1978), Glaister (1982b)), or the reliability of supply of electric current (Telson (1975)).

1.6.4   QUALITY INDICATORS FOR "PUBLIC GOOD" PROPERTIES

As mentioned above, quality indicators can also be taken as indicators for typical "public good" properties of public supply, e.g. the level of education or of health care. Schools or hospital services can then be treated as publicly supplied private goods, where the individually varying demand depends on the quality level, prices and individual income. In my view the above treatment is empirically much more realistic than the assumption of schools or hospital services being public goods, consumed to the same extent by everybody [26].

1.7   OPTIMAL PRICE SCHEDULES

Pricing schedules can follow very different patterns. A uniform price per unit of quantity is only one alternative and, although very common, it is an extreme case. Natural monopolies whose products cannot be resold will typically tend to some sort of price differentiation. Uncertainty and administrative costs prevent firms from fixing different prices for individual customers. However, some standardized forms of price differentiation can be found everywhere in public utility pricing, the best-known being two-part and block tariffs.

In the case of *two-part tariffs* the customer pays a basic fee for the right

---

[26] See the discussion of Usher's (1977) model in section 1.5 above.

to buy any desired amount of the goods at given unit prices. Such tariffs have often been proposed as a means of break-even pricing for decreasing cost industries: the variable charge should equal marginal cost, and the deficit should be financed by the fixed charge, ideally a perfectly discriminating lump-sum tax. Such a pricing procedure is welfare optimal unless we explicitly regard the number of customers as endogenous (Oi (1971), Ng-Weisser (1974), Spremann (1978)).

Block-tariffs define a sequence of prices for successive intervals of quantity demanded. Increasing the number of blocks increases the number of pricing instruments and will therefore never decrease the maximum welfare attainable (Leland-Meyer (1976)).

A price structure which is interesting both theoretically and practically, is one which gives the individual customer the right to choose between two different two-part tariffs, usually a low fixed charge and higher unit prices or vice versa. The theory of this price structure has been investigated by Faulhaber and Panzar (1977). The practice is illustrated by the US-telephone pricing system for local services or by the West German electricity and gas pricing - household tariffs I and II.

All these problems of institutional practice lead to the theoretical question of how to relate the quantities bought to the customer's expenditure in an optimal manner. Consider any customer's expenditures on the consumption of publicly priced goods. These expenditures depend on quantities purchased and on prices, following a functional relationship that must be uniquely defined over all quantities and prices respectively. The functional relationship is not necessarily fixed a priori. We call this a *price schedule*. Now consider an enterprise's board which wants to choose the functional form of this price schedule in a welfare-maximizing way. The welfare-optimal price schedule will not necessarily be linear in quantities. Hence, we speak of "non linear pricing" (Spence (1977), Roberts (1979)). Formally this problem is the same as finding a welfare-maximizing direct-tax function.

Despite the theoretical challenge we have restricted the exposition that follows to *linear (uniform) pricing* because the basic ideas of public pricing can be elaborated best for the simplest possible functional form of a price schedule.

PART ONE: THE BASIC MODEL

CHAPTER 2 ESSENTIAL PARTS OF PUBLIC SECTOR PRICING MODELS

The ideological background of a typical public pricing model is as follows. The approach is basically individualistic, the model being located in a democracy of the US or Western European type.

In *normative approaches* consumers' utilities are aggregated to obtain some measure of "welfare" which can be defined either on the commodity space or on the budget space which depends on prices and individual incomes. In any case, the dependence on qualities can be introduced additionally. Government may attach different weights to the individual utilities, and a combination of government's and individuals' valuations seems to be characteristic for Western-type economic systems.

A similar combination can be found in *positive approaches*. Politico-economic models start from the individual utilities determining the voting behavior on which most of the distribution of political power depends. Bureaucratic value judgements may then be superimposed on the individualistic base. Managerial objectives reckon on individual utilities as the basis of the demand which allows revenue or output to be maximized. Bargaining with trade unions may be superimposed on the individualistic base.

All the above mentioned approaches are relevant to a Western-type economic system which integrates private and public enterprises. Publicly supplied goods are demanded both by consumers and by private enterprises. Public enterprises buy inputs from private enterprises and labor services from consumers. A straightforward way to describe these market interactions are the typical *market clearing conditions*. Welfare optimization under such constraints, moreover, implies some adjustment of public pricing to private pricing, which becomes especially important if the monopolistic competition of the private sector is taken into account. Of course, market disequilibria may also occur, in which case the integration between private and public enterprises follows different lines from the market clearing case.

An additional aspect of the ideological background of public enterprises is the size of the public sector. We could expect the size of the public sector to be endogenously determined, depending on the demand for public supply. This idea could be handled by a theory of nationalization which explicitly gives consumers and private firms the option to decide whether they prefer public or private compliance with their demand. The typical economic theory of public enterprises excludes this problem. The models assume there are public enterprises acting according to some given *technology*. Consumers and private firms are not given the option to establish or abolish public production; they are only given the option to buy or not to buy publicly supplied goods, and to sell or not to sell to existing public enterprises.

Since demand for the public enterprise's output and the supply of inputs to the enterprise are functions of prices and qualities, this could well imply that ultimately the individual customers' decisions determine the size of the public enterprise sector. For the typical public enterprise models, however, this possibility is heavily restricted by explicitly imposing an exogenous *revenue-cost constraint* and by implicitly assuming that public enterprises never go bankrupt.

Summarizing the above framework we have

  – maximization of either welfare or political and managerial objectives

subject to

  – market clearing conditions (or market disequilibrium conditions),

  – the public enterprise's technology, and

a revenue-cost constraint.

A more detailed analysis of these essential parts of any public sector pricing model is given in the following sections.

2.1 OBJECTIVES I: NORMATIVE THEORY

2.1.1 COMMODITY VERSUS BUDGET SPACE

Let welfare depend on individual consumers' utilities. We characterize the consumers by the strictly increasing and concave utility functions $u^h(x^h, q), h = 1, \ldots, H$. Their consumption plans are $x^h = (x_o^h, \ldots, x_n^h)$ where positive quantities denote net demand, negative quantities net supply. $x_o^h < 0$ is consumer h's labor supply. The production plans are assumed to refer to private goods only, as defined by the aggregation rule $\sum_h x_i^h = x_i$, $i \in I$, $I = \{o, \ldots, n\}$. These private goods can be provided publicly or privately.

$q = (q_o, \ldots, q_n)$ is a vector of one-dimensional quality indicators. The individual consumer adapts his demand to the given quality levels. Some quality levels are determined by government, for instance in a welfare maximizing way.

Starting from the above individual utility functions would enable us to define welfare over the "commodity space" by a welfare function [1]

$$W = W(u^1, \ldots, u^H) \qquad \frac{\partial W}{\partial u^h} \geq 0 \qquad h = 1, \ldots, H. \qquad (1)$$

---

[1] For the axiomatic justification of welfare functions see the seminal book of Sen (1970); furthermore see Hammond (1977), Roberts (1980a,b), Seidl (1983).

In optimizing such a welfare function, we typically would expect the relevant board to use individual consumption quantities of public supply as (indirect) policy instruments.

Moreover, quality of public supply could be used as an instrument, as the constraints might directly depend on quality. The resulting marginal conditions would then be transformed, taking into account the individual consumer optima [2].

The reader will have realized that this seemingly direct approach to the topic leads to an indirect treatment of the problem: we would prefer to optimize with respect to prices instead of individual (!) quantities. Therefore we will define welfare over the "budget space", starting from a welfare function

$$W = W(v^1, \ldots, v^H) \qquad \frac{\partial W}{\partial v^h} \geq 0 \qquad h = 1, \ldots, H. \qquad (2)$$

where v^h are the indirect utility functions exhibiting the dependence of the individual optimum utility on prices, on lump-sum income and on the qualities of public supply:

$$v^h(p, q, r^h) := \max_{x^h} u^h(x^h, q) \qquad s.t. \qquad \sum_{i=o}^{n} p_i x_i^h = r^h \qquad h = 1, \ldots, H. \qquad (3)$$

p is a vector of prices $(p_o, \ldots, p_n)$, with p_o normalized to unity. q is a vector of one-dimensional quality indicators $(q_o, \ldots, q_n)$. r^h are given lump-sum incomes, being positive, nil, or negative. If the welfare function is defined over the budget space, we deal in terms of indirect utility functions $v^h(p, q, r^h)$ and Marshallian demand functions $x_i^h(p, q, r^h)$. This not only

---

[2] E.g. replacing $\partial u^h / \partial x_i^h$ with $\mu^h p_i$ where μ^h is the individual marginal utility of lump-sum income r^h.

makes the analytical treatment easier [3], it also permits a more general analysis [4]. Therefore the analysis in this book will be carried out in the "budget space", using welfare functions of type (2).

2.1.2 ALLOCATION VERSUS DISTRIBUTION

The above welfare function describes the board's trade-off between allocation of resources and the distribution of utility among consumers.

We first impose a basic Paretian value judgement by postulating

$$\Lambda^h := \partial W / \partial v^h \geq 0 \qquad h = 1, \ldots, H. \tag{4}$$

Welfare never increases if somebody's utility decreases. This postulate is strengthened by the assumption that W must be strictly increasing in at least one utility level.

The Paretian character of a welfare function with $\Lambda^h \geq 0$ can be seen more explicitly if, instead of choosing a social welfare function, the following alternative problem is considered

$$Max \quad v^1(p, q, r^1) \qquad s.t. \qquad v^h(p, q, r^h) = v^{ho} \qquad h = 2, \ldots, H \tag{5}$$

subject to the market clearing conditions, the public sector's technology and revenue-cost constraint. The individual levels v^{ho} are exogenously given. In

---

[3] Optimization with respect to prices leads directly to the expressions $\partial x_i / \partial p_j$ which can be easily interpreted.

[4] Georgescu-Roegen (1968-69) has shown that corner solutions in the commodity space can be investigated directly in such an analysis. Moreover, individual indifference curves in the commodity space need not be differentiable, only differentiability in the budget space is necessary. See Chipman-Moore (1976, 70-71).

any optimum following (5) there exist Lagrangean multipliers $\widetilde{\Lambda}^h$ which relate to the utility constraints $(\widetilde{\Lambda}^1 := 1)$.

Optimal prices, qualities and quantities will usually differ if we follow (5) instead of maximizing (2) subject to the same constraints. However, after eliminating Λ^h and $\widetilde{\Lambda}^h$ respectively, the marginal conditions on which all our analysis will center are identical in both cases and thus both approaches lead to the *same structure* [5] *of pricing.* Hence, readers who are concerned by the restrictive characteristics of a social welfare function of type (2) may interpret the results as if they were derived using approach (5).

The reader may note that the Lagrangean multipliers $\widetilde{\Lambda}^h$ are always endogenously determined if an optimization according to (5) is performed. The board, however, may influence the values $\widetilde{\Lambda}^h$ by exogenously fixing the individual utility levels v^{ho}. This is where distributional value judgements can be introduced into such an approach.

A similar way of reasoning holds for the constrained optimization of a welfare function (2). From a general point of view the social valuation of individual utility, Λ^h, is *endogenously* determined as result of performing the optimization.

The welfare function, however, does not only imply a Paretian welfare judgement. By choosing the particular functional form of $W(v^1, \ldots, v^H)$ the board can also express any kind of distributional value judgement.

The best-known examples are:

a)   the utilitarian welfare function

$$W = \sum_h v^h. \tag{6}$$

This simple summation of individual utilities has often been critized because it treats individual utilities as equal, and not those variables

---

[5]   The *level* of prices will usually be different.

on which utility depends. Hence, maximizing that sum would favor those who are efficient "utility producers" which does not necessarily imply those egalitarian results one might expect from the board's distributional value judgements. A rich man who gets much pleasure from his income has to be favored as compared to a poor man who is just happy without income. Only if additional assumptions are introduced, e.g. identical individual utility functions with decreasing individual marginal utility of income, do egalitarian results necessarily occur [6].

b) the Rawlsian welfare function

$$W = \min_{h}(v^1, \ldots, v^H). \tag{7}$$

In this case only the utility of the worst-off individual counts, and all other individuals are neglected. It may be noted that Rawls himself presents this idea as only one part of his general criterion of distributive justice. In mathematical economics, however, Rawls views are often reduced to the case of maximizing welfare function (7).

c) intermediate cases

Of course, there are many possible distributional value judgements between the limiting cases of the utilitarian and the Rawlsian welfare functions. The best-known specification of these intermediate cases is due to Atkinson (1970)

$$W = \left[\sum_{h}(v^h)^\nu\right]^{1/\nu} \qquad \nu \le 1 \tag{8}$$

---

[6] Additional problems arise if not incomes, but individual abilities, are taken as exogenous starting points. See Sadka (1976).

where ν measures the inequality aversion. $\nu = 1$ is the utilitarian case; $\nu \to -\infty$ leads to the Rawlsian case. ν between these values allows us to deal with varying inequality aversions of the relevant board.

For reasons of differentiability it is often convenient to restrict the analysis to social welfare functions which are strictly increasing in all individual utilities, $\partial W/\partial v^h > 0$. The Rawlsian case can be approximated by assuming a very high degree of inequality aversion of the politician, for instance, assuming $\nu \to -\infty$ in the case of Atkinson's specification (8).

Before ending this subsection on allocation versus distribution we should mention the particular problem of social versus individual valuations of incomes and utility. If $W(v^1, \ldots, v^H)$ is differentiated with respect to any individual income, we obtain $(\partial W/\partial v^h) \cdot (\partial v^h/\partial r^h)$, where $\partial W/\partial v^h$ is the *social* valuation of individual utility and $\partial v^h/\partial r^h$ is the *individual* marginal utility of lump-sum income. Hence, in general we should avoid economic interpretations of the whole expression, for instance by assuming "the social marginal utility of lump-sum income, $\partial W/\partial r^h$, to decrease with increasing income". If such an interpretation is chosen, it means that at the optimum the politician happens to have chosen the welfare function W in such a way that countervailing effects of individual utility functions are just offset to guarantee that $(\partial W/\partial v^h) \cdot (\partial v^h/\partial r^h)$ is positive, but decreasing with income. The reader should be aware of the complexity of this assumption.

2.1.3   THE CASE AGAINST CONSUMER SURPLUS

This book is based on a general microeconomic analysis because of the theoretical advantages of taking such an approach. Moreover, part IV gives an empirical treatment at a fairly general level. Hence, basing this book on *consumer surplus* is intentionally avoided. The reasons for doing so are given in the present subsection.

After a short, but necessary, definitional exercise we will turn to some particular points of criticism against both Marshallian and Hicksian welfare measures. Hopefully, the reader will be convinced that it is better to avoid welfare concepts which can be attacked on so many grounds [7].

2.1.3.1   DEFINING CONSUMER SURPLUS

Before dealing with particular criticisms of different kinds of consumer surplus we must briefly define them. The quality aspect is suppressed in what follows since its inclusion would not help to solve any of the problems to be discussed. On the contrary: further complicated problems would arise, for instance the particular explanation of integrability conditions if one price and one quality change.

Given the Marshallian demand function of individual h for good i, we define the individual *Marshallian consumer surplus* as the line integral

$$s^h(S, r^h) = \int_S \sum_i x_i^h(\widetilde{p}, r^h) d\widetilde{p} \tag{9}$$

where S denotes the path of integration.

If demand for any particular good depends on its own price only, this measure can be simplified to

$$s^h(p, r^h) = \sum_i \int_{p_i}^{p_i^o} x_i^h(\widetilde{p}_i, r^h) d\widetilde{p}_i \tag{10}$$

which is the well-known "areas under the demand functions" case (where prices change from p^o to p and lump-sum income remains constant at r^h).

---

[7] All criticism below refers to welfare measures for more than one good. The old criticism that consumer surplus can be defined in a one-dimensional world only is wrong.

The Hicksian surplus concepts are defined as follows (again considering price changes from p^o to p and holding income r^h constant): the individual *compensating variation* cv^h is that amount of money received by or from a consumer which leaves him at his original level of welfare although prices have changed.

Consider the decision of an individual consumer in an arbitrarily chosen base period, characterized by given prices p^o and given lump-sum income r^{ho}. The consumer's optimum utility is as follows

$$u^{ho} = \max_{x^{ho}}\left\{ u^h(x^{ho}) \qquad s.t. \qquad \sum_i p_i^o x_i^{ho} = r^{ho}\right\}. \qquad (11)$$

The basic expenditures, $e^{ho} := r^{ho}$, are then compared with those minimal expenditures that enable the rational consumer to attain his basic utility level at present prices [8]

$$e^h(p, u^{ho}) = \min_{x^h}\left\{ \sum_i p_i x_i^h \qquad s.t. \qquad u^h(x^h) = u^{ho}\right\}. \qquad (12)$$

The difference between basic income and these minimal expenditures constitutes those hypothetical income changes that are taken as the welfare measure:

$$cv^h = e^{ho}(p^o, u^{ho}) - e^h(p, u^{ho}). \qquad (13)$$

The *equivalent variation* ev^h is defined analogously, but the welfare level after changing prices is taken as the basis of reference. Consider a proposal to decrease prices. If the proposal comes into operation the consumer

---

[8] Further references on the expenditure function $e^h(\cdot)$ are quoted in Atkinson-Stiglitz (1980, 61). For applications of this function in public finance see Diamond-McFadden (1974). See also section 23.1 below.

reaches a new welfare level and so he is better off. How much money must he be given to agree to a cancellation of this proposal? In other words: the ev^h is the amount of money the consumer requires to reach the new level of welfare at the old prices and is given by

$$ev^h = e^h(p^o, u^h) - e^h(p, u^h) \qquad (14)$$

where u^h is the optimum utility at prices p.

2.1.3.2   THE CASE AGAINST MARSHALLIAN CONSUMER SURPLUS

If consumer surplus is based on Marshallian demand functions it is well-defined only under very restrictive assumptions:

a)   The traditional analysis [9]

Marshallian consumer surplus is only well-defined for homothetic or quasi-linear individual utility functions, or otherwise if we neglect income effects. If utility functions are of a different type or if income effects matter, it is impossible to measure welfare unambigously. Welfare will depend on the path along which prices have changed, either actually in the past, or along some hypothetical path. Such path-dependent welfare measures can by no means be used to compare the welfare implications of different states of the world.

b)   The Bös-Tillmann extension

The case against Marshallian consumer surplus s^h becomes even stronger if we consider a public enterprise which achieves a deficit

---

[9]   Cfr. Hotelling (1932, 1935, 1938), Chipman-Moore (1976). For details see also Bös (1981, 5-11).

(or a profit). If in such a case the financing of the deficit is explicitly considered in an equilibrium model, consumer surplus is only well-defined if there exist particular functional dependencies between individual utility functions and the enterprise's cost function (Bös-Tillmann (1982)). The reason for this result is as follows: The Marshallian consumer surplus is defined along an aggregate demand function. This function depends on individual incomes which, in turn, are modified by the lump-sum taxes which are imposed to finance the deficit. These taxes depend on the deficit which depends on the cost function of the public enterprise. Therefore demand and consumer surplus depend on both individual utilities and the enterprise's costs.

c)   On Willig's "consumer's surplus without apology"

It should be noted that arguments have been advanced recently for using Marshallian consumer surplus. The standard references are Willig (1973a, 1973b, 1976). Willig's analysis establishes well-defined upper and lower bounds for the Marshallian consumer surplus.

For the one-good case Willig (1976) proved that the Marshallian consumer surplus always lies between the two Hicksian surpluses, the compensating and the equivalent variation respectively [10], and that in most empirical analyses these bounds will not be too far from each other. If, therefore, one believes that cv^h or ev^h are "the correct" measures of welfare, one can take s^h as a good approximation, according to Willig's argument. If, on the other hand, one stresses that all surplus concepts can be only approximations, it may be sufficient to show that cv^h, ev^h and s^h are close to each other [11].

---

[10]   This was known before. See Burns (1973, 341).

[11]   A special case had already been pointed out by Glaister (1974) following a result of Deaton (1974): for additively separable utility functions, the compensated and non-compensated elasticities for goods with small budget shares will be close on reasonable empirical assumptions.

The many-good case is rather more complicated. Here the problem of path-dependency arises and, a priori, s^h cannot be taken as an easily measurable proxy for the "correct" but unmeasurable surpluses cv^h and ev^h, respectively [12]. Of course, it is possible to estimate areas under Marshallian demand functions if a particular path of integration is assumed to be given. (Willig (1973b) examines cases in which prices change sequentially.) However, if *all* possible paths of integration are to be admissible, we need additional assumptions regarding the demand functions, as mentioned above in point a) in our case against Marshallian consumer surplus. Hence, Willig's procedure is only satisfactory for an empiricist who is content to look at price paths which actually took place or which he has reason to think are the only ones likely to occur. A theoretician, looking at the uniqueness of a welfare measure at a given state of the world, cannot be satisfied with an n-good analysis which is valid for a given path of prices only. Therefore, we must conclude that Willig's procedure cannot be accepted as an adequate theoretical justification of Marshallian consumer surplus.

2.1.3.3 THE CASE AGAINST THE HICKSIAN WELFARE MEASURES

The "Hicksian surplus" concepts, the compensating variation cv^h and the equivalent variation ev^h avoid the above problems of path-dependency. They are always well-defined (path-independent): at given prices p they have a unique value irrespective of the path along which prices have changed. There are, however, some objections against the Hicksian welfare measures:

---

[12] I disagree with Willig's opinion that correct welfare measurement is possible by cv^h and by ev^h but not by s^h. I believe *all* of these surpluses to be approximations only and therefore no single one of these surplus concepts is a priori better than any other.

a)   the compensating variation may lead to a perverse ranking of alternatives.

If only two states of the world are compared, denoted by "0" and "1", $cv^h(0 \to 1)$ will always be positive if $u^{h1} > u^{ho}$ and negative if $u^{h1} < u^{ho}$.

For any change in prices (at constant income)

$$cv^h(0 \to 1) = -ev^h(1 \to 0). \tag{15}$$

If, therefore, two states of the world are ranked according to these criteria, no problem arises. The individual will choose the state of the world with the higher utility.

However, if more than two states of the world are compared, say 0,1,2, it is well possible that the compensating variation yields perverse rankings, in showing a larger $cv^h(0 \to 1)$ than $cv^h(0 \to 2)$ although $u^{h2} > u^{h1}$ [13]. This possibility of perverse ranking can only be excluded if income does not change *and* not more than two goods are considered. However, the equivalent variation can never rank perversely. This consideration makes ev^h superior to cv^h. For a proof see Bös (1981, 14) [14].

b)   The "nibble paradox"

The surplus concepts are designed to measure gains or losses from economic activities. Actual compensation (payments) is usually not envisaged. The argument is thus based on *potential* Pareto improvements. Therefore, we can concur with Winch (1965) on the following objection to cv^h [15].

---

[13] This was first shown by Foster-Neuburger (1974); see also Hause (1975), Mishan (1976, 1977) and Pauwels (1978).

[14] Some helpful numerical examples can be found in Pauwels (1978).

[15] See also Ng (1979, 1983). Extension of this argument to ev^h is straightforward.

In figure 1 s^h is the area under the Marshallian demand function AB and cv^h is the area under the compensated demand function AF. If the price changes from p^o to p^1, the Marshallian surplus equals $p^o p^1 BA$, the Hicksian $p^o p^1 FA$.

Given the requirement of path-independency these measures must not change if the price changes in small intermediate steps, say from p^o to p^2 and then from p^2 to p^1. As can be seen immediately from the figure this is the case for the Marshallian surplus $(p^o p^2 B'A + p^2 p^1 BB' = p^o p^1 BA)$. For the Hicksian surplus we have to distinguish among different possible paths. If the compensation is actually paid the consumer moves from A to F' and to F and surplus does

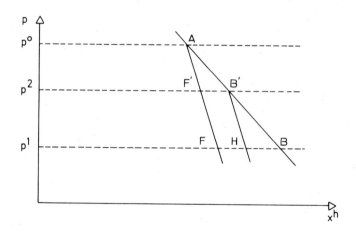

Figure 1

not change $(p^o p^2 F'A + p^2 p^1 FF' = p^o p^1 FA)$. If on the other hand compensation is *not* paid, the consumer first moves to F' if the price changes from p^o to p^2. However, as the compensation is not withdrawn, he will actually consume at B' (F'B' being the income effect). Thus for a change from p^2 to p^1 he will follow the compensated demand function B'H and the Hicksian surplus is increased $(p^o p^2 F'A + p^2 p^1 HB' > p^o p^1 FA)$. If we disaggregate the price change from p^o to p^1 into an infinite number of small steps, cv^h will coincide with s^h. This implies that s^h is superior from a theoretical point of view because the compensation remains hypothetical.

c)   The Boadway paradox

A simple and widely used argument regarding the aggregation of individual consumer surpluses runs as follows: "Until now our investigation was restricted to only one consumer. Adding the compensating variations of all consumers leads to an aggregate consumer surplus. No problems arise as far as addition is concerned, because payments of money can be added without further complications" (Bös (1980)). This yields a justification for the most usual aggregate measures of utility

$$CV = \sum cv^h; EV = \sum ev^h. \tag{16}$$

This simple adding up of individual consumer surpluses has a long tradition, going back to Hicks and to the connection between consumer surplus, expecially CV and EV, and the so called compensation tests. cv^h [16] of any activity is positive for every consumer who gains, and negative for every one who loses. If the politician asks whether an activity is to be undertaken or not, positive $\sum cv^h$ means that, if it is, the potential gainers can compensate the potential losers by adequate money payments and still remain better off. Thus, the simple summing up of individual consumer surpluses reveals whether the potential gainers from an activity can compensate the potential losers.

Many recent critical comments on CV and EV are based on their interpretation as compensation tests. Best known is the Boadway-

---

[16]   The argument for ev^h follows a similar line of reasoning.

paradox (1974) which deals with cases of positive $\sum cv^h$ where nevertheless the potential gainers are not able to compensate the potential losers and still remain better off. Boadway's simplest example starts from an Edgeworth-box for an economy with money (r) and one good (x) as shown in figure 2. An activity which shifts the consumers from K to L is to be evaluated. The new price of x is represented by the slope of the tangent to the indifference curves at L. If every consumer is to stay at his former utility level we obtain $\sum cv^h = ac - bc = ab > 0$. As a shift from K to L represents a pure redistribution it is evident that the potential gainer (1) cannot compensate the potential loser (2) and remain better off: no compensation is possible although $\sum cv^h > 0$!

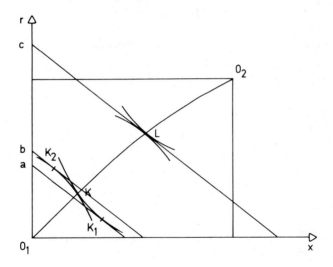

Figure 2

The main reason for this paradox is the following: $\sum cv^h$ may measure gains and losses in states of the economy that cannot be put into practice simultaneously. In our example, for instance, it is impossible to consume simultaneously those quantities of x that correspond to K_1 and K_2 because this would mean consuming more than is available! This objection against $\sum cv^h$ has recently been refined by Schweizer (1980): if cv^h – compensations are (potentially) paid in money there is no reference to the production possibilities of the economy. Thus ranking according to $\sum cv^h$ may lead to the rejection of feasible (= producable) states of the world in favor of infeasible states with higher $\sum cv^h$ [17].

d) . The impossibility of distributional policy based on the Hicksian welfare measures

A sensible analysis of public pricing with distributional objectives cannot employ Hicksian welfare measures. The reason is as follows: distributionally modified public pricing is designed to influence individual utilities by changing "real incomes" [18]. The Hicksian welfare measures hold individuals' utilities constant and presume a complicated hypothetical redistribution of incomes for this purpose.

A model in which a complicated redistribution by lump-sum transfers is assumed to take place, cannot adequately investigate redistribution by public pricing because the effects of both redistribution by lump sums and by public prices overlap and there is no theoretical concept to separate these effects. We simply cannot discern from some marginal conditions whether, say, redistribution by public prices amounts to 1 % of the national income and redistribution by

---

[17] This possibility can be avoided if the compensating payments are defined in goods instead of money (Schweizer following Boadway). The production possibility set cannot be exceeded in such a case.

[18] The importance of redistribution by lump-sum transfers and payments can be seen most clearly when looking at the transition from non-compensated demand in our extended Boiteux model. See section 3.4 below.

lump sums to 70 % or the other way round. Hence, if the redistribution effects of public pricing are to be investigated, we have to make sure there are no redistribution effects of lump-sum transfers, which means we cannot use the Hicksian welfare measures.

Moreover, the Hicksian transfers are typically thought of as hypothetical. In a Hicksian world, therefore, the poor might find that the necessities-of-life are not reduced in price because they all have been given *hypothetical* lump-sum transfers of appropriate amounts.

2.2 OBJECTIVES II: POSITIVE THEORY

There are many possible objective functions which can be adopted in a positive theory of public enterprise. Different objective functions might be used to represent vote maximizing politicians, budget maximizing bureaucrats, and revenue or output maximizing boards of public enterprises. As a general notation for objective functions we use

$$\Phi(p, q, z) \qquad (17)$$

where p is the vector of prices, q of qualities, and z is a vector of "netputs" (outputs minus inputs) of the public enterprise. We assume all these objective functions to be twice continuously differentiable in all prices, qualities and netputs.

The above notation defines the different objective functions over the budget *and* the commodity space, which is a convenient approach for models which take both prices and public netputs as instrument variables. In most cases, however, the particular objectives, as typically formulated by government or by the board, will depend on either prices or netputs. If, for example, government wants to minimize a Laspeyres price index, the objective function can best be specified by means of the usual Laspeyres index formula which includes only prices as variables. If, on the other hand, the board of the enterprise aims at maximizing output, we directly take the output quantities as the only variables, a priori ignoring the supply functions z(p) of the public enterprise. Only a posteriori, after finding the marginal conditions, will we define partial derivatives $\partial z_i / \partial p_e$ which describe the optimal response of public netputs to changing prices.

Most objective functions in positive theory intentionally avoid explicit consideration of utility functions, referring only to *variables which are directly observable,* such as the enterprise's outputs, labor inputs, output prices or wages paid.

Some objective functions in positive theory, however, are defined by explicit reference to individual utility functions

$$\Phi(\cdot) = \Phi(v^1(p,q), \ldots, v^H(p,q)). \tag{18}$$

The best known example is the maximization of votes according to the neoclassical tradition of the economic theory of democracy. In deciding between different political proposals, the voter will choose the alternative that yields the highest utility.

Another type of objective functions in positive theory describes the result of collective bargaining approaches by explicitly referring to the utility functions of those organizations which participate in the bargaining:

$$\Phi(p,q,z) = \Phi(U^1(p,q,z), \ldots, U^K(p,q,z)) \tag{19}$$

where $U^1, \ldots, U^K$ denote the von Neumann-Morgenstern utility functions of the relevant organizations. The best example is the description of a public enterprise under the strong influence of a trade union, where $K = 2$, U^1 being the enterprise's and U^2 the trade union's utility (Gravelle (1984), Rees (1982)).

Last but not least, positive theory can cope with satisficing, instead of optimizing, behavior. In this book we will treat one example where prices are determined by particular accounting axioms based on knowledge of cost functions only. Prices, according to that approach, are not derived from a maximization problem, but are designed for the purpose of sharing the costs incurred among the customers.

2.3 CONSTRAINTS I: MARKETS

We now come to the integration of a public enterprise into the general framework of a market economy. We assume an economy with J private enterprises, $j = 1, \ldots, J$ and one public enterprise. Their production plans are $y^j = (y_o^j, \ldots, y_n^j)$ and $z = (z_o, \ldots, z_n)$, respectively. Positive quantities denote net output, negative quantities net input. This "netput" concept is an improvement upon any approach which deals with final goods only. Products of public enterprises are very often intermediate goods. Transport services, gas, electricity and the products of many (other) nationalized enterprises provide good examples.

The reader should note that the private netputs, y^j, enter our model only through the market clearing or non-clearing constraints. Hence, these market constraints are the decisive link between public and private enterprises. They determine the integration of the public enterprise into the private economy.

The number of private firms, J, is held fixed in our models, which means that the *explicit* consideration of market entry by further private competitors of the public enterprise is excluded. Potential market entry, however, can be treated *implicitly* by assuming that the public enterprise cannot raise profits higher than the costs of entry of potential rivals [19].

---

[19] See subsection 8.2.1 below.

2.3.1   EQUILIBRIUM OF SUPPLY AND DEMAND

The basic model presented in part I of this book assumes that supply and demand are in equilibrium. This restriction is sometimes relaxed in order to investigate particular problems.

In the basic model we have the market clearing conditions [20]

$$\sum_h x_i^h - z_i - \sum_j y_i^j = 0 \qquad i = o, \dots, n. \qquad (20)$$

Any firm's output is used either for consumption or as an input to its own or other firms' production. Consumers supply labor to the private and to the public sector; they buy commodities from private firms and from the public sector. Such a market equilibrium is financially feasible. The net profits of private firms and of the public sector are equal to the sum of lump-sum payments as can be seen easily by multiplying (20) by p_i for every i and adding up to obtain

$$\sum_i \sum_h p_i x_i^h - \sum_i p_i z_i - \sum_i \sum_j p_i y_i^j = 0 \qquad (21)$$

which leads to

$$\sum_h r^h - \Pi - \sum_j \pi^j = 0 \qquad (22)$$

where Π is the deficit or profit of the public enterprise under consideration, and π_j is the profit of firm j. Thus our model implies a total redistribution of private profits to consumers and the public sector. If, however, private and public "profits" lead to an aggregate deficit, consumers are forced to finance it by lump-sum taxes.

---

[20] For the moment it is convenient to suppress all functional dependencies of the different quantities supplied or demanded.

2.3.2   DISEQUILIBRIA OF SUPPLY AND DEMAND

Disequilibrium analysis of public enterprises is characterized by typical institutional and politically generated constraints. The most important cases are as follows:

a) Rationed supply

Public utilities are often obliged to cover demand at given prices, a requirement which can be written as a disequilibrium constraint for $z_i > 0$

$$z_i \geq \sum_h x_i^h - \sum_j y_i^j \qquad i = 1, \ldots, n. \qquad (23)$$

Transportation, gas and electricity provide good examples.

There are many cases where the above constraint may be fulfilled as an equality. A relevant example is where public utilities are not only obliged to cover demand but also to sell their products at comparatively low (welfare maximizing) prices. Assuming demand responds normally to price and that a high deficit is allowed, the above constraint can be fulfilled as an equality. As long as excess supply exists, prices can be reduced in order to increase welfare which will imply an increase in demand until the market is cleared.

On the other hand, disequilibria according to (23) may arise and can be important in practice. Examples are branch lines of European railways which the enterprises are not allowed to close although demand is low, or services which they are obliged to run although it is not worthwhile financially. These examples suggest the practical importance of the inequality constraint (23).

Before leaving the case of excess supply it should be noted that the examples above constitute a buyer's market without the typical prop-

erties of such a market. According to the usual terminology [21] a
buyers' market exists if supply is rationed. In the public utility field,
however, lack of competition on the supply side prevents demand
from exploiting its stronger market position.

b) Rationed demand

For distributional or allocational reasons public outputs, $z_i > 0$,
might be priced very low. To limit the cost of such a policy, government may be willing to accept that demand be rationed

$$z_i \leq \sum_h x_i^h - \sum_j y_i^j \qquad i = 1, \ldots, n. \qquad (24)$$

The German universities provide an example of selling services at
zero prices and rationing demand by a sophisticated system of "nu-
merus clausus".

According to the usual terminology, German universities should be
viewed as providing their services in a sellers' market. However, the
rationing system is built up in such a way that supply cannot exploit
its market position.

c) Mixed cases

Interesting mixed cases occur if demand for publicly supplied goods
fluctuates over time as in the case of demand for energy or transportation services. Covering peak demand would be too expensive.
Rationing demand at all times would not be desirable either. A
compromise would be to require public output, $z_i > 0$, to cover the
off-peak (or the minimal) demand

$$z_i \geq \left[\sum_h x_i^h - \sum_j y_i^j \right]^{min} \qquad i = 1, \ldots, n \qquad (25)$$

---

[21] See, for instance, Malinvaud (1977).

and to tolerate excess demand in periods of higher demand.

d)   Rationed labor markets

Unemployment is an important example of disequilibrium in the market for factors and should be taken into account in public enterprise policy. An individual's labor supply can be treated as rationed according to [22]

$$x_o^h \geq \bar{x}_o^h(L) \tag{26}$$

where $\bar{x}_o^h(L)$ is an exogenously given rationing function, depending on total employment L. This function may even set a consumer's labor supply equal to zero.

2.4   CONSTRAINTS II: PRODUCTION

2.4.1   THE PRODUCTION SIDE OF OUR MODEL

The technology of *private firms* is not explicitly modelled. We assume, however, that the board in the public enterprise has information on the net supply functions $y_i^j(p,q)$ of private firms. This does not imply any particular knowledge of the decision rules used by private firms. In our model the private sector is exogenous and the public enterprise has to accept its behavior and adjust to it, as is usual in a "second best" approach. We always assume private supply functions $y^j(p,q)$ exist even if the private firms are monopolies.

---

[22] To understand why $\geq$ is correct, remember $x_o^h \leq 0$.

The *public enterprise* is assumed to produce efficiently [23] according to a production function

$$g(z, q) = 0 \qquad (27)$$

where $q = (q_o, \ldots, q_n)$ is a vector of one-dimensional quality indicators. By not imposing further restrictions on $g(z, q) = 0$ we allow for decreasing, constant or increasing returns to scale, with respect to the different quantities and qualities.

Special considerations are necessary if a public enterprise is a sales organization, buying privately produced goods and reselling them to consumers or to private firms, at a higher or at a lower price [24]. A priori we could expect the netputs of the distributed goods to be zero as they are bought and resold. The production function would then depend on the labor and capital inputs which are necessary for the distribution of the goods, but since the distributed netputs are zero we would arrive at complicated corner solutions in our models. However, such a modelling of, say, a public warehouse company, would be simply wrong. If we consider a particular period of time, there are some quantities bought and others (re)sold, but inventories also are held, which prevents the netputs from being zero. As the holding of inventories is often one of the main tasks of such sales organizations, particularly in the agricultural sector, the problem of zero netputs can be ignored in what follows.

Defining public enterprise's technology in the above manner implies

---

[23] To produce efficiently in second-best economies is welfare optimal under comparatively weak assumptions.

[24] The brandy monopolies in Austria and in Germany buy alcohol from private producers and resell it to consumers at higher prices. Agricultural sales organizations usually resell products at a lower price, so as to subsidize agricultural branches and/or consumers. In France, FORMA, ONIC and ONIVIC operate as a combination of marketing boards and as a means of subsidizing particular agricultural interests.

several serious assumptions regarding efficiency. In the following subsections
we will discuss these assumptions, distinguishing between X-, Q-, and A-
efficiency (Bös (1978c)).

2.4.2 X-INEFFICIENCY

Excluding production slack by starting from $g(\cdot) = 0$ instead of $g(\cdot) \leq 0$
implies that the public enterprise under consideration produces along the
production possibility frontier only. Points like A, B or C in figure 3 are
considered in our model, points like D or E are excluded. The latter points
are "X-inefficient" according to the terminology due to Leibenstein (1966,
1969, 1976).

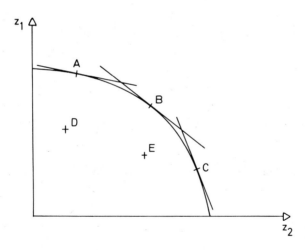

Figure 3

Let the amount of factor inputs be given. Then, X-inefficiency exists if factor inputs can be changed so as to increase the production of some good without reducing the production of any other good.

Explaining such an inefficiency calls for models of the decision processes within the relevant enterprise. We have to consider any single individual within the firm, from part-time blue collar workers to the managers. Any individual chooses that level of labor effort which maximizes his utility. This labor effort generally will not coincide with that which maximizes the firm's profits or minimizes its costs. The owners of the firm often will not be able to solve the complicated underlying principal-agent problems.

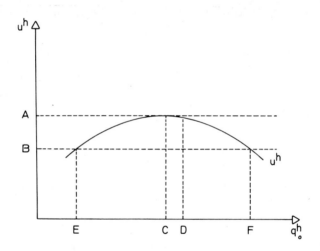

Figure 4

(Explanation: $C - q_o^{h*}$; $D - q_o^h(\text{X-eff})$; E – lower limit of inert area; F – upper limit of inert area)

The main reason for X-inefficiency is the existence of areas of inertia in individual decisions regarding the supply of labor effort. Consider an individual whose labor supply can be described by two variables: x_o^h, working time, and q_o^h, labor effort. The latter variable is a one-dimensional quality indicator of h's labor supply. In dealing with a public enterprise it is plausible to assume labor income $p_o x_o^h$ to be independent of labor effort, q_o^h. The individually optimal labor effort q_o^{h*} in general will differ from q_o^h(X-eff), which would be optimal with respect to an X-efficient production of the enterprise. It seems plausible to assume q_o^h(X-eff) to be near to q_o^{h*} as management recruits employees who are expected to meet the requirements of the various jobs. q_o^h(X-eff) may exceed q_o^{h*} (figure 4 [25])).

In maximizing utility the individual will consider the costs of changing labor effort. Changes in effort occur if the utility increase exceeds these costs. Hence, individual effort may deviate from the optimum q_o^{h*} without any action of individual h induced by this deviation: he or she is trapped in an inert area. In figure 4 the costs of changing effort are assumed to be constant and to amount to AB, leading to an inert area EF.

As we assume q_o^h(X-eff) to be near to q_o^{h*}, the X-efficient labor effort will be located within the inert area. The probability of X-inefficiency of a firm will be greater, the larger the individual inert areas. As X-inefficiency is defined at firm level, we have to aggregate these individual decisions. For an exact theoretical modelling at firm level we would need assumptions on the distribution of the individual deviations between q_o^{h*} and q_o^h(X-eff).

Although Leibenstein formulated his theory for private enterprises, it is of particular applicability for public enterprises. In terms of the above theory of inert areas we could expect X-inefficiency in private enterprises to be less important than in public enterprises, as private enterprises will link incomes with effort more often and in private enterprises the costs of changing labor effort will typically be lower than in public enterprises due to their bureaucratic structures. Figure 5 shows a simple comparison between a private and a public enterprise taking into account the above considerations. Following Leibenstein (1976) we assume a separable utility

---

[25] This figure is taken from Leibenstein (1969, 608).

function $U^h = U^h(Y^h) + U^h(q_o^h)$ where $U^h(Y^h)$ denotes utility from income and $U^h(q_o^h)$ utility from labor effort. In the private economy $Y^h = Y^h(q_o^h)$ is an increasing function of q_o^h, in the public firm Y^h is constant with respect to q_o^h [26].

Note that the size of the inert area of the public firm employee is independent of the level of income Y^h.

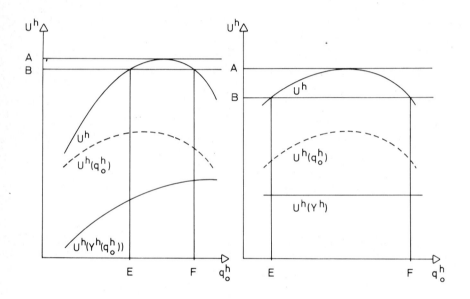

Figure 5a   Figure 5b

The proposition that X-inefficiency is more important in public than in private enterprises has recently been tested in many empirical studies which compare the production efficiency of private and public production. The studies deal with refuse collection, electricity utilities, fire protection,

---

[26] Obviously the same tendency holds, if the public firm links income with labor effort, but to a lesser extent than the private firm.

health care, airlines, and other cases in which the same good is supplied by public and private enterprises. The reader can refer to the recently published surveys of these empirical studies by Borcherding-Pommerehne-Schneider (1982) and by Millward-Parker (1983).

Most of these empirical studies indicate that private production is more efficient than public production. Why does this result occur?

First, public inefficiencies may often be the price of achieving particular *macroeconomic objectives* such as reducing unemployment, or redistributing income. This suggests that the purely accounting view adopted in empirical studies ignores the difference between the one-dimensional efficiency orientation of private firms and the multi-dimensional political, micro- and macroeconomic context in which a public enterprise works.

A different explanation follows Alchian [27]. It accentuates the greater pressure towards efficiency that is due to *ownership rights*. Shareholders may discipline the managers of private enterprises by (the threat of) transferring equities; managers themselves may own equities, which provides a further incentive for them to encourage efficiency. According to this approach, these incentives are absent in public enterprises.

The effect of inappropriate incentives is reinforced by the *lack of competition* in public production. Hence, public enterprises will not be forced to choose the optimum size of the firm [28], nor will they be induced to produce at minimum costs unless they risk losing customers, that is to say, the more elastic the demand the greater the incentive to operate at minimum cost. Recent empirical studies have shown that the efficiency of a public enterprise can be increased substantially by establishing or increasing competition. A good example is given by Caves and Christensen (1980b) using

---

[27] See Alchian (1961).

[28] This means inefficiency with respect to a long-run production possibility frontier. Spann (1977) mentions that public enterprises often are forced to operate at a scale that is predetermined by the given size of a political unit.

the case of the Canadian railways.

Arguments which are perhaps more doubtful stress public enterprises' *bureaucratization* and *risk avoidance*. It is correct that appointment and dismissal of public employees follow more bureaucratic lines as compared with private management. However a comparison of public and private firms of similar size and market position reveals similar patterns of bureaucratic organisation. Nevertheless, attitudes towards risk are assumed to differ: public employees are said to shun riskier investments and particularly innovative activities, and to prefer to pass unnoticed and to assume that errors of commission are more easily recognized than those of omission (Borcherding (1980)). Some empirical studies confirm this hypothesis, the best-known of which compares Australian private and crown banks (Davies (1982)). The counterargument to this view is that if people do not commit their own resources, we would expect them to run risks. There are many examples where the management of public enterprises discounts risks by not evaluating them properly, to the point of brushing them aside as not being serious.

An important task for future public enterprise theory is to deal with the question of how to improve public enterprises' efficiency. The following are promising directions for future research [29]:

- How far can a clarification of public firms' objectives improve efficiency?

- How can competition be improved in the case of publicly supplied goods? Should existing barriers to entry to these markets be abolished? Should auctions of the right to run publicly owned enterprises be undertaken? Can we rely on the mobility of consumers to enforce better efficiency of communal utilities by "voting with their feet"?

- How far does the threat of at least partial de-nationalization im-

---

[29] See Bös (1978c).

prove efficiency? What is the influence of partial de-nationalization on the efficiency of those parts of production that remain
public?

−   How can the internal structure of incentives of public enterprises
    be improved? Could "red tape" be reduced if public enterprises
    engage managers who successfully have run private enterprises?
    Should public enterprises be given more autonomy for their deci-
    sions and in which way? The last question has been dealt with by
    the NEDO-report (1976) and in the discussions on the different
    White papers covering British nationalized industry.

−   Can public enterprises be instructed to follow objective functions
    that imply better incentives regarding efficiency than does welfare
    maximization? The additional instructions necessary to bring
    profit-maximizing public enterprises to a welfare optimal behavior
    has, among others, been shown by Drèze-Marchand (1976) and
    Vogelsang-Finsinger (1979).

2.4.3   Q-EFFICIENCY

Q-inefficiency exists if rational factor input enables increases to be made
in the quality of some good without reducing the quantity or quality of any
other good.

If the technology of the public enterprise is given by $g(z,q) = 0$, then we
can think of Q-efficiency in terms of a production possibility frontier between
quantities z and qualities q. The first best optimum will be characterized
by marginal conditions which call for the equality between marginal rates
of substitution and marginal rates of tranformation, both rates defined with
respect to the trade-off between quantity and quality. Second best optima
will imply differences between the above marginal rates.

There is an important difference between such Q-efficiency and the usual allocative efficiency which can also be characterized by reference to the marginal rates of substitution and transformation (between goods). This difference can be shown most easily with the example of first best optima under non-increasing returns to scale. In the allocative first best optimum both marginal rates are equal to relative prices, which makes it possible to decentralize the economy. This is not the case with Q-efficiency because quality and quantity of any good are characterized by one price only. Hence marginal rates of substitution and transformation between quality and quantity can only be equal to some ratio of price p and a shadow price of quality. Therefore we cannot have the usual decentralized economy, unless quality were sold as a separate commodity with its own price [30].

2.4.4   A-EFFICIENCY

"A-efficiency" is a shorthand for "allocative efficiency". A state of the world is A-efficient if shifting to any other state of the world leads to welfare losses.

Recall figure 3. Points A,B,C can be A-efficient; points D and E are not only X-inefficient but also A-inefficient. Defining technology by $g(\cdot) = 0$ reduces the analysis to points like A,B, or C. The binding technology frontier $g(\cdot) = 0$ instead of $g(\cdot) < 0$ becomes a necessary condition for A-efficiency.

As figure 3 shows, our analysis reduces to comparing points like A,B, or C. Such points are characterized by A-efficiency in production and by the different price ratios by which they are supported.

At this point of our analysis we must deal with the challenging argument that welfare cannot be increased substantially by changing relative

---

[30] In Bös-Genser-Holzmann (1982) we postulate such an explicit distinction between a quality and a quantity price.

prices (i.e. by switching from point A to B or C in figure 3). This argument is due to Harberger (1954). He estimated the welfare losses of non-competitive pricing in the US manufacturing industry to be lower than 0,1% of the gross national product. Some further studies (Schwartzman (1960), Worcester (1973)) confirmed this finding.

The theoretical basis of these estimates is very simple and can be shown by a diagram, as Harberger did.

DD is the market demand function and AC represents constant average costs. z is the output of the particular good (no netput concept is applied in this context). The competitive equilibrium is point C; the equilibrium price OE. The monopolist increases his price to OF which leads to lower demand (point A).

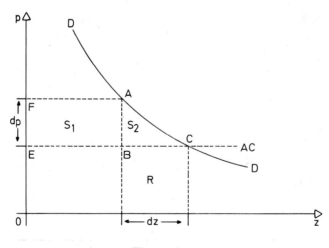

Figure 6

The increased price reduces consumer surplus by S_1 and S_2. However S_1 represents an increase of producer surplus and therefore is not a loss for the society, whereas S_2 is a deadweight loss. R represents resources released by the monopoly. R is not a welfare loss *if* we assume full employment, which means that the resources are simply shifted to other branches of production.

Thus, according to Harberger, only S_2 is a welfare loss. If the demand function is linearly approximated between A and C this loss can be measured by the "little triangle" ABC as

$$\frac{dp \cdot dz}{2}. \tag{28}$$

Added up over all goods and divided by gross national product, this formula can be transformed into

$$L = \frac{1}{2} \cdot \sum_i \left(\frac{dp_i}{p_i} \right)^2 \cdot | \varepsilon_{ii} | \cdot w_i \tag{29}$$

where w_i is the revenue of good i as a percentage of gross national product. Since Harberger assumed the direct-price elasticities of demand ε_{ii} to be equal to -1 in all branches, his low estimates for welfare losses are not surprising.

Because of the ideological significance of the question, Harberger's results have been attacked and discussed vigorously. Recent contributions, the best known of which are due to Bergson (1973) and Cowling-Mueller (1978), contradict Harberger's hypotheses regarding the quantitative importance of allocative inefficiency.

The main points of criticism of the Harberger approach are:

a) The estimation of equilibrium prices for the purpose of comparison, as performed by Harberger, is dubious. He starts from empirical estimations of sales and of rates of profit on capital of the manufacturing industry. Assuming average costs to be constant in the long run, he defines any deviation from the "normal" (=average) rate of profit on capital as a misallocation. The equilibrium prices, then, are given by cost, defined to include these normal profits. This means an underestimation of dp because the average rate of profit takes into account all monopoly profits!

b) The price elasticity of demand and the price change dp are fixed independently of each other. However if the monopolists in question actually have maximized their profits, the identity of marginal revenue and marginal costs implies $(p_i - C_i)/p_i = -1/\varepsilon_{ii}$ where C_i can be equated with the estimation of the competitive price level. Estimating elasticities in this manner typically leads to values that exceed those accepted by Harberger. This again results in an underestimation bias by Harberger (Kamerschen (1966), Cowling-Mueller (1978)). Of course, this is correct only if the firms investigated maximized their profits, which is questionable for some oligopolistic markets (Scherer (1980, 462)).

c) Harberger assumed a single demand elasticity for the monopolistic sector $(\varepsilon = -1)$ [31] and computed dp-values for whole industries, not for single firms. As Bergson (1973) stressed, the welfare losses accrue for every particular product and as disaggregated elasticities typically exceed aggregated ones, this is a further reason for supposing that Harberger underestimated welfare losses due to monopolies.

d) The costs of the acquisition of monopoly power also are neglected by Harberger (Posner (1975) following Tullock (1967)). Empirical studies typically consider this point by adding advertising expenditures to the monopoly profits and by taking S_2 and S_1 as welfare losses: all monopoly profits are redefined as costs and thus as welfare losses of monopolistic market structure [32].

---

[31] Although monopolistic profit maxima are only well-defined for $\varepsilon_{ii} < -1$.

[32] This is quite interesting from the ideological point of view. According to Harberger S_1 means redistribution only and thus monopoly is distributionally important but at the same time allocationally unimportant. According to Posner S_1 means additional costs

e) Harberger dealt with all goods as if they were final goods. If some of the goods are intermediate goods, the welfare loss is increased because the relevant "competitive prices" of the final good have to be lowered [33] due to potentially cheaper inputs. This means that there are additional welfare losses at the final good stage *and* the welfare losses at the intermediate good stage. This argument was mainly presented by Foster (1976) and Scherer (1980).

f) Of course, the assumption of full employment, which allows us to neglect the rectangle R, may be questioned as well, thus raising the issue of the merits of the partial equilibrium approach of Harberger's analysis.

Taking into account these points, Cowling and Mueller (1978) computed monopoly welfare losses for the UK at between 3% and 7% of the Gross Corporate Product of the firms in their sample. For the USA the figures were 3% to 14%. If Bergson's (1973) "simulation" analyses are reduced to the empirically significant values of elasticities (=substitution elasticities between − 4 and − 8), his computations reveal welfare losses between 0,6% and 15% of Gross Domestic Product [34].

The above investigations suggest that the quantitative importance of allocative efficiency is considerably larger than many economists believed for the past two decades. Thus there is good reason for viewing the problems of allocative efficiency as the center of an economic theory of public enterprise.

---

and not profits and thus monopoly is distributionally unimportant but at the same time allocationally important.

[33] Harberger's strange estimation of "competitive prices" (see point (a) above) may under certain circumstances lead to results that point in the opposite direction. See Scherer (1980, 463).

[34] On the other hand Scherer (1980, 464), ignoring points (c) and (d) in the text above, still believes that monopoly welfare losses are rather small, namely between 0,5% and 2% of US Gross National Product, where estimates nearer the lower bound "inspire more confidence".

2.4.5 EFFICIENCY AND COST MINIMIZATION [35)]

The technology frontier $g(z) = 0$ is defined on quantities of netputs, and does not depend on prices. Costs, on the other hand, by definition depend on input prices. Therefore it is impossible to describe problems of cost minimization by using the technology frontier only. Cost functions are defined in such a way that efficiency is necessary but not sufficient for cost minimization.

The inclusion of prices is not the only decisive distinction between the technology frontier and the cost function. The technology can be defined over netput quantities, the cost function can be defined only if inputs and outputs are separated. Therefore, for the following analysis we distinguish labor input $z_o < 0$, other inputs $z_k^- \leq 0$ and outputs $z_k^+ \geq 0$.

The minimum cost of efficient production is derived from the optimization approach

$$\min_{z_o, z_k^-} \mathcal{L} = -p_o z_o - \sum_{k \neq 0} p_k^- z_k^-$$
$$\text{subject to} \tag{30}$$
$$g(z_o, z^-, z^+) = 0 \qquad (\lambda)$$

where λ is the Lagrangean multiplier of the technology constraint.

The resulting marginal conditions

$$- p_o = \lambda(\partial g/\partial z_o)$$
$$- p_k^- = \lambda(\partial g/\partial z_k^-) \tag{31}$$

can be solved to obtain factor demands as functions of outputs and factor prices. These can be used to obtain the cost function

---

[35)] This subsection follows Peters (1985b).

$$C = -p_o z_o^*(z^+, p_o, p^-) \quad - \quad \sum_k p_k z_k^{-*}(z^+, p_o, p^-). \qquad (32)$$

Marginal costs, along this cost function, are defined as

$$C_i := \frac{\partial C}{\partial z_i^+} = -p_o \frac{\partial z_o}{\partial z_i^+} - \sum_{k \neq 0} p_k \frac{\partial z_k^-}{\partial z_i^+}. \qquad (33)$$

As this definition of a cost function implies the validity of the marginal conditions (31), we can substitute into (33) to obtain

$$C_i = \lambda \left(\frac{\partial g}{\partial z_o} \cdot \frac{\partial z_o}{\partial z_i^+} + \sum_{k \neq 0} \frac{\partial g}{\partial z_k^-} \frac{\partial z_k^-}{\partial z_i^+} \right). \qquad (34)$$

From the technology

$$g\big(z_o(z^+, p_o, p^-), z^-(z^+, p_o, p^-), z^+\big) = 0 \qquad (35)$$

we obtain for efficient output changes

$$\frac{\partial g}{\partial z_o} \frac{\partial z_o}{\partial z_i^+} + \sum_{k \neq 0} \frac{\partial g}{\partial z_k^-} \cdot \frac{\partial z_k^-}{\partial z_i^+} + \frac{\partial g}{\partial z_i^+} = 0 \qquad (36)$$

which can be substituted into (34):

$$C_i = -\lambda \frac{\partial g}{\partial z_i^+}. \qquad (37)$$

From (31) we have that $-\lambda = p_o / (\partial g / \partial z_o)$ and therefore marginal costs are given by

$$C_i = p_o \frac{\partial g / \partial z_i^+}{\partial g / \partial z_o} = \frac{\partial g / \partial z_i^+}{\partial g / \partial z_o} \qquad (38)$$

because of $p_o = 1$.

Equation (38) is valid if and only if costs have been minimized, implying the marginal rates of input substitution must be equal to input prices, as follows from (31), considering $p_o = 1$

$$p_k^- = \frac{\partial g/\partial z_k^-}{\partial g/\partial z_o}. \tag{39}$$

If condition (39) is not fulfilled, there is no equality between C_i and the marginal rate of transformation $(\partial g/\partial z_k^+)/(\partial g/\partial z_o)$.

This result is very important because in the Boiteux model, to be described in chapter 3, the above marginal rate of transformation is taken as a proxy for marginal costs. We denote this proxy by c_i, to distinguish it clearly from C_i,

$$c_i := \frac{\partial g/\partial z_i^+}{\partial g/\partial z_o}. \tag{40}$$

Equation (40) is always valid. c_i and C_i coincide if the public enterprise operates at minimum cost, applying (39)[36]. If, however, the public enterprise does not adapt factor inputs to given factor prices in a cost-minimizing way, we obtain

$$\frac{\partial g/\partial z_i^+}{\partial g/\partial z_o} \neq C_i. \tag{41}$$

The same deviation of c_i from C_i prevails if the public enterprise sets input prices which are not equal to the respective marginal rates of factor substitution.

---

[36] Cfr. Boiteux (1956; 1971, 234-239).

2.4.6   LONG-RUN VERSUS SHORT-RUN INVESTIGATIONS

Until now we have not dealt explicitly with the time horizon for which g(z) is assumed to hold. This time horizon matters for the resulting pricing structures. The longer the horizon the more factors of production are variable. In the long run *every* factor of production is variable.

Let g(z) be taken to hold for such a long-run time horizon. Then the dual approach to technology, looking at the monetary costs of the efficient production inputs, leads to *long-run cost functions*. By definition these functions imply the efficient combination of variable inputs, capital stocks and those other inputs whose variation requires time. In other words, the size of the firm is always efficient.

The alternative approach defines g(z) to hold for a short interval of time only. Then some factors of production must be accepted as fixed. The dual approach leads to *short-run cost functions*.

According to the time horizon chosen, long-run and short-run total, marginal and average costs will typically differ. They will coincide only if, for some given output vector $z^+ > 0$, the short-run cost function is applied to a firm which happens to be of optimal size with respect to z^+.

Whether g(z) in the long-run sense or in the short-run sense should be applied is easy to see.

If the optimal capacity can be chosen freely, it is always preferable to choose g(z) in the long-run sense. The reason is simple: for any given vector of outputs, long-run total costs can never exceed short-run total costs, the short-run cost minimization problem being just a constrained version of the long-run cost minimization problem (Varian (1978, 27)).

g(z) in the short-run sense is the appropriate choice for investigating the optimal adjustment to a given structure of fixed factors of production.

The above problems have been discussed extensively in the empirical literature on the topic, and there have been many misunderstandings, as shown in section 24.4 below.

2.5   CONSTRAINTS III: FINANCE

2.5.1   THE GENERAL CONCEPT

Let the public enterprise be restricted by a *revenue-cost constraint*

$$\sum_{i=o}^{n} p_i z_i = \Pi \qquad \Pi \gtreqless 0. \tag{42}$$

$\Pi = 0$ implies break-even pricing; $\Pi < 0$ determines a deficit; $\Pi > 0$ requires public sector profits. Of course, there exist lower and upper bounds for Π. The lowest Π that can be found in practice will correspond to zero tariffs of the public outputs. The highest possible Π corresponds to profit maximizing behavior of the public sector.

Assuming a binding constraint for all cases of Π implies a particular view of the objective of public pricing which may not be familar to the American reader. Let us distinguish two cases using the example of welfare maximization:

- Π exceeds or equals the unconstrained welfare optimal revenue-cost difference. Then an inequality constraint $\sum p_i z_i \geq \Pi$ would be binding and without loss of generality we can assume a priori an equality constraint as is done in (42).

- Π falls below this critical value. In this case, an inequality constraint is not binding. However it may well be possible that, for distributional or other reasons, the politician wants some institutions to follow a policy that leads to such a low Π. Museums

or universities or schools provide examples where it makes sense
not to follow a zero-tariff policy but to fix a Π that is below the
unconstrained welfare optimal value. If, because of their budgetary constraints, the German states (Länder) had to introduce
school fees or university fees, they would certainly choose fees below the unconstrained welfare optimal ones! And these cases can
be treated nicely by assuming an equality constraint as in (42).

In a most general formulation the revenue-cost constraint may depend
on particular prices and qualities, public sector netputs and a vector ρ of
other variables:

$$\Pi = \Pi(p, q, z, \rho). \tag{43}$$

The values of ρ are exogenously given and the public sector has to
adjust to them. Once again, this is typical of a second-best approach. The
fixing of ρ may be due to ideological motives regarding the desired size
of the public sector, to political fears of losing votes because of high public
sector deficits or to economic motives, i.e. opportunity costs of public sector
deficits as compared with alternative uses of resources in the private sector.

To avoid complicated expressions in the marginal conditions of our
model, all derivations in this book are restricted to the following special
cases:

a)

$$\Pi = \Pi(z, \rho), \tag{44}$$

where the inputs are restricted to labor and capital only and it is
assumed that factor prices are given and other prices and qualities
do not to enter the profit constraint. Such a constraint includes profit
limitations that result from fixing a fair return on investment or a
fair profit per unit of output.

b)

$$\Pi = \Pi^o \tag{45}$$

where Π^o is an exogenously fixed value.

Restricting the analysis to the above two cases enables us to skip over many other possible types of revenue-cost constraints which could be analyzed if we started from the general constraint (43). The following two subsections should give the reader an impression of some interesting alternatives. How the relevant marginal conditions have to be changed in the case of these generalizations may be left as an exercise.

2.5.2 AN ALTERNATIVE CONCEPT[37]

Regulatory boards often advise public enterprises to set prices in such a way that a particular percentage of costs is covered. Let us rewrite the production function $g(z) = g(z^- + z^+)$, where $z_i^- = min(0, z_i)$ denote inputs and $z_i^+ = max(0, z_i)$ outputs. Now assume the following revenue-cost constraint

$$R := \sum_{i=o}^{n} p_i z_i^+ = -s \sum_{i=o}^{n} p_i z_i^- =: sC \qquad s > 0 \tag{46}$$

where R is revenue and C is total costs [38].

It has often been overlooked that there are many forms of regulatory control based on some variant of this constraint.

Consider first the case of $0 < s < 1$ where an enterprise is instructed to cover a percentage s of its costs by selling its products, whereas the deficit

---

[37] This subsection is taken from Bös-Tillmann (1983).

[38] It can be seen easily that (46) is a special case of (43).

(1-s) C is financed from elsewhere. Such a regulation typically is imposed on enterprises facing stagnating or declining demand, or on enterprises which are required to sell their products at low prices because of "merit wants" considerations. In both cases it makes sense to define the constraint as an equality: the stagnating industry must recover at least s C from revenues and most probably will not be able to recover more; the merit industry should not recover more than s C but the deficit must not exceed (1-s) C either.

A well known example of the declining market case is Amtrak, which was required to cover 44 percent of operating expenses from fares by the end of the fiscal year 1982 and 50 percent by 1985 (Amtrak Reorganization Act (1979)).

Different institutional models are available for interpreting particular problems of constraint (46) in the case of $0 < s < 1$. The "matching grant" aspect, to use a fiscal federalist term [39], stresses the particular incentive structures of the underlying principal agent relation: what percentage of costs should an enterprise be allowed to achieve best the principal's objectives, taking into account the expected reactions of the agent? The "mixed bureau" aspect, to use a term of Niskanen (1971), considers the enterprise as a bureaucratic entity administering a budget which is financed partly by selling its output and partly by a grant sponsoring authority.

Second, let us *consider the case of s = 1*, the break-even enterprise. Constraint (46) immediately lends itself to an interpretation of the enterprise's behavior when it follows a full cost pricing principle, where total costs can be distributed among the different outputs according to the regulated enterprise's objectives. Moreover, we can interpret the constraint (46) as the simplest form of an adjustment clause [40], as it allows the enterprise

---

[39] Under particular institutional conditions (1-s) C may even be a matching grant in the strict fiscal federalist terminology; e.g., if a federal or state government gives a grant of (1-s) C to a particular local public utility.

[40] See Schmalensee (1979, 121).

simply to react to cost increases by price increases without explicitly asking for a regulatory hearing.

The third interesting case is $s > 1$, the "mark up on cost" or "cost plus" regulation, one of the better-known procedures of government control (see e.g. Bailey-Malone (1970), Bailey (1973)). Although symmetric in its treatment of inputs, such a regulation has been criticized mostly because it may imply incentives for firms to waste resources (depending on the firms' objectives and on the elasticities of demand).

There are many modifications of the basic formula (46) which are mostly designed to deal with different unwanted incentive or disincentive effects of such a constraint. These refinements cannot be treated here in detail.

2.5.3   ON THE OPPORTUNITY COSTS OF FINANCING DEFICITS

The financing of deficits of a public enterprise [41] leads to reduced private consumption and/or private investment. Reducing private investment leads to reduced future consumption. If the rate of return on private investments exceeds the social rate of time preference that is used to discount future consumption, the social evaluation of a unit of reduced investment will exceed that of a unit of reduced consumption. This case of higher opportunity costs (higher shadow prices) of reduced investment is the usual one in practice and turns out to be a typical second-best constraint of public enterprise pricing.

If the production of a public enterprise leads to a deficit, the opportunity costs of such a deficit will depend on the ratio of reduced investment to reduced consumption. This ratio, in turn, will depend on the share of tax or debt financing and on the incidence on consumption and investment

---

[41]   Cfr. Feldstein (1974).

of these methods of financing.

The consequences of different kinds of financing on pricing policy can best be shown if, in a simple model, we start from the assumption that social costs are proportional to the deficit: social costs $= a \sum p_i z_i > 0$. The multiplier $a < 0$ depends on the method of financing the deficit (which affects the extent of the reduction of private investment).

The above considerations can be taken into account when defining the revenue-cost constraint of a public deficit enterprise, $\sum p_i z_i < 0$. The straightforward policy for a government to follow in such a case is the imposition of the constraint

$$\Pi = (1 - a) \sum_{i=o}^{n} p_i z_i \qquad (47)$$

which once again is a special case of the general constraint (43).

CHAPTER 3   NORMATIVE OPTIMUM THEORY

3.1   THE ACTORS AND THEIR INSTRUMENTS

When *Boiteux* published in 1956 his seminal paper on the management of public monopolies subject to budgetary constraints, he was not only a qualified economic theorist, but at the same time manager of the nationalized French electricity industry. He therefore did not visualize his approach as a purely theoretical exercise in welfare economics. Rather, he speculated on the actual applicability of his results and offered rules of thumb for an approximative numerical solution. The applicability of his original model was limited because of the assumption of perfect competition or equivalent behavior in the non-nationalized sector (Boiteux (1971, 233-234)). However, subsequent developments of his model and the version to be presented below allow for a monopolistic private economy. Moreover, Boiteux's restriction to compensated demand is not necessary and we can include income effects and consider public pricing with distributional objectives. For these reasons we have chosen an extended version of the Boiteux model as the best approach to tackle public enterprise theory, for both theoretical and empirical reasons [1].

The main actor in the model is the *board* of a public enterprise which we assume maximizes the welfare function

$$W(v^1, \ldots, v^H) \qquad \partial W / \partial v^h > 0, \qquad h = 1, \ldots, H \qquad (1)$$

where $v^h(p, q, r^h)$ are the individual indirect utility functions.

---

[1] For other extensions of the Boiteux model see Drèze (1984), Drèze-Marchand (1976) Hagen (1979), Marchand-Pestieau-Weymark (1982).

The board has to consider the market economy on the one hand and the government on the other hand.

To take account of the market economy implies taking account of demand, be it demand from consumers or producers. The board must be aware of the existence of many private firms, mostly operating under some sort of monopolistic competition. The following basic model imputes to the board the explicit consideration of market clearing conditions

$$\sum_h x_i^h(p,q,r^h) - z_i - \sum_j y_i^j(p,q) = 0 \qquad i = o,\ldots,n \qquad (2)$$

where positive x_i^h is private net demand [2], positive y_i^j is net supply by a private enterprise and positive z_i is net supply by the public enterprise in question, produced according to a production function

$$g(z,q) = 0. \qquad (3)$$

In addition, we assume some superior authority outside the model, call it *government*. This authority has decided that a particular part of the economy's production has to be run by the public enterprise in question and has given the board of the enterprise the right to set prices of particular goods, which will be labelled $e \in E \subset I$. Moreover, the government has set the public enterprise's minimum profits or maximum deficits, and therefore the board has to act in accordance with the revenue-cost constraint

$$\sum_{i=o}^{n} p_i z_i = \Pi(z,\rho). \qquad (4a)$$

The constraint where profit is fixed, that is

---

[2] Negative x_i^h is private net supply etc.

$$\sum_{i=o}^{n} p_i z_i = \Pi^o \tag{4b}$$

can always be considered as a special case (by simply setting $\partial\Pi/\partial z_i = 0$ for all i).

Taking into account all these constraints, both from the market and from the government, leads to a realistic second-best model. As mentioned above [3], the institutional distribution of responsibility for public pricing is a complex phenomenon of decision sharing between government and public enterprise. In the following we adhere to the hypothesis that the government sets constraints and the board decides on the relevant instruments [4]. The instruments available to the board are as follows.

The *controlled prices* $\{p_e, e \in E \subset I\}$ are a subset of all prices. Prices of goods that are only supplied or demanded by the public enterprise will be controlled in any case. There may exist also non-regulated prices of publicly supplied or demanded goods where the public enterprise has to accept prices which are fixed by private enterprises or by government agencies outside our model. We exclude regulation of wages, p_o [5]. The *uncontrolled prices* $p_i, i \notin E$, are exogenously given which is a sensible assumption in a model which aims to show the appropriate adjustment of public pricing to the given structures of the private economy.

The *controlled net production plans* $\{z_i\}$ are, of course, a subset of all net production plans of the economy $\{z_i, y_i^j\}$. Thus control of prices and control of production refer to parts of the economy only. These parts do not necessarily coincide.

For particular purposes we will suppose that, in addition, the board is

---

[3] See subsection 1.2.3 above.

[4] This basic hypothesis will, for instance, be given up when we deal explicitly with the regulation of marginal-cost or Ramsey pricing. (See sections 7.2 and 8.2 below.)

[5] except in chapter 20, where the influence of trade unions is explicitly considered.

given the opportunity to fix *individual lump-sum incomes* r^h. Needless to say, the analysis is much more realistic if these far-reaching distributional activities are excluded.

Finally, the board controls a subset of all *qualities* $\{q_e, e \in E \subset I\}$. It is plausible to assume that the board controls the qualities of those, and only those, goods whose prices it controls [6]. Private enterprises which supply or demand goods $e \in E$ have to take the publicly fixed quality as given (in the same way as they have to accept the publicly fixed price).

3.2   SOLVING THE MODEL [7]

In the following it will be convenient to follow a stepwise procedure, by first discussing welfare maximizing prices and net production plans, and then extending the analysis to optimal lump-sum incomes. Only at the last stage will we introduce the control of quality.

a)   Optimal prices and quantities

---

[6] Our model can be extended easily to quality regulation of goods which are supplied only privately, e.g. DIN-norms referring to $q_i, i \notin E$. Such problems, however, are beyond the scope of a book on public enterprise economics.

[7] As usual in the public economics literature, we leave open the questions whether: the second order conditions for a maximum are fulfilled; there is a unique optimum; the optimum achieved is a local one only; the optimum derived can actually be realized by decentralized decisions of economic agents. Explicit answers to any of the above questions can be given only if very restrictive assumptions are fulfilled. As the restrictive assumptions cannot be justified by usual microeconomic theory, it is not sensible to treat the above questions in general theoretical analyses. In any empirical case, however, the restrictive assumptions are either fulfilled or not, whence the investigation of the above questions in empirical case studies is always appropriate.

Welfare maximizing controlled prices and net production plans can be obtained by maximizing the following Lagrangean function [8]:

$$
\max_{p_e, z_i} \; \mathcal{L} = W(\cdot) - \sum_{i=o}^{n} \alpha_i \left[\sum_h x_i^h(\cdot) - z_i - \sum_j y_i^j(\cdot) \right] -
$$
$$
- \beta g(\cdot) - \bar{\gamma} \left[(\Pi(\cdot) - \sum_{i=o}^{n} p_i z_i \right]. \tag{5}
$$

The necessary maximum conditions are as follows:

$$
\sum_h \frac{\partial W}{\partial v^h} \frac{\partial v^h}{\partial p_e} - \sum_i \alpha_i \left(\sum_h \frac{\partial x_i^h}{\partial p_e} - \sum_j \frac{\partial y_i^j}{\partial p_e} \right) + \bar{\gamma} z_e = 0 \qquad e \in E \tag{6}
$$

$$
\alpha_i - \beta \frac{\partial g}{\partial z_i} - \bar{\gamma} \left(\frac{\partial \Pi}{\partial z_i} - p_i \right) = 0 \qquad i = o, \dots, n. \tag{7}
$$

As further necessary optimum conditions we obtain the constraints (2) – (4) [9] by differentiating $\mathcal{L}$ with respect to the Lagrangean multipliers. Thus we get a system of as many equations as unknowns. Assuming regularity of this system of equations, the unknowns can be determined.

b)   Optimal lump-sum incomes

In the next step we assume that the board controls also the distribution of lump-sum incomes $\{r^h\}$. Hence it maximizes the Lagrangean function $\mathcal{L}$ not only with respect to prices and quantities, but also

---

[8]   The politician must control at least three prices to avoid degeneration of the optimization approach because of insufficient degrees of freedom. Corner solutions are always excluded.

[9]   Either (4a) or (4b). In the case of (4b) $\partial \Pi / \partial z_i = 0$, as mentioned above.

with respect to the lump-sum incomes [10]. The resulting additional marginal conditions are

$$\frac{\partial W}{\partial v^h}\frac{\partial v^h}{\partial r^h} - \sum_i \alpha_i \frac{\partial x_i^h}{\partial r^h} = 0 \qquad h = 1,\ldots,H. \qquad (8)$$

The unknown prices, quantities, lump-sum incomes and Lagrangean multipliers can be computed from (6), (7) and (8) plus the constraints of the optimization approach. Regularity is, once again, assumed.

c) Optimal qualities [11]

If the board, furthermore, controls qualities q_e, the following additional marginal conditions are obtained by differentiating $\mathcal{L}$ with respect to q_e

$$\sum_h \frac{\partial W}{\partial v^h}\frac{\partial v^h}{\partial q_e} - \sum_i \alpha_i \left(\sum_h \frac{\partial x_i^h}{\partial q_e} - \sum_j \frac{\partial y_i^j}{\partial q_e} \right) - \beta \frac{\partial g}{\partial q_e} = 0 \qquad e \in E. \quad (9)$$

3.3   THE CONDITIONS FOR OPTIMAL PRICES AND QUANTITIES

We first concentrate on prices and quantities alone, neglecting qualities and lump-sum incomes. In this case (6) and (7) plus constraints constitute the relevant system of equations.

Substituting (7) into (6) we obtain

---

[10] The number of controlled prices plus the number of consumers must exceed 2 so as to avoid degeneration of the optimization approach because of insufficient degrees of freedom.

[11] The conditions of avoiding degeneration must always be changed accordingly.

$$\sum_h \frac{\partial W}{\partial v^h} \frac{\partial v^h}{\partial p_e} - \sum_i \left[\beta \frac{\partial g}{\partial z_i} + \bar{\gamma} \left(\frac{\partial \Pi}{\partial z_i} - p_i \right) \right] \left[\sum_h \frac{\partial x_i^h}{\partial p_e} - \sum_j \frac{\partial y_i^j}{\partial p_e} \right] + \bar{\gamma} z_e = 0.$$

(10)

We divide these equations by $\beta_o := \beta \, (\partial g / \partial z_o) > 0$ [12] and define $\lambda^h := (\partial W / \partial v^h)/\beta_o$; $\gamma := \bar{\gamma}/\beta_o$; $c_i := (\partial g / \partial z_i)/(\partial g / \partial z_o)$.

$\lambda^h \geq 0$ is the "normalized" marginal social welfare of individual utility. An equity-conscious politician will choose the welfare function W in such a way that the λ^h increase with decreasing individual utility.

γ is a "normalized" measure of the welfare effects of the size of the public enterprise's deficit. If the revenue-cost constraint Π exceeds the unconstrained welfare-optimal profit, then $0 < \gamma < 1$ [13].

c_i is a shadow price which measures the marginal *labor* costs of publicly producing good i (for $z_i > 0$; otherwise it is a partial marginal rate of transformation). However, as most recent papers on the topic denote c_i as marginal costs, we will adhere to this convention [14].

Using these new symbols the marginal conditions (10) can be rewritten as follows:

$$\sum_h \lambda^h \frac{\partial v^h}{\partial p_e} - \sum_i \left[c_i - \gamma p_i + \gamma \frac{\partial \Pi}{\partial z_i} \right] \left[\sum_h \frac{\partial x_i^h}{\partial p_e} - \sum_j \frac{\partial y_i^j}{\partial p_e} \right] + \gamma z_e = 0. \quad (11)$$

---

[12] Differentiate the Lagrangean function $\mathcal{L}$ with respect to initial endowments of labor z_o, y_o respectively. $\alpha_o > 0$ and $\beta_o > 0$ follow from economic plausibility. See Drèze-Marchand (1976, 67).

[13] This is proved explicitly in chapter 8 for a fixed revenue-cost constraint and in chapter 9 for rate of return regulation.

[14] The connection between c_i and the C_i, the marginal costs proper, has been treated in subsection 2.4.5 above.

For a better economic interpretation we will use the price-cost differences $(p_i - c_i)$ instead of using $(\gamma p_i - c_i)$. Hence we add $(1 - \gamma) \sum_i p_i [\sum_h (\partial x_i^h / \partial p_e) - \sum_j (\partial y_i^j / \partial p_e)]$ on both sides of the marginal conditions (11) to obtain

$$
\sum_h \lambda^h \frac{\partial v^h}{\partial p_e} - (1 - \gamma) \sum_i \sum_h p_i \frac{\partial x_i^h}{\partial p_e} -
$$

$$
- \sum_i \left[c_i - p_i + \gamma \frac{\partial \Pi}{\partial z_i} \right] \left[\sum_h \frac{\partial x_i^h}{\partial p_e} - \sum_j \frac{\partial y_i^j}{\partial p_e} \right] = \qquad (12)
$$

$$
= -\gamma z_e - (1 - \gamma) \sum_i \sum_j p_i \frac{\partial y_i^j}{\partial p_e} \qquad e \in E.
$$

This equation consists of five terms which we shall consider in turn from left to right.

3.3.1   DISTRIBUTIONAL OBJECTIVES

The first two terms reflect *distributional objectives*.

The first term, $\sum_h \lambda^h (\partial v^h / \partial p_e)$, is the social valuation of price changes. This term refers to the *price structure*, its absolute value being high for necessities and low for luxuries. This can be seen most easily after applying Roy's identity:

$$
\sum_h \lambda^h \frac{\partial v^h}{\partial p_e} = -\sum_h \lambda^h x_e^h \cdot \frac{\partial v^h}{\partial r^h} \qquad e \in E. \qquad (13)
$$

In the following it will be convenient to define a "distributional characteristic" of any good $e \in E$ as a distributionally weighted sum of individual consumption shares:

$$F_e := \sum_h \lambda^h \frac{\partial v^h}{\partial r^h} \cdot \frac{x_e^h}{x_e}. \tag{14}$$

The social valuation of changes in the individual lump-sum incomes, $\lambda^h(\partial v^h/\partial r^h)$, will be a decreasing function of individual incomes, thereby bringing about the distributional weighting mentioned above. For a similar reasoning see Feldstein (1972 a,b,c) and Atkinson-Stiglitz (1980, 387, 469).

The second term refers to the *price level*. It does not include any particular distributional differentiation between necessities and luxuries. Its absolute value is larger, the smaller γ. Typically, a smaller γ will result from a lower Π. The lower Π, the lower the level of prices [15]: to take a simple example, the level of prices of a welfare maximizing deficit enterprise will be lower than that of a perfect monopolist.

Formally, we apply the Slutsky equation to this second term [16]

$$(1-\gamma)\sum_i\sum_h p_i \frac{\partial x_i^h}{\partial p_e} = (1-\gamma)\left[\sum_i\sum_h p_i \frac{\partial \hat{x}_i^h}{\partial p_e} - \sum_i\sum_h p_i x_e^h \frac{\partial x_i^h}{\partial r^h}\right] =$$
$$= -(1-\gamma)\sum_h x_e^h, \tag{15}$$

where $\hat{x}_i^h$ denotes compensated demand. The reader should recall that for any individual h the compensated expenditures for all goods do not react to price changes $(\sum_i p_i(\partial \hat{x}_i^h/\partial p_e) = 0)$. Moreover, differentiating the individual budget constraint always yields $\sum_i p_i(\partial x_i^h/\partial r^h) = 1$. Hence the first two terms can be rewritten as follows

[15] "Level of prices" may be interpreted as referring to some adequately defined price index. It does not necessarily imply $\partial p_e/\partial\Pi > 0$ for all $e \in E$.

[16] Low prices will typically imply high demand x_e, which reinforces the tendencies mentioned in the text.

$$-F_e x_e + (1 - \gamma)x_e, \tag{16}$$

the first term referring to the price structure and the second to the price level.

3.3.2   ALLOCATION IN THE PUBLIC SECTOR

, The third and the fourth terms of (12) reflect the problems of *allocation in the public sector*. They center on the question of whether and how far prices should deviate from marginal costs, as expressed by $(p_i - c_i)$. In recent decades theoretical interest has shifted from marginal-cost pricing to second-best prices which deviate from marginal costs. The Boiteux model itself is an important step in that direction, with its stress on the revenue-cost constraints of the public sector. In our version of Boiteux's model these constraints are represented by $\gamma \, z_e$ and by $\gamma \, \partial\Pi/\partial z_i$, the latter term reflecting possible distortions caused by choosing revenue-cost constraints which are asymmetric with respect to different kinds of inputs (or outputs). As these distortions mostly refer to inputs, it is often convenient to define "modified" marginal costs as

$$\tilde{C}_i = c_i + \gamma \frac{\partial \Pi}{\partial z_i}. \tag{17}$$

However, allocation in the public sector does not only depend on the supply side but also on the price sensitivity of demand for publicly supplied goods. This can be clarified by defining $z_i^D(p)$ [17] as "demand for public supply" which implies

---

[17] The net supply z_i in the market clearing condition (2) does not depend directly on any other variable of the model because z_i is an instrument variable. After determining the optimal z_i from the optimization approach (5), we can define consumer net demand z_i^D as depending on prices.

$$\frac{\partial z_i^D}{\partial p_e} := \sum_h \frac{\partial x_i^h}{\partial p_e} - \sum_j \frac{\partial y_i^j}{\partial p_e}. \tag{18}$$

Note that z_i^D is a normal, "Marshallian" demand function and not a "Hicksian" compensated one.

3.3.3 THE PUBLIC ENTERPRISE AND THE PRIVATE SECTOR

The fifth term in (12) reflects the *adjustment of public enterprise pricing to monopolistic structures in the private economy.*

The term vanishes if the private sector is perfectly competitive because profit-maximizing price-taking firms follow Hotelling's lemma which leads to $\sum_i p_i(\partial y_i^j/\partial p_e) = 0$.

The term does not vanish if the private sector follows noncompetitive pricing. Such practices can best be described by price-cost margins which can be introduced into our analysis as follows. Consider $c_i^j := -dy_o^j/dy_i^j$, the marginal costs of producing good i in firm j at the optimum (for $y_i^j > 0$; otherwise c_i^j is a partial marginal rate of transformation). c_i^j can be interpreted as "producer prices". In the case of efficient production

$$\sum_i c_i^j \frac{\partial y_i^j}{\partial p_e} = 0 \qquad j = 1, \ldots, J. \tag{19}$$

Hence the following expansion is valid (Hagen (1979)):

$$(1-\gamma)\sum_i\sum_j p_i \frac{\partial y_i^j}{\partial p_e} = (1-\gamma)\sum_i\sum_j (p_i - c_i^j) \frac{\partial y_i^j}{\partial p_e} \qquad e \in E \tag{20}$$

which clearly shows that private price-cost margins influence public prices.

Incorporating these definitions and reformulations of the five terms in our basic marginal conditions, we can rewrite equation (12) as [18]

$$
F_e x_e - (1 - \gamma) x_e + \sum_i (\tilde{C}_i - p_i) \frac{\partial z_i^D}{\partial p_e} =
$$
$$
= \gamma z_e - (1 - \gamma) \sum_i \sum_j (c_i^j - p_i) \frac{\partial y_i^j}{\partial p_e} \qquad e \in E. \tag{21a}
$$

For any good e which is neither supplied nor demanded by private firms, but by the public sector only $(z_e = x_e)$, equation (21a) simplifies to

$$
\sum_i (\tilde{C}_i - p_i) \frac{\partial z_i^D}{\partial p_e} = (1 - F_e) z_e - (1 - \gamma) \sum_i \sum_j (c_i^j - p_i) \frac{\partial y_i^j}{\partial p_e} \qquad e \in E. \tag{21b}
$$

It seems natural to think of a public enterprise's policy within the general framework given by (21). This means that we

- look at the interaction between public and private supply;
- include distributional welfare judgements;
- start from the usual, non-compensated demand for public supply and consider the possibility of regulatory distortions.

It is rather surprising that the conventional literature did not follow this framework, which suggests itself naturally. It was not until 1956-57 that Lipsey-Lancaster stressed the interaction between the public and private sectors. And it was not until 1972 that Martin Feldstein stressed the distributional component of the problem. Moreover, the allocative elements of our framework have been narrowly analyzed by the exclusive concentration on compensated demand functions. The basic philosophy behind

---

[18] after multiplying by –1.

this emphasis on allocation is the underlying assumption that public pricing is not an appropriate instrument for redistribution. When dealing with compensated demand only, it is assumed that incomes are redistributed optimally by some sort of compensating lump-sum payments even though the empirical feasibility of such payments is at least questionable. Moreover, the consumer surplus approaches, which are often employed, do not make this basic redistributional procedure explicit, thereby hiding the implied value judgements.

Not only the importance of lump-sum transfers but also the conceptual weakness of this traditional procedure can be revealed by considering explicitly the redistribution required to obtain compensated demand functions in the Boiteux model.

3.4 COMPENSATING FOR INCOME EFFECTS

Consider now a board that controls the distribution of lump-sum incomes and computes the optimum on the basis of (6), (7), (8) and the relevant constraints. The marginal condition (8)

$$\frac{\partial W}{\partial v^h}\frac{\partial v^h}{\partial r^h} - \sum_i \alpha_i \frac{\partial x_i^h}{\partial r^h} = 0 \qquad h = 1, \ldots, H \qquad (8)$$

can be transformed by substituting Roy's identity. We obtain

$$\frac{\partial W}{\partial v^h}\frac{\partial v^h}{\partial p_e} = -\sum_i \alpha_i x_e^h \frac{\partial x_i^h}{\partial r^h} \qquad h = 1, \ldots, H \qquad e \in E. \qquad (8a)$$

Incomes are redistributed in such a way that for each consumer the weighted sum of all income effects that result from changing price p_e is equated to the board's valuation of the individual's utility change because of the change in the price p_e. Hence, at this optimum, distributional valuations and all income effects cancel out. This implies the elimination of all distributional considerations from the pricing structure, the optimal income distribution being guaranteed by the optimal choice of lump-sum incomes r^h, leaving only the task of allocation for the public pricing structure. At the same time all income effects are eliminated from the pricing structure, leading to a concentration on substitution effects, i.e. on compensated demand.

Formally we substitute (8a) into (6) and denote

$$\frac{\partial \hat{z}_i}{\partial p_e} = \left[\sum_h \left(\frac{\partial x_i^h}{\partial p_e} + x_e^h \frac{\partial x_i^h}{\partial r^h} \right) - \sum_j \frac{\partial y_i^j}{\partial p_e} \right] \qquad i = o,\ldots,n \qquad e \in E \quad (22)$$

where $\hat{z}_i(p)$ is the "compensated aggregate demand" for public supply of good i [19].

The resulting equations

$$-\sum_i \alpha_i \frac{\partial \hat{z}_i}{\partial p_e} + \overline{\gamma} z_e = 0 \qquad e \in E, \qquad (23)$$

can be transformed analogously to the above "non-compensated" case [20] to obtain

---

[19] The reader should note that the integrability conditions are not necessarily fulfilled for demand $\hat{z}_i$. $\partial \hat{z}_i / \partial p_e$ equals $\partial \hat{z}_e / \partial p_i$ only if $\sum_j \partial y_i^j / \partial p_e = \sum_j \partial y_e^j / \partial p_i$ which is the case for perfect competition in the private economy only (Hotellings lemma). However, our model explicitly takes into account the possibility of private monopolistic pricing.

[20] In this transformation it is necessary to add $(1-\gamma) \sum_i p_i (\partial \hat{z}_i / \partial p_e)$ on both sides of the marginal conditions. For the further transformation of the right-hand side the reader may note that $\sum_i p_i (\partial \hat{z}_i / \partial p_e) = -\sum_i \sum_j p_i (\partial y_i^j / \partial p_e)$, because for compensated demand $\sum_i \sum_h p_i (\partial \hat{x}_i^h / \partial p_e) = 0$.

$$\sum_i (\tilde{C}_i - p_i)\frac{\partial \hat{z}_i}{\partial p_e} = \gamma z_e - (1 - \gamma)\sum_i \sum_j (c_i^j - p_i)\frac{\partial y_i^j}{\partial p_e} \qquad e \in E. \quad (24)$$

These are the basic marginal conditions for the case of compensated demand.

3.5 THE CONDITIONS FOR OPTIMAL QUALITY

3.5.1 ON CONSUMERS' AND PRODUCERS' QUALITY CHOICE

Modelling quality is complicated because there is no counterpart to the usual duality between prices and quantities. The same price typically refers to quantity and quality, and there is no differentiation between a quantity and a quality price, which would facilitate the analysis.

For the above reasons it is necessary to deduce some fundamental properties of consumers' and producers' quality choice before transforming the relevant marginal conditions.

First we must extend *Roy's identity* so as to include qualities [21]. Consider an optimum state of the world, characterized by prices p^*, qualities q^* and optimal income r^{h*}. Consumer h can attain optimum utility u^{h*}. Now consider the dual problem. The expenditure function $e^h(p, q, u^{h*})$ denotes the minimal expenditures which enable the consumer to attain the constant utility level u^{h*}:

---

[21] For the case without quality see e.g. Varian (1978, 93).

$$e^h(p, q, u^{h*}) = \min_{(x^h)} \left\{ \sum_i p_i x_i^h \ \bigg| \ u^h(x^h, q) = u^{h*} \right\}. \tag{25}$$

Hence the following identity holds

$$u^{h*} = v^h(p, q, e^h(p, q, u^{h*}))^{22)}. \tag{26}$$

The interpretation of this equation is that for any arbitrary set of prices and qualities, the consumer can achieve optimum utility u^{h*} if he is given the minimal income which he needs to obtain u^{h*}.

Let us now differentiate this identity with respect to some quality q_e:

$$0 = \frac{\partial v^h(p^*, q^*, r^{h*})}{\partial q_e} + \frac{\partial v^h(p^*, q^*, r^{h*})}{\partial r^h} \cdot \frac{\partial e^h(p, q, u^{h*})}{\partial q_e}. \tag{27}$$

Rearranging (27) we obtain a formula similar to Roy's identity, that is

$$\frac{\partial v^h(\cdot)/\partial q_e}{\partial v^h(\cdot)/\partial r^h} = -\frac{\partial e^h(\cdot)}{\partial q_e}. \tag{28}$$

This result, although interesting in itself, raises further issues: what interpretation can be given to $\partial e^h/\partial q_e$ and can this partial derivative be rearranged to obtain a relationship similar to $\partial e^h/\partial p_e = x_e^h$? There are several ways of approaching this problem.

a)   At the optimum, prices will depend on qualities. Under the strong assumption that the inverse demand functions

$$p_i = f_i^h(q, x^h, r^h) \tag{29}$$

---

22) By starting from this specification of v^h we make sure that we obtain Marshallian demand functions in what follows.

exist, we can consider the expenditure functions at the optimum

$$e^h(f^h(q, x^h, r^h), q, u^{h*}).\tag{30}$$

Now let the consumer optimally adapt to qualities, i.e. let him behave as if he could choose the cost-minimizing quality levels q_e. Minimizing e^h with respect to q_e implies

$$\sum_i \frac{\partial e^h}{\partial p_i} \cdot \frac{\partial f_i^h}{\partial q_e} + \frac{\partial e^h}{\partial q_e} = 0.\tag{31}$$

Using Shephard's lemma we obtain

$$\frac{\partial e^h}{\partial q_e} = -\sum_i \nu_{ie}^h x_i^h\tag{32}$$

where the $\nu_{ie}^h = \partial f_i^h / \partial q_e$ measure the price-quality effects. If some particular quality influences its own price only, the above result reduces to

$$\frac{\partial e^h}{\partial q_e} = -\nu_{ee}^h x_e^h\tag{33}$$

which is nicely analogous to the differentiation of an expenditure function with respect to a single price: once again, the influence is the greater, the higher consumer's consumption of the respective good. The parameter ν_{ee}^h gives the necessary transformation from the quality to the quantity and expenditure spaces.

ν_{ee}^h is usually expected to be positive (Sheshinski (1976))[23]. Hence, $\partial e^h / \partial q_e$ will typically be negative: utility is maintained at lower

---

[23] The second derivative of the inverse demand function $\partial f_i^h / \partial q_i \partial x_i^h$ is more complicated. If this derivative is negative, quality and quantity can be regarded as substitutes; if it is positive, they can be regarded as complements (Sheshinski (1976)).

expenditures, the consumer being compensated by the higher quality level.

b) A further interpretation of $\partial e^h/\partial q_e$ assumes an individual quality-quantity trade-off as follows

$$\tilde{f}^h(q, x^h) \leq 0. \tag{34}$$

According to this constraint, the consumer's options are not only restricted by an income ceiling but also by particular limitations in the choice of qualities.

The best example refers to quality levels q which are measured in units of time, as is usual in transportation economics where lower waiting and travelling times are taken as the best proxies for higher quality. In these cases the constraint (34) simply reads as

$$\sum_e q_e x_e^h \leq Q - Q(\neg e) \tag{35}$$

where $e \in E$ are the goods supplied by the transportation enterprise, Q is an upper limit of time for any flow of consumption, say 24 hours, and $Q(\neg e)$ is time devoted to consumption of non-transportation goods and leisure. The usual analysis treats both Q and $Q(\neg e)$ as exogenous variables (Glaister (1982b)).

Given such a quality transformation constraint, the consumer is restricted in minimizing his expenditures so as to achieve utility u^{h*}. Consider, therefore, the expenditure function at the optimum and let the consumer optimally adapt to qualities, i.e. let him behave as if he could choose the optimal quality levels q_e

$$\min_{q_e} e^h(p, q, u^{h*}) \qquad \text{subject to} \qquad \tilde{f}^h(q, x^h) \leq 0. \tag{36}$$

Restricting ourselves to the economically interesting interior solutions we obtain the following necessary conditions for the expenditure function to be optimal with respect to qualities

$$\frac{\partial e^h}{\partial q_e} = \nu^h \left(\frac{\partial \tilde{f}^h}{\partial q_e} + \sum_i \frac{\partial \tilde{f}^h}{\partial x_i^h} \cdot \frac{\partial x_i^h}{\partial q_e} \right) \qquad e \in E \qquad (37)$$

where $\nu^h \leq 0$ is the Lagrangean multiplier of the above optimization approach. The optimum conditions become more appealing if we concentrate on a public transportation enterprise which is constrained by (35). Then the expenditure function follows the condition

$$\frac{\partial e^h}{\partial q_e} = \nu^h \left(x_e^h + \sum_{i \in E} q_i \frac{\partial x_i^h}{\partial q_e} \right) \qquad e \in E. \qquad (38)$$

This short treatment of the microeconomics of optimal quality must not be concluded without some consideration of the *production side*.

In equilibrium, production will be influenced by qualities in a twofold way:

- — it costs more to produce a given quantity of some good the higher its quality (direct influence);

- — changing quality leads to changing demand which, in turn, influences the costs of production (indirect influence).

Quality influences on a public enterprise's production are as follows:

- — the direct influence is expressed by c_{qe}, the marginal labor costs of an increase in quality q_e

$$c_{qe} := \frac{\partial g / \partial q_e}{\partial g / \partial z_o}; \qquad (39)$$

–   the indirect influence is expressed by

$$\sum_i \tilde{C}_i \frac{\partial z_i^D}{\partial q_e} \qquad \text{in the case of non-compensated demand} \qquad (40)$$

or, alternatively, by

$$\sum_i \tilde{C}_i \frac{\partial \hat{z}_i}{\partial q_e} \qquad \text{in the case of compensated demand} \qquad (41)$$

where $\partial z_i/\partial q_e$ is defined in a similar way to that in which $\partial z_i/\partial p_e$ was defined above. The exact definitions follow in the next subsection.

It is a little more complicated to deal with quality influences on private enterprise production. We assume private enterprises adjust to those qualities q_e which are determined by the public enterprise. Consider the production function of the j-th private enterprise, $g^j(y^j,q) = 0$. As efficiency is maintained for all price and quality changes, we obtain the following condition

$$\sum_e \left(\sum_i \frac{\partial g^j}{\partial y_i^j} \cdot \frac{\partial y_i^j}{\partial p_e} \right) dp_e + \sum_e \left(\frac{\partial g^j}{\partial q_e} + \sum_i \frac{\partial g^j}{\partial y_i^j} \cdot \frac{\partial y_i^j}{\partial q_e} \right) dq_e = 0 \qquad (42)$$

which, after division by $\partial g^j/\partial y_o^j$, is fulfilled if

$$\sum_i c_i^j \frac{\partial y_i^j}{\partial p_e} = 0 \qquad\qquad e \in E \qquad (19)$$

and

$$c_{qe}^j + \sum_i c_i^j \frac{\partial y_i^j}{\partial q_e} = 0 \qquad\qquad e \in E. \qquad (43)$$

$c_{qe}^j := (\partial g^j / \partial q_e)/(\partial g^j / \partial y_o^j)$ are marginal costs of increasing quality at constant quantities y_i^j (direct influence).

$\sum_i c_i^j (\partial y_i^j / \partial q_e)$ measures the indirect influence on costs, [24] via changing y_i^j.

Having formulated the consumers' and producers' quality choices we can now analyse the marginal conditions which can be derived from optimizing welfare with respect to qualities (under the usual constraints).

3.5.2 OPTIMAL QUALITIES, PRICES AND QUANTITIES [25]

The board of the public enterprise dealing with quality has to consider the additional marginal conditions [26]

$$\sum_h \frac{\partial W}{\partial v^h} \cdot \frac{\partial v^h}{\partial q_e} - \sum_i \alpha_i \left(\sum_h \frac{\partial x_i^h}{\partial q_e} - \sum_j \frac{\partial y_i^j}{\partial q_e} \right) - \beta \frac{\partial g}{\partial q_e} = 0 \qquad e \in E. \quad (9)$$

After substituting (7) and transforming as usual, we obtain

$$\sum_h \lambda^h \frac{\partial v^h}{\partial q_e} - (1-\gamma) \sum_i \sum_h p_i \frac{\partial x_i^h}{\partial q_e} -$$

$$- \sum_i \left[c_i - p_i + \gamma \frac{\partial \Pi}{\partial z_i} \right] \left[\sum_h \frac{\partial x_i^h}{\partial q_e} - \sum_j \frac{\partial y_i^j}{\partial q_e} \right] = \qquad (44)$$

$$= c_{qe} - (1-\gamma) \sum_i \sum_j p_i \frac{\partial y_i^j}{\partial q_e} \qquad e \in E.$$

---

[24] Recall $c_i^j := (\partial g^j / \partial y_i^j)/(\partial g^j / \partial y_o^j)$.

[25] In this subsection lump-sum incomes are exogenously given; they are treated endogenously in subsection 3.5.3 below.

[26] In this case the board considers (6), (7) and (9) plus constraints (2), (3) and (4).

These are the basic equations on qualities in the same way as eqs. (12) are the basic equations on prices. "Basic" means that the economic interpretation of eqs. (44) centers on quality whereas the interpretation of eqs. (12) centers on prices (nothwithstanding the fact that qualities, prices, and quantities are always determined together by the same system of equations). The degree of complexity of eqs. (44) is similar to eqs. (12). They consist of five terms which we shall consider now, reading from left to right.

3.5.2.1   SOCIAL VALUATION OF QUALITY CHANGES

The first term describes the social valuation of changing quality. It is convenient to denote

$$Q_e := -\sum_h \lambda^h \frac{\partial v^h}{\partial q_e} \qquad e \in E. \tag{45}$$

Q_e can be transformed by using the extended version of Roy's identity we described in the last subsection. Applying the general formula (28) we obtain

$$Q_e = \sum_h \lambda^h \frac{\partial v^h}{\partial r^h} \frac{\partial e^h}{\partial q_e} \qquad e \in E. \tag{46}$$

The social valuation of changing lump-sum incomes, $\lambda^h(\partial v^h/\partial r^h)$, will usually decrease with increasing lump-sum income, reflecting the distributional considerations of the enterprise's board. However $\partial e^h/\partial q_e$ is very likely to increase with increasing lump-sum income, reflecting the higher sensitivity to quality of higher-income earners. Hence, in general we cannot say whether Q_e is higher or lower for a typical necessity than for a luxury.

This is not a surprising result. If higher-income earners are more sensitive to quality, the explicit inclusion of quality in our optimization must imply a stronger weighting of higher-income earners' tastes. A board which does not want such an indirect favoring of higher-income earners must choose a W which gives a higher value to $\partial W / \partial v^h$ for lower-income earners. Hence, the achievement of a particular degree of redistribution [27] calls for different social welfare functions depending on the inclusion or exclusion of quality problems [28].

For reasons of completeness let us next mention the second term of (44). It is very easy to handle. Differentiating the individual consumer's budget constraint $\sum_i p_i x_i^h - r^h = 0$ with respect to quality q_e, we can see that

$$\sum_i p_i \frac{\partial x_i^h}{\partial q_e} = 0. \qquad e \in E. \qquad (47)$$

Therefore this second term vanishes.

3.5.2.2 QUALITY ALLOCATION IN THE PUBLIC SECTOR

The third and the fourth terms of (44) reflect the problems of quality allocation in the public sector, and the influence of quality allocation on the price-cost margins. The third term can be rewritten by using the definition (17) of $\widetilde{C}_i = c_i + \gamma \left(\partial \Pi / \partial z_i \right)$ and by defining

---

[27] The degree of redistribution is meant to be defined with respect to some concentration measure (Lorenz, Gini etc.) applied to the individual utilities v^h.

[28] As we could well expect, substituting for $\partial e^h / \partial q_e$ does not help to solve the above problems but only shows them up once again. Therefore it may be left to the reader as an exercise to insert either (32), or (33), or (37), or (38) into (46) and to consider the consequences.

$$\frac{\partial z_i^D}{\partial q_e} := \sum_h \frac{\partial x_i^h}{\partial q_e} - \sum_j \frac{\partial y_i^j}{\partial q_e} \qquad e \in E, \tag{48}$$

similarly to (18). The fourth term, c_{qe}, is already given in its definitive form.

The interpretation of the third and fourth term of (44) is complicated because the qualities q_e do not appear explicitly, but in the optimum influence all relevant variables, even the prices p! Moreover, $(\widetilde{C}_i - p_i)$ also are of central importance in the marginal conditions (12), whence we should always interpret the marginal conditions (12) and (44) together, for instance by substituting for $(\widetilde{C}_i - p_i)$ from (12) into (44). In the general formulation the result of such a procedure is a tedious formula which cannot be interpreted straightforwardly, but in special cases the procedure may lead to nice results as shown later in the book with examples of particular price-quality choices.

3.5.2.3   THE PUBLIC ENTERPRISE AND THE PRIVATE SECTOR

The fifth term in (44) reflects the adjustment of the public enterprise to the private economy. The problems of interpretation are similar to those just mentioned. Generally the economic interpretation is easier if eq. (43) is added to obtain a corrected fifth term as follows

$$(1 - \gamma)\sum_j c_{qe}^j + (1 - \gamma)\sum_i \sum_j (c_i^j - p_i)\frac{\partial y_i^j}{\partial q_e}. \tag{49}$$

Introducing the new definitions and reformulations above we can rewrite (44), the basic equations on qualities, in the following way

$$\sum_i (\tilde{C}_i - p_i) \frac{\partial z_i^D}{\partial q_e} =$$

$$= -[c_{qe} + Q_e] - (1 - \gamma) \sum_j c_{qe}^j - (1 - \gamma) \sum_i \sum_j (c_i^j - p_i) \frac{\partial y_i^j}{\partial q_e} \qquad (50)$$

which corresponds to (21) above.

3.5.3 COMPENSATING FOR INCOME EFFECTS

Let us now give the board the right to control the distribution of lump-sum incomes $\{r^h\}$ [29]. The basic equations on qualities (44) can be transformed by the use of the optimum conditions for lump-sum incomes

$$\frac{\partial W}{\partial v^h} \frac{\partial v^h}{\partial r^h} - \sum_i \alpha_i \frac{\partial x_i^h}{\partial r^h} = 0 \qquad h = 1, \ldots, H. \qquad (8)$$

Substituting the quality extended version of Roy's identity yields

$$\frac{\partial W}{\partial v^h} \cdot \frac{\partial v^h}{\partial q_e} = -\sum_i \alpha_i \frac{\partial e^h}{\partial q_e} \frac{\partial x_i^h}{\partial r^h} \qquad h = 1, \ldots, H \qquad e \in E. \qquad (51)$$

The incomes are redistributed in such a way that for each consumer the weighted sum of all quality induced income effects is equated to the board's valuation of the quality induced utility change. Hence, the board's valuation and the quality induced income effects cancel out.

---

[29] In this case the board takes into account (6), (7), (8) and (9) plus constraints (2), (3) and (4).

Formally, we substitute (51) into (44) and define

$$\frac{\partial \hat{z}_i}{\partial q_e} := \left[\sum_h \left(\frac{\partial x_i^h}{\partial q_e} + \frac{\partial e^h}{\partial q_e} \cdot \frac{\partial x_i^h}{\partial r^h} \right) - \sum_j \frac{\partial y_i^j}{\partial q_e} \right] \qquad e \in E \qquad (52)$$

where $\hat{z}_i$ is compensated demand, compensation referring to prices and qualities.

The basic conditions on quality can then be written as follows [30]:

$$\sum_i (\tilde{C}_i - p_i) \frac{\partial \hat{z}_i}{\partial q_e} = - \left[c_{qe} + (1 - \gamma) \sum_h \frac{\partial e^h}{\partial q_e} \right] - $$

$$- (1 - \gamma) \sum_j c_{qe}^j - (1 - \gamma) \sum_i \sum_j (c_i^j - p_i) \frac{\partial y_i^j}{\partial q_e} \qquad e \in E. \qquad (53)$$

These are the basic equations on qualities in the same way as eqs. (24) are the basic equations on prices, if in both cases income effects are excluded. Once again, both (24) and (53) are parts of the same system of equations and can only be solved simultaneously.

Comparing (50) and (53) shows that the optimal lump-sum redistribution leads to a shift from non-compensated to "quality compensated" demand. It also excludes the social valuations of individual incomes, which can be seen if we substitute $Q_e = \sum_h \lambda^h (\partial v^h / \partial r^h)(\partial e^h / \partial q_e)$ for $(1 - \gamma) \sum_h (\partial e^h / \partial q_e)$. Hence, optimal qualities and optimal prices no longer reflect those distributional features which tend to favor necessities and to burden luxuries.

---

[30] Differentiating the budget constraint $\sum_i p_i x_i^h = r^h$ we obtain $\sum_i p_i (\partial x_i^h / \partial r^h) = 1$. This property is used to transform $(1-\gamma) \sum_h \partial e^h / \partial q_e \sum_i p_i \partial x_i^h / \partial r^h = (1-\gamma) \sum_h \partial e^h / \partial q_e$.

CHAPTER 4   POSITIVE OPTIMUM THEORY

The theory and application of welfare optimal public pricing have been criticized for a number of reasons, in particular, for the normative character of the welfare function W, the excessive information requirements and the lack of incentives for efficiency.

It is often argued that the Bergsonian welfare function should be abandoned because it is a purely normative concept and public pricing theory should be based on the actual objectives of the relevant economic agents. For example, politicians may be interested in winning votes, bureaucrats in maximizing their budgets. Managers of public enterprises may try to maximize output or revenue instead of welfare. Labor unions may try to induce public enterprises to follow a policy which maximizes labor inputs or wages (subject to relevant constraints).

If we postulate objectives to represent the interests of these groups, the information requirements will be lower than those of the normative approach as there is no need to go back to the social valuation of individual utilites.

Moreover, we can also ignore lump-sum transfers which, if they were to be made, would require data which cannot be obtained. In contrast, if revenue or output is maximized, or if a Laspeyres price index is minimized (given some revenue-cost constraint), the required data are readily available. This implies that it is possible to ascertain whether the objectives, e.g. of politicians and managers, have been achieved. In contrast, "maximum welfare" is an abstract concept. A typical board might find it both unattractive and not feasible to follow such an abstract guideline. In claiming managerial success the board would prefer to be able to rely on high output or revenue figures of the preceding year, or the number of employees in public production. A management which only pleads that it worked for the public welfare might give the impression of being less dynamic and of using "welfare" as an excuse for its poor economic performance.

For these reasons boards in practice will tend to apply the objectives usually postulated in the economics of political choice and in managerial economics. Table 1 shows which positive theory objectives are explicitly treated in this book.

We now present the theoretical analysis of public pricing with such objectives.

We use $\Phi(p, q, z)$ as general notation for any objective function of positive pricing. Φ may be the number of votes, the size of the bureaucratic budget, output, revenue etc.

---

[1] We restrict ourselves to the regulation of output prices, $e = m+1, \ldots, n$. The only exceptions are energy pricing (chapter 18) and the explicit consideration of wage regulation if trade union interests are explicitly considered (chapter 20).

[2] z_i, $i = m+1, \ldots, n$, denote outputs ($z_i \geq 0$).

[3] $\partial z_k^D / \partial p_e$ does not result from directly differentiating z_k, but from defining $\partial z_k^D / \partial p_e := \sum_h \partial x_k^h / \partial p_e - \sum_j \partial y_k^j / \partial p_e$. Now assume normally reacting demand for energy, $\partial z_k^D / \partial p_k < 0$, and complementarity of energy and other goods, $\partial z_k^D / \partial p_e < 0$, $e \neq k$. The above signs hold regardless of whether $z_k > 0$ (public energy supply case) or $z_k < 0$ (private supply case). Additionally we assume normally reacting supply of energy, $\partial y_k^j / \partial p_k < 0$, $j \in K$, and, once again, complementarity of energy and other goods, $\partial y_k^j / \partial p_e < 0$, $e \neq k$, $j \in K$

[4] In this case the numeraire must not be labor, but some other good.

TABLE 1: POSITIVE THEORY OBJECTIVES

objective	objective function to be maximized(Φ)	$\frac{\partial \Phi}{\partial z_i}$	$\frac{\partial \Phi}{\partial p_e}$ 1)
votes (chapter 16)	$f(v^1,...,v^H)$	0	$\sum_h \frac{\partial f}{\partial v^h} \cdot \frac{\partial v^h}{\partial p_e} < 0$
"discretionary" budget (chapter 17)	$\sum_{m+1}^n p_i z_i + BUD(z_{m+1},...,z_n)$ 2)	0 inputs $p_i + \frac{\partial BUD}{\partial z_i} > 0$ outputs	$z_e > 0$
output (chapter 18)	$\sum_{m+1}^n z_i$	0 inputs 1 outputs	0
revenue (chapter 18)	$\sum_{m+1}^n p_i z_i$	0 inputs $p_i > 0$ outputs	$z_e > 0$
energy (supplied by private firms $j \in K$; ch.18)	$z_k - \sum_h x_k^h(\cdot) +$ $+ \sum_{j \notin K} y_k^j(\cdot)$	0 $\forall i \neq k$ 1 $i=k$	$-(\frac{\partial z_k^D}{\partial p_e} + \sum_{j \in K} \frac{\partial y_k^j}{\partial p_e}) > 0$ 3)
energy (publicly supplied; ch.18)	$-\sum_h x_k^h(\cdot) + \sum_j y_k^j(\cdot)$	0	$-\frac{\partial z_k^D}{\partial p_e} > 0$ 3)
Laspeyres price index (ch.19)	$-\sum_{m+1}^n p_i x_i^o / \sum_{m+1}^n p_i^o x_i^o$	0	$-x_i^o / \sum_{m+1}^n p_i^o x_i^o < 0$
combined manager and trade union interests (ch.20)	$U^1(z_{m+1},...,z_n)$ $+ U^2(p_o,z_o)$ 4)	$U_z^2 < 0$ $i=o$ $U_i^1 > 0$ outputs	$U_p^2 > 0$ $i=o$ 0 outputs

The environment, in which the board is assumed to be working, is treated in the same way as in the Boiteux model (chapter 3). There is an economy with H utility maximizing consumers, J private enterprises and a public sector. The board once again chooses prices $\{p_e\}$, qualities $\{q_e\}$, and production plans $\{z_i\}$, given the production technology, market clearing constraints and a revenue-cost constraint. Many objectives of political and managerial economics require explicit differentiation between inputs and outputs. We have to include such differentiation in our model. $z_i \leq 0$ $i = 0, \ldots, m$ denote public inputs and $z_i \geq 0$ $i = m+1, \ldots, n$ denote public outputs.

The above assumptions impute to the board an optimizing approach characterized by the following Lagrangean

$$\max_{p_e, q_e, z_i} \; \mathcal{L} = \Phi(p, q, z) - \sum_{i=o}^{n} \alpha_i \left[\sum_h x_i^h(p, q, r^h) - z_i - \sum_j y_i^j(p, q) \right] - $$
$$- \beta g(z, q) - \overline{\gamma}(\Pi(z, \rho) - \sum_i p_i z_i). \tag{1}$$

Differentiating $\mathcal{L}$ with respect to the instrument variables [1] leads to the following system of necessary conditions for an optimum

$$\frac{\partial \Phi}{\partial p_e} - \sum_{i=o}^{n} \alpha_i \frac{\partial z_i^D}{\partial p_e} + \overline{\gamma} z_e = 0 \qquad\qquad e \in E \tag{2}$$

$$\frac{\partial \Phi}{\partial q_e} - \sum_{i=o}^{n} \alpha_i \frac{\partial z_i^D}{\partial q_e} - \beta \frac{\partial g}{\partial q_e} = 0 \qquad\qquad e \in E \tag{3}$$

$$\frac{\partial \Phi}{\partial z_i} + \alpha_i - \beta \frac{\partial g}{\partial z_i} - \overline{\gamma}\left(\frac{\partial \Pi}{\partial z_i} - p_i \right) = 0 \qquad\qquad i = o, \ldots, n \tag{4}$$

---

[1] We always implicitly assume that politicians use sufficiently many instruments as to avoid degeneration of the optimization approach because of a lack of degrees of freedom.

where we have made use of the definitions of $\partial z_i^D/\partial p_e$ and $\partial z_i^D/\partial q_e$, as presented in $(3-18)$ and $(3-48)$.

These marginal conditions can be transformed in the usual way. After dividing all conditions by $\beta_o := \beta(\partial g/\partial z_o)$, we transform eqs. (4) into

$$\frac{\alpha_i}{\beta_o} = \left(\widetilde{C}_i - \gamma p_i - \frac{1}{\beta_o}\frac{\partial \Phi}{\partial z_i}\right) \qquad i = o,\ldots,n \qquad (5)$$

where γ and $\widetilde{C}_i$ are defined as in chapter 3.

We will always define the chosen objective function $\Phi(p,q,z)$ in such a way that $\beta_o > 0$. γ, which enters (5) as part of $\widetilde{C}_i$, will be positive if the objectives are defined as above and if the prescribed profit exceeds the unconstrained Φ-optimizing profit. $\gamma < 1$ can be deduced as usual as long as the objective function does not depend directly on labor inputs.

Substituting (5) into (2) and (3), we obtain two groups of conditions for optimal prices and qualities

$$\sum_{i=o}^{n}\left(\widetilde{C}_i - \gamma p_i - \frac{1}{\beta_o}\frac{\partial \Phi}{\partial z_i}\right)\frac{\partial z_i^D}{\partial p_e} = \gamma z_e + \frac{1}{\beta_o}\frac{\partial \Phi}{\partial p_e} \qquad e \in E \qquad (6)$$

$$\sum_{i=o}^{n}\left(\widetilde{C}_i - \gamma p_i - \frac{1}{\beta_o}\frac{\partial \Phi}{\partial z_i}\right)\frac{\partial z_i^D}{\partial q_e} = -c_{qe} + \frac{1}{\beta_o}\frac{\partial \Phi}{\partial q_e} \qquad e \in E \qquad (7)$$

where c_{qe} is defined as in $(3-39)$. To obtain price-cost differences in the left-hand terms we substract $(1-\gamma)\sum_i p_i(\partial z_i^D/\partial p_e)$ and $(1-\gamma)\sum_i p_i(\partial z_i^D/\partial q_e)$ on both sides of the respective marginal conditions. The result is as follows:

$$\sum_{i=o}^{n} \left(\tilde{C}_i - p_i - \frac{1}{\beta_o} \frac{\partial \Phi}{\partial z_i} \right) \frac{\partial z_i^D}{\partial p_e} =$$

$$= \gamma \, z_e - (1 - \gamma) \sum_{i=o}^{n} p_i \frac{\partial z_i^D}{\partial p_e} + \frac{1}{\beta_o} \frac{\partial \Phi}{\partial p_e} \qquad e \in E \tag{8}$$

$$\sum_{i=o}^{n} \left(\tilde{C}_i - p_i - \frac{1}{\beta_o} \frac{\partial \Phi}{\partial z_i} \right) \frac{\partial z_i^D}{\partial q_e} =$$

$$= -c_{qe} - (1 - \gamma) \sum_{i=o}^{n} p_i \frac{\partial z_i^D}{\partial q_e} + \frac{1}{\beta_o} \frac{\partial \Phi}{\partial q_e} \qquad e \in E. \tag{9}$$

Using eqs. $(3 - 15)$ and $(3 - 20)$, we obtain

$$\sum_i p_i \frac{\partial z_i^D}{\partial p_e} = \sum_i p_i \left[\sum_h \frac{\partial x_i^h}{\partial p_e} - \sum_j \frac{\partial y_i^j}{\partial p_e} \right] =$$

$$= -x_e - \sum_i \sum_j (p_i - c_i^j) \frac{\partial y_i^j}{\partial p_e} \qquad e \in E \tag{10}$$

and analogously, applying eqs. $(3 - 43)$ and $(3 - 47)$,

$$\sum_i p_i \frac{\partial z_i^D}{\partial q_e} = -\sum_j c_{qe}^j - \sum_i \sum_j (p_i - c_i^j) \frac{\partial y_i^j}{\partial q_e} \qquad e \in E. \tag{11}$$

Substituting the expressions in (10) and (11) into equations (8) and (9) we obtain the general price and quality conditions

$$\sum_{i=o}^{n} \left(\tilde{C}_i - p_i - \frac{1}{\beta_o} \frac{\partial \Phi}{\partial z_i} \right) \frac{\partial z_i^D}{\partial p_e} = \gamma z_e + (1 - \gamma) x_e +$$

$$+ (1 - \gamma) \sum_i \sum_j (p_i - c_i^j) \frac{\partial y_i^j}{\partial p_e} + \frac{1}{\beta_o} \frac{\partial \Phi}{\partial p_e} \qquad e \in E \tag{12}$$

$$\sum_{i=o}^{n} \left(\tilde{C}_i - p_i - \frac{1}{\beta_o} \frac{\partial \Phi}{\partial z_i} \right) \frac{\partial z_i^D}{\partial q_e} = -c_{qe} + (1 - \gamma) \sum_i c_{qe}^j +$$

$$+ (1 - \gamma) \sum_i \sum_j (p_i - c_i^j) \frac{\partial y_i^j}{\partial q_e} + \frac{1}{\beta_o} \frac{\partial \Phi}{\partial q_e} \qquad e \in E. \tag{13}$$

The reader will note that the adjustment of public prices and qualities to monopolistic structures in the private economy follows the same lines as in the normative approach. Therefore we need not repeat explicitly all the results when dealing with positive approaches. It is more convenient to concentrate on those terms of the respective marginal conditions where positive approaches actually differ from normative ones. For that purpose we neglect all interdependencies between the public and the private sector. We therefore assume:

a) only prices of publicly supplied goods are controlled [2];

b) the private sector is perfectly competitive; goods with publicly controlled prices are neither supplied nor demanded by private firms.

Under these assumptions we obtain the following structure of public prices and qualities [3]

$$\sum_{i=o}^{n} \left[\tilde{C}_i - p_i - \frac{1}{\beta_o} \frac{\partial \Phi}{\partial z_i} \right] \frac{\partial z_i^D}{\partial p_e} = z_e + \frac{1}{\beta_o} \frac{\partial \Phi}{\partial p_e} \qquad e \in E \tag{14}$$

---

[2] This assumption could be given up to investigate public pricing of goods which are only produced in the private sector. Such investigations, however, are beyond the scope of this book on public enterprise economics.

[3] Recall $c_{qe}^j + \sum_i c_i^j (\partial y_i^j / \partial q_e) = 0$ from (3-43). For perfect competition in the private sector, moreover, $\sum_i p_i (\partial y_i^j / \partial q_e) = 0$.

$$\sum_{i=o}^{n}\left[\widetilde{C}_i - p_i - \frac{1}{\beta_o}\frac{\partial \Phi}{\partial z_i}\right]\frac{\partial z_i^D}{\partial q_e} = -c_{qe} + \frac{1}{\beta_o}\frac{\partial \Phi}{\partial q_e} \qquad\qquad e \in E. \qquad (15)$$

Part III, on positive public enterprise economics, will concentrate on this system of marginal conditions.

CHAPTER 5   NORMATIVE PIECEMEAL THEORY

5.1   ON THE DIFFERENCE BETWEEN OPTIMUM AND PIECEMEAL POLICIES

In chapter 3 we presented the conditions for optimal prices, qualities and lump-sum incomes. In practice, the prices and qualities set by a public enterprise which assumes the payment of lump-sum incomes, are likely to be suboptimal. Switching to the optimal set of prices and qualities would typically require a total rearrangement of all relevant variables.

Such a once-and-for-all policy may often be impossible or unwanted. Political reasoning might suggest the choice of some step-wise course, which is less exposed to criticisms by the opposition and the media. Economically, the public enterprise's board might fear the disturbance of consumption habits by abrupt policy changes. The latter argument is closely connected with the informational requirements of public pricing policies. A board which tries to achieve an optimum in a once-and-for-all policy has to have full information on market demand functions, its competitors' supply functions and its own cost functions and those of its competitors. Even a well-informed board will have knowledge of these functions only in the neighborhood of its *present situation*.

The board facing the above problems will turn to a piecemeal policy. The optimum being unknown, and possibly far away, the board starts from given prices, qualities and lump-sum incomes, the level and structure of which will usually not be optimal, and searches for small price and quality changes which increase welfare. If lump-sum incomes are available as instruments, we can also integrate the analysis of changes in lump sums into such a piecemeal framework.

The welfare increasing piecemeal policy in a Boiteux world has to be market-clearing and technologically and financially feasible. Any small step has to consider the usual constraints, as treated in the previous chapters of this book.

A theory of piecemeal policy yields *sufficient* conditions for welfare improvements, contrary to an optimum theory which yields *necessary* conditions which are fulfilled at the optimum. Let us give a simple example. The optimum Ramsey pricing policy tells us that it is a necessary condition for an optimum that price-cost margins are fixed according to an inverse elasticity rule. A piecemeal Ramsey policy tells us that, given some public prices, near the optimum but still non-optimal, an increase of the price-cost margin of a price-inelastic good is a sufficient condition for a welfare improvement [1].

The above exposition should not mislead the reader into expecting too much from piecemeal policy. If the present situation is far from the welfare optimum, there are so many different ways to increase welfare that clear-cut rules, comparable to our optimum rules, usually will *not* be obtainable. Therefore the general results of a *theory* of piecemeal policy are disappointing. This does not mean that a theory of piecemeal policy is unimportant. After specifying all relevant functions, it may well serve as the basis for the board's decisions on how to proceed step by step.

As the general results are disappointing, it is not necessary to deal in full detail with all different possible cases of changing prices, qualities, and lump-sum incomes. We shall restrict the analysis to one particular case, namely, to small changes of prices (and the correponding small changes of quantities). The extension to changing qualities and lump-sum incomes is straightforward.

---

[1] However, this property need not always hold for all welfare-increasing price changes along a path from non-optimal prices to optimal prices.

5.2 WELFARE IMPROVEMENTS WITH NON-TIGHT CONSTRAINTS

Welfare improvements are "non-tight" if they are performed under inequality constraints.

Consider a board which is guided by the following welfare function

$$W(v^1, \ldots, v^H) \tag{1}$$

where $v^h(p, q, r^h)$ are the indirect utilities which depend on variable prices and on constant qualities and lump-sum incomes.

At the starting point of our analysis, prices p_e and quantities z_i are set in a market clearing and technologically and financially feasible way:

$$\sum_h x_i^h(p, q, r^h) - z_i - \sum_j y_i^j(p, q) = 0 \qquad i = o, \ldots, n \tag{2}$$

$$g(z, q) = 0 \tag{3}$$

$$\Pi(z, \rho) = \sum_{i=o}^{n} p_i z_i. \tag{4}$$

The board intends to increase welfare

$$\Delta W(v^1, \ldots, v^H) > 0 \tag{5}$$

by small changes of prices Δp_e [2] and of quantities Δz_i, always remaining in the Boiteux world. Let us assume that along any path of price and quantity

---

[2] The uncontrolled prices are assumed to remain constant ($dp_i = 0 \ \forall i \notin E$).

changes all markets must remain in equilibrium; the technology and budget constraints are weakened to inequalities.

The above problem is very complicated because we do not know the functional shape of the different "reaction functions": neither do we know exactly how welfare reacts to price and quantity changes, nor do we know exactly how the constraints alter. As shown in figure 7, $\Delta W = 0$ may be some arbitrary, non linear function in a $(\Delta p_1, \Delta p_2)$-space, going through the status quo point X.

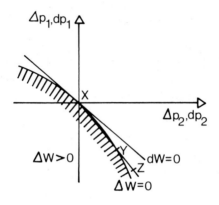

Figure 7

Usually, this problem is solved by linearizing all "reaction functions", using the total differentials [3]. Then our problem consists of finding price changes dp_e and quantity changes dz_i which fulfill the following conditions [4]:

---

[3] For another approximation which takes into account also second-order terms, see Hammond (1984).

[4] We always assume that enough prices and quantities are changed to avoid overdetermination.

$$dW = \sum_e \sum_h \frac{\partial W}{\partial v^h} \frac{\partial v^h}{\partial p_e} dp_e > 0 \tag{6}$$

$$\sum_e \sum_h \frac{\partial x_i^h}{\partial p_e} dp_e - dz_i - \sum_e \sum_j \frac{\partial y_i^j}{\partial p_e} dp_e = 0 \qquad i = o, \ldots, n \tag{7}$$

$$\sum_i \frac{\partial g}{\partial z_i} dz_i \leq 0 \tag{8}$$

$$\sum_i \left(\frac{\partial \Pi}{\partial z_i} - p_i \right) dz_i - \sum_e z_e dp_e \leq 0. \tag{9}$$

Consider a feasible direction of price changes, represented by the ray X Y Z in figure 7 [5]. As $\Delta W = 0$ is non-linear, a point like Z actually does not improve welfare although it is shown as welfare-improving under the approximation $dW > 0$. All points between X and Y, however, are welfare improving. Hence, if the step $(\Delta p_1, \Delta p_2)$ along any feasible ray is small enough, there will be a welfare improvement. Denoting proportional changes of both (all) prices along such a ray by "s" we obtain

$$\exists s > 0 \; : \; \forall s' < s \mid W(p) < W(p + s' dp) \; ; \; s' > 0. \tag{10}$$

The above result implies that there is always some possible welfare improvement as long as the step taken is sufficiently small. This result is valid for all rays in the non-closed space $dW > 0$. It is not valid for $dW = 0$ which is tangential to $\Delta W = 0$. Therefore only $dW > 0$ is sensible, not $dW \geq 0$.

---

[5] The following analysis deals with W only, ignoring the constraints for welfare-improvement. They could easily be inserted into figure 7, but would not alter the economic reasoning in favor of $dW > 0$.

It is not only condition (6), $dW > 0$, which causes particular problems. Let us also examine conditions (7) – (9). These conditions are sensible because we assumed the enterprise started from a market clearing and technologically and financially feasible situation. Without this assumption, changing prices and quantities according to (7) – (9) would imply switching from an infeasible situation to another which may also be infeasible, and we have no economic rationale for such a change.

For *finite* changes of prices and quantities, conditions (7) – (9) normally do not guarantee that the new situation is still market-clearing and technologically and financially feasible. Only for infinitesimal changes dp_e and dz_i is such an outcome guaranteed [6]. For sufficiently small steps we may hope that the outcome is almost always welfare improving.

As welfare improving finite price and quantity changes may lead away from allocative efficiency, one could even doubt that there is any connection between a piecemeal policy as described above and an optimum policy, given the formulation of the Boiteux model. Fortunately Farkas' "theorem of the alternative" enables us to show that such a connection exists. For this purpose we condense the analysis to piecemeal *pricing* policies, and assume that the piecemeal quantity changes always secure market equilibria, given the price changes. The economic reasoning requires solving explicitly (7) for dz_i to obtain

$$dz_i = \sum_e \sum_h \frac{\partial x_i^h}{\partial p_e} dp_e - \sum_e \sum_j \frac{\partial y_i^j}{\partial p_e} dp_e = \sum_e \frac{\partial z_i^D}{\partial p_e} dp_e. \qquad (11)$$

After substituting for dz_i in (8) and (9) we obtain the system

$$A_o^T (dp_e) = \left(\sum_h \frac{\partial W}{\partial v^h} \frac{\partial v^h}{\partial p_e} \right)^T (dp_e) > 0 \qquad (12)$$

---

[6] The same is trivially valid if all relevant functions in eqs. (7) – (9) are linear in p and z.

$$A_1^T(dp_e) = \left(\sum_i \frac{\partial g}{\partial z_i} \frac{\partial z_i^D}{\partial p_e}\right)^T (dp_e) \leq 0 \qquad (13)$$

$$A_2^T(dp_e) = \left(\sum_i \left(\frac{\partial \Pi}{\partial z_i} - p_i\right) \frac{\partial z_i^D}{\partial p_e} - z_e\right)^T (dp_e) \leq 0 \qquad (14)$$

where (dp_e) is the vector [7] of price changes; A_o, A_1, A_2 are gradient vectors which are defined as can be seen in $(12) - (14)$.

It is convenient to denote the set of feasible welfare-improving price changes by $\Omega(dp_e)$:

$$\Omega(dp_e) = \left\{(dp_e) \mid A_o^T(dp_e) > 0; A_1^T(dp_e) \leq 0; A_2^T(dp_e) \leq 0\right\}. \qquad (15)$$

After this preparatory work we are ready to apply Farkas' theorem to our problem. This theorem belongs to the family of theorems which state that either a system of homogeneous linear equations has a solution *or* a related system of inequalities has a solution, but never both. For an exact mathematical presentation and comparison of the different "theorems of the alternative" see Mangasarian (1969).

The special case of Farkas' theorem to be applied to our problem is as follows. For each given matrix $A = (A_1, A_2)^T$ and each vector A_o [8] either

I $\qquad A_o^T \xi > 0, \qquad A^T \xi \leq 0 \qquad$ has a solution ξ

II $\qquad A\chi = A_o, \qquad \chi \geq 0$ [9] $\qquad$ has a solution χ

---

[7] Principally we define vectors as column vectors; A^T means the transpose.

[8] $A_o \neq 0$ is a sort of trivial condition in our case; otherwise the whole problem of welfare improvement is not well-defined.

[9] $\chi \geq 0$ means that all components of vector χ must be non-negative, and so the case of all components equal to zero is not excluded.

but never both.

To apply the above theorem to our problem, we define $\xi := (dp_e)$ and A_o, A_1, A_2 as before. Then it can be seen easily that the piecemeal policy conditions (12) – (14) satisfy case I of Farkas' theorem.

What about case II of Farkas' theorem? Defining $\chi \equiv (\beta, \bar{\gamma})^T$, this case implies

$$A_0 - \beta A_1 - \bar{\gamma} A_2 = (0) \qquad (16a)$$

where (0) is an adequately defined vector consisting of zero elements. This system of equations can be written as

$$\left(\sum_h \frac{\partial W}{\partial v^h} \frac{\partial v^h}{\partial p_e} \right) - \beta \left(\sum_i \frac{\partial g}{\partial z_i} \frac{\partial z_i^D}{\partial p_e} \right) - \bar{\gamma} \left(\sum_i \left(\frac{\partial \Pi}{\partial z_i} - p_i \right) \frac{\partial z_i^D}{\partial p_e} - z_e \right) = (0)$$

or equivalently

$$\sum_h \frac{\partial W}{\partial v^h} \frac{\partial v^h}{\partial p_e} - \sum_i \left[\beta \frac{\partial g}{\partial z_i} + \bar{\gamma} \left(\frac{\partial \Pi}{\partial z_i} - p_i \right) \right] \frac{\partial z_i^D}{\partial p_e} + \bar{\gamma} z_e = 0 \quad \text{for all} \quad e \in E.$$

$$(16b)$$

This result is identical with our necessary optimum conditions (3 – 10)!

The application of Farkas' theorem to our problem shows therefore that either (12) – (14) hold or (16), but never both. Hence, there is always a possibility for welfare improving price changes unless the existing prices are welfare optimal under the given constraints. This shows the connection between piecemeal and optimum theory [10].

The economic meaning of the piecemeal-policy conditions (12) – (14), and of their connection with the optimum conditions (16), can be best illustrated by means of a graphical exposition.

---

[10] Because of $\chi \geq 0$, the Lagrangean multipliers must be non-negative, $\beta, \bar{\gamma} \geq 0$.

Figure 8a shows the contours of the conditions (12) – (14) for two price changes dp_1, dp_2. The hatching indicates the location of the halfspaces which are generated by the above conditions. All price changes that start from the status quo X and move into the set $\Omega(dp_e)$ are welfare-improving under the chosen constraints.

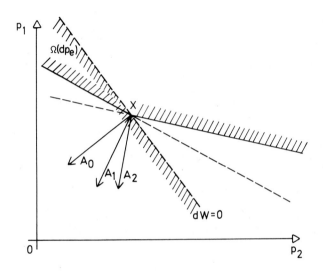

Figure 8a

In the case of figure 8b the situation is rather different. The intersection of the three halfspaces that are generated by (12) – (14) is empty [11]. No welfare-improving price changes are possible; point X is a welfare optimum. Graphically such a situation is always given if A_o lies between A_1 and A_2. Analytically, in that case A_o, A_1 and A_2 can be written as a non-negative

---

[11] Remember that $dW=0$ itself is *not* part of the halfspace generated by (12). Hence the intersection is actually empty. (Otherwise the intersection would have consisted of point X.)

linear combination

$$A_o = \beta A_1 + \overline{\gamma} A_2 \qquad\qquad \beta, \overline{\gamma} \geq 0 \qquad\qquad (17)$$

which is the well-known optimum condition [12].

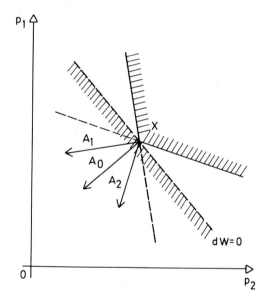

Figure 8b

[12] We do not explicitly deal with degenerate cases where either χ_1 or χ_2 equals zero.

5.3 WELFARE IMPROVEMENTS WITH TIGHT TECHNOLOGY CONSTRAINT

Matters become more complicated if more of the relevant constraints have to hold as equalities. The best example is offered by the case of a tight technology constraint whence the welfare improving price changes should satisfy the following conditions

$$A_o^T(dp_e) > 0 \qquad\qquad (18)$$

$$A_1^T(dp_e) = 0 \qquad\qquad (19)$$

$$A_2^T(dp_e) \leq 0 \qquad\qquad (20)$$

where the vectors A_o, A_1, A_2 and (dp_e) have the same meaning as before. We denote the set of feasible welfare-improving price changes by $\tilde{\Omega}(dp_e)$:

$$\tilde{\Omega}(dp_e) = \{(dp_e) \mid A_o^T(dp_e) > 0; A_1^T(dp_e) = 0; A_2^T(dp_e) \leq 0\}. \qquad (21)$$

In that case Farkas' theorem is inapplicable, but Motzkin's theorem of the alternative can be used [13]. The special case of that theorem to be applied is as follows. For each given vectors A_o [14], A_1 and A_2, either

I $\qquad A_o^T\xi > 0, \qquad A_1^T\xi = 0, \qquad A_2^T\xi \leq 0 \qquad$ has a solution ξ or

---

[13] See once again Mangasarian (1969) for mathematical details. Diewert (1978) and Weymark (1979) have applied Motzkin's theorem to tax reforms.

[14] Once again, $A_o \neq 0$ must be fulfilled. Not only for mathematical reasons, but also for economic reasons, as our problem is only well-defined for $A_o \neq 0$.

II $\chi_o A_o + \chi_1 A_1 - \chi_2 A_2 = 0; \quad \chi_o > 0, \chi_1 \gtrless 0, \chi_2 \geq 0$ has a solution
χ.

If the vector $\chi = (\chi_o, \chi_1, \chi_2)$ is normalized as to yield $\chi = (1, -\beta, \bar\gamma)^{15)}$, it can be seen easily that Motzkin's theorem is applicable to the above problem of tight welfare improvements. Once again, there is some possibility for welfare improving price changes [16] according to (18) – (20) unless the prices are already optimal.

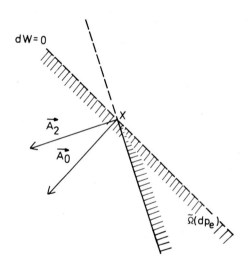

Figure 9

The graphical illustration of the piecemeal-policy conditions (18) – (20) is a little more difficult than in the case of improvements under non-tight constraints because at least three prices must be changed and hence a three-

---

[15] Motzkin's theorem does *not* imply a particular sign of β; $\bar\gamma \geq 0$ is, once again, implied.

[16] At least three prices must be changed, otherwise the problem is overdetermined.

dimensional presentation is required. However, there is a technique which allows an easier graphical presentation. Consider changing three prices. We know that all price changes must take place along the plane $A_1(dp_e) = 0$. Typically this plane will intersect the two halfspaces generated by $A_o(dp_e) > 0$ and $A_2(dp_e) \leq 0$.

To draw figure 9 we rotate the plane $A_1(dp_e) = 0$ until it coincides with the page [17]. The figure shows the contours of conditions (18) and (20).

$\vec{A}_o$ and $\vec{A}_2$ are projections of the gradient vectors into the plane $A_1(dp_e) = 0$. All price changes along this plane that start from the status quo X and move into the set $\widetilde{\Omega}(dp_e)$ are welfare increasing under the chosen constraints.

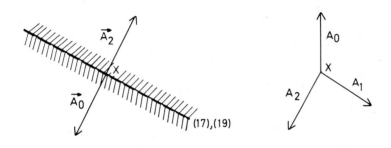

Figure 10a   Figure 10b

It is not easy to show graphically the typical optimum case [18]. Take again a three price case where the conditions (18) – (20) are three-dimensional hyperplanes. Then in the typical optimum case all three planes intersect along one straight line, all three gradient vectors being vertical on this

---

[17] Because of this rotation we cannot explicitly denote axes of a system of coordinates in such a case.

[18] where χ_o, χ_1 and $\chi_2 \neq 0$.

line. Looking vertically at the plane $A_1(dp_e) = 0$ yields figure 10a; looking vertically at the line of intersection of all three planes yields figure 10b. As all planes intersect along the same line, two degrees of freedom are lost, in other words, A_o, A_1 and A_2 are linearly dependent

$$A_o = -(\chi_1/\chi_o)A_1 + (\chi_2/\chi_o)A_2 \qquad (22)$$

where $(\chi_1/\chi_o) = -\beta$ and $(\chi_2/\chi_o) = \overline{\gamma}$.

5.4   ON WELFARE -IMPROVING INCREASES OF PUBLIC INEFFICIENCY [19]

Given an inefficient initial situation, one would a priori expect piecemeal recommendations which associate welfare improvements with reductions of inefficiency. This a priori expectation is wrong. It may well be possible that the first steps of piecemeal policy should go in the direction of further increases of inefficiency, and not towards decreasing inefficiency until some subsequent stage of policy.

The above statement can be proved easily. Given tight market clearing constraints [20], but non-tight technology and budget constraints, i.e.

$$g(z) < 0 \qquad (23)$$

$$\Pi(z,\rho) - \sum_i p_i z_i < 0, \qquad (24)$$

---

[19] See Peters (1985a).

[20] If market disequilibria are allowed, the normative piecemeal theory does not lead to a meaningful analysis, in contrast to many cases of the positive piecemeal theory. See section 6.2 below.

the first step of piecemeal policy should follow the steepest ascent of the objective function ("gradient projection method" [21])):

$$(dp_e) = \sum_h \frac{\partial W}{\partial v^h} \frac{\partial v^h}{\partial p_e}. \tag{25}$$

The economic implications of this gradient projection method are as follows. Substitute Roy's identity to obtain

$$(dp_e) = -\sum_h \frac{\partial W}{\partial v^h} \frac{\partial v^h}{\partial r^h} x_e^h. \tag{26}$$

The resulting price changes are higher, the higher the quantities consumed (x_e^h) and the higher the social valuation of consumption. The latter will typically imply larger price reductions of necessities [22].

Any further economic interpretation of the above piecemeal policy explicitly has to consider the technology and the budget constraints. We rewrite these constraints using dummy variables $DV_1, DV_2 > 0$

$$\tilde{g}(z, DV_1) = g(z) + DV_1 = 0 \tag{27}$$

$$\tilde{\Pi}(z, p, \rho, DV_2) = \Pi(z, \rho) - \sum_i p_i z_i + DV_2 = 0. \tag{28}$$

We postulate the validity of these constraints along any piecemeal policy path whence the following linear approximations hold [23]

---

[21] See Luenberger (1973, 247-254).

[22] The reader should compare eq. (26) on piecemeal price changes, and the "distributional characteristic" of the optimum policy, as defined in eq. (3-14).

[23] By substituting (11) we explicitly consider the market clearing conditions.

$$\sum_e \sum_i \frac{\partial \tilde{g}}{\partial z_i} \frac{\partial z_i^D}{\partial p_e} dp_e + \frac{\partial \tilde{g}}{\partial DV_1} dDV_1 = 0 \tag{29}$$

$$\sum_e \left[\sum_i \frac{\partial \tilde{\Pi}}{\partial z_i} \frac{\partial z_i^D}{\partial p_e} + \frac{\partial \tilde{\Pi}}{\partial p_e} \right] dp_e + \frac{\partial \tilde{\Pi}}{\partial DV_2} dDV_2 = 0. \tag{30}$$

To transform the above approximations, we first differentiate (27) and (28) with respect to z_i and DV_i, respectively:

$$\frac{\partial \tilde{g}}{\partial z_i} = \frac{\partial g}{\partial z_i} \; ; \; \frac{\partial \tilde{g}}{\partial DV_1} = 1, \tag{31}$$

$$\frac{\partial \tilde{\Pi}}{\partial z_i} = \frac{\partial \Pi}{\partial z_i} - p_i \; ; \; \frac{\partial \tilde{\Pi}}{\partial p_e} = -z_e \; ; \; \frac{\partial \tilde{\Pi}}{\partial DV_2} = 1. \tag{32}$$

Secondly we recall that price changes (dp_e) follow the gradient of the welfare function as shown in (26).

Welfare-improving price changes, therefore, can be characterized by the following changes of the dummies:

$$dDV_1 = \sum_e \sum_i \sum_h \frac{\partial W}{\partial v^h} x_e^h \frac{\partial v^h}{\partial r^h} \frac{\partial g}{\partial z_i} \frac{\partial z_i^D}{\partial p_e} \tag{33}$$

$$dDV_2 = \sum_e \sum_h \frac{\partial W}{\partial v^h} x_e^h \frac{\partial v^h}{\partial r^h} \left\{ \sum_i \left(\frac{\partial \Pi}{\partial z_i} - p_i \right) \frac{\partial z_i^D}{\partial p_e} - z_e \right\} \quad . \tag{34}$$

Let us first interpret equation (33). The derivatives on the right-hand side have different signs, namely

- $\partial W / \partial v^h \geq 0$ (value judgement in the welfare function)
- $\partial v^h / \partial r^h > 0$ (property of an indirect utility function)

-   $\partial g / \partial z_i > 0$ (property of the production function)
-   $\partial z_i^D / \partial p_e \lessgtr 0$ (if z_i and z_e are outputs $i \neq e$: typically positive for substitutes, negative for complements).

Hence, the sign of dDV_1 cannot be determined uniquely: increasing inefficiency, $dDV_1 > 0$, cannot be excluded as a possible candidate for welfare-improving price changes.

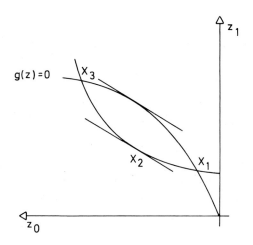

Figure 11a

The worst is yet to come: the paradoxical case of increasing inefficiency is likely to occur. Consider a single price change dp_e. Any tendencies towards $dDV_1 < 0$ come from the own price effect $\partial z_e^D / \partial p_e < 0$, or from the cross price effects of complements. All cross effects with respect to substitutes tend towards $dDV_1 > 0$. The more disaggregated a model, the more likely the occurence of the above paradoxical result.

Figure 11a corroborates the probability of paradoxical results. For a one input-one output model of a public monopoly, we consider the technology frontier $g(z)$[24], and an aggregate offer curve, connecting the consumption bundles (z_o, z_1) the consumers would choose at different possible price ratios [25].

X_3 is the optimum. Any piecemeal policy which starts somewhere between X_1 and X_2 will first imply increasing inefficiency because the distance between the technology frontier and the offer curve increases if one moves from X_1 towards X_2. Only if the piecemeal policy starts somewhere between X_2 and X_3 will decreasing inefficiency be the appropriate choice.

Let us now turn to eq. (34). $dDV_2 > 0$ implies that the public enterprise's excess revenues $(\Sigma_i p_i z_i - \Pi)$ are increased. Such a case seems to be a poor candidate for welfare improvements because typically we would expect this policy to be associated with higher public prices, which should reduce, and not increase, welfare. However, once again we cannot exclude paradoxical results.

An example can be found easily. We know from (34) that $dDV_2 > 0$ if

$$\sum_i \frac{\partial \Pi}{\partial z_i} \frac{\partial z_i^D}{\partial p_e} > z_e + \sum_i p_i \frac{\partial z_i^D}{\partial p_e} \quad \text{for all } e \quad . \tag{35}$$

Now consider the case of a fixed revenue-cost constraint Π^o whence $\partial \Pi / \partial z_i = 0$ for all i. Then $dDV_2 > 0$ if the effects of complements are predominant and in addition if demand is highly responsive and if the output of publicly supplied goods is not too large. – However, one should not be too concerned about such a possibility. Empirical evidence indicates that the predominance of complements is rather unusual. Substitutes are found more often, and in the case where substitution effects are predominant the above paradoxical result will not hold.

---

[24] Without limitation of generality figure 11a uses a convex technology frontier.

[25] The positive intersect of the offer curve and the z_1-axis can be explained by assuming a positive Σr^h in the initial situation.

5.5   PIECEMEAL POLICY RECOMMENDATIONS:
GENERAL RULES FOR SOME SPECIAL CASES

The theory elaborated above yields interesting insight into piecemeal improvements of welfare and its connection with optimum policy. But the results on piecemeal price changes do not lend themselves to straightforward economic interpretation. They are valuable for practical application, but leave the neoclassical theoretician disappointed. There exist, however, some special cases where piecemeal pricing policies can be interpreted in an economically satisfactory way. The best-known case, to be treated in the present section, deals with price changes with optimal adjustments of quantities and lump-sum incomes [26].

Consider the board of a public enterprise which intends to improve welfare by changing prices, quantities and lump-sum incomes. Qualities are assumed as constant. The condition for a welfare improvement can therefore be written as follows

$$dW = \sum_e \sum_h \frac{\partial W}{\partial v^h} \frac{\partial v^h}{\partial p_e} dp_e + \sum_h \frac{\partial W}{\partial v^h} \frac{\partial v^h}{\partial r^h} dr^h > 0 \quad . \tag{36}$$

The piecemeal policy may be constrained by the market clearing and technology conditions. There is no budget limitation.

We again linearize the relevant constraints by applying total differentiation:

$$\sum_h \sum_e \frac{\partial x_i^h}{\partial p_e} dp_e + \sum_h \frac{\partial x_i^h}{\partial r^h} dr^h - dz_i - \sum_j \sum_e \frac{\partial y_i^j}{\partial p_e} dp_e = 0 \qquad i = o, \dots, n \tag{37}$$

---

[26] A second very special way to apply piecemeal policy techniques uses an alleged similarity between the total differential of demand functions and the left hand side of pricing formulas in compensated demand cases. See section 8.4 below.

$$\sum_i \frac{\partial g}{\partial z_i} dz_i = 0 \quad . \tag{38}$$

Solving (37) for dz_i and substituting into (38) yields

$$\sum_i \frac{\partial g}{\partial z_i} \left\{ \sum_e \frac{\partial z_i^D}{\partial p_e} dp_e + \sum_h \frac{\partial x_i^h}{\partial r^h} dr^h \right\} = 0 \quad . \tag{39}$$

We could now apply Motzkin's theorem as above. However, this would not lead to further results on piecemeal policy recommendations. Therefore, we restrict ourselves to a very special case of the above piecemeal policy approach.

For any given prices p we assume that the public enterprise chooses quantities z_i and incomes r^h in a welfare-maximizing way:

$$\left. \max_{z_i, r^h} W \right|_{p,q} - \sum_i \alpha_i \left(\sum_h x_i^h - z_i - \sum_j y_i^j \right) - \beta g(\cdot). \tag{40}$$

The marginal conditions are

$$\alpha_i - \beta \frac{\partial g}{\partial z_i} = 0 \qquad i = o, \dots, n \tag{41}$$

$$\frac{\partial W}{\partial v^h} \frac{\partial v^h}{\partial r^h} - \sum_i \alpha_i \frac{\partial x_i^h}{\partial r^h} = 0 \qquad h = 1, \dots, H. \tag{42}$$

The validity of these additional conditions enables us to transform $dW > 0$ as follows:

$$dW = \sum_e \sum_h \frac{\partial W}{\partial v^h} \frac{\partial v^h}{\partial p_e} dp_e + \sum_h \frac{\partial W}{\partial v^h} \frac{\partial v^h}{\partial r^h} dr^h$$

$$= -\sum_e \sum_h \frac{\partial W}{\partial v^h} \frac{\partial v^h}{\partial r^h} x_e^h dp_e + \sum_h \frac{\partial W}{\partial v^h} \frac{\partial v^h}{\partial r^h} dr^h$$

$$= \sum_h \frac{\partial W}{\partial v^h} \frac{\partial v^h}{\partial r^h} \left(dr^h - \sum_e x_e^h dp_e \right)$$

$$(42) \quad = \sum_h \sum_i \alpha_i \frac{\partial x_i^h}{\partial r^h} \left(dr^h - \sum_e x_e^h dp_e \right)$$

$$(41) \quad = \sum_h \sum_i \beta \frac{\partial g}{\partial z_i} \frac{\partial x_i^h}{\partial r^h} \left(dr^h - \sum_e x_e^h dp_e \right)$$

$$(39) \quad = -\sum_i \sum_e \beta \frac{\partial g}{\partial z_i} \left(\frac{\partial z_i^D}{\partial p_e} + \sum_h x_e^h \frac{\partial x_i^h}{\partial r^h} \right) dp_e$$

$$= -\sum_i \sum_e \beta \frac{\partial g}{\partial z_i} \frac{\partial \hat{z}_i}{\partial p_e} dp_e.$$

Therefore we can conclude

$$-\sum_{i=o}^{n} \sum_{e \in E} c_i \frac{\partial \hat{z}_i}{\partial p_e} dp_e > 0 \Rightarrow dW > 0. \tag{43}$$

For an economic interpretation of the above condition we transform the left-hand side of (43) as follows. To obtain price-cost differences, we simultaneously add and subtract $\sum_i p_i(\partial \hat{z}_i / \partial p_e)$, for any good e, and use the property

$$\sum_i p_i \frac{\partial \hat{z}_i}{\partial p_e} = -\sum_i \sum_j p_i \frac{\partial y_i^j}{\partial p_e} \tag{44}$$

(because $\sum_i p_i(\partial \hat{x}_i / \partial p_e) = 0$).

Now consider first a *perfectly competitive private economy* for which $\sum_i p_i(\partial y_i^j/\partial p_e) = 0$ for any private firm. Price changes are welfare improving in this case if

$$\sum_e \sum_i (p_i - c_i) \frac{\partial \hat{z}_i}{\partial p_e} dp_e > 0. \tag{45}$$

We know from (45) that either welfare improving price steps dp_e are possible, or that prices are optimal, in which case

$$\sum_{i=o}^n (p_i - c_i) \frac{\partial \hat{z}_i}{\partial p_e} = 0 \qquad e \in E. \tag{46}$$

For a perfectly competitive private economy the relevant optimum is the marginal-cost optimum. Details on the piecemeal policy on its way towards the marginal-cost optimum will be given in section 7.4 below.

Consider second a private economy which is not perfectly competitive but where the *private* enterprises achieve profits, $\pi^j > 0$. Let the piecemeal policy dp_e be neutral with respect to private profits

$$d\pi^j = \sum_e \left\{ y_e^j + \sum_i p_i \frac{\partial y_i^j}{\partial p_e} \right\} dp_e = 0 \qquad \text{for all j} \tag{47}$$

and hence

$$\sum_i \sum_j p_i \frac{\partial y_i^j}{\partial p_e} = -\sum_j y_e^j = -y_e. \tag{48}$$

Note that $\sum_e y_e dp_e$ is the impact incidence [27] on private profits of the piecemeal pricing policy.

---

[27] In the sense of Musgrave (1959, 230).

We obtain the following condition for welfare-improving price changes

$$\sum_e \left\{ \sum_i (p_i - c_i) \frac{\partial \hat{z}_i}{\partial p_e} - y_e \right\} dp_e > 0 \tag{49}$$

showing a dependency on the price effects $\partial \hat{z}_i / \partial p_e$ and on the impact incidence on private profits of the piecemeal pricing policy.

The optimum which corresponds to the above piecemeal policy can be characterized by the marginal conditions

$$\sum_{i=o}^{n} (p_i - c_i) \frac{\partial \hat{z}_i}{\partial p_e} = y_e \qquad e \in E. \tag{50}$$

It can be seen clearly that this optimum is *not* a marginal-cost optimum, but decisively depends on the impact incidence of public pricing on private sector profits. The result, of course, rests on our assumption of constant private profits. Considering Walras' law this assumption is a type of substitute for a public sector profit constraint and we therefore obtain a pricing rule which appears to resemble Ramsey pricing.

CHAPTER 6   POSITIVE PIECEMEAL THEORY

6.1   IMPROVEMENTS WITH TIGHT AND NON-TIGHT CONSTRAINTS

As we could expect, most positive piecemeal analyses lead to similar results as the normative analyses presented in chapter 5.

Consider, for instance, an initial state where prices p_e and quantities z_i are fixed in a market clearing, technologically and financially feasible way, the relevant constraints being fulfilled as equalities. Along any piecemeal policy path all markets must remain in equilibrium; the technology and budget constraints are weakened to inequalities.

The value of an adequately chosen objective function $\Phi(p, q, z)$ will increase if price changes dp_e and quantity changes dz_i [1] fulfill the following conditions:

$$d\Phi = \sum_e \frac{\partial \Phi}{\partial p_e} dp_e + \sum_i \frac{\partial \Phi}{\partial z_i} dz_i > 0 \qquad (1)$$

$$\sum_e \sum_h \frac{\partial x_i^h}{\partial p_e} dp_e - dz_i - \sum_e \sum_j \frac{\partial y_i^j}{\partial p_e} dp_e = 0 \qquad i = o, \dots, n \quad (2)$$

$$\sum_i \frac{\partial g}{\partial z_i} dz_i \le 0 \qquad (3)$$

---

[1]   As in chapter 5 we always hold qualities constant in this chapter.

$$\sum_i \left(\frac{\partial \Pi}{\partial z_i} - p_i \right) dz_i - \sum_e z_e dp_e \leq 0. \tag{4}$$

Solving the market clearing conditions for dz_i, and substituting into (1), (3), and (4), we obtain

$$B_o^T(dp_e) = \left(\frac{\partial \Phi}{\partial p_e} + \sum_i \frac{\partial \Phi}{\partial z_i} \frac{\partial z_i^D}{\partial p_e} \right)^T (dp_e) > 0 \tag{5}$$

$$B_1^T(dp_e) = \left(\sum_i \frac{\partial g}{\partial z_i} \frac{\partial z_i^D}{\partial p_e} \right)^T (dp_e) \leq 0 \tag{6}$$

$$B_2^T(dp_e) = \left(\sum_i \left(\frac{\partial \Pi}{\partial z_i} - p_i \right) \frac{\partial z_i^D}{\partial p_e} - z_e \right)^T (dp_e) \leq 0. \tag{7}$$

Clearly, Farkas' theorem can be applied to this system of conditions [2], showing the connection between positive piecemeal and optimum theory. After replacing dW with $d\Phi$, figures 8a and 8b of the previous chapter apply directly.

A similar reasoning applies in case of a tight technology constraint, making use of Motzkin's theorem [3] and of figures 9 and 10 in the preceding chapter.

---

[2] See section 5.2 above.

[3] See section 5.3 above.

6.2 THE TRADE-OFF BETWEEN EFFICIENCY AND MARKET EQUILIBRIUM

6.2.1 TRENDS TOWARDS PRODUCTION INEFFICIENCY WITH MARKETS IN EQUILIBRIUM

We saw in section 5.4 that increasing production inefficiency can be a necessary step to improve welfare. Let us now ask whether similar paradoxical results can occur in the positive piecemeal approach. The question is by no means trivial. It is often suggested in political discussion that positive approaches to public pricing are preferable to normative approaches because the former postulate maximands which can be observed directly and therefore provide better incentives for efficiency in production. Such an argument sounds very plausible because many positive theory objectives are directly linked with produced quantities. Welfare, on the other hand, is directly linked to consumed quantities whence we could expect market equilibria to be of greater importance in piecemeal normative than in piecemeal positive theory. The following analysis shows to what extent efficiency improvements are of greater importance in positive than in normative piecemeal theory.

Consider an initial situation with tight market clearing conditions

$$z_i = \sum_h x_i^h(p, q, r^h) - \sum_j y_i^j(p, q) \qquad i = o, \dots, n, \qquad (8)$$

but non-tight technology and budget constraints

$$\tilde{g}(z, DV_1) = g(z) + DV_1 = 0 \qquad (9)$$

$$\tilde{\Pi}(z, p, \rho, DV_2) = \Pi(z, \rho) - \sum_i p_i z_i + DV_2 = 0 \qquad (10)$$

where DV_1, $DV_2 > 0$ are dummy variables, measuring the public firm's inefficiency and excess revenues.

Assume these conditions hold not only in the initial situation, but also along any piecemeal policy path. Direct application of the gradient projection method to $\Phi(p, q, z)$ leads to a complicated result [4] which does not lend itself to further economic interpretation. Hence, we substitute the market equilibria $z_i = z_i^D(p, \cdot)$ into the positive theory objective function

$$\widetilde{\Phi}(p, q) := \Phi(p, q, z) \tag{11}$$

and let prices change along the steepest ascent of the objective function $\widetilde{\Phi}$

$$dp_e = \frac{\partial \widetilde{\Phi}}{\partial p_e} = \frac{\partial \Phi}{\partial p_e} + \sum_i \frac{\partial \Phi}{\partial z_i} \frac{\partial z_i^D}{\partial p_e} \tag{12}$$

where the derivatives $\partial \Phi / \partial z_i$ and $\partial \Phi / \partial p_e$ vary from objective function to objective function, as shown explicitly in table 1, chapter 4.

As the non-tight technology and budget constraints are assumed to hold along any policy path, we obtain the following linear approximations [5]:

$$dDV_1 = -\sum_e \sum_i \frac{\partial g}{\partial z_i} \frac{\partial z_i^D}{\partial p_e} \frac{\partial \widetilde{\Phi}}{\partial p_e} \tag{13}$$

---

[4] According to Luenberger (1973) the only binding constraints (8) determine the formula for the optimal price and quantity changes dp and dz as follows:

$$\begin{pmatrix} dp \\ dz \end{pmatrix} = \{I - \nabla_M [\nabla_M^T \nabla_M]^{-1} \nabla_M^T\} \begin{pmatrix} \partial \Phi / \partial p \\ \partial \Phi / \partial z \end{pmatrix}$$

where I is a unit matrix, ∇_M is the gradient matrix of the market clearing conditions with respect to prices and quantities, $\partial \Phi / \partial p$ and $\partial \Phi / \partial z$ are the gradient vectors of the objective function.

[5] Analogously to section 5.4 above.

$$dDV_2 = -\sum_e \sum_i \left\{ \left(\frac{\partial \Pi}{\partial z_i} - p_i \right) \frac{\partial z_i^D}{\partial p_e} - z_e \right\} \frac{\partial \widetilde{\Phi}}{\partial p_e} \qquad (14)$$

where the market equilibria $z_i = z_i^D(p, \cdot)$ have been substituted.

Let us concentrate on decreasing or increasing inefficiency [6].We know from (13) that changes in inefficiency depend on the relevant objective function, via $\partial \widetilde{\Phi} / \partial p_e \lessgtr 0$, on the price effects, $\partial z_i^D / \partial p_e \lessgtr 0$, and on the production effects, $\partial g / \partial z_i > 0$. Since these partial derivatives are multiplied by each other, it is impossible to obtain any general cqnclusions as to whether ppsitive piecemeal theory requires decreasing or increasing inefficiency. We cannot exclude the paradoxical result that increasing inefficiency is best along some parts of the piecemeal policy path, nor can we definitely conclude which positive theory objectives provide the best incentives for efficiency.

Nevertheless, some typical characteristics of piecemeal policy can be shown with the help of two examples. Both examples describe some initial situation which is characterized by particular price responses. Results for such a situation can be found by applying eq. (13). The reader should always remember that the results which follow hold only for such an initial state. Along the path towards the optimum we expect all cases of decreasing inefficiency to vanish, at least at the very last step towards the optimum [7].

The two examples are as follows:

Case (I), "predominant substitute relations"
Assume the own price effects of demand are not too high *and* predominant substitutional relations are more likely than predominant complementary relations [8]. Assume the price effects interact in such a way that the second term in (12) always takes the same sign as the components of $(\partial \Phi / \partial z)$, and

---

[6] The interpretation of (14) is similar to that of (13). However, it is even more complicated to obtain any results.

[7] As usual, we exclude the possibility of interior optima.

[8] Complementarities, for instance in the case of energy minimization, can easily disturb that pattern.

dDV_1 takes the opposite sign to that of the components of $(\partial\widetilde{\Phi}/\partial p)$ [9].

Case (II), "ignore the cross-elasticities"
$(\partial z_i^D/\partial p_e = 0;\ \partial z_e^D/\partial p_e < 0$ by excluding inverse reactions of demand). This is just the opposite of case (I). The second term in (12) always takes the opposite sign as $\partial\Phi/\partial z_e$, and dDV_1 takes the same sign as the components of $(\partial\widetilde{\Phi}/\partial p)$.

Although the assumptions of case (I) seem to be realistic for many cases of public supply, case (II) has a historical tradition as an aid for interpreting public pricing [10].

Let us first interpret *case (I)*. We obtain

$$\partial\widetilde{\Phi}/\partial p_e < 0 \qquad \text{for maximization of votes, and}$$
$$\text{for minimization of price indices;} \qquad (15)$$

$$\partial\widetilde{\Phi}/\partial p_e > 0 \qquad \text{for budget, output, revenue maximization,}$$
$$\text{and for energy minimization;} \qquad (16)$$

$$\partial\widetilde{\Phi}/\partial p_e \lessgtr 0 \qquad \text{for the combined manager-trade union}$$
$$\text{objective.} \qquad (17)$$

Hence, we expect *increasing inefficiency* if votes are maximized or if price indices are minimized. These results are consistent with those derived from the welfare approach of chapter 5. The reason is that vote maximization refers explicitly to individual utilities, as does welfare. And it is well-

---

[9] Recall from table 1, chapter 4, that for any objective function all $\partial\Phi/\partial z_i$ are either positive or negative or zero, but never mixed. The same is valid for $\partial\Phi/\partial p_e$. The only exception is the combined manager trade-union objective.

[10] The "inverse elasticity rule" is the best-known application. See subsection 8.1.1.

known that every price index can be seen as a sort of welfare measure [11].
Therefore we should not be surprised that vote and price index optimization
imply similar tendencies towards efficiency as does welfare maximization.

On the other hand, we expect *decreasing inefficiency* if budget, output
or revenue is to be maximized. This result shows the existence of higher
efficiency incentives from those positive theory objectives which concentrate
on prices and quantities sold by the firm instead of on customers' utilities.

Energy minimization is another objective which leads to decreasing
inefficiency. This result could be expected if we think of inefficiency in
terms of waste and energy inputs are assumed to be lower, the less waste
occurs. Yet this result is also surprising since energy minimization as such
is an objective which discriminates between different inputs, and would be
expected to cause inefficiencies.

The inefficiency incentives which result from the combined manager-
trade union objective cannot be determined unambigously. There are two
trade-offs [12]:

(a)   a trade-off between the trade union's interest in wages and the public
      firm's interest in output. Increasing inefficiency occurs if a trade
      union (over)accentuates wage policy in a public firm which is not too
      eagerly engaged in increasing its outputs;

(b)   a trade-off between the trade union's interest in employment and
      its interest in wages, the interest in employment pointing towards

---

[11]   The easiest way to grasp this connection is to compare a true cost of living index
with the Hicksian compensating variation.

[12]   Substituting from table 1, chapter 4, leads to $\partial\tilde{\Phi}/\partial p_o = U_p^2 + U_z^2(\partial z_o^D/\partial p_o)$ which
will be positive if the union's interest in wages dominates ($U_p^2 > 0$), and negative if the
union's interest in employment dominates ($U_z^2 < 0$), as $\partial z_o^D/\partial p_o$ is positive.
$\partial\tilde{\Phi}/\partial p_e = \sum_i U_i^1(\partial z_i^D/\partial p_e) < 0$; $e,i = m+1,...,n$, on the other hand, depend on the firm's
interest in output only ($U_i^1 > 0$). $\partial z_i^D/\partial p_e < 0$ because of the complementarity assumption
of case (I).

increasing efficiency and the interest in wages towards increasing inefficiency.

It should be noted that these trade-offs change considerably if market disequilibria are allowed, as the following subsection will show.

Let us now *consider case (II)* where all cross-price effects are neglected. In that case we obtain

$\partial\widetilde{\Phi}/\partial p_e < 0$ for maximization of votes,

                   minimization of price indices,

                   maximization of output;   (18)

$\partial\widetilde{\Phi}/\partial p_e > 0$ for energy minimization (public supply);   (19)

$\partial\widetilde{\Phi}/\partial p_e \lessgtr 0$ for budget and revenue maximization,

                   energy minimization (private supply),

                   combined manager and trade union interest.[13] (20)

The results of case (II), therefore, are not simply opposite to those of case (I). The utility related objectives, votes and price indices, indicate a tendency towards increasing efficiency. The same tendency prevails for output maximization, which thereby exhibits the most pronounced incentive towards efficiency of all positive theory objectives. Budget and revenue maximization may still exhibit incentives towards efficiency if the own price effect is not too low. The combined manager-trade union interest, again, leads to indeterminate results.

Once again, the usual reminder holds that the above tendencies need not prevail along the whole path of piecemeal policy.

---

[13] In this case $\partial\widetilde{\Phi}/\partial p_e < 0$ for $e \neq 0$; $\partial\widetilde{\Phi}/\partial p_e > 0$ for $e = 0$.

6.2.2 PRODUCTION EFFICIENCY WITH MARKETS IN DISEQUILIBRIUM

Until now we have always assumed that markets are in equilibrium. The present subsection shows that the above mentioned tendencies towards increasing inefficiency result from the necessity to observe the market equilibrium constraints.

For this purpose we consider an initial situation with non-tight market, technology and budget constraints

$$\tilde{m}_i(z_i, p, r^h, DV_{oi}) = \sum_h x_i^h(p, r^h) - z_i - \sum_j y_i^j(p) + DV_{oi} = 0 \qquad (21)$$

$$\tilde{g}(z, DV_1) = g(z) + DV_1 = 0 \qquad (22)$$

$$\tilde{\Pi}(z, p, \rho, DV_2) = \Pi(z, \rho) - \sum_i p_i z_i + DV_2 = 0. \qquad (23)$$

Employing the gradient projection method, price *and* quantity changes are as follows:

$$dp_e = \frac{\partial \Phi}{\partial p_e} \; ; \; dz_i = \frac{\partial \Phi}{\partial z_i}. \qquad (24)$$

This piecemeal policy does not change the prevailing degree of inefficiency if votes are maximized or if a Laspeyres price index is minimized. Both objectives do not depend on quantities z_i and therefore (24) implies $dz_i = 0$. As the quantities remain unchanged, the degree of inefficiency represented by DV_1 in (22) also remains unchanged. There is no trade-off between inefficiency and market disequilibrium in the cases of vote and price index optimization [14].

---

[14] The same result holds for welfare maximization.

However, such a trade-off exists if positive theory objectives depend on quantities z_i. For an analysis of these cases, we assume that the non-tight constraints (21) – (23) hold along any piecemeal policy path. Therefore we obtain as linear approximations

$$dDV_{oi} = \frac{\partial \Phi}{\partial z_i} - \sum_e \frac{\partial z_i^D}{\partial p_e} \frac{\partial \Phi}{\partial p_e} \qquad i = o, \ldots, n \qquad (25)$$

$$dDV_1 = -\sum_i \frac{\partial g}{\partial z_i} \frac{\partial \Phi}{\partial z_i} \qquad (26)$$

$$dDV_2 = -\sum_i \left(\frac{\partial \Pi}{\partial z_i} - p_i \right) \frac{\partial \Phi}{\partial z_i} + \sum_e z_e \frac{\partial \Phi}{\partial p_e}. \qquad (27)$$

Let us begin the economic interpretation with the most interesting result: if a positive theory objective is monotonically increasing in z_i, there is a tendency towards decreasing inefficiency [15]. This result is based on eq. (26) where $dDV_1 < 0$ if $(\partial g/\partial z_i) > 0$ and $(\partial \Phi/\partial z_i) \geq 0$, strictly positive for at least one z_i. For a plausible explanation of this effect see figure 11b. There are two curves in figure 11b: the offer curve which represents the market equilibrium and the production possibility frontier which represents efficiency. In previous analyses we followed the offer curve from X_1 to X_2, which yielded inefficiency. The present analysis allows us to approach more directly the production possibility frontier by moving within the hatched area and ignoring the offer curve.

The only exception may result from the trade union's influence [16]. We encounter a trade-off between the trade union's interest in employment and the public firm's in output. Too intensive accentuation of employment targets may drive the public firm into inefficiency unless it is seriously aware of its own output targets. The trade union's interest in wage increases

---

[15] There is only one exception which is considered in the following paragraph.

[16] If $U_z^2 < 0$ outweighs the influence of public firm's $U_i^1 > 0$, $i = m+1,...,n$.

does not influence this efficiency trade-off, but the equilibrium on the labor market only.

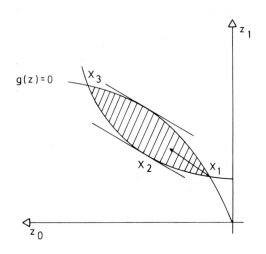

Figure 11b

Positive theory's higher incentives towards efficiency may be questionable if they are accomplished at the cost of increasing market disequilibria ($dDV_{oi} > 0$).

As we could expect, this result occurs with certainty if output is maximized. Output maximizing public firms, therefore, face the well-known bias of quantitatively producing as much as possible, but missing the market.

It is impossible to state in general which objectives will always lead to increasing or decreasing disequilibria in all markets. However tendencies towards a trade-off between efficiency and market equilibria are also prevalent in many other cases. Once again, cases (I) and (II) may serve as examples. The results are shown in table 2.

TABLE 2: SIGN OF dDV_{oi} [17]

Objective	Case (I)	Case (II)
Votes	$+$	$-$
Budget$(i = m + 1, \ldots, n)$	$\overset{+}{-}$	$+$
Output	$+$	$+$
Revenue$(i = m + 1, \ldots, n)$	$\overset{+}{-}$	$+$
Energy (private supply)$(i \neq k)$[18]	$-$	$+$
Energy (public supply)	$-$	$+$
Price index	$+$	$-$
Manager and trade union $i = 0$[19]	$-$	$-$
$\quad i = m + 1, \ldots, n$	$+$	$+$

Whereas most results of table 2 are self-evident, we should deal more extensively with the combined manager and trade union objective. In all markets but the labor market there is a tendency towards increasing disequilibria. The reason is simple. The firm's part of this objective function is a monotonically increasing function of output. The union's part depends on

---

[17] $+$ means $dDV_{oi} > 0$; $-$ means $dDV_{oi} < 0$; $\overset{+}{-}$ means the sign is indeterminate.

[18] For $i = k$ the private monopolistic supplier will always guarantee the equilibrium in the energy market.

[19] If p_i is an instrument variable we assume the price effect $\partial z_o^D / \partial p_o > 0$.

the labor market variables only. Hence for all markets but the labor market, this objective function has the same effect as output maximization. On the labor market, however, the union's interest involves a tendency towards decreasing market disequilibria.

It is fitting that we close this section by reminding the reader, once again, that caution is required when dealing with the above cases (I) and (II). A tendency towards increasing market disequilibria typically will not hold along the whole piecemeal policy path. Somewhere along this path the above tendency has to switch, and piecemeal policy must imply decreasing market disequilibria, at least at the last step towards the optimum.

PART TWO: PUBLIC PRICING POLICIES FOR WELFARE MAXIMIZATION

A   BASIC RULES

CHAPTER 7   MARGINAL-COST PRICING

7.1   OPTIMUM POLICY

7.1.1   THE THEORETICAL BASIS AND PRACTICAL EXAMPLES

We begin with the most conventional case. Let us assume that

a)   only prices of publicly produced goods are controlled; uncontrolled prices equal marginal costs c_i in the public sector [1];

b)   the private sector is perfectly competitive;

c)   the distribution of lump-sum incomes is optimally chosen, hence we deal with compensated demand;

d)   there is no revenue-cost constraint on the public sector;

e)   quality levels are fixed.

Then the marginal conditions (3-24) reduce to

---

[1]   If only output prices are regulated, this assumption implies equality of c_i and C_i for all net outputs. See subsection 2.4.5 above.

$$\sum_{i \in E}(p_i - c_i)\frac{\partial \hat{z}_i}{\partial p_e} = 0 \qquad e \in E. \qquad (1)$$

This can be interpreted as a homogeneous system of equations in the unknown variables $(p_i - c_i)$. If we assume the matrix $\partial \hat{z}_i / \partial p_e$ to be regular [2], we obtain the well-known marginal-cost pricing rule

$$p_i = c_i(z) \qquad i \in E. \qquad (2a)$$

This rule requires the enterprise to set all controlled prices equal to the marginal costs c_i which are defined as the marginal rates of transformation between output or input i and labor. Moreover, as all uncontrolled prices also equal the respective marginal costs c_i, production is always cost-minimizing, implying equality of c_i and C_i, the marginal costs proper [3]. Therefore we can conclude that

$$p_i = C_i(z) \qquad i \in E. \qquad (2b)$$

This rule is normatively valid for any kind of public enterprise: for competitive public enterprises (nationalized steel industries, communal breweries etc.) as well as for natural monopolies (e.g. telephone, electricity, gas supply).

With this in mind it is not surprising to find a wide range of proposals for the practical application of marginal-cost pricing:

- nationalized enterprises in general (White Paper (1967) for the UK; the project failed – see NEDO (1976); the White Paper (1978) avoided any explicit pricing rule);

---

[2] The Slutsky matrix never has full rank. However, our approach deals with a part of the economy only ($e \in E$; $E \subset I$).

[3] See subsection 2.4.5 above.

- electricity (papers by Boiteux and his team are collected in Nelson (1964); for Electricité de France see also Quoilin (1976); for the UK Turvey (1968, 1971));

- railways (frequently suggested since Hotelling's (1938) seminal paper);

- television (Samuelson (1964) opposing Minasian (1964) given the assumption of zero marginal costs for TV);

- telephone, theater, airports etc.

7.1.2 DEFICITS UNDER MARGINAL-COST PRICING

The marginal-cost pricing rule is a challenge for economists, regarding both theory and practice, because it provides a theoretical justification for public supply with permanent deficits. This consequence of marginal-cost pricing results if there exist strict local scale economies (as defined below). This is of considerable importance since, according to empirical studies, much of public enterprises' production takes place under scale economies.

The concept of a "welfare optimal" deficit is contrary to the widespread belief that deficits always mean mismanagement of public enterprises. The theoretical justification of deficits provided by marginal-cost pricing does not justify mismanagement. Marginal-cost prices are only one part of the solution of an optimization model which also gives normative instructions for optimal quantities of outputs and inputs thereby prescribing cost minimization [4].

Let us consider more closely the conditions required for such a welfare-optimal deficit. It can be shown that strict *local* increasing returns to scale are a sufficient *and* necessary condition for a marginal-cost pricing deficit.

---

[4] How to transpose these solutions into regulatory practice will be discussed extensively in section 7.2 below.

The proof is comparatively simple although we deal with a multiproduct enterprise. The reason for this simplicity lies in the particular definition of marginal costs in our extended Boiteux model which allows a straightforward definition of local increasing returns to scale which directly depends on marginal costs [5].

For this purpose we solve the production function $g(z) = 0$ so as to obtain $z_o = z_o(z_1, \ldots z_n) = z_o(z.)$ whence $\partial z_o / \partial z_i = -(\partial g / \partial z_i)/(\partial g / \partial z_o) = -c_i$. We define strict local increasing returns to scale by an adequately chosen elasticity of production [6]

$$\varepsilon(z) = \lim_{s \to 1} \frac{s}{z_o(sz.)} \frac{\partial z_o(sz.)}{\partial s} < 1. \tag{3}$$

This is an elasticity of the labor input with respect to the scale parameter s. The production function exhibits increasing returns to scale if labor input increases by a smaller proportion than all netputs $z_1, \ldots, z_n$.

Transforming the above definition yields

$$\begin{aligned}
\varepsilon(z) &= \lim_{s \to 1} \frac{s}{z_o(sz.)} \sum_{i=1}^{n} \frac{\partial z_o(sz.)}{\partial (sz_i)} \cdot z_i \\
&= \frac{1}{z_o} \cdot \sum_{i=1}^{n} \frac{\partial z_o(z.)}{\partial z_i} z_i \\
&= -\frac{1}{z_o} \cdot \sum_{i=1}^{n} c_i z_i.
\end{aligned} \tag{4}$$

Strict local increasing returns to scale are therefore given if [7]

---

[5] The general proof is more complicated as shown by Baumol (1976, 1977), and Panzar-Willig (1977a).

[6] For a similar procedure see Intriligator (1971, 181-2).

[7] Recall $z_o < 0$ when transforming $\varepsilon(z) < 1$.

$$z_o + \sum_{i=1}^{n} c_i z_i < 0. \tag{5}$$

From the marginal-cost pricing deficit

$$\sum_{i=o}^{n} p_i z_i = \sum_{i=o}^{n} c_i z_i = z_o + \sum_{i=1}^{n} c_i z_i < 0, \tag{6}$$

it can be seen that $\varepsilon(z) < 1$ is equivalent to the case of a marginal-cost pricing deficit [8].

Strict *global* increasing returns, on the other hand, are only a sufficient, but not a necessary, condition for deficits under marginal-cost pricing in multiproduct enterprises. Deficits can arise also if returns to scale are decreasing in some parts and increasing in others.

7.1.3 MARGINAL-COST PRICING AND GENERAL EQUILIBRIA

Recently there has been a revival of interest in the theory of marginal-cost pricing under economies of scale [9].

First, the *existence* of marginal-cost pricing equilibria is challenged (Beato (1982), Cornet (1982)): how can such an optimum be achieved by decentralized decisions of economic agents? Will marginal-cost pricing firms go bankrupt because of losses? Will consumers go bankrupt if they are liable

---

[8] If the technology is represented by a cost function, the above result occurs for strictly decreasing ray average costs (see Baumol (1976)).

[9] The main points of this discussion will be mentioned briefly, although existence problems are not handled at all in the Boiteux framework. Mentioning those recent papers gives us an opportunity to stress some shortcomings of the Boiteux approach.

as shareholders of public enterprises? In the Boiteux approach this problem is solved by assuming (optimal) lump-sum taxes which finance possible deficits. Although this is a satisfactory way of dealing with an allocative optimum, it is not a satisfactory way of dealing with decentralization because there are no a priori arrangements that assure positive individual incomes, given any distributions of profits and endowments. To overcome this problem, we must consider special distributions (Beato (1982)). Further research should concentrate on the existence of marginal-cost pricing equilibria if public deficits are financed by taxes on goods and factors in inelastic supply (the old Hotelling proposal) or by two-part tariffs, where the fixed parts, aggregated over all customers, must be such as to cover the difference between total costs and the revenue which would result from marginal-cost pricing.

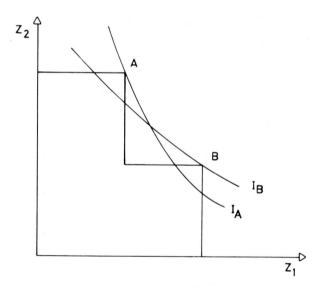

Figure 12

Second, the *optimality* of marginal-cost pricing is challenged (Guesnerie (1975), Brown-Heal (1979, 1980a, 1980b), Tillmann (1981)). If the production possibilities are non-convex, marginal-cost equilibria may fail to be Pareto optima. The literature tries to find conditions under which at least one equilibrium is Pareto efficient. However, there exist examples showing that even in very simple cases such conditions cannot be found. The best example can be given by using Brown-Heal's (1979) figure for a two-consumer, one-producer economy.

Let the production possibility frontier of the non-convex economy be as shown in the figure. The Scitovsky social indifference curve through A is denoted I_A. If endowments and the relative price change, the social indifference curve also changes, say from I_A to I_B. This implies a new equilibrium at B. Both A and B are equilibria because they fulfill the first-order conditions, but are not Pareto optimal. Whether such problems arise depends on the endowments of the consumers because they affect the social indifference curves and their possible intersection.

7.1.4 LONG-RUN VERSUS SHORT-RUN MARGINAL-COST PRICING; JOINT INPUTS; SOCIAL COSTS

Depending on the particular specification of technology $g(z)$, there are different meanings that can be attributed to marginal costs:

a) $g(z)$ can be defined in a short-run or in a long-run sense, depending on the variability of inputs over time [10]. The resulting problems of short-run versus long-run marginal-cost pricing have been discussed intensively in the empirical literature [11].

b)   Similar problems arise if the technology $g(z)$ comprises specific inputs for any good to be produced *and* joint inputs which are necessary

---

[10]   As dealt with in subsection 2.4.6 above.

[11]   Some of the problems of this discussion are treated in our empirical section 24.4 below.

for the production of more than one good. The empirical literature
explicitly stresses the importance of including the optimal capacity
choice if marginal-cost pricing is to be applied [12].

c) It has often been postulated that marginal-cost pricing should equate
prices to *social* marginal costs in the sense used in cost-benefit analysis. The application of marginal-cost pricing, then, raises the usual
practical problems: the empirical estimation of spillovers, intangibles, the choice of the rate of time preference or rate of opportunity
costs. Of course, the technology $g(z)$ could be understood as including all the above effects. However, in the framework of our general
model this procedure is by no means straightforward. There is no
need to include *external effects*, as the interaction with the rest of
the economy is explicitly modelled so as to ensure Pareto efficiency.
Intangibles cannot be measured in any case. Hence, if necessary, we
could include some warning of the presence of intangibles in verbal
supplementary remarks, but it is not helpful to include intangibles
in the model. The choice of the *discount factor*, on the other hand,
remains of importance. However, our model is a static one. Elsewhere we have shown explicitly the importance of discount rates on
public pricing and on subsidizing of public enterprises (Bös-Tillmann-
Zimmermann (1984)).

7.1.5   THE PROBLEM OF CROSS-SUBSIDIZATION[13]

Before marginal-cost pricing can be applied in practice, we must always
consider carefully what is to be understood as a "good" in the sense of our
analysis. In practice we can start from a comparatively narrow conception

---

[12] See for instance Glaister (1976a).

[13] As cross-subsidization is of particular interest in the case of a given revenue-cost
constraint, a more extended discussion of this problem may be found in subsection 8.1.2.

(e.g. different categories of seats in theaters) or from a comparatively broad conception (regional unitary tariffs for railways, electricity, gas and certain postal services).

The term "broad conception" means unitary pricing for a good, in spite of different costs for various parts of production, and in spite of differences in the demand for this good. Unitary pricing thereby leads to internal subsidization. If, for instance, a unitary tariff is collected for local traffic (determined by marginal costs of total local traffic), long-distance users will be subsidized by short-distance users and, as well, users of less frequented lines by users of heavily frequented lines, etc.

If such an internal subsidization is unwanted, we have to split our good into different goods with different prices depending on the marginal costs of the newly defined different goods. Usually, this will lead to cases of joint-cost production.

7.2   REGULATING MARGINAL-COST PRICES

7.2.1   COMPETITIVE PUBLIC ENTERPRISES

If prices are set by the market, and the public enterprise produces under decreasing returns to scale, profit maximization will directly lead to marginal-cost pricing; if additionally all other enterprises produce under non-increasing returns to scale the welfare optimum can be easily decentralized.

This is not valid if the public enterprise produces under increasing returns to scale. Economic theory offers different solutions for the case in which an enterprise produces under a deficit.

Assume that all potential firms have the same technology g(z) and that input prices are given. Now define the locus M which separates the regions of subadditive technology [14] (quantities below M) and superadditive

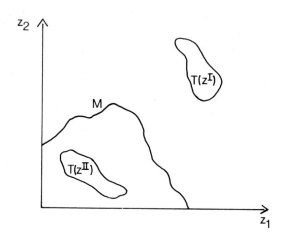

Figure 13

technology (quantities above M) [15]. Now consider the region of all output vectors that can generate a total revenue equal to or exceeding the total costs of the industry. The location of this region depends on the interrelation between demand and costs. If this region is outside and far to the right of M in figure 13 $(T(z^I))$, production by more than one enterprises will be optimal (cost minimizing). If in such a case the enterprises that are actually in the market make profits, these profits will be restrained by potential entrants. If

---

[14] In terms of cost functions subadditivity is given if for any two output vectors $z^{+'}$ and $z^{+''}$ we obtain $C(z^{+'}+z^{+''}) < C(z^{+'})+C(z^{+''})$. To define strict superadditivity one has to replace $<$ with $>$ in the above cost inequality.

[15] See Baumol-Fischer (1978).

they have deficits, the marginal producers will leave the market. In the long run the producers will produce along M and break even. This mechanism solves the deficit problem and determines the optimal number of firms [16].

In the case of region $(T(z^{II}))$ such a solution cannot be found and the elimination of marginal producers will continue until monopolistic structures prevail in the particular market, in which case the profit maximizing quantities and prices are defined for increasing returns to scale. An alternative to these private monopolistic structures can be seen in the establishment of a public enterprise.

7.2.2 REGULATING NATURAL MONOPOLIES

To investigate the regulation of marginal-cost pricing in an empirically relevant environment, we assume the income distribution to be optimal. In the theoretical framework of the Boiteux model this assumption implies that optimal lump-sum incomes r^h are chosen by the government [17], whence we consider compensated demand $\hat{z}_i(\cdot)$ [18]. Available instruments are the n+1 quantities $(\hat{z}_i)$ and the k regulated prices $(p_e) = (p_1, \ldots, p_k)$ which we always assume to refer to net outputs.

Now consider the following problem. The appropriate government agency feels obliged to optimize welfare, but lacks information on the demand for the firm's products and, even worse, on the costs of production. The firm typically wants to maximize profits, output or revenue, and tries

---

[16] For further details see Baumol-Fischer (1978).

[17] In empirical studies this problem typically is excluded by starting from a representative consumer, in which case any explicit computation of individual lump-sum incomes is avoided.

[18] We exclude the difficult problems that, for instance in cases of increasing returns to scale, there might exist no unique solution of our Boiteux model or no solution at all and treat the problems of regulation only for cases where a unique welfare optimum exists.

to hide information from government in order to reach its own objectives as best as possible. Given this principal-agent relation, we must find regulatory rules which force the enterprise to achieve the government's objective although the enterprise follows its own interest and is not obliged to inform government about all details of its demand and cost functions. Only demand and cost data, not necessarily functions, of past periods are thought of as being known to both the enterprise and the controlling government agency.

There are many different possibilities for a government to fix regulatory rules, where in all cases we must consider government's informational requirements, and public enterprise's incentive effects.

The most important *informational* problem refers to the cost function which enterprises often are not willing to disclose. Information on costs is particularly difficult to be obtained by the government especially if fixed costs have to be imputed to the different goods the public firm produces. Moreover, the government agency and the public enterprise will have to stipulate which kind of cost function they want to consider in their respective activities. Otherwise the government may set welfare maximizing prices based on social cost considerations, whereas the public enterprise may maximize profit considering private costs or apply social cost criteria which are inconsistent with those of the government.

The *incentive* problem will be considered by looking at the degrees of freedom the public enterprise's board is given after regulation, and which can be used to maximize profits, revenue, or output, instead of welfare.

a) *First case of regulation*: delegating the maximization of social welfare to the public enterprise itself, giving the enterprise the right to optimize welfare in the Boiteux framework, by means of (p_e) and (z_i), taking into account those particular assumptions which lead to marginal-cost pricing [19].

---

[19] Recall that the lump-sum incomes r^h are assumed to be optimally fixed by the

The government's information requirements are low because they relate only to the ex-post control of the firm. The firm's incentives to maximize welfare also are low because the firm is left with $k+n+1$ degrees of freedom, k prices and $n+1$ quantities, which can be used to maximize profits, output or revenue. Profit maximization might be detected easily by government control. But output or revenue maximization is much more complicated to detect by someone who is not fully informed of the relevant demand and cost functions, because these objectives lead to low pricing strategies of the public firm, which might be difficult to distinguish from welfare optimal low pricing.

To deal with the lack of incentives of the firm, the government will tend to be more precise in its regulatory activities.

b) *Second case of regulation*: the government sets k welfare-optimal output prices, the board chooses $n+1$ netput quantities.

The government's information requirements are high because computing welfare-optimal prices p_e presupposes knowledge of the shape of the demand functions for the relevant goods and of the cost function of the public enterprise.

The board's incentives for welfare maximization are not particularly high. Assuming all z_i are used as instruments of the public enterprise, the board is given exactly $n+1$ degrees of freedom. The board could use these degrees of freedom to maximize revenue or outputs, which would typically imply some distortions.

The same problems as in the price-setting case arise if the government sets a certain amount of welfare-optimal netput quantities, say m, whereas the board chooses k prices and the remaining $n+1-m$ quantities. Hence, this kind of regulation does not help either.

Therefore, apart from setting prices or quantities, the government has to instruct the board to follow particular regulatory rules. These rules

---

government.

should be as simple as possible, but must be sufficient to guarantee the welfare-optimum.

c) *Third case of regulation*: the government sets k prices [20] and particular regulatory rules which must be obeyed by the firm.

The best-known of these rules is called the *MC-rule*: the government instructs the board to extend production until marginal costs are equal to the fixed prices

$$c_e(z) = p_e = \bar{p}_e \qquad e \in E, \qquad (7)$$

the bar indicating that prices (p_e) are exogenously given to the board.

The board's degrees of freedom are clearly reduced by the MC-rule. However there remain many degrees of freedom because $c_e(z)$ depends on all outputs and inputs $z = (z_o, \ldots, z_n)$. If all z_i are used as instruments, the board is given as many degrees of freedom as the number of all goods minus the number of regulated prices.

Hence, the MC-rule is not sufficient to guarantee the achievement of the marginal-cost pricing welfare optimum by independent decisions of the government and of the board. Let us therefore extend the regulatory activity.

The *efficiency rule*, to be added to the MC-rule, is as follows. The government instructs the board to achieve the welfare optimal profit of deficit $\overline{\Pi}^o$ [21] and to produce efficiently.

The board, then, has to follow the production function $g(z) = 0$, or equivalently $z_o = z_o(z_1, \ldots z_n) = z_o(z.)$ with the well-known property

---

[20] The case of the government setting m quantities could be treated analogously.

[21] The government optimizes welfare without any revenue-cost constraint. The resulting marginal-cost prices imply a particular welfare -optimal profit or deficit $\overline{\Pi}^o$. For the public enterprise, facing the efficiency rule, this profit or deficit $\overline{\Pi}^o$ is exogenously given.

$\partial z_o / \partial z_i = -(\partial g / \partial z_i)/(\partial g / \partial z_o) = -c_i$. As the profit or deficit is exogenously fixed, the board faces the following constraint

$$\overline{\Pi}^o = z_o + \sum_{i=1}^n p_i z_i \; ; \; d\overline{\Pi}^o = 0. \tag{8}$$

But then

$$d\overline{\Pi}^o = \sum_{i=1}^n \frac{\partial z_o}{\partial z_i} dz_i + \sum_{i=1}^n p_i dz_i = \sum_{i=1}^n (p_i - c_i) dz_i = 0. \tag{9}$$

This condition can only be met if the MC-rule is fulfilled and if $p_i = c_i$ for all $dz_i, i \notin E$, which guarantees the achievement of the welfare optimum. The remarkable feature of such a regulatory rule is the necessity to inform the enterprise about the deficit or profit it has to achieve.

The combination of the MC-rule and the efficiency rule seems to be quite common in economic practice. The reason is simple: the government always has to plan its budget in advance. Therefore it is always sensible to instruct the public enterprise to achieve that deficit which is provided for in the budget.

Although the above way of regulating marginal-cost prices leads to the welfare optimum and implies reasonable incentives for the board, one is inclined to search for regulatory procedures with even better incentives for the board. The straightforward candidate for this is the *profit rule*, to be added to the MC-rule: the government obliges the enterprise to choose all $z_i, i \notin E$, in a profit maximizing way,

$$\text{choose } \Pi^* = \max_{z_i (i \notin E)} \left\{ \sum_i p_i z_i \mid g(z) = 0 \right\}. \tag{10}$$

As the prices $p_i, i \notin E$, are given by the market, a quasi-equilibrium situation arises [22], and the board will choose netputs so as to equate marginal costs c_i, $i \notin E$, to prices. Unfortunately, however, the board might have the incentive not to follow this approach. In case of non-increasing returns to scale, everything goes the right way, the above rules implying a profit maximum. In the case of increasing returns to scale, however, the above marginal conditions imply a profit *minimum*, as can be seen from the second-order conditions [23].

For this purpose we solve the production function for z_o and differentiate $\Pi = z_o(z_1, \ldots, z_n) + \sum_1^n p_i z_i$ with respect to z_i, $i \notin E$. The first-order conditions

$$\left(\frac{\partial z_o}{\partial z_i} + p_i\right) = (p_i - c_i) = 0 \qquad i \notin E, \qquad (11)$$

added to the MC-rule, lead to second-order conditions

$$d\Pi^2 = dz.^T \nabla^2_{z.} dz. \qquad (12)$$

where $\nabla^2_{z.} = (\partial^2 z_o)/(\partial z_i \partial z_k)$ is the Hessian matrix of the production function $z_o = z_o(z_1, \ldots z_n)$. In the case of increasing returns to scale, $z_o(\cdot)$ is a convex function, $\nabla^2_{z.}$ is positive semidefinite and hence $d\Pi^2 \geq 0$. Therefore the optimum achieved is a profit minimum. In the case of non-increasing returns to scale the contrary is true.

However, we do not believe that on the basis of the above result public enterprises should be instructed to *minimize* profits [24] because the practice of such a regulation will typically induce the firm to produce inefficiently,

---

[22] This implies the assumption that the public enterprise is not a monopoly, but perfectly competitive, with respect to all goods $i \notin E$.

[23] If the board of the enterprise is obliged to minimize costs by using z_i, $i \notin E$, the approach leads to a cost maximum in the case of increasing returns to scale.

[24] Other authors are sometimes willing to accept profit minimization as a regulatory rule, see Wiegard (1978).

neglecting our theory which explicitly excludes inefficiencies. Therefore regulation by combining the MC-rule and the profit rule should only be applied for non-increasing returns to scale industries, in which case the firm actually achieves the welfare optimum by finding its profit maximum.

The government's information requirements are therefore increased. Before instructing the firm to apply the profit rule plus MC-rule, the government must know whether the firm produces under increasing returns. However, most probably this information will be obtainable from the firm's cost data of earlier periods.

Finally, we should discuss the common regulation of combining the MC-rule and the *"meet-all-demand"* rule: the firm is instructed to sell as much net outputs as consumers and private firms demand and to buy as much net inputs as they offer. The latter instruction could also be termed a *"buy-all-supply"* rule. Hence, quantity rationing of customers' demand or supply is forbidden by the meet-all-demand rule. Price rationing is forbidden by the MC-rule.

The government's information requirements are not higher than in the other cases of combining different regulatory rules we mentioned previously.

Recall that the MC-rule leaves us with n+1–k degrees of freedom. Additionally introducing the k equations of the meet-all-demand rule [25],

$$z_e = x_e - y_e \qquad e \in E, \qquad (13)$$

we obtain a system of equations which is either underdetermined or overdetermined depending on whether $k \gtrless n + 1 - k$. In the case of underdetermination, there may still be distortions if a board uses some or all of the remaining degrees of freedom to maximize, say, output or revenue. In the case of overdetermination, the enterprise cannot follow all regulatory rules.

---

[25] As usual, x_e is total private demand of good e, y_e is total private production of good e.

However, even if $k = n + 1 - k$, the achievement of a welfare-optimum is not guaranteed. Although there are no degrees of freedom left, there is no reason why the board should choose all quantities so as to obtain $c_i(z) = p_i$ for $i \notin E$. The MC-rule might then be fulfilled, but at "wrong" quantities.

d) *Fourth case of regulation*: the government does not set prices or quantities, but regulatory rules only. The board chooses prices (p_e), and quantities (z_i).

The combination of three regulatory rules, namely

- choose prices at marginal costs,
- achieve a given profit or deficit Π^o by efficient production, *and*
- meet all demand at the resulting prices,

is sufficient to eliminate degrees of freedom which could be used by the board to deviate from the welfare optimum. In the case of non-increasing returns to scale, the MC-rule, profit-rule, and meet-all-demand rule, taken together, can be used as an alternative system of regulation to achieve the marginal-cost pricing optimum.

e) *Fifth case of regulation*.

A different way of regulating marginal-cost prices has been proposed by Finsinger-Vogelsang (1981). Their subsidy adjustment process reckons on the firm's interest in maximizing the discounted flow of profits, where profit is defined as revenue minus costs plus government subsidies. We assume demand and cost functions to be constant over time. The firm chooses its prices at the beginning of any period and meets all demand which arises at these prices. Let us restrict the presentation to the usual case of starting prices p(0) above marginal costs. These prices are thought of as representing the state of the world without regulation.

The government does not restrict the firm's free choice of prices, but gives subsidies which increase with decreasing prices. It begins with a first period subsidy of

$$SUB(1) = z^+(0) \cdot [p(0) - p(1)] \tag{14}$$

and afterwards always pays

$$SUB(t) = SUB(t-1) + z^+(t-1) \cdot [p(t-1) - p(t)] \quad t = 2, \ldots, \tag{15}$$

where t is the index of time, SUB is the subsidy and z^+ is the vector of publicly supplied outputs. After successively substituting for the earlier periods, in any period T the subsidy can be written as

$$SUB(T) = \sum_{t=1}^{T} z^+(t-1) \cdot [p(t-1) - p(t)] \quad T = 1, \ldots . \tag{16}$$

When determining subsidies SUB($\cdot$), the government needs relatively little information, especially since the subsidies do not depend on costs.

The firm, on the other hand, is stimulated to maximize welfare. The subsidy (16) consists of accumulated rectangles under the demand functions, and therefore approximates consumers' surplus, measured between the starting prices p(0) and the present prices p(T). The after subsidy profits of the firm are therefore an approximation to the sum of consumers' and producer's surplus in period T. The maximum of this sum is obtained at marginal-cost prices. Hence, it always pays for the firm to lower its prices until they equal marginal costs. The firm will prefer to lower the prices in small steps in order to skim off consumers' surplus as far as possible. However, as future subsidies and profits are discounted, these small steps are prevented from becoming infinitesimally small.

It should be noted that the firm's incentives are achieved by paying consumers' surplus to the public firm, which may imply unwanted distributional consequences. The amount of subsidy paid to the firm will depend on the firm's starting prices p(0) and therefore we expect the firm to try to start from prices chosen as high as possible [26].

7.3   CONSEQUENCES FOR ALLOCATION, DISTRIBUTION, AND STABILIZATION

Owing to its derivation from the unconstrained maximization of welfare, marginal-cost pricing leads to what is called a *first-best allocation of resources*. This is the crux of the merit of marginal-cost pricing, and we should note in particular the following two consequences.

– Marginal-cost pricing leads to first-best utilization of capacity especially if we take into consideration the identity of short-run and long-run marginal costs in cases of optimal investment decisions of public enterprises.

– If public *and* private enterprises follow marginal-cost pricing, the allocation between publicly and privately produced goods is first best [27]. Such a result influences the *size of the public sector*. In the case of increasing returns to scale it leads to an extension of the public sector beyond that associated with cost covering prices, because in such a case marginal-cost prices have to be lower than cost-covering prices and demand for publicly supplied goods will be greater.

---

[26] If the management is not interested in maximizing the firm's profit, but in maximizing its own income, similar incentives can be obtained by paying the managers an additional income which approximates the changes of consumers' and producer's surplus (Finsinger-Vogelsang (1981, 399-401)).

[27] If private enterprises set prices above marginal costs the public enterprise can minimize welfare losses only by giving up marginal-cost pricing as well.

Income redistribution is not the main objective of marginal-cost pricing.

This does not mean that marginal-cost pricing has no distributional consequences at all:

– In the case of increasing returns to scale, the comparatively low price level may be distributionally positive if the publicly supplied goods are mainly consumed by low-income earners. However, because in our model the public deficits are financed by lump-sum taxes, a regressive impact of these taxes may offset the above mentioned positive effects.

– Splitting up one good into different goods (as in the case of peak load pricing [28]) may have distributional consequences, although in general we cannot say what these consequences will be. Comparing uniform marginal-cost pricing for a composite good with differentiated marginal-cost pricing for every single good we may point out the following distributional effects: typical peak-load pricing with higher peak prices will burden lower-income earners if the peak demand comes mainly from those groups (who cannot shift to off-peak demand as easily as higher-income earners). If the different goods are characterized by differences in quality [29], marginal-cost pricing will favor lower-income earners if marginal costs of "first class" goods exceed marginal costs of "second class" goods at least in the neighborhood of the optimum. These possibilities show clearly that we cannot draw general conclusions.

As far as the *stabilization aspects* are concerned, it has often been asserted that marginal-cost pricing is a built-in stabilizer.

The typical argument is as follows (Thiemeyer (1964)): assume a public one-product enterprise producing under increasing marginal costs at the point of intersection with average costs. Demand compatible marginal-cost

---

[28] For details see chapter 14.

[29] For details see subsection 1.6.1 and section 15.1.

prices and average-cost prices then coincide (point A in fig. 14). If we start from this point, a fall in demand (recession) will lead to a fall in marginal-cost prices, but to a rise in average-cost prices as shown by the demand function D"D" in fig. 14. If demand rises (boom), marginal-cost prices will rise more than average-cost prices as shown by the demand function D'D'. The comparatively lower prices in recession and comparatively higher prices in boom periods can be regarded as anticyclical.

This built-in stabilizing effect is a special case and does not hold in general. If we consider the boom period only, we can see that:

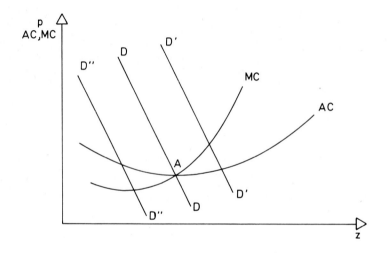

Figure 14

   –   The above argument is not valid in the case of scale economies where both marginal and average costs decrease, marginal costs falling faster than average costs.

   –   The argument applies to the short-run only. In the long-run the public enterprise will start to invest in order to regain the point of minimum average costs.

–   We need to ask how the public enterprise spends the revenue it receives from selling its products at higher prices. If the revenue is spent on additional investment or labor, for instance on overtime, there is no decrease in total demand but only a lag effect.

–   The stabilizing effects depend on the market structure. A monopolistic public enterprise, selling at higher prices to consumers, withdraws private purchasing power; selling at higher prices to producers, it reduces their profits or increases inflationary pressure: the effect on stabilization may be regarded as positive. Competitive public enterprises, on the other hand, selling at higher prices, allow other producers to increase their profits, and increase inflationary pressure: the effect on stabilization is negative.

7.4   PIECEMEAL POLICY

In deriving marginal-cost pricing as a special result of the extended Boiteux model, we started from particular assumptions, a) to e) above. Let us now introduce the same assumptions into the piecemeal policy model and assume quantities and lump-sum incomes to be optimally adjusted to any price changes.

As shown in chapter 5, we then obtain eq. (5–45). Welfare will be increased by changing prices according to the sufficient condition

$$\sum_{e \in E} \sum_{i \in E} (p_i - c_i) \frac{\partial \hat{z}_i}{\partial p_e} dp_e > 0. \qquad (5-45)$$

The above formula shows, once again, all the intricacy of piecemeal policy recommendations. After introducing so many restrictive assumptions we would have expected the result that welfare always increases if the price-cost margin of some good $e \in E$ is lowered in absolute value. Unfortunately, such a result cannot be corroborated by inequality (5–45). Consider the following example: there is some arbitrary initial situation where all prices are above the respective marginal costs. Some good, $e \in E$, is a substitute for all other goods, $\partial \hat{z}_i / \partial p_e > 0$ for all $i \in E$, $i \neq e$. In that case welfare increases if dp_e is positive, which implies increasing the deviation of p_e from c_e. Of course, such a result cannot hold along the complete path of price changes towards the optimum, but at least it cannot be excluded from the piecemeal policy analysis.

' To obtain more appealing economic results, we need further (!) assumptions. Two well-known examples are shown in the following [30].

Assume, *first*, that all prices change in proportion to the existing distortions $(dp_e = (p_e - c_e)ds)$. Welfare increases if

$$\sum_{e \in E} \sum_{i \in E} (p_i - c_i) \frac{\partial \hat{z}_i}{\partial p_e} (p_e - c_e)ds > 0 \qquad (17)$$

which only is fulfilled if $ds < 0$ [31]: an equal relative reduction of all price marginal-cost differences increases welfare. If all prices move towards marginal costs in proportion to the existing distortions, welfare increases. Here, at last, is the long wished for result that welfare increases if marginal-cost pricing is approached.

---

[30] For further details of this approach see Dixit (1975), Green (1975), Hatta (1977), Hagen (1979), Kawamata (1974), Wiegard (1980).

[31] We assume that at least one price does not equal marginal costs. We postulate that the matrix $(\partial \hat{z}_i / \partial p_e)$ has full rank and is negative semidefinite. For the latter property consider $(\partial \hat{z}_i / \partial p_e) = (\partial \hat{x}_i / \partial p_e) - \Sigma_j (\partial y_i^j / \partial p_e)$, the first matrix being negative semidefinite as a part of the Slutsky substitution matrix, the second matrix being positive semidefinite as a sum of the matrices of the second derivatives of the individual firms' profit functions which is known to be convex in prices in case of perfect competition.

Assume, *second*, some particular good $e \in E$ whose price-cost margin $\Theta_e := (p_e - c_e)/p_e$ in the initial situation does not exceed the price-cost margins of its complements, but exceeds the price-cost margins of its substitutes. Let the other prices be constant.

Then $dp_e < 0$ increases welfare. The proof is as follows. Split [32)]

$$\sum_{i \in I} \Theta_i p_i \frac{\partial \hat{z}_i}{\partial p_e} dp_e > 0 \tag{18}$$

into complements and substitutes

$$\left\{ \sum_{k \in IC} \Theta_k p_k \frac{\partial \hat{z}_k}{\partial p_e} + \sum_{i \in IS} \Theta_i p_i \frac{\partial \hat{z}_i}{\partial p_e} \right\} dp_e > 0 \tag{19}$$

where

$$IC = \{k \mid \Theta_k \geq \Theta_e \ ; \ \partial \hat{z}_k / \partial p_e < 0\}$$
$$IS = \{i \mid \Theta_i < \Theta_e \ ; \ \partial \hat{z}_i / \partial p_e \geq 0\}$$
$$IC \cup IS = I.$$

Using the particular properties of compensated demand we know that

$$\Theta_e \left\{ \sum_{k \in IC} p_k \frac{\partial \hat{z}_k}{\partial p_e} + \sum_{i \in IS} p_i \frac{\partial \hat{z}_i}{\partial p_e} \right\} = 0 \tag{20}$$

and substracting (20) from (19) yields

$$\left\{ \sum_{k \in IC} (\Theta_k - \Theta_e) p_k \frac{\partial \hat{z}_k}{\partial p_e} + \sum_{i \in IS} (\Theta_i - \Theta_e) p_i \frac{\partial \hat{z}_i}{\partial p_e} \right\} dp_e > 0. \tag{21}$$

[32)] Recall $\Theta_i = 0$ for $i \notin E$ because of our assumption b) in subsection 7.1.1. That property enables us to proceed from (5–45) to (18).

Our assumptions imply that $dp_e < 0$ increases welfare. The intuitive appeal of this result can be seen if all Θ_i and Θ_k are positive. Then welfare increases if some price p_e is lowered so as to approach the respective marginal costs c_e. Such a change brings Θ_e closer to the price-cost margins of the substitutes, Θ_i, but farther away from the price-cost margins of the complements, Θ_k.

CHAPTER 8   RAMSEY PRICING

8.1   OPTIMUM RAMSEY POLICY

8.1.1   THEORETICAL BASIS

Let us now consider the case where

a) only prices of publicly produced goods are controlled; uncontrolled prices equal marginal costs c_i in the public sector [1];

b) the private sector is perfectly competitive;

c) the distribution of lump-sum incomes is optimally chosen, hence we deal with compensated demand;

d) *the public enterprise is restricted by an exogenously fixed deficit or profit* Π^o; [2] and

e) quality levels are fixed.

Then the marginal conditions (3–24) reduce to

$$\sum_{i \in E} (p_i - c_i) \frac{\partial \hat{z}_i}{\partial p_e} = -\gamma z_e \qquad e \in E \qquad (1)$$

where $\gamma \neq 0$. For the most relevant case where Π^o exceeds the unconstrained welfare-optimal profit, $0 < \gamma < 1$ [3].

---

[1] If only output prices are regulated, this assumption implies equality of c_i and C_i for all netputs. See subsection 2.4.5 above.

[2] The extension to $\Pi(z,\rho)$ is straightforward.

[3] Remember from the general presentation of the Boiteux model that $\alpha_o > 0$ and

It is quite common to find the following transformations of this Ramsey-condition in the public economics literature:

$$a)^{4)} \quad \sum_{i \in E} t_i S_{ie} = -\gamma \hat{z}_e \qquad\qquad e \in E \qquad\qquad (1a)$$

where $t_i = p_i - c_i$ and $S_{ie} = \partial \hat{z}_i / \partial p_e$ is the Slutsky substitution effect. This transformation is well known from the theory of optimal indirect taxation.

$$b)^{5)} \quad \sum_{i \in E} \Theta_i \eta_{ei} = -\gamma \qquad\qquad e \in E \qquad\qquad (1b)$$

where $\Theta_i = (p_i - c_i)/p_i$ is the price-cost margin and $\eta_{ei} = (\partial \hat{z}_e / \partial p_i)(p_i / \hat{z}_e)$ is the compensated price elasticity of demand. This transformation is mostly used for two-product public enterprises where γ can be eliminated to obtain the condition

$$\frac{\Theta_1}{\Theta_2} = \frac{\eta_{22} - \eta_{12}}{\eta_{11} - \eta_{21}}. \qquad\qquad (1c)$$

Ramsey pricing is characterized by a particular trade-off between the level of prices and the structure of prices.

$\beta_o > 0$. Now assume a fixed profit constraint Π^o which exceeds unconstrained welfare-optimizing profit. Differentiate $\mathcal{L}$ (in (3-5)) with respect to Π^o. $\partial \mathcal{L} / \partial \Pi^o = -\bar{\gamma} < 0$ follows from economic plausibility (and from the appropriate Kuhn-Tucker formulation of the problem). Therefore $\gamma > 0$. Moreover, (3-7) yields $\alpha_o / \beta_o = 1 - \gamma$ because $\partial \Pi / \partial z_o = 0$ in our case. Hence $1 - \gamma > 0$ and $\gamma < 1$. If, on the other hand, Π^o falls below the unconstrained welfare-optimizing profit, $\gamma < 0$.

[4)] For these transformations remember that $z_e(p,(r^h(p,u^{h*}))) = \hat{z}_e(p,(r^h))$. Hence at the optimum the right hand side of eqs. (1) equals $\hat{z}_e$.

[5)] Recall that the Slutsky substitution effects are symmetric, $\partial \hat{x}_i / \partial p_e = \partial \hat{x}_e / \partial p_i$. Because of assumption b), moreover, $\partial y_i^j / \partial p_e = \partial y_e^j / \partial p_i$ and therefore $\partial \hat{z}_i / \partial p_e = \partial \hat{z}_e / \partial p_i$.

The *level of prices* is primarily influenced by the value of Π^o chosen. Ramsey pricing therefore can stand for low pricing as well as for high pricing policies, for deficit enterprises, cost-covering ones, or for profit-making enterprises. All or some prices can fall below marginal costs to bring about a deficit Π^o. The lower and the upper bound of Π^o, as mentioned above, are widely separated. Hence, Ramsey prices range from zero tariffs to unconstrained profit maximizing prices. The economic consequences of pricing under revenue-cost constraints depend on the concrete choice of Π^o. The usual exclusive concentration on the structure of prices prevents many economists from realizing that! Low Π^o will imply a low pricing level and, if demands react normally, a comparatively large public sector. Low Π^o may imply cheaper prices of publicly provided goods in order to help low income earners. This argument is mainly relevant if Π^o refers to a single public enterprise the outputs of which are mainly demanded by low-income earners.

What about the *structure of prices?* Recall that the public sector has to observe a revenue-cost constraint and to meet all demand. Hence the board must consider the price elasticities of demand for the different goods. The less price elastic a good, the easier can its price be increased in order to achieve Π^o because the public sector need not be too afraid of losing its customers. If, on the other hand, a good is comparatively price elastic, the customers will leave the market if the price is increased. The board will therefore refrain from large price increases of very price elastic goods.

Of course, cross price elasticities may destroy this basic pattern. However, the above considerations suggest a similarity between the Ramsey price structure and the price structure of a profit maximizing monopolist , which can be shown easily. Assume a monopolist who calculates his profit maximizing prices p_e, $e \in E$, considering production possibilities $g(z) = 0$ and acting along compensated demand functions $\hat{z}_e(p)$. He will choose the following price structure [6]:

---

[6] Following Drèze (1964, 31) we solve the production function $g(z)=0$ to obtain

$$\sum_{i \in E} (p_i - c_i) \frac{\partial \hat{z}_i}{\partial p_e} = -\hat{z}_e \qquad\qquad e \in E. \qquad (2)$$

Therefore Ramsey pricing converges to monopoly pricing if $\gamma \to 1$ and if the monopolist takes account of compensated demand functions.

Hence a board which chooses Ramsey pricing behaves as if it were an unconstrained profit maximizing monopolist who inflates all compensated price elasticities by a factor $1/\gamma$ [7].

If Π^o exceeds the unconstrained welfare-optimal revenue-cost difference, the inflating factor is $1/\gamma > 1$. The board has to overestimate all price elasticities and thus react more carefully than a monopolist would, being more anxious not to lose customers, which implies a lower level of prices than for a profit maximizing monopolist.

For the sake of completeness we must deal also with the case of Π^o below the unconstrained welfare-optimal revenue-cost difference. In this case the inflating factor $1/\gamma$ is negative. The board behaves like a monopolist who changes the signs of all price elasticities.

$z_o = z_o(z_1, \ldots z_n)$; $\partial z_o / \partial z_i = -(\partial g / \partial z_i)/(\partial g / \partial z_o)$. A monopolist's optimization is as follows ($z_i = z_i(p)$!):

$$max_{p_e} \sum_{i=1}^n p_i z_i + p_o z_o(z_1, \ldots, z_n).$$

Therefore

$$z_e + \sum_{i=1}^n p_i \frac{\partial z_i}{\partial p_e} + p_o \sum_{i=1}^n \frac{\partial z_o}{\partial z_i} \frac{\partial z_i}{\partial p_e} = 0 \qquad e \in E$$

which can be transformed into

$$\sum_{i=1}^n (p_i - c_i) \frac{\partial z_i}{\partial p_e} = -z_e \qquad e \in E \quad .$$

Now remember that we always assume $p_i = c_i$ $\forall i \notin E$ and that the monopolist acts along compensated demand functions $\hat{z}_e(p)$.

[7] Divide (2) by γ and set $(\partial \hat{z}_i / \partial p_e)/\gamma = (\partial \hat{z}_i / \partial p_e)^{infl}$ $\forall$ i, e. The compensated price elasticities are then obtained by multiplying each partial derivative by the corresponding price/compensated quantity ratio. $\eta_{ie}^{infl} = (1/\gamma)\eta_{ie}$ follows.

It may be noted in passing that it seems to be implausible that the above mentioned properties of Ramsey pricing can serve directly as a basis for *regulating* public pricing. [8]

We must not be conclude this subsection without mentioning a very special, but particularly well-known, case of Ramsey pricing. If we neglect totally all cross price elasticities of demand $(\partial \hat{z}_i / \partial p_e = 0; i, e \in E; i \neq e)$, the Ramsey price structure reduces to the famous *"inverse elasticity rule"*

$$\frac{p_e - c_e}{p_e} = -\frac{\gamma}{\eta_{ee}} \qquad e \in E \qquad (3)$$

where η_{ee} is the own compensated price elasticity of demand. In this special case any price-cost margin is proportional to its inverse price elasticity.

The price-cost margin of a good is larger, the smaller the absolute value of its price elasticity. As the compensated elasticities are always negative, all prices lie either above or below marginal costs. The case of positive price-cost margins may, for instance, be achieved by a break-even constraint for a public enterprise working under increasing returns to scale. The case of negative price-cost margins is plausible for public enterprises that have to follow "low pricing procedures" [9].

The economic consequences of the inverse elasticity rule are different for positive and for negative price-cost margins. The case of positive price-cost margins leads to relatively higher prices of price inelastic goods and to relatively lower prices of price elastic goods. The case of negative price-cost margins leads to the contrary. Now assume that goods mainly bought by lower-income consumers are comparatively price inelastic (whether this is the case must be ascertained empirically – Timmer (1981)). Then lower income consumers are burdened in the case of positive price-cost margins

---

[8] See subsection 8.2.2 below.

[9] Equations (3) show clearly that, for prices above marginal costs, $\gamma > 0$, and for prices below marginal costs $\gamma < 0$. But, of course, this does not hold generally if all cross price elasticities are taken into account, as in (1).

and favored in the case of negative ones.

8.1.2   CROSS-SUBSIDIZATION

The cross-subsidization problem of multiproduct enterprises refers to the relation between the revenues and the costs that are attributed to the individual goods or to combinations among them. The best presentation of the problem uses a game-theoretic approach (Faulhaber (1975)). If a public enterprise produces n' goods, we denote by "N" any "coalition" of goods, either individual goods, or combinations of more than one good, or the "coalition of the whole" n'. We denote a vector z^{+N} with entries

$$z_i^{+N} = \begin{cases} z_i^+ & i \,\varepsilon N \\ 0 & \text{otherwise.} \end{cases} \tag{4}$$

Denote revenue of the public enterprise by R and costs by C. Then for a *break-even* enterprise that is characterized by

$$R(z^{+n'}(p)) = C(z^{+n'}(p)) \tag{5}$$

we can identify "subsidizers" where

$$R(z^{+N}(p)) \geq C(z^{+N}(p)) \tag{6}$$

and subsidized coalitions where the contrary holds. This definition applies to any kind of cost function [10].

---

[10] In contrast Faulhaber (1975) restricts his analysis to subadditive cost functions because he is mainly interested in price structures of break-even enterprises where no coalition is a subsidizer but all benefit from being part of the enterprise. This formulation of the cross-subsidization problem was the starting point of the discussion on sustainability of natural monopolies.

It follows that some good or some coalition of goods is a cross subsidizer if it can "go it alone" and make a profit.

The concrete computation of (6) is quite complicated for public enterprises facing interrelated demand (z^{+N} always depends on all prices p!) and facing joint production [11].

The break-even case, however, is only one particular case of Ramsey pricing. And there may well exist cross-subsidization in cases of public enterprises with deficits or profits. Therefore, we should extend Faulhaber's terminology.

The straightforward extension is as follows. If the revenue-cost ratio of an enterprise is exogenously given, denoted by $R^o (R^o > 0)$:

$$\frac{R(z^{+n'}(p))}{C(z^{+n'}(p))} = R^o, \tag{7}$$

we can identify "subsidizers" where

$$\frac{R(z^{+N}(p))}{C(z^{+N}(p))} \geq R^o \tag{8}$$

and subsidized coalitions where the contrary holds. This definition again applies to any kind of cost function. And, needless to say, the computational problems are the same.

According to this extension in deficit enterprises goods with a nearly cost-covering price subsidize goods with a price which covers only 50% of the costs attributed to the production although this problem cannot be handled by a "go it alone"–test and there is no problem of a possible lack of sustainability. Moreover, it implies that in a profitable enterprise some

---

[11] Recently developed cost-sharing algorithms that make computation of $C(z^{+N}(p))$ possible also follow game-theoretic approaches, especially the Shapley-value. See Littlechild (1970), Billera-Heath-Raanan (1978).

goods may be subsidized although the prices are cost covering and they could "go it alone". In the long run this problem will, of course, only exist if entry to this market is forbidden.

Let us conclude by pointing out that the problem of cross-subsidization is of no importance from the point of view of welfare economics. If optimal pricing includes any kind of cross-subsidization (of the Faulhaber type or of an extended type), then that cross-subsidization should be accepted.

8.2.   REGULATING RAMSEY PRICES[12)]

The main dichotomy between alternative kinds of regulation can be seen as follows:

a)   The Ramsey optimization problem is solved by the public enterprise alone. All relevant variables, such as prices, quantities, and qualities are controlled by the public enterprise. Sometimes this applies even to the revenue-cost difference, provided it stays within certain acceptable limits. Regulation is only intended to lead the public enterprise itself to act according to Ramsey guidelines. This approach has the advantage of minimal information requirements for the public authority [13)]. However, it gives rise to incentive problems. A direct prescription to apply the Ramsey optimization will most probably not be the best way to achieve the Ramsey optimum. The objectives of the public enterprise may point in a different direction, thus making the situation unstable because we expect the public enterprise to deviate from the Ramsey optimum as soon as the control of the pub-

---

[12)] "Ramsey pricing" always refers to eqs. (1) which are a special case of marginal conditions (3-24).

[13)] The government's information requirements are reduced to that information which is necessary for the ex-post control of the public enterprise.

lic authority is weakened. Therefore, we should ask: do there exist better possibilities than direct prescription of Ramsey optimization to induce a public enterprise to follow Ramsey prices? This can only be the case if the environment of the public enterprise is changed, for instance by allowing market entry.

b) Sharing of responsibility between the public authority and the public enterprise means that the Ramsey optimum is not attained by one economic agent acting alone. Some variables are set by the public authority, others by the public enterprise. The government may, for instance, set Ramsey prices, and the public enterprise produce and sell those quantities that are demanded at these prices. Information requirements are increased "a priori" as compared with the approach outlined in a), because two agents solve optimization problems and need information. However, as we shall see, there exist many different possibilities for a government to set variables relevant for a public enterprise's decision range. These different policies can, in turn, be compared with each other from the point of view of the information needed by the government and of the incentives offered to the public enterprise.

8.2.1 REGULATION BY CHANGING THE ENVIRONMENT

Recently Baumol and others [14] have stressed the sustainability of natural monopolies. Assume a monopoly working under particular cost advantages [15]: what kind of pricing will protect the monopoly from losing its

---

[14] See Baumol- Bailey-Willig (1977), Panzar-Willig (1977b).

[15] According to Baumol-Bailey-Willig (1977) two cost attributes guarantee sustainability: strictly decreasing ray average costs and transray convex costs. The first assumption means a strong form of economies of scale, the second one a strong form of economies of scope (cost savings from complementarities in production).

monopolistic position through new entrants into the market? If we define sustainability as "a stationary equilibrium set of product quantities and prices which does not attract rivals into the industry" [16], it can be proved that

- Ramsey prices are sufficient for sustainability if the natural monopoly's profit does not exceed the entry costs of potential rivals;

- other price vectors may lead to sustainability, but the enterprise needs global information on the demand and cost functions for its products to find them.

The sustainability theory has been developed primarily for regulated private firms. The theory has no application to public enterprises if either free entry is forbidden legally or if no private firm is willing to enter because the public firm works at a permanent deficit or at profits which fall below the entry costs of any potential rival. The latter point is especially relevant for public deficit firms. According to the sustainability theory public monopolies could be brought to Ramsey pricing simply by the threat of potential de-nationalization of all or of parts of its production. As bureaucracies want to keep their monopolistic position, such a regulation would imply Ramsey pricing, the maximum achievable profit being given by the entry costs of potential rivals. The main policy suggestions of such an "invisible hand" approach to public enterprise regulation are

- less control, less regulatory rules:

- restrictions on internal subsidization (the most profitable parts of public supply are most exposed to potential entry).

8.2.2   REGULATION IN A GIVEN ENVIRONMENT

In general, the regulation of Ramsey prices can be treated in the same

---

[16]   Baumol-Bailey-Willig (1977, 350).

way as the regulation of marginal-cost prices.

First case of regulation: the government totally shifts the Ramsey optimization problem to the public firm. The government's information requirements are low, but equally low are the firm's incentives to maximize welfare. Hence, this case of regulation is not likely to be very successful.

Second case of regulation: the government sets prices or netput quantities. The government's information requirements are high; but the firm is left with many degrees of freedom which can be used, for example, to maximize profits.

Third case of regulation: the government sets k prices *and* particular regulatory rules. The MC-rule has to be replaced with the *Ramsey-rule* which consists of k rules on the pricing structure and one rule on the price level, i.e. the revenue-cost constraint which determines whether prices on average have to be low or high. The public firm faces the following problem:

$$\sum_{i \in E}(p_i - c_i)\frac{\partial \hat{z}_i}{\partial p_e} = -\gamma z_e \qquad e \in E$$

$$\sum_{i=o}^{n} p_i z_i = \Pi^o \qquad\qquad\qquad (9)$$

where the prices $p_i, i \in E$ are exogenously given [17].

If the firm faces fixed prices *and* the Ramsey rule, it is left with as many degrees of freedom as the number of all goods exceeds the number of regulated prices. Hence, once again, further regulatory rules should be added to the above Ramsey rule to obtain the optimum. The efficiency rule – produce efficiently at given $\overline{\Pi}^o$ [18] – absorbs the degrees of freedom which remain after fixing prices and imposing the Ramsey rule because the firm will equate marginal costs $c_i, i \notin E$ to those prices p_i which are

---

[17] The case of the government fixing m quantities could be treated analogously.

[18] See eqs. (7-8) and (7-9).

given exogenously by the market. Hence, by decentralized decisions of the government and of the public enterprise, precisely that welfare optimum is attained which we treated above [19].

If a meet-all-demand rule is added to the Ramsey rule, the system of equations will usually be over- or underdetermined, as in our earlier case of the regulation of marginal-cost pricing [20].

Fourth case of regulation: the government does not set prices or quantities, but regulatory rules only. Here, the government has to combine the Ramsey rule, the efficiency rule and the meet-all-demand rule so as to obtain the desired welfare optimum. The government's information requirements are not exceedingly high.

Fifth case of regulation: the government makes use of the similarity between the Ramsey-price structure and the perfect monopoly pricing structure, and advises the public enterprise *to inflate all demand elasticities by a common factor* $1/\gamma > 1$ *and then to behave like a profit-maximizing monopolist* (Drèze-Marchand (1976)).

There are three main objections to this proposal: first, the information requirements do not differ from those in the cases of setting prices or setting quantities, as the Ramsey optimization problem must be solved by the government to find the exact value of γ. Second, any profit maximizer will apply Marshallian demand functions and not compensated ones. Hence, the firm always faces an incentive to deviate from the above rule to optimize normal instead of compensated profit. Correct incentives could only be achieved by inflating factors which vary among commodities, depending on the varying income effects. Third, the proposal seems to include a strategy for the enterprise to cheat itself by computing profits on the basis of elasticities which the enterprise knows to be wrong. Thus there will always

---

[19] See subsection 8.1.1.

[20] A profit rule is meaningless in the Ramsey case as maximizing profit under a given profit constraint makes no sense.

be a tendency for the firm's board to switch to the correct elasticities or to give false information to the government agency.

Sixth case of regulation: finally, we must mention the *regulatory adjustment process* discussed by Vogelsang and Finsinger (1979). This process, applicable to enterprises under inreasing returns to scale, reduces the government's information requirements and is based on the profit-maximizing behavior of the enterprise, thus yielding positive incentive effects. The government regularizes the set of prices the enterprise is allowed to choose. These prices are at most cost covering if applied to the quantities sold in the period before:

$$\text{RAP}_t = \{p \mid p_t^T z_{t-1}^+ - C(z_{t-1}^+) \leq 0\} \tag{10}$$

where RAP is the set of regulatory adjusting prices. t denotes time, z^+ is the vector of publicly supplied outputs and p an adequately defined price vector. Demand and cost functions are assumed to be constant over time. Prices are set by the firm at the beginning of any period. The firm meets all demand at these prices.

The public enterprise then maximizes the profits of period t

$$\max_{p_t \in RAP_t} [\bar{p}_t^T z_t^+ - C(z_t^+)] \tag{11}$$

which may be positive. The profit-maximizing quantities (z_t^+) serve as the basis for finding the prices p_{t+1} of the next period. It can be shown that this iterative process converges to break-even Ramsey-prices [21].

---

[21] For criticism of the assumptions of this approach, and for extensions, using modified incentive structures, see Sappington (1980) and Gravelle (1981, 1982b).

8.3   INFLUENCE OF RAMSEY PRICES ON ALLOCATION, DISTRIBUTION, AND STABILIZATION

It is impossible to derive general results on allocative, distributional, and stabilization effects of Ramsey prices because all the consequences will depend on the amount of Π^o. Whether Ramsey prices will exceed or fall below marginal-cost prices will be determined by Π^o. Results can only be derived for given Π^o.

Considering $\Pi^o = 0$, in the case of increasing returns to scale, at least one Ramsey price will exceed marginal cost. If cross-price elasticities can be neglected, all Ramsey prices exceed marginal costs. With respect to *optimal allocation* this will lead to a shrinking public sector as compared with marginal-cost prices, where a revenue-cost constraint does not exist [22].

The *distributional consequences* of Ramsey pricing depend, first, on the *level of prices*. A public enterprise may, for instance, be constrained to work under deficit ($\Pi^o < 0$) to hold the price level of its products low in order to subsidize its low-income customers. Second, the *price structure* has to be considered. Here we have to ask whether the prices are above or below their marginal costs, as shown above by the example of the "inverse elasticity rule".

General results concerning the *stabilization consequences* of Ramsey prices cannot be formulated. These consequences will depend on the relevant elasticities of demand in business cycles. It will not be possible to obtain concrete results unless we build a dynamic model to investigate the relevant cases. There will be quite different consequences for stabilization policy if we consider cases of revenue-cost constraints other than cost covering. In such cases we can assume $\Pi^o \neq 0$ to vary anticyclically and to cause stabilization effects by means of optimal price or quantity instructions to

---

[22] The same tendency will prevail if we compare Ramsey prices with optimal two-part tariffs. Whereas the fixed charge as a lump-sum tax does not influence the first-best marginal conditions, a Ramsey price higher than the marginal-cost prices will.

the public enterprise.

8.4 A PIECEMEAL–POLICY INTERPRETATION OF THE RAMSEY OPTIMUM

Some of the best-known interpretations of Ramsey pricing follow a piecemeal approach. Consider a situation where the controlled prices change by dp_e and the uncontrolled prices remain constant. Then the total differentials of the demand functions $\hat{z}_e = \hat{z}_e(p)$ are as follows

$$d\hat{z}_e(p) = \sum_{i \in E} \frac{\partial \hat{z}_e}{\partial p_i} dp_i \qquad e \in E. \tag{12}$$

Let all price changes be proportional to the difference between price and marginal cost, that is,

$$dp_i = (p_i - c_i)ds \qquad i \in E \tag{13}$$

where $ds < 0$ implies that prices move towards marginal costs [23] and $ds > 0$ implies the contrary.

Substituting into (1) yields

$$-\gamma\hat{z}_e = \sum_{i \in E}(p_i - c_i)\frac{\partial \hat{z}_i}{\partial p_e} = \sum_{i \in E}(p_i - c_i)\frac{\partial \hat{z}_e}{\partial p_i} = \frac{1}{ds}\sum_{i \in E}\frac{\partial \hat{z}_e}{\partial p_i}dp_i = \frac{1}{ds}d\hat{z}_e(p)$$

$$\tag{14}$$

and by rearranging we obtain

---

[23] Prices which exceed marginal costs are lowered; prices which are below marginal costs are increased.

$$d\hat{z}_e = -\gamma \, \hat{z}_e \, ds \qquad e \in E. \tag{15}$$

This is one of Boiteux's (1956, 1971) main results for a second-best optimum: The price marginal-cost deviations are proportional to those infinitesimal variations in price that entail a proportional change in the demands for all publicly provided goods. This proportional change in demand may, however, imply that for some goods demand increases, although the own price decreases or vice versa [24]. Consider the following example: Π^o exceeds the unconstrained revenue-cost difference. Hence, $\gamma \in (0,1)$. Assume $ds > 0$. Recall that, for a given Π^o, some prices may exceed marginal costs, some others may fall short of them. The proportional price changes then imply increasing as well as decreasing prices. But the quantities change in the same direction: demand decreases, even for those goods whose prices decrease. The reason for such a demand response is straightforward. If the relevant good k is relatively unresponsive to its own price, but quite responsive to the prices of other goods that are complements, its second-best price may fall below marginal costs even if other prices exceed marginal costs. In such a case the proportional price change implies increasing the prices of complements which may imply a fall in the demand for good k even though its own price decreases.

A very common alternative interpretation going back to Ramsey (1927) concerns the case of the transition from second-best to marginal-cost pricing [25]: at a second-best optimum the relative deviations of second-best quantities from those quantities that would have been demanded if the goods were sold at marginal-cost prices are equal for all goods. Usually the authors add some remarks on the empirical applicability of such a result: if the public enterprise sells every good, not at the present price but at a price given

---

[24] Of course $\partial \hat{z}_e / \partial p_e$ is always negative. However, as we are considering simultaneous changes of all prices, the cross-price effects may overcompensate this direct effect.

[25] This is a special case of (15) where we start from marginal-cost pricing and integrate over ds from -1 (p^{MC}) to 0 (p^{Ramsey}). Then $[\hat{z}_i(p^{MC}) - \hat{z}_i(p^{Ramsey})]/\hat{z}_i(p^{Ramsey}) = \gamma \; \forall i$.

by the marginal cost of the present production, it will not be in a state of second-best optimum if the relative shifts of demand for the various goods turn out to be different.

However, the Boiteux-Ramsey interpretation of second-best quantities is an approximation only, contrary to our interpretation of second-best prices. As we use the total differential (12), all following results are strictly valid only for infinitesimal deviations from marginal-cost pricing or for demand functions which are linear in prices. This raises the question whether the prominence given to this approach, for instance in papers on optimal commodity taxation (Diamond (1975), Mirrlees (1975)), is warranted.

204

CHAPTER 9   RATE OF RETURN REGULATION

9.1   AN INTUITIVE INTRODUCTION

Since a fixed profit constraint Π^o is totally exogenous, it involves frequently recurring regulatory review processes, especially in inflationary times. Asking a government to change constraints is always a tedious procedure, leading to regulatory lags and a waste of time and other resources by the enterprise's board. Thus, it seems to be a more economic and flexible procedure to limit profits by fixing the maximum return on investment (in real terms) [1]. This procedure can be found often in regulatory practice, e.g. in the United States and in different proposals of the British White Papers on Nationalised Industries (1967, 1978). Moreover, this kind of regulation has been the subject of intensive analysis from the early paper by Averch and Johnson (1962) to the more recent book by Mrs. Bailey (1973). These examples suggest that rate of return regulation is relevant for public as well as for regulated private enterprises. Public enterprises may consider the rate of return limitation as a constraint on welfare maximization in the framework of our Boiteux model. Regulated private enterprises will typically treat it as a constraint on profit maximization. The results of both approaches can be compared.

Let the government fix a maximum rate of return on investment (for short "rate of return"). The definition of this rate of return discloses a capitalistic bias as it implicitly assumes all profits to be earned by the capital inputs only: the rate of return equals profit plus capital costs per unit of capital. Capital is assumed implicitly to earn its own costs and the whole profit:

---

[1] Other profit constraints which are partly endogenous include fixing a "fair" markup on cost or fixing a "fair" profit per unit of output. See Bailey-Malone (1970) for the resulting allocational inefficiencies.

$$\text{Rate of Return} = \frac{\text{Profit} + \text{Capital Costs}}{\text{Capital Input}}. \tag{1}$$

By fixing a maximum rate of return the government restricts the enterprise's profit. From (1) we see easily that the maximum profit allowed, given a maximum allowed rate of return, is given by

$$\text{Profit} = (\text{Rate of Return} - \text{Interest Rate}) \quad \times \quad \text{Capital Input}. \tag{2}$$

Such a profit constraint evidently differs from a "neutral" constraint Π^o because of its asymmetric treatment of the inputs. Compared with the neutral constraint, rate of return regulation will typically distort the capital-labor input ratio. The output prices of the multiproduct public sector or regulated private enterprise will be distorted as well.

Proceeding to a more concise notation we separate outputs $z_i^+ \geq 0$ from inputs which we aggregate into labor input $\ell > 0 (= -z_o)$ and capital input $\kappa > 0$. The respective prices are p_e, $e \in E$, p_o and p_κ, the input prices being fixed. Since capital and labor are perfectly divisible in production, the necessary inputs depend on the output quantities as follows

$$\ell = \ell(z^+), \quad \kappa = \kappa(z^+); \quad \left(\frac{\partial \ell}{\partial z_i^+}, \frac{\partial \kappa}{\partial z_i^+} \right) >> 0 \tag{3}$$

where $z^+ = (z_i^+)$ is the vector of the outputs.

Fixing a rate of return, d, restricts profit in the following way

$$\sum_i p_i z_i^+ - p_o \ell - p_\kappa \kappa = (d - p_\kappa)\kappa. \tag{4}$$

As in the case of a fixed constraint we will always choose a binding profit limitation. Of most interest, once again, is the case of a profit constraint that exceeds the unconstrained welfare maximizing level. However, even this case may well imply a deficit. Hence, we cannot conclude a priori whether $(d - p_\kappa) \gtreqless 0$.

9.2 A MORE RIGOROUS TREATMENT

Pricing under rate of return regulation can be seen as a special case of our Boiteux model solution (3-24). We again assume that

a) only prices of publicly produced goods are controlled [2];

b) the private sector is perfectly competitive;

c) the distribution of lump-sum incomes is optimally chosen, hence we deal with compensated demand;

d) *the public enterprise is restricted by a binding rate of return constraint;* and

e) quality levels are fixed.

Then the marginal conditions (3-24) reduce to

$$\sum_{i=o}^{n}(p_i - \widetilde{C}_i)\frac{\partial \hat{z}_i}{\partial p_e} = -\gamma \, z_e^+ \qquad\qquad e \in E \qquad\qquad (5)$$

where the modified marginal costs $\widetilde{C}_i$ equal

---

[2] We do not introduce the assumption $p_i = c_i$ for all $i \notin E$ because this chapter deals with modified marginal costs $\widetilde{C}_i$, whence the response of all goods $i = o,...,n$ influences public pricing even if $p_i = c_i$. The summation in (9-5) is over $i = o,...,n$ and not over $i \in E$ as in chapters 7 and 8.

$$\widetilde{C}_i = c_i + \gamma(d - p_\kappa)\frac{\partial \kappa}{\partial z_i^+} = p_o\frac{\partial \ell}{\partial z_i^+} + \gamma(d - p_\kappa)\frac{\partial \kappa}{\partial z_i^+} \tag{6}$$

using the definitions of $\widetilde{C}_i$ and of c_i.

If the regulated profit exceeds the unconstrained welfare-maximizing one, $0 < \gamma < 1$ [3]. The limiting cases refer to marginal-cost pricing ($\gamma = 0$) and to a rate of return regulated but profit maximizing monopolist ($\gamma = 1$).

The pricing structure (5) resembles the Ramsey result, replacing c_i with $\widetilde{C}_i$. Hence, the enterprise's board will once again behave like a profit maximizing monopolist who inflates all compensated price elasticities by a factor $1/\gamma$. However, the board not only takes account of the shadow prices c_i, but also of the marginal capital inputs, weighted by the difference between the rate of return and the interest rate. This asymmetric treatment of labor and capital is due to the asymmetric profit constraint.

The welfare maximizing board will always set prices in such a way that it *undercapitalizes* compared with the efficient capital-labor ratio. This implies that prices for labor-intensive goods are too low and vice versa.

The reason is that the board is not interested in profit, but in welfare. And the best strategy to maximize welfare is to keep the profit $(d - p_\kappa)\kappa$ low by low capital inputs. Then the "level of prices" can be kept lower and welfare increased.

The totally exogenous profit constraint Π^o, on the other hand, always leads to an efficient capital-labor ratio because it treats inputs symmetrically. This is an important theoretical advantage of Ramsey regulation as compared with rate of return regulation. This theoretical advantage, however, has to be balanced against the practical disadvantages mentioned in the introduction to this chapter. These disadvantages may be more important for practical application as we do not know the exact empirical

---

[3] $\gamma > 0$ can be shown as follows: differentiate $\mathcal{L}$ in the presentation of the Boiteux model (eq. (3-5) above): $\partial \mathcal{L}/\partial d = -\bar{\gamma} < 0$. Because of $\beta(\partial g/\partial z_o) > 0$ we obtain $\gamma > 0$.

relevance of the theoretically inefficient input choices.

9.3   WELFARE VERSUS PROFIT MAXIMIZATION: THE AVERCH-JOHNSON EFFECT

The analysis and practice of US rate of return regulation concerns profit maximization rather than welfare maximization. Hence, we should compare this approach with the Boiteux case.

For this purpose we consider a profit maximizing *board* of a public or private enterprise, setting prices p_e and output quantities z_i^+. We exclude lump-sum transfers. This exclusion can be justified ideologically: we do not want to give the profit maximizing enterprise the right to control the income distribution in order to maximize its profits. Hence, the enterprise is restricted to one-part tariffs and not allowed to set different income deductions and transfers for individuals as the fixed part of two-part tariffs.

The board considers the market equilibria for all outputs. In our partial approach, however, there is no need for the firm to consider the equilibrium of the labor and capital markets. The technology is introduced into the model by assuming that $\ell(z^+)$ and $\kappa(z^+)$ are factor demand functions.

The maximum profit the board is allowed to make depends on the rate of return, as fixed by the *government*. To deal with the most relevant case, we assume this rate of return to exceed the interest rate, since otherwise the enterprise would have to achieve a deficit (and a private enterprise would leave the market). On the other hand, the rate of return must be chosen in such a way that the profit permitted falls below the unconstrained monopoly profit. Under these conditions the profit constraint will always be binding.

Hence, we assume the enterprise solves the following optimization problem:

$$\max_{p_e, z_i^+} \mathcal{L} = \sum_i p_i z_i^+ - p_o \ell - p_\kappa \kappa - \sum_i \alpha_i \left[x_i(p) - z_i^+ - y_i(p) \right] -$$
$$- \delta \left[(d - p_\kappa)\kappa - \left(\sum_i p_i z_i^+ - p_o \ell - p_\kappa \kappa \right) \right] \tag{7}$$

which yields the first-order conditions

$$\sum_i (p_i - \widetilde{C}_i) \frac{\partial z_i^{+D}}{\partial p_e} = -z_e^+ \qquad e \in E \tag{8}$$

where the modified marginal costs $\widetilde{C}_i$ equal

$$\widetilde{C}_i = p_o \frac{\partial \ell}{\partial z_i^+} + \left[p_\kappa + \frac{\delta}{1+\delta}(d - p_\kappa) \right] \frac{\partial \kappa}{\partial z_i^+}. \tag{9}$$

The Lagrangean multiplier in this case is $-1 \le \delta \le 0$, the limiting cases being

- zero profits ($\delta = -1$; $d = p_\kappa$) and

- monopoly profits ($\delta = 0$) [4].

For the monopolist $\widetilde{C}_i$ reduces to $C_i = p_o(\partial \ell / \partial z_i^+) + p_\kappa(\partial \kappa / \partial z_i^+)$ as can be seen easily by substituting $\delta = 0$ into (9). In C_i both inputs are treated symmetrically, in $\widetilde{C}_i$ the price of capital is reduced by the factor $\delta(d - p_\kappa)/(1 + \delta) < 0$.

Hence, the rate of return regulated profit maximizer behaves as if he were an unconstrained monopolist who underestimates the price of capital.

---

[4] The sign and range of this Lagrangean multiplier are a much discussed aspect of the Averch-Johnson literature. For details, proofs and references see Bailey (1973, 25-8; 73-4; 80). - It should be mentioned that this restriction of the range of δ does not necessarily imply $\partial \delta / \partial (d - p_\kappa) > 0$ although the above mentioned interpretation may suggest that.

This property of our pricing formula corresponds to the well-known Averch-Johnson effect of over-capitalization resulting from this kind of regulation.

The resulting price structure reduces the prices of capital-intensive goods. The price of any good, p_e, will be lower, the higher, ceteris paribus, its marginal capital intensity of production [5]. The rate of return regulation, therefore, does not only imply a suboptimal structure of inputs but also a suboptimal structure of outputs because of a distortion of output prices resulting from regulation. This effect vanishes only if the constraint is non-binding as then the enterprise will follow the usual perfect monopoly price structure which does not imply any miscalculation of the price of capital. (If $\delta = 0, \widetilde{C}_i$ reduces to C_i.) This reveals a puzzling feature of the rate of return regulation: if the enterprise is restricted in its ability to maximize profits, it will misallocate inputs and outputs. If it is not so restricted, it will allocate inputs and outputs correctly, albeit monopolistically.

Thus the misallocation does *not* decrease if a regulated enterprise is confronted with a lower difference between the rate of return and the interest rate. (This has been a decisive counterargument to Klevorick's (1966) proposal of a "graduated rate of return" that diminishes with increasing capital input.) In our case it cannot be shown whether the miscalculation of the price of capital inputs increases or decreases when the difference between the rate of return and the interest rate decreases.

The production technology, as introduced by the simple assumptions (3), influences the miscalculation of the price of capital. Whereas no more need be said as far as neoclassical technologies are concerned, we should say more about the case of fixed coefficients of production. Consider a firm which, because of its profit target, moves along expansion paths of Leontief technologies for every good e:

---

[5] For a proof substitute (9) into (8) and solve for p_e. Differentiating p_e with respect to the marginal capital intensity of production leads to the result in the text.

$$\frac{\partial \ell}{\partial z_e^+} = k_e \frac{\partial \kappa}{\partial z_e^+}.$$
(10)

Then $\widetilde{C}_e$ is as follows:

$$\widetilde{C}_e = p_o k_e \frac{\partial \kappa}{\partial z_e^+} + \left(p_\kappa + \frac{\delta}{1+\delta}(d - p_\kappa) \right) \frac{\partial \kappa}{\partial z_e^+}$$
(11)

and there will still be a distorting effect influencing the output price structure. The profit maximizing rate of return regulated firm will still behave like a monopolistic who underestimates the price of capital inputs and thus the price structure will differ from that of an unconstrained monopolist.

Of course, this miscalculation will not imply suboptimal *input* combinations in the production of any single good as the enterprise follows the expansion paths (10), regardless of the structure of input prices. However, the prices of *outputs* are still distorted in favor of capital intensive goods. The firm that is confronted with Leontief technologies for any good can maximize its profit by changing the composition of produced goods towards higher capital intensity of its total production. This is the Averch-Johnson effect regarding a multiproduct enterprise under Leontief technology.

We should mention once again that the Averch-Johnson inefficiencies vanish if an exogenous profit constraint Π^o is fixed. However, a definite answer on whether Ramsey or rate of return regulation is superior is impossible, just as it was in the case of welfare maximization. There is no clear-cut empirical evidence that the Averch-Johnson effect actually matters. See Joskow-Noll (1980) for further references.

CHAPTER 10   PRICING WITH DISTRIBUTIONAL AIMS

10.1   PRICES VERSUS TAXES

In many European countries public pricing is not only considered as an instrument of allocation policy, but also as an instrument of distribution policy. The most favorable conditions for this approach prevail if different classes of goods can be identified which typically are demanded by consumers with different incomes: first and second class railway or hospital accommodation provide good examples. We could think also of a nationalized enterprise producing small cars for low- income consumers and large cars for high-income consumers and deviating from allocatively optimal pricing by reducing the price of small cars at the expense of large cars.

Such a pricing policy favors low-income earners and it avoids the need for a direct means test and the associated costs of implementing such a system of distributional pricing. Moreover, the consumers are still given the freedom to choose the good they prefer. A rich man who likes to chat with less rich people is not prohibited from using a second class railway compartment.

However, we must examine the following two main objections against the use of public pricing as means of income redistribution:

a) First, *liberal economists* often oppose distributionally modified public pricing. They view progressive income taxation or income subsidies as the most effective instruments of income redistribution and wish to restrict public sector pricing to the allocational objectives only. ("Why do you want to favor poor people simply because they go by railway? If you regard them as poor give them money" as A.A. Walters formulated it in a personal discussion with the author some years ago.)

The traditional liberals argue that income taxation distorts the labor-leisure decision only, whereas distributional public prices distort relative prices throughout the economy. They contend that a rich man, reflecting upon his labor-leisure choice, does not only consider the marginal income tax rate on additional income, but also that he has to pay more for certain goods than a poor man. By whatever means he is deprived of a dollar, the disincentive effect on his labor effort will be the same. Hence, public pricing is an inferior instrument of redistribution. For the same degree of redistribution it leads to the same welfare losses from distorting labor-leisure choices as an income tax, but it leads to additional welfare losses because of distorted relative prices for goods (Ng (1984)).

However, it can be shown that this conclusion is not valid:

– If we assume a social welfare function with the usual distributional weighting of individual incomes, and that income taxation *and* public pricing are available policy instruments, the level of social welfare which can be achieved must be greater than or at least the same as that which can be attained when an income tax is the only policy instrument. This result takes account of the disincentive effects of both progressive taxation and distributional pricing. There is, however, a special case where optimal prices equal marginal costs. This implies that pricing is restricted to the allocation task and the redistribution task has to be achieved by the income tax only. The optimality of marginal-cost pricing, however, depends on very restrictive assumptions, namely, constant returns to scale and utilities which are weakly separable between labor and all goods together. These assumptions are highly implausible and therefore public prices will usually have to consider distributional objectives and income taxation will not be the only, and hence superior, instrument of redistribution (Bös (1984)).

– It is worth noting that the argument of the liberal economists did not presuppose fiscal illusion. It seems likely that they would have found that it varies with the way in which revenue is raised (taxes, prices etc.). Moreover, fiscal illusion can be particularly relevant when price differences are associated with quality differences. The absence of fiscal illusion in this case would require the purchaser to distinguish between that part of the higher price which is due to quality and that which is due to redistribution.

b) *Social democrats*, on the other hand, oppose distributional public prices because they do not depend on personal means unlike, for example, the payment of income taxes. The rich man in the second class railway offers a good example. Moreover, distributional price differentiation typically implies some quality differentiation which has often been critized for ideological reasons, which stress the merits of uniform public supply of schooling, health etc.

However, there are counter-arguments to these conclusions:

–   distributional pricing can be tied to individual income by using an explicit means test;

–   quality differentiation can be restricted to a few classes of different goods, or even totally be avoided if it seems appropriate for distributional reasons.

10.2   FELDSTEIN PRICING

Let us consider the following special case of the generalized Boiteux model:

a) only prices of publicly produced goods are controlled;

b) the private sector is perfectly competitive;

c)   *all lump-sum incomes are exogenously given, and we are dealing with
     non-compensated demand;*

d)   there is a revenue-cost constraint, either an exogenously given Π^o or
     an endogenized $\Pi(z, \rho)$; and

e)   quality levels are fixed.

The reasons for combining the above assumptions are as follows:

We must first make sure that public prices are the actual instruments of
distribution policy. Therefore we have to exclude those lump-sum transfers
which are the distributional instruments in the earlier sections on marginal-
cost pricing, Ramsey-pricing, and rate of return pricing. Public pricing with
distributional objectives must be located in a world of Marshallian demand
functions, not in a world of compensated demand functions (assumption c)
above).

Next we have to consider the financial difficulties the enterprise's board
will encounter if it applies distributional pricing: revenue will tend to fall,
perhaps below costs, because any internal subsidization of the poor is limited
by the possibility that the rich leave the market totally or switch to the
consumption of lower priced goods. Large redistributional effects will thus
lead to a marked increase in the demand for low-priced goods and a marked
decrease in the demand for high-priced goods, implying a tendency towards
a deficit. Hence, we must always include a profit constraint for the public
enterprise, be it total profit or the rate of return (assumption d) above).

The financial difficulties would become even worse if private competitors were allowed to enter the public enterprise's markets. Needless to say,
these competitors would concentrate on supplying those goods which are
intended to play the role of internal subsidizers. This problem will become
more important, the more profitably some of the publicly supplied goods
can be priced.

Let us, first, exclude this particular problem by introducing the additional assumption that goods with publicly controlled prices are neither

supplied nor demanded by private firms. Then, given assumptions a) to e) the marginal conditions (3-21b) reduce to:

$$\sum_{i=o}^{n}(p_i - \widetilde{C}_i)\frac{\partial z_i^D}{\partial p_e} = -(1 - F_e)z_e \qquad\qquad e \in E \qquad (1)$$

The reader should recall that z_i^D represents *non-* compensated demand and F_e the distributional characteristics (3-14)

$$F_e := \sum_{h}\frac{x_e^h}{x_e}\lambda^h\frac{\partial v^h}{\partial r^h} \qquad\qquad e \in E. \qquad (2)$$

The distributional characteristic of any good is higher, the larger is its share of consumption by lower-income people: quantities x_e^h of a necessity are given the higher weights λ^h; moreover $\partial v^h/\partial r^h$ will be higher for lower income. Hence F_e will usually be higher for a necessity than for a luxury, implying a tendency towards lower prices of necessities. Pricing according to (1) may be denoted "Feldstein pricing" as Feldstein (1972 a,b,c) was the first to emphasize distributional equity considerations in public sector pricing.

The most general interpretation of the distributional price structure (1) once again can be given by comparing this price structure with that of the perfect monopolist [1]. The distributionally oriented board behaves as if it were a monopolist who inflates each price elasticity of demand η_{ie} by $1/(1 - F_e)$ [1a]. This pricing behavior is more complicated than in the Ramsey case because typically there will exist as many different inflating factors as publicly priced goods.

---

[1] Ignoring the difference between c_i and $\widetilde{C}_i$.

[1a] Divide (1) by $(1-F_e)$ and define $(\partial z_i^D/\partial p_e)/(1-F_e)=(\partial z_i^D/\partial p_e)^{infl.}$. Elasticities can then be obtained easily by multiplying each partial derivative with the corresponding price/quantity ratio p_e/z_i^D.

The operation of this procedure can be illustrated most easily if we neglect cross-price effects. Then the pricing rule is as follows:

$$(p_e - \tilde{C}_e)\frac{\partial z_e^D}{\partial p_e} = -(1 - F_e)z_e \qquad (3)$$

If we exclude inverse demand responses by assuming $\partial z_e^D/\partial p_e < 0$ then the price of good e will exceed the modified marginal costs $\tilde{C}_e$ if $1 > F_e > 0$ and fall below $\tilde{C}_e$ if $F_e > 1$.

For a price above marginal costs the inflating factor $1/(1 - F_e)$ will be positive and will increase with increasing F_e. The demand response must therefore be overestimated and the degree of over-estimation increases with increasing social valuation of individual consumption as reflected in F_e. Above all, the demand response of necessities must be over-estimated because monopolistic pricing always implies greater care in the pricing of goods with higher demand elasticities.

If, on the other hand, the price falls below marginal costs, the inflating factor $1/(1 - F_e)$ will be negative and will again increase with increasing F_e. This implies once again a tendency to reduce the price of necessities.

An interesting extension of the above distributional pricing formula arises if the regulated goods are supplied or demanded also by private firms.

Then public prices have to be determined according to a special case of (3-21a):

$$\sum_{i=o}^{n}(p_i - \tilde{C}_i)\frac{\partial z_i^D}{\partial p_e} = -(1 - F_e)x_e - \gamma(z_e - x_e) \qquad e \in E. \qquad (4)$$

As we could expect, this formula shows that some price must not only be reduced for distributional reasons, but also because of competition by private firms. This trade-off can be seen directly by looking at eqs. (4).

Cheaper prices for necessities are brought about by higher F_e or, equivalently, by lower $(1 - F_e)x_e$. The price of good e is also reduced if $\mid z_e - x_e \mid$ increases, i.e. if the consumption from private supply is greater (for outputs $x_e > z_e$ and positive γ).

Competition by private firms becomes more important, the more profitably some publicly supplied goods can be priced. In the above formula this tendency is revealed by the influence of γ which typically will be higher, the higher the permitted public revenue-cost difference Π.

It is interesting to note that γ influences the pricing *structure* [2] only if private market entry is explicitly considered in the model. Eqs. (1) do not contain γ, but eqs. (4) do.

10.3   COMPARING DISTRIBUTIONAL AND ALLOCATIVE PRICING

Assume a public enterprise which employs the Boiteux model to determine prices (p_e) and quantities (z_i), the revenue-cost difference being restricted to Π^o. The enterprise's board is given the choice between Ramsey pricing (including the optimal determination of lump-sum incomes (r^h)) and "Feldstein" pricing (accepting lump-sum incomes (r^h) as exogenously fixed).

Ramsey pricing

$$\sum_{i \in E}(p_i - c_i)\frac{\partial \hat{z}_i}{\partial p_e} = -\gamma\, z_e \qquad\qquad e \in E \qquad\qquad (8-1)$$

is usually thought of as "the" pure allocative pricing rule.

---

[2] γ does, of course, influence the optimal absolute values of the prices in any case.

"Feldstein" pricing [3]

$$\sum_{i \in E} (p_i - c_i) \frac{\partial z_i^D}{\partial p_e} = -(1 - F_e) z_e \qquad\qquad e \in E \qquad\qquad (5)$$

is usually thought of as "the" distributional pricing rule.

Both pricing rules have been derived from the same basic model. Therefore, our first conclusion must be the following: if the social welfare function $W(v^1, \ldots, v^H)$ is the same in both cases, Ramsey prices are at least as effective with respect to the achievement of distributional objectives as Feldstein prices. This weak distributional dominance of Ramsey pricing is due to the fact that both approaches optimize the same objective function under the same constraints, but with different instrument variables, the set of Feldstein instruments being a proper subset of the set of Ramsey instruments.

The above paradoxical result shows the importance of using compensated demand in the Ramsey case and non-compensated demand in the Feldstein case. However, it seems a little unfair to compare Ramsey and Feldstein pricing using the same welfare function. Let us therefore follow the usual tradition and compare

- Ramsey pricing as the policy of a distributionally neutral board, $\partial W / \partial v^h = 1$ for all h, and

- Feldstein pricing as the policy of a distributionally oriented board, $\partial W / \partial v^h > 0$.

The fixed revenue-cost difference Π^o is assumed identical in both cases [4].

Needless to say, Feldstein pricing by definition leads to a distributionally optimal result with respect to the above objective function and the

---

[3] For this explicit comparison between Ramsey and Feldstein pricing we additionally assume that uncontrolled prices equal marginal costs c_i in the public sector.

[4] The following text of this subsection is taken from Bös (1983).

given constraints. But how good are these distributional results if they are compared with Ramsey prices? *Will Feldstein prices always favor necessities more than Ramsey prices do?*

To examine this issue we restrict the analysis to two publicly priced goods:

- good 1 (for example, "first class") is a luxury. A comparatively high percentage of the quantity x_1 is bought by higher- income consumers. It has a numerically high price elasticity of demand because of easy substitutability and because lower-income consumers of this good are very sensitive to price increases;

- good 2 (for example, "second class") is a necessity. A comparatively high percentage of the quantity x_2 is bought by lower-income consumers. It has a numerically low price elasticity of demand [5].

Moreover, we assume that income effects are not very important (ideally equal to zero), and cross-price elasticities are neglected.

Usually, the necessity will be favored if Feldstein pricing is applied. However, there may exist perverse cases where the maximization of a distributionally oriented welfare function leads to higher prices for necessities than the maximization of the neutral welfare function under the same revenue-cost constraint. These possible perversities depend on the fact that favoring lower-income groups in this model does not differentiate between incomes but between goods.

Usually the shifts in the price-cost margins are used as proxies for the shifts in the prices. Let us for the moment accept this approximation. Let us consider only cases where both prices exceed marginal costs [6]. Then the necessity is favored if

---

[5] In practical applications of our theoretical model one should, however, always carefully check whether these assumptions are fulfilled.

[6] Other possible cases are dealt with in Bös (1981, 96-7, 100.).

$$\Delta P(F) > \Delta P(R) \qquad (6)$$

where F refers to Feldstein and R to Ramsey, and the meaning of $\Delta P(\cdot)$ is as follows:

$$\Delta P(F) = \left[\left(p_1^F - c_1^F\right)/p_1^F\right] \bigg/ \left[\left(p_2^F - c_2^F\right)/p_2^F\right] = \frac{\varepsilon_{22}}{\varepsilon_{11}} \cdot \frac{(1 - F_1)}{(1 - F_2)} \qquad (7)$$

where ε_{ii} are the non-compensated price elasticities of demand, i = 1,2 .

$$\Delta P(R) = \left[\left(p_1^R - c_1^R\right)/p_1^R\right] \bigg/ \left[\left(p_2^R - c_2^R\right)/p_2^R\right] = \frac{\eta_{22}}{\eta_{11}} \qquad (8)$$

where η_{ii} are the compensated price elasticities of demand, i = 1,2.

Therefore, the necessity is favored relatively if

$$\frac{\varepsilon_{22}}{\varepsilon_{11}} \cdot \frac{(1 - F_1)}{(1 - F_2)} > \frac{\eta_{22}}{\eta_{11}} \qquad (9)$$

where the elasticities ε_{ii} are considered at the Feldstein optimum, the elasticities η_{ii} at the Ramsey optimum.

Looking at above inequality, we see that the necessity may be relatively expensive under Feldstein pricing for the following two reasons:

a) η_{22}/η_{11} may exceed $\varepsilon_{22}/\varepsilon_{11}$. The distributional objectives aim at a lower price for the necessity. This typically implies a numerically lower elasticity ε_{22}. However, the allocative "inverse elasticity structure" which also is implied in the Feldstein rule, means a tendency towards a price increase of the necessity. It can be seen immediately from (9) that such changes of the elasticities work against lower Feldstein prices of the necessity.

Usually this difficulty is overcome by the assumption that the elasticities are identical for the comparison (9), $\varepsilon_{ii} = \eta_{ii}$ for i = 1,2.
This assumption can be justified only if we restrict ourselves to cases
where income effects do not matter and where a politician is unwill-
ing to change prices abruptly for fear of political disturbances and
therefore only compares Ramsey prices and Feldstein prices that are
not far from each other. Needless to say there may exist many cases
where this does not hold and where the above mentioned change of
elasticities may lead to unexpected results.

b) There may exist cases of a perverse ranking of the "distributional
characteristics" F_i.

Let us assume identical elasticities $\varepsilon_{ii} = \eta_{ii}$. Then (9) reduces to
$F_1 < F_2 < 1$ [7], which implies

$$\sum_h \left\{ \left[x_1^h W'(r^h) \right] \Big/ \left(\sum_k x_1^k \right) \right\} < \sum_h \left\{ \left[x_2^h W'(r^h) \right] \Big/ \left(\sum_k x_2^k \right) \right\} \qquad (10)$$

where $W'(r^h) = \lambda^h (\partial v^h / \partial r^h)$ is the marginal social valuation of the
individual lump-sum income r^h, and is assumed to be a decreasing
function of income r^h.

There will exist many cases where this condition holds, because we
have assumed that the weights $W'(r^h)$ decrease with increasing income and that x_1 is demanded mainly by higher-income earners and
x_2 mainly by lower-income earners. But we can think easily of combinations of x_i^h and $W'(r^h)$ that do not fulfill these conditions. The
reader should recall that we only assumed that "a comparatively
high percentage" of total demand comes from higher (lower) income

---

[7] The other mathematically possible solution of reducing (9) in case of $\varepsilon_{ii} = \eta_{ii}$ is
excluded by the assumption that both prices exceed marginal costs.

earners. Therefore we have neither excluded purchases of necessities by higher-income earners nor purchases of luxuries by lower-income earners. Moreover we have only assumed that $W'(r^h)$ is a decreasing function of incomes. We have not included any assumptions on $W''(r^h)$.

A simple numerical example for $F_1 > F_2$ is as follows: define a necessity as a good where more than 50 % of the total quantity is consumed by lower-income earners, and conversely for a luxury. Take an economy with 5 income earners, y = (10, 15, 20, 30, 35), which means an average income of 22. Thus the first three income earners are lower-income earners. Assume a social marginal valuation of the individual incomes $W'(r^h)$ = (1; 0,8; 0,6; 0,55; 0,5) for the income distribution mentioned above. Now choose consumption shares of the necessity as (20%; 10%; 25%; 22,5%; 22,5%) which implies that 55% of the consumption comes from lower-income earners. Choose consumption shares of the luxury as (25%; 10%; 10%; 27,5%; 27,5%) which implies that 55% of the consumption comes from higher-income earners. - The distributional characteristic for the luxury then is $F_1 = 0,68$, and for the necessity, $F_2 = 0,67$.

The comparison of Feldstein versus Ramsey pricing remains incomplete if it is restricted to the above consideration. Relaxing the earlier assumption on cross-price effects and the restriction of our comparison (9) to price-cost margins, we get the following additional reasons for why Feldstein prices might make the necessity more expensive.

c) Cross-price elasticities

If $\Delta P(F)$ and $\Delta P(R)$ are assumed to depend on the cross-price elasticities of demand as well (allowing also for the income effects in case of the non-compensated elasticities ε_{ij} [8]), general conclusions on

---

[8] See Feldstein (1972a); corrected version of p. 33, footnote 7 in American Economic Review 62 (1972, 763).

a comparison between Feldstein and Ramsey prices become next to impossible.

d)   Returns to scale

Until now, our comparison has not focussed on the prices themselves, but on the ratios of price-cost margins. However a lower price-cost margin may imply a higher price if the marginal costs change correspondingly. This can be a further reason why Feldstein prices of a necessity may exceed Ramsey prices. If additional quantities of the necessity can only be produced at increasingly higher marginal costs, it will become more and more difficult to achieve distributional objectives by low pricing of the necessity. This tendency will be reinforced if considerable economies of scale prevail in the production of the luxury.

B   INTERDEPENDENCIES WITH THE PRIVATE ECONOMY

CHAPTER 11   ADJUSTMENT TO MONOPOLISTIC PRICING IN THE PRIVATE SECTOR

11.1   THE SECOND–BEST ISSUE: ADJUSTMENT TO, VERSUS INTERFERENCE IN, THE PRIVATE ECONOMY

Let some prices in the private economy deviate from marginal costs because of the monopoly power of some entrepreneurs, because of the application of rule of thumb (e.g. mark-up) pricing, or because of commodity taxation. Any of these cases will be called "monopolistic pricing", the degree of monopoly being measured by the positive price-cost margin

$$\Theta_i^j := (p_i - c_i^j)/p_i > 0 \qquad i = 1,\ldots,n; \quad j = 1,\ldots,J. \tag{1}$$

If these prices cannot be, or are not, brought down to marginal costs, then the second-best philosophy tells us that in general the prices of the other goods also must deviate from marginal costs in order to obtain maximal welfare. The rationale is that the attainable welfare in an economy is maximized if the price structure corresponds to the relative scarcity of goods. Such a correspondence will, in general, be approximated better if unavoidable distortions are compensated by other distortions than if the rest of the economy does not react to these distortions [1].

---

[1] In a second-best model *typically* all conditions for the optimum differ from the corresponding conditions for the Pareto optimum. The seminal paper by Lipsey-Lancaster

Lipsey-Lancaster (1956-57) and Green (1962) were the first to articulate some challenging hypotheses on public pricing in a monopolistic environment. This second-best approach to public pricing was attacked subsequently because it seemed to take as unalterable the fact that prices in the private economy cannot be brought down to marginal costs and therefore required that public prices adjust to the private degrees of monopoly. In turn, this seemed to imply a public pricing policy that did everything to enable private monopolists to make profits. If privately and publicly priced goods are substitutes, public prices must be increased to mitigate the competition with the monopoly. If they are complements, public prices must be reduced to make the joint purchase of both goods cheaper, which again helps the private enterprise. Opponents argued that this meant the "abdication of economic policy".

These objections partly miss the point. They may be valid if a public enterprise actually adjusts its price structure to a perfect private monopolist. However, monopolistic pricing in the private sector, as defined above, refers to all enterprises whose prices exceed marginal costs. Usually there will exist many cases of politically acceptable positive price-cost margins. Then the chosen structure of public prices only implies the best possible way to restore price relations that indicate the relative scarcity of goods. Therefore, publicly priced substitutes have to be more expensive to restore at least partly the price relations that would have prevailed in the absence of private monopolistic pricing. On the other hand, publicly priced complements have to be cheaper: if public prices remained at marginal costs, the "composite" price for both complements would be farther from the price relations that would have prevailed in the absence of private monopolistic pricing.

Objections to adjusting public pricing to private pricing can be criticized for yet another reason. It is true that this approach assumes private price-cost margins to be exogenously given and public ones to be endoge-

---

(1956-57) is confusing in this respect. Page 11 incorrectly states that *all* Paretian conditions must be altered. Page 27 correctly states that this holds "*in general*".

nously adjusted. However, this does not imply that the public sector has no influence on the private economy. For example, assume the public price-cost margins to be lower than those in a private industry producing substitutes. This will decrease the demand for the privately supplied goods although the public sector does not follow marginal-cost pricing. One should always consider the adjustment of the private economy to public pricing which is also included in our approach. The importance of this feedback will, of course, depend on the relative size of the public and the private sectors of the economy.

The adjustment of public pricing to typical private pricing can be treated in general and in partial microeconomic models.

a) The predominant theoretical approach is concerned with public and private pricing in a *general microeonomic model*, in our case in the extended Boiteux model. This approach will be treated in section 11.2 below.

b) Typical *partial analyses* consider duopolistic or oligopolistic market structures where one of the participants is the public sector (Rees (1976, 1984), Bös (1981, chapter 5), Beato-Mas-Colell (1984)). Such analyses show public and private pricing to depend on the different possible strategies of the economic agents involved, as shown in section 11.3 below.

11.2 A MODEL FOR PUBLIC PRICES IN AN IMPERFECT MARKET ECONOMY

Dealing with a special case of the extended Boiteux model, we must once again clarify the particular assumptions which characterize the following analysis:

a)   only prices of publicly produced goods are controlled [2];

b)   *the private sector is not perfectly competitive;*

c)   the distribution of lump-sum incomes is optimally chosen, hence we shall deal with compensated demand;

d)   the revenue-cost difference is considered alternatively as constrained and as non-constrained;

e)   quality levels are fixed.

Then the marginal-conditions (3-24) of the extended Boiteux-model hold:

$$\sum_i (p_i - \tilde{C}_i) \frac{\partial \hat{z}_i}{\partial p_e} = -\gamma\, z_e - (1 - \gamma) \sum_i \sum_j (p_i - c_i^j) \frac{\partial y_i^j}{\partial p_e} \qquad e \in E. \quad (2)$$

For the economic interpretation of this pricing structure we first assume a revenue-cost constraint which exceeds unconstrained profits ($\gamma > 0$). For any single price p_e equation (2) can be rewritten as

$$p_e = \tilde{C}_e - \frac{\gamma z_e}{\partial \hat{z}_e / \partial p_e} - \sum_{i \neq e} (p_i - \tilde{C}_i) \frac{\partial \hat{z}_i / \partial p_e}{\partial \hat{z}_e / \partial p_e} -$$
$$- (1 - \gamma) \sum_i \sum_j (p_i - c_i^j) \frac{\partial y_i^j / \partial p_e}{\partial \hat{z}_e / \partial p_e}; e \in E. \quad (3)$$

Hence, the controlled price p_e will usually differ from marginal costs. The second term on the right hand side of (3) measures the effects of the revenue-cost constraint and implies the expected tendency for the price p_e to

---

[2] The analysis can be extended easily to price control of goods which are only produced privately. (Set $z_e = 0$ and $\partial \hat{z}_e / \partial p_e = 0$ in eqs. (2).)

exceed the marginal costs of producing good e in the public sector (because $\gamma > 0, \partial \hat{z}_e / \partial p_e < 0$). The last two terms on the right hand side, the "reallocation effects" (Hagen (1979)) imply a unique tendency for price p_e to exceed $\widetilde{C}_e$ if all prices exceed the respective marginal costs and if good e is a net substitute for all other goods ($\partial \hat{z}_i / \partial p_e > 0, \partial y_i^j / \partial p_e > 0 \quad \forall i \neq e$). Complementarities between good e and (some) other goods point in the opposite direction; there is no general answer in this case.

Let us *secondly* consider public pricing without a binding budget constraint, but with given price distortions in the private economy. The general interpretation of this case is straightforward and can be left to the reader. (Set $\gamma = 0$ in (3)). One special interpretation, however, must be treated more extensively. Assume the mark-up for any good i to be identical for all private firms and for the public sector

$$
\begin{aligned}
&\Theta_i = (p_i - c_i)/p_i = (p_i - c_i^j)/p_i \qquad i = 1, \ldots, n, ; j = 1, \ldots, J \\
&\Theta_o = 0.
\end{aligned}
\tag{4}
$$

The theoretical literature on the topic usually tries to account for such parallel behavior by referring to identical commodity taxation.

Then (2) can be written as follows

$$
\Theta_e p_e \frac{\partial \hat{x}_e}{\partial p_e} = - \sum_{i \neq e} \Theta_i p_i \frac{\partial \hat{x}_i}{\partial p_e} \qquad e \in E.
\tag{5}
$$

As the compensated expenditures for all goods do not respond to price changes ($\Sigma_k p_k (\partial \hat{x}_k / \partial p_e) = 0$), we obtain

$$
\Theta_e = \sum_{i \neq e} \Theta_i w_{ie} \qquad e \in E,
\tag{6}
$$

where

$$w_{ie} = p_i(\partial \hat{x}_i/\partial p_e) \ / \ \sum_{k \neq e} p_k(\partial \hat{x}_k/\partial p_e); \qquad \sum_{i \neq e} w_{ie} = 1. \qquad (7)$$

The price-cost margin Θ_e is a weighted average of all other Θ_i. This implies that the optimal price-cost margin lies somewhere between the minimum and the maximum price-cost margin if good e is a net substitute for all other goods. With some modifications this result can be found in Green (1962), Bergson (1972), Hatta (1977), Kawamata (1977), Wiegard (1978, 1979), Hagen (1979).

It seems unlikely that this celebrated result merits the attention given to it, for two reasons:

a) Exogenously fixing $\Theta_i = \Theta_i^j$ for all i and j implies the exogenous determination of variables that are endogenously determined in the model: the optimal values of Θ are the result of the optimization approach! An equality of Θ_i and Θ_i^j can only result by chance or from particular theoretical assumptions regarding the private sector which we have avoided deliberately in this section. Moreover, there is no economic justification for introducing this identity of mark-ups as additional constraints in our optimization approach.

b) The result is only valid if good e is a net substitute for all other goods, which is empirically not very plausible. There exist many net complementarities between regulated and non-regulated goods. Take e.g. the situation of demand for different goods that are relevant for producing transportation services. Publicly priced railway services are substitutes for private motor-car traffic, publicly priced toll roads or petrol are complements to private motor-car traffic. The demand for regulated airline tickets is complementary to the demand for hotel services, as often there is a joint demand for both.

11.3   A DUOPOLY MODEL FOR PUBLIC PRICES

Partial analyses must be centered on duopolistic or oligopolistic structures where one of the participants is a public enterprise. The great advantage of such an analysis is that it reveals the whole range of possible outcomes as depending on the different possible reactions of the economic agents concerned.

Whereas in the extended Boiteux model there is only one optimal adjustment of welfare to private monopolistic pricing, there are different optimal adjustments of welfare in the duopoly model, depending on the different types of behavior of the duopolists. The economic intuition behind these different concepts can be shown best if we restrict ourselves to the following simplified analysis.

Consider two players of a game:

- a public enterprise, setting prices p_e, $e \in E$. The board is interested in maximizing welfare, choosing its instruments (p_e), $(z_i\ i \neq m)$, (r^h) in a market-clearing and technologically feasible way;

- a private firm, setting prices p_m, $m \in M \subset I$. The firm is interested in maximizing profits, defined as its revenue-cost difference $\tau_m = \sum_i p_i y_i^m$.

The following optimization approaches will be presented analytically in a comparatively general manner. The analytical presentation deals with substitutes as well as complements, decreasing cost functions as well as increasing, and various assumptions about the behavior of demand. However, typical neoclassical "well behaved" functions are assumed to exist. – Figure 15a illustrates a typical configuration for substitute goods, increasing marginal costs of both enterprises, and well behaved demand functions.

We define the duopoly problem over the budget space and thus any action of the public firm depends on its own price p_e and on the price $p_m^E(p_e)$ which the private firm is expected to set when responding to the public firm's price. On the other hand, any action of the private firm depends on its own price p_m and on the price $p_e^E(p_m)$ the public firm is expected to set when responding to private firm's price. "E" stands for "expected response" because any firm when setting its own price starts from some particular assumption of how the other firm will respond.

The public enterprise, therefore, maximizes the following Lagrangean function

$$\max_{p_e, z_i\ i\neq m\ ,r^h} \mathcal{L} = W(v^h(p_e, p_m^E(p_e), r^h)) - \sum_{i\neq m} \alpha_i \left[\sum_h x_i^h(p_e, p_m^E(p_e), r^h) \right.$$
$$\left. - z_i - \sum_j y_i^j(p_e, p_m^E(p_e)) \right] - \beta g(z) - \overline{\gamma} \left[\Pi(\cdot) - \sum_i p_i z_i \right] \tag{8}$$

where all variables which are held constant are suppressed in the notation of the functional dependencies [3]. $z_m = 0$ implies the assumption that good m is not used as an input of the public firm. It is only the price reactions which constitute the particular duopoly problem.

The resulting price structure is relatively complicated as it contains all possible reactions of the private firm.

$$\sum_{i\neq m} (p_i - \tilde{C}_i)\left(\frac{\partial \hat{z}_i}{\partial p_e} + \sum_m \frac{\partial \hat{z}_i}{\partial p_m} \cdot \frac{\partial p_m^E}{\partial p_e} \right) = -\gamma\left(z_e + \sum_m z_m \frac{\partial p_m^E}{\partial p_e} \right)$$
$$- (1 - \gamma)\left\{ \sum_{i\neq m} \sum_j (p_i - c_i^j)\left(\frac{\partial y_i^j}{\partial p_e} + \sum_m \frac{\partial y_i^j}{\partial p_m} \cdot \frac{\partial p_m^E}{\partial p_e} \right) \right. \tag{9}$$
$$\left. + \sum_m (p_m - c_m^m)\left(\frac{\partial \hat{x}_m}{\partial p_e} + \frac{\partial \hat{x}_m}{\partial p_e} \cdot \frac{\partial p_m^E}{\partial p_e} \right) \right\} \qquad e \in E.$$

---

[3] $v^h(p_e, p_m^E(p_e), r^h) := v^h(\bar{p}_o, \bar{p}_1, ..., p_e, ..., p_m^E(p_e), ..., \bar{p}_n, \bar{q}_1, ...\bar{q}_n, r^h)$ and analogously for the demand functions $x_i^h(\cdot)$ and $y_i^j(\cdot)$.

The price structure becomes much simpler if a particular strategic behavior of the private firm is assumed by specifying $p_m^E(p_e)$. Before doing so, however, we must treat the private firm's optimization in a general form. Substitute $x_m = y_m^m, m \in M$ because of the monopolistic market structure $(z_m = 0)$ to obtain [4]

$$\max_{p_m, y_i^m} \sum_m p_m x_m(p_e^E(p_m), p_m) + \sum_{i \notin M} p_i y_i^m \quad s.t. \quad g(x_m(\cdot), y_{i \notin M}^m) \qquad (10)$$

where $g(\cdot)$ denotes the private firm's production function.

This optimization leads to the following price structure [5]

$$\sum_{k \in M} (p_k - c_k^m) \left(\frac{\partial x_k}{\partial p_m} + \sum_e \frac{\partial x_k}{\partial p_e} \frac{\partial p_e^E}{\partial p_m} \right) = -x_m \qquad m \in M \qquad (11)$$

which is the extension of the monopolistic pricing rule we expected after including the reaction of the public firm.

We have now defined the general framework for duopoly pricing. We are interested in the type of behavior the duopolists will choose within this framework. The first approach we shall examine assumes *Cournot-type behavior* of both firms: each firm treats the price of the other firm as fixed at each stage of the pricing process. The public firm assumes p_m not to respond to changes of p_e, and the private firm assumes p_e not to respond to changes of p_m:

---

[4] $x_m(\cdot) = x_m(\bar{p}_o, \bar{p}_1, \dots, p_e^E(p_m), \dots, p_m, \dots, \bar{p}_n, \bar{q}_1, \dots, \bar{q}_n, \bar{r}^1, \dots, \bar{r}^H)$.

[5]   Differentiation of the respective Lagrangean $\mathcal{L}$ with respect to y_i^m yields

$p_i - \lambda(\partial g/\partial y_i^m) = 0 \qquad i \notin M$.

We use one of these marginal conditions, namely

$\lambda(\partial g/\partial y_o^m) = p_o = 1$

to replace λ in the conditions resulting from $\partial \mathcal{L}/\partial p_m$, and define as usual

$c_k^m = (\partial g/\partial y_k^m)/(\partial g/\partial y_o^m) = (\partial g/\partial x_k)/(\partial g/\partial y_o^m)$.

$$\frac{\partial p_m^E}{\partial p_e} = 0 \quad ; \quad \frac{\partial p_e^E}{\partial p_m} = 0 \qquad e \in E, \ m \in M. \tag{12}$$

Under these assumptions the general pricing rules (9) and (11) reduce to

$$\sum_{i \neq m} (p_i - \tilde{C}_i) \frac{\partial \hat{z}_i}{\partial p_e} = -\gamma z_e - (1 - \gamma) \left\{ \sum_{i \neq m} \sum_j (p_i - c_i^j) \frac{\partial y_i^j}{\partial p_e} + \right.$$
$$\left. + \sum_m (p_m - c_m^m) \frac{\partial \hat{x}_m}{\partial p_e} \right\} \qquad e \in E \tag{13}$$

$$\sum_{k \in M} (p_k - c_k^m) \frac{\partial x_k}{\partial p_m} = -x_m \qquad m \in M. \tag{14}$$

Equation (13) resembles the usual welfare-optimal adjustment of public to private pricing as shown in equation (2). Its interpretation could, therefore, follow the lines of the preceding subsection. Equation (14) is the well-known monopoly pricing rule. Prices will usually exceed marginal costs, depending on the uncompensated demand elasticities.

For a graphical representation consider figure 15a where (13) and (14) refer to the equations above. (13) connects the welfare-maximizing prices p_e if p_m is given. $W^{o\prime}$ and $W^{o\prime\prime}$ are iso-welfare lines. Point W is the welfare maximum. Of course an upper limit for p_e exists where the public enterprise loses all customers ($z_e = 0$). (14) connects the profit maximizing prices p_m if p_e is given. $\pi_m^{o\prime}$ and $\pi_m^{o\prime\prime}$ are iso-profit lines. The absolute profit maximum is located on the line $z_e = 0$ where the public enterprise has left the market (point π_m).

Given Cournot-type behavior of both firms, the resulting prices can be obtained analytically by solving (13) and (14) for p_e and p_m; graphically we obtain point A in figure 15a.

The following alternative approach is due to Stackelberg. *Stackelberg-type behavior* is asymmetric. One duopolist takes the active position, the other duopolist adjusts to the actions of the active player.

Suppose, first, the *public enterprise is the active player.* Taking the active position means it expects the private firm to

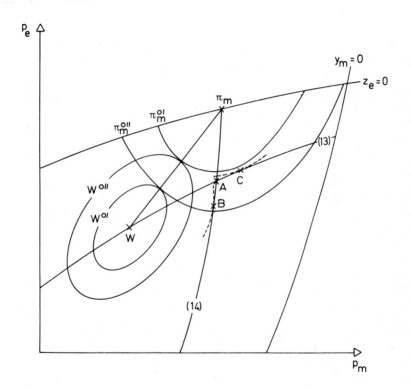

Figure 15a

respond to the public prices. The passive position, as taken by the private firm, means it does not expect the public firm to respond to the private firm's price changes:

$$\frac{\partial p_m^E}{\partial p_e} \neq 0 \quad \text{(active position)};$$

$$\frac{\partial p_e^E}{\partial p_m} = 0 \quad \text{(passive position)}; \qquad e \in E, \; m \in M.$$

$$(15)$$

Analytically we obtain prices according to the marginal conditions (9) and (14). Graphically the result is point B in figure 15a which is the welfare maximum given the private firm's adherence to eq. (14) [6].

If the *private enterprise is the active player* the contrary holds. The active private firm expects public prices to respond to private prices. The passive public firm does not expect private prices to respond to public ones:

$$\frac{\partial p_e^E}{\partial p_m} \neq 0 \quad \text{(active position)};$$

$$\frac{\partial p_m^E}{\partial p_e} = 0 \quad \text{(passive position)}; \qquad e \in E, \; m \in M.$$

$$(16)$$

Analytically, eqs. (11) and (13) result from this sort of Stackelberg-type behavior. Graphically point C in figure 15a is obtained, which is the profit maximum, given the public firm's adherence to eq. (13).

A somewhat different approach to the duopoly game assumes that the players behave so as to obtain *Pareto-optimal outcomes*: outcomes where increasing welfare is only possible at decreasing profit and vice versa. (In figure 15a the set of Pareto optimal outcomes is the contract curve $W\pi_m$.) Rather than interpreting this result as the outcome of joint maximization

---

[6] In our figure 15a playing actively leads to higher welfare (profit) than playing passively. However, there exist situations where the contrary may result, although this is counterintuitive. See Krelle (1976, I, 239-278; especially 265-267).

it is better to distinguish between active and passive strategies similar to those postulated in Stackelberg-type behavior.

First, let the *public enterprise be the active player* [7]. Assume that the public enterprise in question intends to restrict the profit of the private enterprise to a fixed maximal amount

$$\pi_m = \sum_i p_i y_i^m \leq \pi_m^o \qquad 0 < \underline{\pi}_m^o < \pi_m^o < \bar{\pi}_m^o \qquad (17)$$

where $\underline{\pi}_m^o$ is the threshold value for the private enterprise to stay in the market and $\bar{\pi}_m^o$ is the Cournot monopoly profit.

This means assuming that the public enterprise has a threat strategy to bring the private enterprise to a profit less than or equal to π_m^o. This threat strategy may lead to extraordinarily low public prices in order to break the private monopoly power, or to other administrative or legal actions that can be set in motion by the public enterprise.

The private firm is expected to maximize profits, given constraint (17), and therefore the constraint can be regarded as binding for the optimization approach of the public enterprise. Hence we obtain

$$\sum_{k \in M} \frac{\partial \pi_m}{\partial p_k} dp_k + \sum_{f \in E} \frac{\partial \pi_m}{\partial p_f} dp_f = 0. \qquad (18)$$

If only one public price and one monopoly price change, we obtain a special case of (18):

---

[7] For the sake of completeness we should mention the possibility of an *active private enterprise* following a profit maximizing strategy conceding a certain welfare level to the public enterprise. However, this approach is not as plausible as the case of the active public enterprise.

$$\left.\frac{dp_m}{dp_e}\right|_{\pi_m^o} = \frac{\partial p_m^E}{\partial p_e} = -\frac{\partial \pi_m/\partial p_e}{\partial \pi_m/\partial p_m}(\pi_m^o). \qquad (19)$$

The public enterprise, on the other hand, is not expected to respond to the private firm's price, as it takes the active position. Hence, in the case of (19), the Pareto optimum with an active public firm is characterized by

$$\frac{\partial p_m^E}{\partial p_e} = -\frac{\partial \pi_m/\partial p_e}{\partial \pi_m/\partial p_m}(\pi_m^o) \quad \text{(active position)};$$

$$\frac{\partial p_e^E}{\partial p_m} = 0 \quad \text{(passive position)}; \quad e \in E, m \in M. \qquad (20)$$

Analytically we are once again back at solving conditions (9) and (14), but with the special specification of the private firm's price response due to its profit limitation.

The above approach avoids the usual objections to the idea that public enterprises adjust to private pricing because it accentuates the active position of the public enterprise and its ability and willingness to prevent exploitation of consumers by the private firm.

It is instructive to examine the above mentioned *threat strategy* of the public firm a little more extensively and to ask wether the private firm could use some counter-threats.

Consider figure 15b and assume point A to be the desired Pareto-optimum. The public firms concedes a profit $\pi_m^{o\prime}$ to the private firm, expecting it to set its price according to point A. If the private firm decides to set some other price, the public firm has the threat strategy of going down to point B, maliciously reducing private profit as much as possible without suffering any reduction in welfare. The hatched line starting in W connects those threat strategies of the public firm.

However, the private firm also has some threat potential [8]. Knowing price p_e corresponds to point **A**, it could decide to set its price according to point **C**, maliciously reducing welfare without having to suffer any reduction

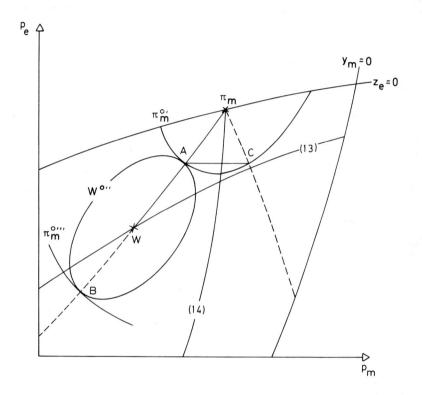

Figure 15b

---

[8] Some hypothetical threat strategies of the private firm could be constructed in the same way as the public firm's threat strategies. These strategies are hypothetical, because they refer to cases where the duopoly has ceased to be a duopoly.

in its profit. Hence, pricing according to C is a threat strategy of the private firm. For other public prices similar possibilities exist for the private firm, as shown by the hatched line going through C.

Considering the public firm's possibilities we can safely assume that the private firm cooperates by choosing price p_m according to point A, assuming such a cooperative solution can be justified by the fact of the asymmetric risk of public and private firms. Only the private firm can go bankrupt in a price war with the public firm. This is the ultimate threat potential of the public firm.

CHAPTER 12   ADJUSTMENT TO RATIONED MARKETS

The existence of rationed markets means that the market clearing conditions of the Boiteux model are disturbed. The disturbances are caused by a lack of flexibility on the demand side or the production side of the economy, or both. Sticky prices may be one of the reasons for these failures.

The best way of modelling such failure is to take a typical second-best approach. The model does not explain the causes of failures of demand and production, but takes them as given. The resulting disturbances are introduced as exogenous influences in the model. By way of an example, we do not formulate explicitly which demand or cost-side influences prevent some people from being employed. Rather we assume there is disequilibrium because of fixed prices for labor and (some) other goods in the private sector and therefore consumers are rationed in their employment decision.

There are many situations where rationed markets are relevant for public enterprise theory. Two important cases are presented below.

12.1   RATIONED LABOR MARKET

12.1.1   INDIVIDUAL EMPLOYMENT CONSTRAINTS

In the recent situation of public enterprises most Western European governments rank employment problems first. What is the role of public pricing in such a situation? Should the public enterprise reduce the prices of labor-intensive goods, thereby accepting the resulting welfare losses associated with departing from first-best pricing? We have already mentioned that the rate of return regulation for welfare maximizing public enterprises implies this result. However because such a policy assumes an exogenously given rate of return, the problem at issue here is dealt with only implicitly in that context.

The high ranking of employment problems suggests we must explicitly consider employment as an instrument variable.Taking this approach we assume the public sector is large enough to warrant treating total employment L as macro-variable instrument. To develop a realistic model of the recent economic situation we should abandon the usual equilibria in the labor and private commodity markets and instead deal with equilibria under rationing (Malinvaud (1977)).

Following Drèze (1984) we assume the individual supply of labor is constrained as follows [1]

$$x_o^h \geq \bar{x}_o^h(L) \qquad h = 1, \ldots, H; \qquad \sum \bar{x}_o^h = L \qquad (1)$$

where $L < 0$ is total labor demand by private and public firms. $\bar{x}_o^h(L)$ is an exogenously given rationing function which is assumed to be differentiable. In the following we assume this constraint to be binding. The excess supply of labor is assumed to result from fixed prices of (some) privately supplied goods, and a fixed wage rate, respectively.

The consumer maximizes his direct utility $u^h(x^h)$ given the prices and his fixed labor and lump-sum income. The resulting individual demand functions are $x_i^h(p, r^h, \bar{x}_o^h(L)) =: x_i^h(p, r^h, L)$. The rationing of labor supply implies that the individual demand for any good depends on the total labor demand.

---

[1] If, for instance, an individual wants to work 40 hours per week, it is possibly constrained to work 20 hours only $(\bar{x}_o^h)$ or less. For the direction of the inequality remember $x_o^h < 0$.

We assume excess supply of labor and therefore

$$w_R^h < p_o = 1. \tag{2}$$

The reservation wage w_R^h is defined as the marginal rate of substitution between labor and income

$$w_R^h := \frac{\partial u^h / \partial x_o^h}{\partial u^h / \partial r^h}(\bar{x}_o^h). \tag{3}$$

At the reservation wage the consumer voluntarily would supply $\bar{x}_o^h$. In the case of excess supply of labor $\bar{x}_o^h$ is lower in absolute value than the voluntary labor supply x_o^h; therefore the reservation wage must be lower than the market wage rate, which explains the assumption in (2).

The compensated employment effect of demand, $\partial \hat{x}_i^h / \partial L$, can be derived from the identity of Marshallian and Hicksian demand at the lump-sum income $r^h = e^h(p, \bar{x}_o^h, u^{h*}) : x_i^h(p, r^h, L) = \hat{x}_i^h(p, u^{h*}, L)$. Differentiation with respect to L yields

$$\frac{\partial x_i^h}{\partial L} + \frac{\partial x_i^h}{\partial r^h} \frac{\partial e^h}{\partial \bar{x}_o^h} \frac{\partial \bar{x}_o^h}{\partial L} = \frac{\partial \hat{x}_i^h}{\partial L}. \tag{4a}$$

We differentiate the expenditure function $e(\cdot) = p_o \bar{x}_o^h + \sum_1^n p_i \hat{x}_i^h$ with respect to the individual employment $\bar{x}_o^h$. Using the envelope theorem [2] we obtain

$$\frac{\partial e^h}{\partial \bar{x}_o^h} = p_o - \frac{\partial u^h / \partial \bar{x}_o^h}{\partial u^h / \partial r^h} = 1 - w_R^h. \tag{5}$$

Substituting (5) into (4a) yields

---

[2] Consider the Lagrangean $\mathcal{L} = p_o \bar{x}_o^h + \sum_1^n p_i x_i^h - \lambda(u^h(\bar{x}_o^h, x^h) - u^{h*})$ where $\lambda = \partial e / \partial u^{h*}$. Differentiating $\mathcal{L}$ with respect to $\bar{x}_o^h$ yields $\partial \mathcal{L} / \partial \bar{x}_o^h = p_o - \lambda(\partial u / \partial \bar{x}_o^h) = \partial e / \partial \bar{x}_o^h$ where the far right equation is based on the envelope theorem.

$$\frac{\partial \hat{x}_i^h}{\partial L} = \frac{\partial x_i^h}{\partial L} + \frac{\partial x_i^h}{\partial r^h}(1 - w_R^h)\frac{\partial \bar{x}_o^h}{\partial L}. \qquad (4b)$$

The indirect utility function is $u^h(x_i^h(p, r^h, \bar{x}_o^h), \bar{x}_o^h) =: v^h(p, r^h, \bar{x}_o^h(L)) =: v^h(p, r^h, L)$. Its dependence on the employment L is as follows. Recall that at the consumer optimum $\nu^h = u^{h*}$. Therefore

$$\frac{\partial v^h}{\partial r^h}\frac{\partial e^h}{\partial \bar{x}_o^h}\frac{\partial \bar{x}_o^h}{\partial L} + \frac{\partial v^h}{\partial L} = 0 \text{:} \qquad (6a)$$

Substituting (5) into (6a) we obtain

$$\frac{\partial v^h}{\partial L} = (w_R^h - 1)\frac{\partial v^h}{\partial r^h}\frac{\partial \bar{x}_o^h}{\partial L}. \qquad (6b)$$

The rationed labor supply, moreover, influences the net supply of private firms, and this relationship can be written as $y_i^j = y_i^j(p, L), i \geq 1$. The private firms' demand for labor, in turn, will typically be lower than their demand in the absence of rationing, whence $y_o^j = y_o^j(p, L)$. Public net supply and demand are also influenced by the rationing of individual labor supply. However, the quantities z_i are taken as instruments and therefore the functional dependencies are not specified a priori, but well-defined at the optimum.

The board chooses optimal prices p_e, optimal input and output quantities z_i (including public labor input z_o), optimal lump-sum transfers r^h and optimal total employment L. The quality levels are held constant. The board considers the usual constraints, the rationed labor-market equilibrium being defined as follows:

$$L = z_o + \sum_j y_o^j(p, L). \qquad (7)$$

Hence, the board solves the problem:

$$\max_{p_e, r^h, z_i, L} \mathcal{L} = W\left(v^h(p, r^h, L)\right) - \alpha_o\left[L - z_o - \sum_j y_o^j(p, L)\right] -$$

$$- \sum_{i=1}^n \alpha_i\left[\sum_h x_i^h(p, r^h, L) - z_i - \sum_j y_i^j(p, L)\right] - \qquad (8)$$

$$- \beta g(z) - \bar{\gamma}\left[\Pi(\cdot) - \sum_{i=o}^n p_i z_i\right].$$

We obtain the following result [3]:

$$\sum_{i=1}^n (\gamma\, p_i - \tilde{C}_i)\frac{\partial \hat{z}_i}{\partial L} = (1 - \gamma)\frac{\partial z_o}{\partial L} \qquad (9a)$$

$$\sum_{i=1}^n (p_i - \tilde{C}_i)\frac{\partial \hat{z}_i}{\partial p_e} = -\gamma\, z_e - (1 - \gamma)\sum_{i=o}^n \sum_{j=1}^J (p_i - c_i^j)\frac{\partial y_i^j}{\partial p_e} \qquad e \in E. \qquad (9b)$$

In (9a) the compensated response of demand z_i to total employment is defined as

$$\frac{\partial \hat{z}_i}{\partial L} := \sum_h \left[\frac{\partial x_i^h}{\partial L} + \frac{\partial x_i^h}{\partial r^h}(1 - w_R^h)\frac{\partial \bar{x}_o^h}{\partial L}\right] - \sum_j \frac{\partial y_i^j}{\partial L}. \qquad (10a)$$

The response of public sector employment z_o to total employment is defined as

---

[3] It is possible to neglect the term $\gamma(\partial\Pi/\partial z_o)\Sigma_j(\partial y_o^j/\partial p_e)$ because $\partial\Pi/\partial z_o = 0$ for the empirically relevant cases of a fixed revenue-cost constraint and for a rate of return regulation.

$$\frac{\partial z_o}{\partial L} = 1 - \sum_j \frac{\partial y_o^j}{\partial L}. \tag{10b}$$

The condition (9a) can be interpreted after some further transformations. We use the property of the compensated response $\partial \hat{z}_i / \partial L$

$$\sum_{i=1}^{n} p_i \frac{\partial \hat{z}_i}{\partial L} = -\sum_{i=1}^{n} \sum_{h=1}^{H} p_i w_R^h \frac{\partial x_i^h}{\partial r^h} \frac{\partial \bar{x}_o^h}{\partial L} - \sum_{i=1}^{n} \sum_{j=1}^{J} p_i \frac{\partial y_i^j}{\partial L}$$

to obtain

$$\sum_{i=1}^{n} (p_i - \tilde{C}_i) \frac{\partial \hat{z}_i}{\partial L} = (1 - \gamma) \left[1 - \sum_{i=1}^{n} \sum_{h=1}^{H} p_i w_R^h \frac{\partial x_i^h}{\partial r^h} \cdot \frac{\partial \bar{x}_o^h}{\partial L} \right]$$
$$- (1 - \gamma) \sum_{i=o}^{n} \sum_{j=1}^{J} (p_i - c_i^j) \frac{\partial y_i^j}{\partial L}. \tag{9a'}$$

This formula reflects an adjustment of public prices to the monopolistic private pricing and also an adjustment to the labor market disequilibrium, as expressed by the first term of the right-hand side of (9a'). A general interpretation of this term cannot be given. A particular specification of the rationing scheme $\bar{x}_o^h(L)$ may therefore be helpful. The individual rationing is more serious the lower the individual reservation wage. Hence an increase in the overall employment should favor an employee more, the lower w_R^h. A useful benchmark, therefore, is the following specification

$$\frac{\partial \bar{x}_o^h}{\partial L} = \frac{s}{w_R^h}$$

where $s > 0$ is a proportionality factor. This factor is determined by the aggregation property

$$\sum_h \frac{\partial \bar{x}_o^h}{\partial L} = 1 \ \rightarrow \ s = \frac{1}{\sum_h (1/w_R^h)}.$$

Hence the rationing depends on the relative reservation wages

$$\frac{\partial \bar{x}_o^h}{\partial L} = \frac{1}{\sum_{h'} (w_R^h / w_R^{h'})}.$$

Substituting this specification into (9a') we obtain

$$\sum_{i=1}^{n} (p_i - \tilde{C}_i) \frac{\partial \hat{z}_i}{\partial L} = (1-\gamma)(1-sH) - (1-\gamma) \sum_{i=o}^{n} \sum_{j=1}^{J} (p_i - c_i^j) \frac{\partial y_i^j}{\partial L}. \quad (9a")$$

H is the number of consumers. The factor $s \in (0, 1/H]$, and therefore $sH \in (0,1]$. sH is higher, the higher the overall employment.

The adjustment of public pricing to changes in the overall employment, therefore, depends on $(1-\gamma)(1-sH)$. For ease of exposition, we consider prices above marginal costs only.

We can see the following trade-off between employment and pricing policy. If we approach a high level of overall employment $(sH \to 1)$, the right-hand side of (9a") becomes lower. This can only be achieved by also reducing the left-hand side. Such a reduction can be brought about by reducing the prices of complements to leisure $(\partial \hat{z}_i / \partial L > 0)$ [4] and increasing the prices of complements to labor $(\partial z_i / \partial L < 0)$. The result is an increase in the demand for leisure, whence we can conclude that prices have been changed in order to reduce the overall employment. This interpretation suggests that typically we will obtain an interior solution for L which is somewhere below full employment. If, however, we approach a low level of overall employment $(sH \to 0)$, the right-hand side of (9a") increases and the board will increase the prices of complements to leisure and reduce the prices of complements to labor. Prices are changed in order to increase the overall employment.

---

[4] The definitions of complements to leisure and labor used in the text are unusual albeit the straightforward definitions to deal with equation (9a").

Let us now turn to the interpretation of the marginal conditions (9b). Surprisingly, they are identical with the conditions (11-2) [5]. Hence, rationing individual labor supply does not influence the qualitative results on the structure of prices we have derived in chapter 11. Quantitatively, of course, prices will differ depending on the rationing scheme.

The result we have obtained depends decisively on the form of individual rationing. As labor is allocated according to a binding scheme $\bar{x}_o^h$, this labor allocation cannot be influenced by changes in the public prices. Hence there is no rationale for changing the structure of prices in order to influence the labor market. Such a rationale exists, however, if we deal with an economy where the overall employment is constrained, but where the individuals are given the option to choose the utility maximizing labor supply. This case is treated in the next subsection.

12.1.2   AN OVERALL EMPLOYMENT CONSTRAINT

If we want to obtain a pricing structure which directly reflects the optimal response of public pricing to a disequilibrium in the labor market, we should not treat overall employment as an instrument variable and we should not apply the individual rationing scheme of the Drèze model. We should rather assume that overall employment is exogenously given at a level $\overline{L}$. Hence, the public firm has to accept the constraint

$$\overline{L} \le \sum_h x_o^h(p, r^h). \tag{11}$$

The individuals are allowed to choose the utility maximizing labor supply x_o^h. We assume that in the absence of the constraint (11) the total labor

---

[5] Recall $p_o = c_o$ and assume once again $\partial \Pi / \partial z_o = 0$.

supply $\sum x_o^h$ would be higher in absolute value than $\overline{L}$. Hence the labor market constraint will be binding.

Prices, quantities and lump-sum incomes have to be chosen in such a way that the utility maximizing labor supplies of the consumers add up to the exogenously given employment level $\overline{L}$. The resulting optimization approach is

$$\max_{p_e, r^h, z_i} \mathcal{L} = W(v^h(p, r^h)) - \sum_{i=o}^{n} \alpha_i \left[\sum_h x_i^h(p, r^h) - z_i - \sum_j y_i^j(p) \right] -$$

$$- \alpha_{n+1} \left[\overline{L} - \sum_h x_o^h(p, r^h) \right] - \beta g(z) - \tag{12}$$

$$- \overline{\gamma} \left[\Pi(\cdot) - \sum_{i=o}^{n} p_i z_i \right].$$

We obtain the following structure of public pricing

$$\sum_{i=1}^{n} (p_i - \tilde{C}_i) \frac{\partial \hat{z}_i}{\partial p_e} = -\gamma z_e - \frac{\alpha_{n+1}}{\beta_o} \frac{\partial \hat{x}_o}{\partial p_e} -$$

$$- (1-\gamma) \sum_{i=o}^{n} \sum_{j=1}^{J} (p_i - c_i^j) \frac{\partial y_i^j}{\partial p_e} e \in E. \tag{13}$$

The ratio of Lagrangean multipliers, α_{n+1}/β_o is positive because $\alpha_{n+1} = -\partial W/\overline{L} > 0$ and $\beta_o := \beta(\partial g/\partial z_o) > 0$. [6] (13) is identical with (11-2) except for the term $(\alpha_{n+1}/\beta_o)(\partial \hat{x}_o/\partial p_e)$. The result in (13) reflects the adjustment of public pricing to disequilibria in the private commodity markets (far right term) and the influence of the employment constraint on public sector pricing [7]: there is a tendency to reduce the price of complements

---

[6] For the sign of α_{n+1} recall $\overline{L}<0$. For $\beta_o>0$ see section 3.3, footnote 12.

[7] The reader may explicitly solve (13) for a particular price p_e as we have done in (11-3). Then the following economic interpretation follows immediately.

to leisure $(\partial \hat{x}_o/\partial p_e < 0)$ and to increase the price of complements to labor $(\partial \hat{x}_o/\partial p_e > 0)$.

If lump-sum incomes are not available instruments, the optimization of (12) with respect to public prices and quantities leads to a pricing structure which is identical with (3-21) except for the term $(\alpha_{n+1}/\beta_o)(\partial \hat{x}_o/\partial p_e)$ and the labor market constraint influences the price structure in the same way as in the model presented in the text. However, for a direct comparison with the results of chapter 11 and of the preceding subsection 12.1.1 the inclusion of lump-sum incomes as instruments is necessary.

12.2   CAPACITY LIMITS OF PUBLIC TRANSPORTATION

Transportation capacity limits are of critical importance during times of peak demand. Traffic demand for public buses or underground is rationed. Congestion causes queues at bus stops because of delayed arrival of buses. On the other hand, private peak traffic is also rationed. People will anticipate the traffic jam, and will have to invest more time in travel. The following model integrates the rationing of public and of private peak traffic.

We label public peak traffic by "n". Therefore $x_n^h > 0$ is consumer h's demand, $y_n^j < 0$ private producer j's demand, $z_n > 0$ public supply. Public off-peak traffic is one of the many goods $i \in I$ which are part of the model, but in which we are not particularly interested.

In dealing with private traffic we have to distinguish between marketed and non–marketed services.

Marketed traffic services are produced by private enterprises and sold to consumers and to private and to public enterprises at a market price or at a regulated price (taxis etc.). These services are also included in our model as some of the many goods $i \in I$. To keep our model simple, we do not include these services explicitly into the capacity constraint.

Non-marketed private traffic is "produced" by the traffic user at the moment of use. There is no market price or regulated price. In fact, demand for non-marketed private traffic is revealed in the demand for those goods and services the private consumer or producer needs for the "production" of traffic. Hence, traffic demand is revealed indirectly as the demand for automobiles, petrol etc. Moreover, if a consumer or a private producer "produces" such non-marketed traffic services, this production requires labor as an input. Private producers evaluate these labor inputs at the wage rate, $p_o = 1$. Consumers are assumed to ignore their own labor input.

We label private non–marketed peak traffic by "n+1" because it is a good which is revealed only indirectly by demand for other goods $i \in \{o, 1, \ldots, n\}$. There is no price for "good n+1" and no "market" equilibrium. However we specify two "production" functions, namely,

$$x^h_{n+1} = x^h_{n+1}(x^h_1, \ldots, x^h_{n-1}) \quad ; \quad x^h_{n+1} > 0 \tag{14}$$

as the consumers' production function, and

$${}^{,j}{}_{\cdot} = y^j_{n+1}(y^j_o, y^j_1, \ldots, y^j_{n-1}) \quad ; \quad y^j_{n+1} < 0 \tag{15}$$

as the private producers' production function.

Consumers' optimal consumption choices and producers' optimal input/output choices can be written as usual, referring to good $i = \{o, \ldots, n\}$. Good n+1 enters the consumption and production plans only indirectly, via consumption or input of automobiles, petrol etc.

Both public and private traffic require infrastructure. However, public traffic requires less infrastructure for the same quantity of passenger miles: for example, the present UK highways would provide sufficient infrastructure for motor traffic even at the summer holiday weekends if everybody used public buses instead of private cars. Hence we postulate the following demand function for infrastructure, i.e. for capacity

$$CAP = CAP(x_n - y_n; x_{n+1} - y_{n+1})^{8)}$$
$$(CAP > 0;\ CAP_1, CAP_2 > 0;\ CAP_1 < CAP_2). \tag{16}$$

This demand will not be met totally by the available capacity. Hence we assume an exogenously given capacity limit $\overline{CAP}$ which restricts the peak transportation services

$$\overline{CAP} \geq CAP(x_n - y_n; x_{n+1} - y_{n+1}). \tag{17}$$

As our analysis deals with peak traffic, we assume this constraint to be binding.

Consider the Boiteux model for the case of constrained peak traffic. The board chooses optimal prices p_e, quantities z_i, and lump-sum transfers r^h. The quality levels are, once again, held constant. The resulting optimization approach is as follows [9]

---

[8] As usual $x_i = \Sigma_h x_i^h$, $y_i = \Sigma_j y_i^j$.

[9] To avoid the tedious treatment of corner solutions, we assume every consumer to consume $x_n^h > 0$ and $x_{n+1}^h > 0$. This assumption can be justified by thinking of consumers as households where, e.g., the man uses the private car to go to business and the wife uses the public bus for shopping or vice versa.

$$\max_{p_e, r^h, z_i} \mathcal{L} = W(v^h(p, r^h)) -$$

$$- \sum_{i=o}^{n} \alpha_i \left[\sum_h x_i^h(p, r^h) - z_i - \sum_j y_i^j(p) \right] -$$

$$- \alpha_{n+1} \left[\overline{CAP} - CAP \left(z_n; \sum_h x_{n+1}^h(p, r^h) - \sum_j y_i^j(p) \right) \right] - \qquad (18)$$

$$- \beta g(z) - \overline{\gamma} \left[\Pi(\cdot) - \sum_{i=o}^{n} p_i z_i \right].$$

We obtain the following structure of prices

$$\sum_{i=o}^{n} (p_i - \widetilde{C}_i) \frac{\partial \hat{z}_i}{\partial p_e} + \frac{\alpha_{n+1}}{\beta_o} \left(CAP_1 \frac{\partial \hat{z}_n}{\partial p_e} + CAP_2 \frac{d(\hat{x}, y)_{n+1}}{dp_e} \right) =$$

$$= -\gamma \, z_e - (1 - \gamma) \sum_{i=o}^{n} \sum_{j=1}^{J} (p_i - c_i^j) \frac{\partial y_i^j}{\partial p_e} \quad e \in E. \qquad (19)$$

Prior to the detailed economic interpretation of this structure of prices we have to clarify the exact meaning of some of the symbols used.

First, α_{n+1}/β_o is a marginal rate of substitution between labor and capacity. This can be shown as follows. Remember that $\beta_o := \beta(\partial g/\partial z_o) = -\partial W/\partial \bar{z}_o > 0$, where $\bar{z}_o$ is the initial endowment of labor in the public sector. Differentiating the Lagrangean function $\mathcal{L}$ with respect to $\overline{CAP}$ yields $\alpha_{n+1} = -\partial W/\partial \overline{CAP} < 0$. Therefore the ratio of the parameters $\alpha_{n+1}/\beta_o = \partial \bar{z}_o/\partial \overline{CAP}$ (at constant W) is negative. This marginal rate of substitution between labor and capacity is large (in absolute value) if the social valuation of the capacity limit is large, which is more probable the lower the capacity limit $\overline{CAP}$. In such a case the welfare loss from foregoing one unit of capacity can only be compensated by a large increase in the available labor endowment in the public sector.

Second, we have defined a "compensated" price effect of total peak traffic as follows [10]

$$\frac{d(\hat{x}, y)_{n+1}}{dp_e} := \sum_h \frac{dx_{n+1}^h}{dp_e} + \sum_h x_e^h \frac{dx_{n+1}^h}{dr^h} - \sum_j \frac{dy_{n+1}^j}{dp_e}. \qquad (20)$$

In doing so we had to consider that the "production functions" $x_{n+1}^h(\cdot)$ and $y_{n+1}^h(\cdot)$ depend on prices in the following way

$$\frac{dx_{n+1}^h}{dp_e} = \sum_{i=1}^{n-1} \frac{\partial x_{n+1}^h}{\partial x_i^h} \cdot \frac{\partial x_i^h}{\partial p_e} \quad ; \quad \frac{dy_{n+1}^j}{\partial p_e} = \sum_{i=o}^{n-1} \frac{\partial y_{n+1}^j}{\partial y_i^j} \cdot \frac{\partial y_i^j}{\partial p_e}. \qquad (21)$$

We assume the price effect $d(\hat{x}, y)_{n+1}/dp_e$ to be positive for substitutes for private peak traffic, as for instance for public peak traffic. The effect is assumed to be negative for complements, for instance for petrol which can be considered as one of the goods $e \in E$ if its price is controlled by the public sector [11].

Let us now turn to the economic interpretation of public sector pricing when peak traffic is constrained by a capacity limit. We transform (19) to obtain

---

[10] We cannot use the symbol $d\hat{z}_{n+1}$, because ex definitione there is no public supply z_{n+1} in our model.

[11] We skip over all institutional details of controlling the petrol price like direct setting of the price or indirect control via taxation, and possible earmarking of tax revenues for the expansion of capacity.

$$p_e = \tilde{C}_e - \frac{\gamma \, z_e}{\partial \hat{z}_e / \partial p_e} - \sum_{i \neq e} (p_i - \tilde{C}_i) \frac{\partial \hat{z}_i / \partial p_e}{\partial \hat{z}_e / \partial p_e} -$$

$$- (1 - \gamma) \sum_{i=o}^{n} \sum_{j=1}^{J} (p_i - c_i^j) \frac{\partial y_i^j / \partial p_e}{\partial \hat{z}_e / \partial p_e} - \tag{22}$$

$$- \frac{\alpha_{n+1}}{\beta_o (\partial \hat{z}_e / \partial p_e)} \left(CAP_1 \frac{\partial \hat{z}_n}{\partial p_e} + CAP_2 \frac{d(\hat{x}, y)_{n+1}}{dp_e} \right) \qquad e \in E.$$

This pricing structure can be compared with equation (11–3). Public prices therefore depend on

- marginal costs;

- a "Ramsey term", implying a dependence of prices on their own price elasticity of demand;

- the "reallocation terms" which relate prices p_e to price-cost margins, both in the public and in the private sector; and

- a capacity term, measuring the influence of p_e on the capacity utilization.

Both the Ramsey and the reallocation terms have the usual sign. The Ramsey term typically implies a tendency for p_n to exceed marginal costs. The reallocation terms would imply a tendency for p_n to exceed marginal costs if all other prices exceeded the respective marginal costs *and* if public production were a net substitute for all other goods. The latter assumption is very implausible. Transportation usually is complementary to many other goods. Hence, the reallocation terms might imply a tendency towards low public peak prices.

Let us now turn to the capacity term. First, we obtain the expected result that the capacity term is more important, the larger the marginal rate of substitution between labor and capacity, in absolute value. The more restrictive the capacity limit, the more relevant its influence on public pricing.

In the following we distinguish among three different groups of goods which are publicly controlled: public peak traffic, substitutes for peak traffic, and complements to peak traffic.

The price of *public peak traffic* must be lower, the less public traffic influences capacity (CAP_1) and the more private traffic does (CAP_2). The influence of private utilization of capacity, moreover, depends on a ratio of price effects, reflecting the influence of changing p_n on both private and public peak traffic. The relevant price effects, however, are not independent of each other. An increase in p_n will typically shift traffic from the public to the private transportation modes; the more sensitively public traffic responds to p_n, the more sensitively will private traffic respond. This interdependence can be shown easily. We denote the total traffic by TV which consists of public and private traffic (all variables measured in the same units, for instance passenger miles):

$$TV = z_n + x_{n+1} + y_{n+1}. \qquad (23)$$

Differentiation with respect to the public peak fare yields

$$\frac{\partial TV}{\partial p_n} = \frac{\partial z_n}{\partial p_n} + \frac{d(x,y)_{n+1}}{dp_n} \qquad (24)$$

and we obtain

$$\frac{d(x,y)_{n+1}/dp_n}{\partial z_n/\partial p_n} = -1 + \frac{\partial TV/\partial p_n}{\partial z_n/\partial p_n}. \qquad (25)$$

Since a reduction in public fares typically increases the traffic volume, we assume $\partial TV/\partial p_n < 0$ [12] Moreover, we assume income effects are small

---

[12] $(\partial TV/\partial p_n)/(\partial z_n/\partial p_n) < 1$ is guaranteed by our assumption that public and private peak traffic are substitutes and that demand for public peak traffic does not react inversely to its own price. The influence of CAP_2 on the fare of public peak traffic, therefore, cannot turn over to the contrary.

and therefore non-compensated price effects approximate compensated effects. Now substitute (25) into the capacity term for the public fare p_n, to determine the extent to which increases in the traffic volume, resulting from low public fares, restrict the use of low fares policies.

Let us now consider publicly controlled *prices of peak traffic substitutes* $(\partial \hat{z}_n / \partial p_e > 0, \; d(\hat{x}, y)_{n+1}/dp_e > 0)$. They must be lower, the more public and private peak traffic influence capacity. The private utilization of capacity will have a greater effect because of $CAP_2 > CAP_1$. The resulting low prices for peak traffic substitutes is a familiar result of the peak-load pricing literature. The peak traffic substitutes are typically the off-peak transportation services, and their low prices are designed to shift demand from peak to off-peak times.

The opposite result is obtained for publicly controlled *prices of peak traffic complements* $(\partial \hat{z}_n / \partial p_e < 0, \; d(\hat{x}, y)_{n+1}/dp_e < 0)$. They must be higher, the more public and private peak traffic influence capacity. Once again, CAP_2 will be more influential. It is interesting that higher prices of peak traffic complements, for instance a higher price for petrol, burden both private and public peak traffic although the public peak traffic utilizes less capacity. Furthermore, lower utilization of capacity by the public peak traffic leads to a lower price for petrol which, in turn, favors also the private peak traffic in spite of its heavy utilization of capacity.

C TIME–DEPENDENT PRICING

CHAPTER 13 PRICING THROUGH TIME AND ADJUSTMENT CLAUSES

The rapid inflation of the seventies has increased the interest in pricing rules through time. The more rapidly input prices increase, the more quickly must output prices be adjusted and the more important are profit losses because of regulatory lags. This challenge of the seventies has brought about theoretical as well as practical responses.

The *theoretical response* has been to develop a dynamic analysis of public pricing: the models derive a path of prices through time which optimizes an integral over the welfare function at the different points of time, given relevant constraints. Using discrete or continuous control theory, an optimal path of prices $p_e(t)$, t being the index of time, can be found. A simple example of such an analysis is given by Crew–Kleindorfer (1979, chapter 7).

The basic idea of such a theory is the instantaneous optimal adjustment of prices over the whole horizon. This constitutes the difference between these dynamic models and a static analysis applying the Boiteux model period by period. This theoretical difference has a characteristic institutional counterpart. A static analysis is the appropriate theory for describing the common system of setting prices by discretionary actions, such as those determined by rate hearings. A dynamic theory describes an ideal adjustment path. Hence the dynamic theory of public pricing can be regarded as the basis of automatic adjustment clauses.

Sophisticated adjustment clauses are of a stochastic nature: neither government nor the board of the public sector know whether some or all input prices will change at time t; there is uncertainty about future factor prices. The problems which arise from this uncertainty have been investigated explicitly for fuel-adjustment clauses which provide for automatic adjustment in output prices in response to changes in the factor prices of fuel and gas but not in response to other factor prices. Assume a technology where fuel and capital inputs can be substituted ex ante, but where their ratio is fixed ex post. The future price of fuel is uncertain at the time the fuel-capital ratio is chosen. The fuel-adjustment clause implies a sharing of the risk resulting form the uncertain factor price, reducing both the firm's expected profit and the regulator's expected welfare compared with the case of certainty (Baron–DeBondt (1981)). The fuel-adjustment clause can lead the firm to an inefficient fuel-capital ratio. Moreover, the incentive to choose the least-cost fuel supply can be reduced. These problems are relevant primarily in cases of decreasing returns to scale because in this case the profit from increasing output price exceeds the additional cost from the inefficient input combination. However, this effect appears only if the output price is adjusted immediately or after a short time. Hence, the above inefficiencies can be avoided by extending the "collection lag" if the firm is not permitted to collect the adjusted price until after some time (Baron–DeBondt (1979)).

The *practical response* to these problems in the US has been to apply or to propose adjustment clauses for electricity utilities and the Bell telephone companies. They are either fuel-adjustment clauses, or general factor-price adjustment clauses, permitting the firm to adjust automatically to increases in all factor prices. The first type of adjustment clause weakens incentives for the efficient choice of inputs, whereas the latter avoids this bias. Both types of adjustment clauses, however, weaken incentives for the regulated firm to increase its productivity. Hence, some proposals permit automatic output price increases only in so far as the weighted input price increases exceed the rate of increase of productivity (Kendrick (1975), Sudit (1979)). The price increase of any input is weighted by the respective share of that input in total costs. Productivity is measured either by man-hour per output (Kendrick) or by a Divisia index of total factor productivity change [1] (Sudit). To avoid

---

[1] This is the difference between the sum of the percentage changes in physical outputs

controversies between firm and regulator over the accuracy and reliability of actual company-specific data, Sudit proposes that the adjustment clause be based on market reference input prices and industry productivity trends.

In a multiproduct enterprise, moreover, the *many* adjustment paths of the different prices have to be compatible with the *overall* productivity incentives of the firm. Sudit therefore suggests (i) individual price changes which are determined by minimizing a quadratic loss function, postulating automatically adjusted price increases to be as close as possible to certain desirable levels of price changes, as defined by the regulator, and (ii) an overall adjustment formula which restricts the weighted sum of individual price changes to the weighted sums of input price changes minus factor productivity changes, the weights being the respective revenue and cost shares.

Recently the advantages and disadvantages of the practical application of adjustment clauses have been discussed intensively. Proponents argue that damage to firms from regulatory lags is reduced and competitiveness between regulated and non-regulated industries is restored. Opponents, on the other hand, stress the implied abandonment of regulatory control, the resulting inefficiencies and the reduction of built-in-stabilizing effects of regulatory lags. They argue that problems like profit squeeze of regulated firms could equally well be diminished by granting them interim relief.

---

weighted by their respective shares in total revenue and the sum of the percentage changes in physical inputs weighted by their respective share in total costs (Sudit (1979, 60)).

CHAPTER 14   PEAK–LOAD PRICING

14.1   SETTING THE PROBLEM

Consider goods for which *demand* fluctuates cyclically over time, both daily and seasonally. Electricity or gas demand peaks in the morning, at noon and in the evening, and is highest in winter. Local bus and underground services are used most intensively between 7 to 9 a.m. and 4 to 7 p.m. Air and rail traffic have a holiday demand peak; telecommunication has a business demand peak. In all these cases it is impossible to use off-peak production to serve peak demand because the goods are not storable, at least not at reasonable costs.

The *supply* side of such goods also has special features. The production typically is characterized by high fixed costs and low variable costs; there are many cases of increasing returns to scale. In other words, the characteristics of "natural monopolies" are often present: enterprises producing those goods could keep others out of the market by their pricing policy and still make profits. For these reasons the goods are produced either by nationalized or by regulated public utilities.

In practice such public utilities are often required to meet all demand, however high it may be. (There are some theoretical arguments to justify this requirement.) A public utility which charges only one price for its output will therefore face a trade-off between fairly high capacity costs and a fairly high price. Profit maximizing as well as welfare maximizing monopolies have used systems of price differentiation to cope with this trade-off.

The *simplest rule of thumb* in our peak-load case is based upon the distinction between operating and capacity costs: only consumers who are responsible for the capacity costs should pay for them. Hence peak demand has to pay operating plus capacity costs whereas off-peak demand is priced at the low operating costs only. This price structure is designed to increase off-peak demand, and to encourage a more uniform utilization of capacity and to increase welfare, including the welfare gains from not driving people out of the market.

The welfare optimality of this rule of thumb has been verified by Steiner (1957) and Williamson (1966), albeit under very restrictive assumptions. There are at least two periods of fixed length, each characterized by a given demand function $x_e(p_e)$. For a given price, demand within any period is assumed to be constant ("time independent demand"). The chosen cost function is of the simplest possible type, namely a fixed proportions technology, leading to constant operating costs and constant capacity costs.

There is, however, an interesting counterexample to this simple model. Assume that peak and off-peak demand do not differ very much and that capacity costs are very high. At a single price there may be an undesired peak/off-peak structure of demand. The public utility introduces peak-load pricing and follows the above mentioned rule of thumb. The off-peak price falls drastically because the capacity costs are assumed to be very high. The peak price increases drastically. This may imply a *shifting peak* where the former off-peak demand becomes the new peak demand and vice versa. An empirical example is the German "Moonlight-tariff" for phoning after 10 p.m. It was abolished in 1981 because it led to an intensive demand peak between 10 and 11 p.m. Under the restrictive assumptions on cost functions mentioned above, welfare optimal pricing requires a price discrimination which equates peak and off-peak demand. Off-peak demand has to pay a share of capacity costs.

The plausibility of the above mentioned rules should not prevent us from recognizing that their validity rests on their very restrictive assumptions. They do not remain valid if we work with the usual neoclassical cost functions (Panzar (1976)), or allow for time-dependent demand.

We therefore require a more general model of the peak-load problem. A priori we might consider applying the usual Boiteux model of public pricing.

This would involve classifying demand in different periods as different goods so that demand is time-independent within each period. We obtain peak-load marginal-cost pricing rules, peak-load Ramsey-pricing rules etc. The peak-load problem turns out to be a special case of joint production and by always considering the optimal input choice we can find an optimal mix between operating and capacity costs.

Practical problems can arise if too many periods are distinguished, but the approach seems to provide a straightforward theoretical solution of the peak-load problem (Bös (1981, 31-33)). It is, however, a little superficial to treat the peak-load problem in this way. Were the approach appropriate, it would be difficult to understand the immense interest in the peak-load problem in the last five or ten years (as surveyed in Crew–Kleindorfer (1979), Mitchell–Manning–Acton (1977) and Turvey–Anderson (1977), to mention a few outstanding recent books).

What, then, is the reason for developing a special theory of peak-load pricing? It is the following peak-load trilemma:

- First, the government does not want too many prices because this leads to high information and administrative costs and to uncertainty for consumers [1]. Hence the length of the periods chosen is such that demand does not depend on prices alone, but fluctuates within the periods as well, either stochastically [2], or deterministically depending on an index of time ("time-dependent demand").

- Second, the government wants to avoid high peak prices, mostly because of distributional considerations. High peak prices for local transport may disadvantage the lower-income working population most and not the better-off car owner.

---

[1] With microprocessing, the technical possibilities of adequate metering would allow for many more periods than was the case previously.

[2] Electricity demand, for instance, depends heavily on weather.

–   Third, the government wants to meet all demand because relia-
    bility is an important quality characteristic of public supply.

The direct application of the Boiteux model does not come to terms
with time-dependent demand although it deals adequately with points two
and three. Hence we must extend our usual Boiteux approach to the case of
time-dependent demand. Moreover, recent peak-load theory avoids condition three of the trilemma and accepts excess demand and rationing, arguing
that it may be welfare optimal to accept excess demand instead of excessive
spending on the capacity costs of public utilities or applying peak prices
which are too high.

14.2   A MODEL WITH EXCESS DEMAND AND RATIONING

We treat the peak-load problem in a particular version of the Boiteux
model. The public sector consists of one firm producing one good, say
electricity. The market demand for this good varies among the periods of
the day. These periods are labelled $e \in E$. The number of periods and
their respective length, L(e), are exogenously fixed. The board uses the
instruments p_e and z_i to maximize welfare under relevant constraints [3].

We want to show the trade-off between rationing by price and rationing
by quantity. This trade-off would be distorted if the board were allowed to
apply lump-sum transfers $\{r^h\}$ or $\{r_e^h\}$, as such transfers would introduce a
further means of rationing: "rationing by redistribution", shifting purchasing power from peak to off-peak demand. Let us therefore exclude lump-sum
transfers.

To deal with the peak-load problem we define all demand and supply
quantities x_e and z_e per unit of time in a period (say, the demand in one

---

[3] Qualities q_e are assumed to be constant.

second). This method of definition enables us to come to terms with fluctuations of demand within a given period $e \in E$. Quantities of all other goods $i \notin E$ are defined as usual.

The *quantity demanded per unit of time*, x_e, depends on the period price and on time in an additively separable way (Dansby (1975)) [4][5]:

$$x_e(p_e, t_e) = x_e(p_e) + \tau(t_e) \qquad e \in E. \tag{1}$$

The demand depends on the price p_e which is the same for all units of time (moments) of period e. It does not depend on prices in other periods: no cross price elasticities enter our formulas [6]. On the other hand, demand is allowed to fluctuate within the period, depending on t_e, the index of units of time (moments) of period e, $t_e \in e$. The price effect of demand is invariant with respect to time and the time effect is invariant with respect to the period price.

The time-dependent demand $\tau(t_e)$ is defined over the interval $[0, \tau_e^{max}]$. Both $\tau = 0$ and $\tau = \tau_e^{max}$ may occur at one, or more than one, moment of time in the interval e. In other words, there may be one, or more than one, cyclical movement of demand $\tau(t_e)$ during period t_e. We assume that the board knows all these fluctuations, whence it can compute the density function $f_e(\tau)$ of time-dependent demand. This density function measures the relative frequency of a particular demand τ, taken together from all

---

[4] The derivations of our model can be applied analogously to the case of stochastic demand $x_e = x_e(p_e, u)$, where u is a random variable. Our specification corresponds to the additive stochastic demand function $x_e = x_e(p_e) + u$. For further discussion of these problems see Brown–Johnson (1969), Visscher (1973), and Carlton (1977).

[5] It is possible to give up the additive structure of time–dependent demand and to prove most results for more general demand functions (Watzke (1982)).

[6] They can be introduced easily into our derivations. However, the interpretation of the resulting price structure (18) becomes far more complicated. Hence we follow the usual tradition of the stochastic pricing literature and suppress them.

cyclical fluctuations in period t_e. The corresponding distribution function may be denoted $F_e(\tau)$.

The *quantity supplied per unit of time*, z_e, is assumed to be time-independent. It is constant within a period, but may differ between periods. As we deal with outputs only, $z_e \geq 0$. With respect to the other quantities $z_i, i \notin E$, all our conventions hold. They are defined with respect to the usual time horizon of production, i.e. over all periods $e \in E$. Hence the production function equals

$$g(z) = g(z_e L(e), z_i \big|_{i \notin E}) = 0 \tag{2}$$

and we can define modified marginal costs

$$\tilde{C}_e = \left[\frac{\partial g / \partial z_e}{\partial g / \partial z_o} + \gamma \frac{\partial \Pi}{\partial z_e} \right] L(e) > 0; \quad \tilde{C}_i \big|_{i \notin E} = \left[\frac{\partial g / \partial z_i}{\partial g / \partial z_o} + \gamma \frac{\partial \Pi}{\partial z_i} \right] > 0. \tag{3}$$

The market may be *in equilibrium or in disequilibrium* [7]. Both excess demand and excess supply are possible, resulting in rationing of demand or supply. However, for political reasons the extent of demand rationing will be constrained. The welfare optimal choice of output may well imply that during some periods demand is always rationed. Consumers, however, would not be willing to accept a telecommunication system which is rationed all day long and unrationed between 0 and 5 a.m. only. As a matter of fact, such a low level of electricity, gas or telephone supplies in single periods is undesirable and usually leads to adverse reactions from customers. The quality structure of public utilities' supply obviously is influenced by political considerations. The government will be afraid of losing votes, of campaigns against electricity blackouts etc. Hence it requests the enterprise's board explicitly to consider *reliability constraints*. The straightforward choice of a reliability constraint in our model is [8] :

---

[7] For all goods $i \notin E$ the market equilibria are assumed to hold as usual.

[8] As these constraints will reduce the extent of rationing, they can be thought of

$$z_e - x_e(p_e) \geq 0. \qquad e \in E. \qquad (4)$$

This constraint obliges the board to cover at least the time-independent basic demand $x_e(p_e)$ in any period. Demand rationing is restricted to the time-dependent demand $\tau(t_e)$.

For expositional clarity we split supply z_e into the "minimum" supply z_e^m which just covers the time-independent basic demand, and the "additional" supply z_e^a which is consumed by time-dependent demand:

$$z_e^m = x_e(p_e); \qquad z_e^m + z_e^a = z_e \qquad e \in E. \qquad (5)$$

Rationing of demand refers to supply z_e^a only. Therefore, at any point of time the public enterprise will sell the following quantity

$$S(e, t_e) := z_e^m + min[\tau(t_e), z_e^a] \qquad e \in E, \qquad (6)$$

whence its revenue-cost constraint is as follows [9] :

$$\sum_{e \in E} \int_{t_e \in e} p_e S(e, t)dt + \sum_{i \notin E} p_i z_i = \Pi(\cdot) \qquad (7)$$

or equivalently

$$\sum_e p_e L(e) \left\{ z_e^m + \int_0^{z_e^a} \tau \, f(\tau)d\tau + z_e^a \left(1 - F(z_e^a)\right) \right\} + \sum_{i \notin E} p_i z_i = \Pi(\cdot). \qquad (8)$$

as a surrogate for explicitly regarding administrative rationing costs (Crew–Kleindorfer (1979, 91)). – In stochastic models of peak-load pricing such constraints have been dealt with since Meyer (1975) by saying that the probability of excess demand at any moment e must not exceed a level ε_e.

[9] The exact specification of $\Pi(\cdot)$ is $\Pi(z_e L(e); z_i|_{i \notin E}; \rho)$.

Let us now turn to demand rationing and its social valuation. Demand is rationed if there is excess demand, $E > 0$, where

$$E(e, t_e) := max\{\tau(t_e) - z_e^a, 0\} \qquad e \in E. \tag{9}$$

The usual peak-load literature deals with different *theoretical* alternatives to rationing: consumers are either excluded randomly or with respect to their willingness to pay, usually measured by the individual consumer surplus or by the compensating variation. In the latter case rationing may exclude people in order of the lowest or highest willingness to pay until capacity is exhausted.

These are theoretical solutions of the rationing problem and can be handled nicely in the peak-load calculus. Practical rationing, for instance of telephone calls etc., follows other criteria. Hence we will not adopt one of these concepts, but use a more general concept to formulate the welfare losses of rationing.

We start from a *social welfare function per unit of time* $W(p, t_e)$ depending on both controlled and uncontrolled prices. According to the usual definition, welfare is defined on the assumption that all consumers who are willing to pay the price p_e are being served. Hence, welfare accrues unreduced in moments without excess demand. With respect to moments of rationing, however, the board has to consider an adequately reduced welfare $\Gamma(E(e, t_e)) \cdot W(p, t_e)$ where $\Gamma(E)$ can be take values between 0 and 1. This is a fairly general formulation of welfare losses from rationing: the function $\Gamma(E)$ may represent individual consumers' actually accruing welfare losses but also the board's valuation of such losses. By normalization $\Gamma(E) = 1$ if there is no excess demand. However, the board may decide to set $\Gamma(E) = 1$ even if $E > 0$, thus totally ignoring welfare losses from rationing. On the other hand, the board may decide to value welfare losses from rationing at more than the individual consumer losses; in the limiting case assuming $\Gamma(E) = 0$ as soon as $E > 0$. Usually, the board will follow some middle course, in particular it may follow the actual losses [10].

Aggregating over all moments of time and over all periods we obtain the board's total welfare measure

$$
\widetilde{W}(p, z) = \sum_{e \in E} \int_{t_e \in e} \Gamma(E(e,t)) \cdot W(p,t) dt
$$

$$
= \sum_{e \in E} L(e) \left\{ \Gamma(0) \int_{0}^{z_e^a} W(p, \tau) f(\tau) d\tau \right. \tag{10}
$$

$$
\left. + \int_{z_e^a}^{\tau_e^{max}} \Gamma(\tau - z_e^a) W(p, \tau) f(\tau) d\tau \right\}.
$$

We follow the usual peak-load literature and assume the social welfare function to be a consumer surplus, whence

$$
\frac{\partial W}{\partial p_e} = -x_e(p_e, t_e). \tag{11}
$$

We now substitute the special welfare function $\widetilde{W}$ into the Boiteux model, and consider the reliability constraints (4), the rationed market equilibrium of public supply (5) and the revenue-cost constraint (7). We obtain the following optimization approach:

---

[10] Some particular cases of rationing cannot be expressed directly by $\Gamma(E)$ if the board takes the actual individual losses as a measure of the relevant social welfare losses. Random rationing, for instance, can only be expressed by a function $\Gamma(E,x) = (1-E/x)$. The extension of our derivations to such a case is straightforward, albeit a little tedious.

$$
\max_{\substack{p_e, z_i, \\ z_e, z_e^m, z_e^a}} \mathcal{L} = \widetilde{W}(p, z) - \sum_{e \in E} \alpha_e(x_e(p_e) - z_e^m) -
$$

$$
- \sum_{i \notin E} \alpha_i \left[\sum_h x_i^h(p) - z_i - \sum_j y_i^j(p) \right] -
$$

$$
- \beta g(z) - \overline{\gamma} \left[\Pi(\cdot) - \sum_{e \in E} \int_{t_e \in e} p_e S(e, t) dt - \sum_{i \notin E} p_i z_i \right] -
$$

$$
- \sum_{e \in E} \delta_e(z_e - z_e^m - z_e^a). \tag{12}
$$

The following first-order conditions hold:

$$
\frac{\partial \mathcal{L}}{\partial p_e} = -L(e) \int_0^{\tau_e^{max}} \Gamma(E) x_e(p_e, \tau) f(\tau) d\tau - \alpha_e \frac{\partial x_e}{\partial p_e} - \sum_{i \notin E} \alpha_i \frac{\partial z_i^D}{\partial p_e} +
$$

$$
+ \overline{\gamma} L(e) \left[z_e^m + \int_0^{z_e^a} \tau f(\tau) d\tau + z_e^a(1 - F(z_e^a)) \right] = 0 \quad e \in E, \tag{13}
$$

$$
\frac{\partial \mathcal{L}}{\partial z_i} = \alpha_i - \beta \frac{\partial g}{\partial z_i} - \overline{\gamma} \left(p_i - \partial \Pi / \partial z_i \right) = 0 \qquad i \notin E, \tag{14}
$$

$$
\frac{\partial \mathcal{L}}{\partial z_e} = -\beta \frac{\partial g}{\partial z_e} L(e) - \overline{\gamma} \partial \Pi / \partial z_e L(e) - \delta_e = 0 \qquad e \in E, \tag{15}
$$

$$
\frac{\partial \mathcal{L}}{\partial z_e^m} = \alpha_e + \overline{\gamma} p_e L(e) + \delta_e = 0 \qquad e \in E, \tag{16}
$$

$$\frac{\partial \mathcal{L}}{\partial z_e^a} = - L(e) \int_{z_e^a}^{\tau_e^{max}} \Gamma'(\tau - z_e^a) W(p, \tau) f(\tau) d\tau +$$

$$+ \overline{\gamma} \, L(e) \, p_e [1 - F(z_e^a)] + \delta_e = 0 \quad e \in E.$$

$$(17)^{11)}$$

What is the economic meaning of these marginal conditions?

First, they show that in our model it is *welfare optimal to have excess demand*. This can be proved by contradiction. Assume an optimum without any excess demand, whence $z_e^a = \tau_e^{max}$. Then the integral in (17) vanishes, and so does $\overline{\gamma} L(e) p_e [1 - F(z_e^a)]$, because by definition $F(\tau_e^{max}) = 1$. Therefore eqs. (17) could only be fulfilled if $\delta_e = 0$. But, because of (15), $\delta_e = 0$ implies $\widetilde{C}_e = 0$ which contradicts our assumption $\widetilde{C}_e > 0$. Therefore $z_e^a = \tau_e^{max}$ is ruled out and there must exist excess demand at the welfare optimum. Only if demand is time-independent, supply always equals demand, because $z_e^a = 0$ and $z_e^m = z_e = x_e(p_e)$ from eq. (5) [12).

We now examine the *pricing implications* of peak-load effects. Applying the usual type of transformations we obtain the following pricing rule:

$$(\widetilde{C}_e - p_e) \frac{\partial x_e}{\partial p_e} L(e) + \sum_{i \notin E} (\widetilde{C}_i - p_i) \frac{\partial z_i^D}{\partial p_e} =$$

$$= \int_{t_e} \left[\gamma(z_e^m + S(e,t)) - \frac{\Gamma(E)}{\beta_o} x_e \right] dt -$$

$$- (1 - \gamma) \left[p_e \frac{\partial x_e}{\partial p_e} L(e) + \sum_{i \notin E} p_i \frac{\partial z_i^D}{\partial p_e} \right], \quad e \in E.$$

$$(18)$$

[11) After cancelling $\Gamma(0) W(p, z_e^a) f(z_e^a) - \Gamma(z_e^a - z_e^a) W(p, z_e^a) f(z_e^a)$ in the derivation of the welfare function, and $z_e^a f(z_e^a) - z_e^a F\prime(z_e^a)$ in the derivation of the profit constraint.

[12) In this case the aggregation constraints on z_e must be omitted in the optimization approach (12).

The particular properties of peak-load pricing can be seen more easily if we follow the usual peak-load literature and suppress the relations to other public outputs or inputs. Our interpretation therefore focuses on the price structure

$$(\tilde{C}_e - p_e)\frac{\partial x_e}{\partial p_e}L(e) = \int\limits_{t_e} \left[\gamma(z_e^m + S(e,t)) - \frac{\Gamma(E)}{\beta_o}x_e\right]dt -$$

$$- (1-\gamma)p_e\frac{\partial x_e}{\partial p_e}L(e), \qquad e \in E. \tag{19}$$

The main economic meaning of this formula will be indicated for the limiting case $\gamma = 1$. (It is left to the reader to consider further limiting cases.) If in such a case the board is as sensitive as to set $\Gamma(E) = 0$ if $E > 0$,[13] the pricing rule reduces to

$$(\tilde{C}_e - p_e)\frac{\partial x_e}{\partial p_e} = \frac{L(\Psi_e)}{L(e)}z_e + \frac{\beta_o - 1}{\beta_o}\frac{L(\Psi_e^c)}{L(e)}\bar{x}_e^c \qquad e \in E, \tag{20}$$

where $L(\Psi_e)$ is the time span of excess demand, and $L(\Psi_e^c)$ is its complement, $L(\Psi_e) + L(\Psi_e^c) = L(e)$. $\bar{x}_e^c$ is the average demand per unit of time in period Ψ_e^c. The right-hand side of (20) is a weighted average of $S(e, t_e)$. A profit-maximizing monopolist who faces the reliability constraints follows similar conditions, but uses the arithmetic mean of $S(e, t_e)$. For $\beta_o \to \infty$ therefore welfare maximization and profit maximization lead to the same result. Hence, for large β_o the board concentrates on rationing by high prices, reducing the extent of rationing by quantity.

If, on the other hand, the board is totally insensitive with respect to rationing $[\Gamma(E) = 1$ if $E > 0]$, the pricing formula becomes:

---

[13] Differentiability, in that case, can be achieved by replacing the discontinuous function $\Gamma(E)$ by a sequence Γ_k of differentiable functions converging to $\Gamma(E)$. Under the assumption that the sequence of quantities is convergent, the limit system of quantities can be characterized by (20).

$$(\tilde{C}_e - p_e)\frac{\partial x_e}{\partial p_e} = \frac{L(\Psi_e)}{L(e)}(z_e - \overline{x}_e/\beta_o) + \frac{\beta_o - 1}{\beta_o}\frac{L(\Psi_e^c)}{L(e)}\overline{x}_e^c =$$
$$= \frac{\beta_o - 1}{\beta_o}\overline{x}_e^{act} - \overline{E}(e) \qquad e \in E \tag{21}$$

where $\overline{x}_e$ is the average demand per unit of time in period Ψ_e ; $\overline{x}_e^{act}$ is the actual demand per unit of time, $\overline{x}_e^{act} = \int_{t_e} x_e(t)dt/L(e)$; $\overline{E}(e)$ is the average excess demand per unit of time, $\overline{E}(e) = \int_{t_e} E(e,t)dt/L(e)$. For small $\beta_o(\beta_o < 1)$ prices fall below marginal costs. We obtain low prices: the board concentrates on rationing by quantity, reducing the extent of rationing by prices. Prices above marginal costs are obtained if $\beta_o > 1$ and if the excess demand is not too large.

One central question remains: will peak prices exceed off-peak prices in our model? There is no general answer to this question, but we can show the conditions for such a result to occur.

Consider two periods only, e(peak) and e(off-peak), and assume the following relations to hold:

$$z_{e(\text{peak})} \geq x_{e(\text{peak})}^m > z_{e(\text{off-peak})} \geq x_{e(\text{off-peak})}^m. \tag{22}$$

Now consider the right-hand side of the pricing rule (19). z_e increases if we switch from off-peak to peak. This means a *tendency* for the difference quotient

$$\Delta(\text{right-hand side of}(19))/\Delta x_e^m, \tag{23}$$

to be positive. There always exist values of γ which are large enough and of $\Gamma(E)$ which are small enough to ensure that this tendency becomes effective for the whole difference quotient (23). Then

$$\Delta(\text{left-hand side of}(19))/\Delta x_e^m > 0 \tag{24}$$

must also hold.

This implies a higher difference between price and marginal cost in the peak period *if* the price effect $\partial x_e / \partial p_e$ is unchanged in spite of the change from off-peak to peak or does not change too sharply. And if, additionally, marginal peak costs exceed marginal off-peak costs, higher peak prices are obtained.

The following conditions are sufficient for higher peak than off-peak prices:

- government fixes a sufficiently high budget requirement;

- the enterprise's board is sufficiently sensitive to excess demand and rationing;

- the price effect of peak demand does not differ too much from that of off-peak demand;

- marginal peak costs do not fall below marginal off-peak costs.

This result indicates the crucial importance of the particular assumptions of those older theories on peak-load pricing according to which higher peak prices were always superior.

D   PUBLIC PRICING WHEN QUALITY MATTERS

CHAPTER 15   DIFFERENT APPROACHES TOWARDS OPTIMAL QUALITY

15.1   QUALITY I: DISTINGUISHING DIFFERENT GOODS

According to the Arrow-Debreu tradition a good must be described exhaustively with respect to time, location and quality. This definition of a good is more precise than the colloquial definition. Different qualities constitute different goods which can be sold at different prices.

Public enterprises' actual quality differentiation very often can be described adequately by the above theoretical approach. First, those nationalized firms which are competitive with private enterprises offer the usual differentiated supply, be it different types of automobiles, sorts of steel, etc. Second, public utilities often subdivide the market by distinguishing between different goods. Examples include electric current for business and for households (with different reliability of supply), special or normal delivery of letters, and all applications of peak-load pricing. Some public utilities, moreover, apply a particular sort of monopolistic price differentiation by distinguishing different classes of goods, like first and second class railway or hospital accommodation.

Assuming different qualities to be different goods, labelled $e \in E$ or $i \in E$, we can apply all pricing rules we have treated in the previous chapters. However, some special problems arise with respect to this application.

A preliminary question relates to the *degree of disaggregation*: to what extent should the public enterprise subdivide its market by distinguishing between different goods? This question has to be answered before applying models of optimal allocation because optimal allocation can be defined for any degree of disaggregation. From a theoretical point of view it is always possible to increase welfare by further disaggregation. However such a procedure leads to additional costs. At the optimal degree of disaggregation the welfare gains equal the marginal costs of further disaggregation. In practice the rule of thumb is to stop if further disaggregation does not change the result significantly. Very often, however, only two goods are distinguished e.g. day and night current, or peak and off-peak traffic.

Further questions relate to the *specific properties of supply and demand* in case of quality differentiation:

- The relevant goods are typically substitutes for each other; then in applying various models of the previous chapters we have to take the substitute case. This implies, inter alia, a high probability of welfare-optimal increases in *inefficiency* (section 5.4)

- In many cases of quality differentiation, the cross-price elasticities will be comparatively high; in those cases we must not apply approaches which neglect cross elasticities.

- The differentiated quality case often lends itself to price differentiation with distributional objectives.

- We typically deal with joint production, and all the difficult problems of imputation of fixed costs arise.

- Adding up quantities of different goods makes economic sense if these goods "satisfy the same wants" at different levels of quality. Only that property of public supply allows multiproduct enterprises to follow a strategy of maximizing total output [1].

- Goods which are distinguished by quality only are typically close

---

[1] See chapter 18 below.

substitutes. Hence in special cases demand for good i can be met by supply of good j, for instance if second class railway passengers are allowed to use first class seats at a second class price after all second class seats have been occupied [2].

15.2 QUALITY II: USING CONTINUOUS QUALITY INDICATORS

15.2.1 ON THE SIGNIFICANCE OF SUCH AN ANALYSIS

The use of one-dimensional quality indicators is a superior approach if the explicit quality-price trade-off is a central concern of a public enterprise. Such a theory is best suited to answer questions of the following type (always taking account of the permissible deficit):

- should the bus fare be increased or should the number of buses serving the route be decreased?

- should the electricity price per kw-h be increased or should the reliability of supply be decreased?

- should the fees of some school be increased or should the number of teachers per pupil be decreased?

When presenting an extended version of the Boiteux model in chapter 3, we considered explicitly the optimum conditions for one-dimensional quality indicators $q = (q_0, \ldots, q_n)$. The economic interpretation of these conditions is still deficient because in the previous chapters we held quality fixed. Using

---

[2] The usual market clearing conditions, in that case, would have to be replaced with one condition only, implying $\Sigma_i \Sigma_h x_i^h - \Sigma_i z_i - \Sigma_i \Sigma_j y_i^j = 0$ with Lagrangean parameter α whence $\widetilde{C}_i - \gamma p_i = \alpha/\beta_o$ has to be constant for all goods i included in the above market clearing constraint.

the marginal conditions on quality presented in chapter 3, we can explicitly investigate how the pricing rules of chapters 7 to 14 change if quality is chosen optimally. However, the theoretical results of such a procedure are somehow disappointing.

Quality q_e itself never appears explicitly in the marginal conditions, it only has an implicit influence on other variables, as shown by the respective partial derivatives such as $\partial z_i/\partial q_e$. Hence, any statement on quality q_e can only be of an indirect type. Prices p_e, on the contrary, always appear directly in the marginal conditions, which allows statements of a direct type.

This does not mean that the consideration of quality indicators is without interest. First, the introduction of quality indicators shows the restricted validity of the marginal-cost or Ramsey rules etc. Second, the theory is very useful if the relevant quality responses are specified, i.e. for any econometric investigation.

Because of the above difficulties of interpretation, the following analysis is restricted to the question of how the best-known basic rules of public sector pricing change if quality indicators are considered.

For this purpose remember the five assumptions we used to deduce basic rules from the general model of chapter 3. The narrowest formulation was presented at the beginning of chapter 7 on marginal-cost pricing:

a)   only prices of publicly produced goods are controlled; uncontrolled prices equal marginal costs c_i in the public sector [3)];

b)   the private sector is perfectly competitive;

c)   the distribution of lump-sum incomes is optimally chosen, hence we deal with compensated demand;

d)   there is no revenue-cost constraint on the public sector;

[3)] If only output prices are regulated, this assumption implies equality of c_i and C_i for all net outputs. See subsection 2.4.5 above.

e) quality levels are fixed.

15.2.2 THE CASE THAT CORRESPONDS TO MARGINAL–COST PRICING

To deal with optimal quality, we give up assumption e), but maintain assumptions a) to d). The resulting pricing rule has to consider the marginal conditions (7–1)

$$\sum_{i \in E}(p_i - c_i)\frac{\partial \hat{z}_i}{\partial p_e} = 0 \qquad e \in E \qquad (7-1)$$

and the following special case of the marginal conditions (3–53) [4)]

$$\sum_{i \in E}(p_i - c_i)\frac{\partial \hat{z}_i}{\partial q_e} = c_{qe} + \sum_h \frac{\partial e^h}{\partial q_e} \qquad e \in E. \qquad (1)$$

Let us assume both matrices $(\partial \hat{z}_i/\partial p_e)$ and $(\partial \hat{z}_i/\partial q_e)$ have full rank. The optimal prices and qualities can then be obtained by solving the total system of marginal conditions which consists of the two subsystems that have been presented above.

In that case, (7–1) directly implies marginal-cost prices, whence a solution of the whole system of marginal conditions can only be achieved if

$$c_{qe} = -\sum_h \frac{\partial e^h}{\partial q_e} \qquad e \in E. \qquad (2)$$

Thus we obtain a marginal condition for first-best qualities. In the marginal-cost price optimum the qualities have to be expanded until the

---

[4)] Recall $c_{qe}^j + \Sigma_i c_i^j (\partial y_i^j/\partial q_e) = 0$ from (3-43). For perfect competition in the private sector, moreover, $\Sigma_i p_i (\partial y_i^j/\partial q_e) = 0$. Moreover, because of assumption d) we obtain $\gamma = 0$.

marginal quality costs equal the total welfare gains as measured by the changes of the expenditure functions.

This condition reflects the public-good properties of the qualities. c_{qe} is the marginal rate of transformation between quality and labor, see eq. (3-39). As the wage rate is normalized to unity, it is also a marginal rate of transformation between quality and income earned in the public sector ($p_0 z_0$). Each individual $\partial e^h / \partial q_e$ is a marginal rate of substitution between quality and the individual lump-sum income, see eq. (3-28). The first-best qualities, therefore, require the equality of a marginal rate of transformation and the sum of individual marginal rates of substitution, both rates defined between quality and income. This condition resembles the Samuelson condition on public goods. The relevant incomes, however, are defined differently in the transformation rate and in the substitution rates.

15.2.3   THE CASE THAT CORRESPONDS TO RAMSEY PRICES

Remember again our usual five assumptions a) – e), and abandon assumptions e) *and* d). We consider an optimal quality choice in the presence of a fixed revenue-cost constraint Π^0. The resulting pricing rule is the corresponding case to Ramsey pricing.

We have to consider the marginal conditions (8-1)

$$\sum_{i \in E}(p_i - c_i)\frac{\partial \hat{z}_i}{\partial p_e} = -\gamma z_e \qquad\qquad e \in E \qquad\qquad (8-1)$$

and the following special case of the marginal conditions (3-53)

$$\sum_{i \in E}(p_i - c_i)\frac{\partial \hat{z}_i}{\partial q_e} = c_{qe} + (1-\gamma)\sum_{h}\frac{\partial e^h}{\partial q_e} \qquad\qquad e \in E. \qquad\qquad (3)$$

We assume, once again, that both matrices $(\partial \hat{z}_i / \partial p_e)$ and $(\partial \hat{z}_i / \partial q_e)$

have full rank. The Ramsey prices and qualities can then be obtained by solving the total system of marginal conditions which consists of the two subsystems that have been presented above.

How to interpret the resulting ,qualities and prices? Remember the interpretation of Ramsey pricing in chapter 8: an enterprise's board following Ramsey pricing behaves like a monopolist who miscalculates all price elasticities of demand by the same factor $1/\gamma$. We could therefore expect a similar result to hold if a profit-maximizing monopolist and a welfare-maximizing public enterprise under budget constraint do not only set optimal prices, but also optimal qualities.

Consider a monopolist who calculates his profit maximizing prices p_e, and qualities $q_e, e \in E$, considering production possibilities g(z,q) $= 0$ and acting along compensated demand functions $\hat{z}_e(p,q)$. His profit optimum is characterized by the following two systems of marginal conditions [5]

$$\sum_{i \in E}(p_i - c_i)\frac{\partial \hat{z}_i}{\partial p_e} = -z_e \qquad\qquad e \in E. \tag{4}$$

$$\sum_{i \in E}(p_i - c_i)\frac{\partial \hat{z}_i}{\partial q_e} = c_{qe} \qquad\qquad e \in E. \tag{5}$$

Hence we can still conclude that the welfare maximizing board behaves as if it were an unconstrained profit maximizing monopolist who inflates all compensated price elasticities by $1/\gamma$. In the usual case of $1/\gamma > 1$ [6] the board will react more carefully in the price space than a monopolist would, overaccentuating consumers' price responses. With respect to quality, the

---

[5] Write the production function as $z_0 = z_0(z_1(p,q),...,z_n(p,q),q)$ and consider $\partial z_0/\partial z_i = -(\partial g/\partial z_i)/(\partial g/\partial z_0) = -c_i$ and $\partial z_0/\partial q_e = -(\partial g/\partial q_e)/(\partial g/\partial z_0) = -c_{qe}$. The monopolistic optimum then follows from an optimization approach $max_{p_e,q_e} \sum_{i=1}^n p_i z_i(\cdot) + p_0 z_0(\cdot)$. Remember that $p_i = c_i$ for all $i \notin E$ and that the monopolist applies compensated demand functions.

[6] Π^0 exceeds the unconstrained welfare-optimal revenue-cost difference.

profit maximizer neglects consumer welfare gains, the welfare maximizer takes them into account. As these gains are measured by the negative $\sum_h \partial e^h / \partial q_e$, we may conclude that the welfare maximizer behaves like a monopolist who underestimates the marginal quality costs c_{qe} which implies a tendency towards higher qualities.

15.2.4   PRICING WITH DISTRIBUTIONAL AIMS

We now abandon assumptions e) *and* c). Hence, we deal with the optimal quality choice in the presence of a revenue-cost constraint Π^o and in the presence of uncompensated demand. As the distribution of lump-sum incomes is exogenously given, the distributional value judgements of government cannot lead to a redistribution of incomes, but are explicitly reflected by the public price and quality structure. We exclude private demand and supply of publicly controlled goods e. This additional assumption could easily be given up, as shown for optimal pricing in chapter 10.

Consider the marginal conditions (10-1)

$$\sum_{i \in E} (p_i - c_i) \frac{\partial z_i^D}{\partial p_e} = -(1 - F_e) z_e \qquad e \in E \qquad\qquad (10-1)$$

and the following special case of conditions (3-50)

$$\sum_{i \in E} (p_i - c_i) \frac{\partial z_i^D}{\partial q_e} = Q_e + c_{qe} \qquad e \in E. \qquad\qquad (6)$$

As in the case of Ramsey pricing, we can compare these two systems of equations with corresponding equations which result from profit maximization. The welfare maximizing board behaves as if it were a profit maximizer who inflates all price elasticities by factors $1/(1 - F_e)$. With respect to quality the profit maximizer neglects the welfare gains of the consumers,

Q_e, which are explicitly considered by the welfare maximizer. As in the Ramsey case this implies an underestimation of the marginal quality costs ($Q_e < 0$) which implies a tendency towards higher qualities.

15.2.5 ADJUSTMENT TO MONOPOLISTIC STRUCTURES IN THE PRIVATE ECONOMY

Consider the pricing rule which includes the possibility that uncontrolled prices deviate from their respective marginal costs in the public and in the private sector. We deal with compensated demand, obtaining the systems of equations (3-53) and (11-2):

$$\sum_i (p_i - c_i) \frac{\partial \hat{z}_i}{\partial p_e} = -\gamma \, z_e$$

$$- (1 - \gamma) \sum_i \sum_j (p_i - c_i^j) \frac{\partial y_i^j}{\partial p_e} \quad e \in E \tag{11-2}$$

$$\sum_i (p_i - c_i) \frac{\partial \hat{z}_i}{\partial q_e} = c_{qe} + (1 - \gamma) \sum_h \frac{\partial e^h}{\partial q_e}$$

$$+ (1 - \gamma) \sum_j c_{qe}^j - (1 - \gamma) \sum_i \sum_j (p_i - c_i^j) \frac{\partial y_i^j}{\partial q_e} \quad e \in E. \tag{3-53}$$

The optimal prices and qualities can be found by simultaneously solving these two systems of equations.

PART THREE: POSITIVE THEORY: PUBLIC PRICING
POLICIES TO ACHIEVE POLITICIANS'
AND MANAGERS' AIMS

A   POLITICIANS AND BUREAUCRATS

CHAPTER 16   WINNING VOTES[1)]

Pricing of public utilities tends to be one of the major determinants of the political climate in local communities. Local politicians try to postpone until after the next election any price increases for local public transportation, for gas and electricity. The popularity of any local politician seems to be at stake if local public utilities work inefficiently or if price increases are in the offing.

Consider a politician who chooses public prices so as to maximize votes. We expect such a policy to favor the interests of lower income groups because in any economy the incomes of more than 50 % of the population fall short of the average income. However, there are different ways of favoring lower income consumers by public pricing. Examples range from cheaper railway or local bus fares for retired people, school children and students, to lower basic rates for the telephones of lower income consumers; from different 1st and 2nd class railway fares or hospital fees to lower school fees for lower income earners.

Which kind of price differentiation should the politician pursue ? There

---

[1)] Parts of this chapter are taken from Bös-Zimmermann (1983).

are at least the following three possibilities:

— Direct differentiation between *lower-income* and *higher- income* consumers (e.g. if the recipient has to prove that his income falls below a particular threshold value in order to be eligible to pay a lower price).

— Differentiation between different *classes* or *groups* of consumers who differ with respect to their income although not in every case (e.g. retired and non-retired, students and non-students etc.).

— Differentiation between *goods* which are demanded more by lower income than by higher income consumers (although, again, not necessarily in every case, e.g. as with the distinctions between 1st and 2nd class railway or hospital services).

Different classifications can be treated in a uniform framework after adequate definition of output. Consider a simple example: to deal with differentiation between social groups, we define students' demand for local traffic as x_1, the old-age pensioners' demand as x_2, other people's demand as x_3. We should note that the differentiation among groups (and goods, respectively) is one of the instruments of the politician who is in search of political support. However, after this differentiation of goods has taken place we can always find prices for them which maximize votes.

In a democratic context the political choice is only well-defined if there are at least two alternatives. Consider therefore *two price systems*, p and p^*, both market clearing and technologically feasible and subject to the same profit constraint Π. Because of the identical constraints, vote maximization has to consider the trade-off frontier where some prices p_i are lower than p_i^*, and some others are higher. The trivial cases of $p << p^*$ or $p >> p^*$ are excluded.

Assume $\{p_e\}$ to be the instruments of a politician who wants to max- imize votes and $\{p_e^*\}$ to be a given reference price system. Various insti- tutional stories can be told to rationalize this reference price system, for example, we have at least the following two possibilities: according to one we treat public pricing in a two-party competition model, according to the other we treat it in the context of a monopoly approach of public choice. In the first, p^* would be the price system offered to the voter by the other political party [2]. In the second, p^* would be a sort of "reversion policy" that will apply if the price system p is not supported by a majority, similar to Romer-Rosenthal's (1979) agenda-setter model. Finally p^* can simply mean the present system of prices. In that case we describe a referendum on public pricing or a demoscopic opinion poll.

Regardless of which of the above versions we adopt, any politician will always be interested in finding that platform p which the greatest possible number of people prefers to p^* [3].

Voters, however, do not decide on economic criteria alone. Therefore, we assume an individual h to vote for a price system p if

$$\omega^h + s^h \geq 0. \tag{1}$$

ω^h measures the "economic" component of the voter's decision, the utility gain or loss from price system p

$$\omega^h(p, r^h) := v^h(p, r^h) - v^h(p^*, r^h). \tag{2}$$

s^h , on the other hand, measures the "sympathy" or "antipathy" component of his decision. Some individual might not be willing to vote for platform p which increases his utility because he "does not like" the politician who proposes price system p. On the other hand, somebody may be willing to

---

[2] This implies Cournot-type behavior of the political duopolists. Note that we do not deal with a voting equilibrium where both parties react to each other. Only under very restrictive assumptions will such equilibria exist, e.g. under a generalized single-peakedness concept for voting decisions on multidimensional issues.

[3] If p^* happens to be the vote-maximizing price system, the politician will apply $p=p^*$. This case of indifference is excluded in the text.

vote for platform p which diminishes his utility because the proposal comes from "his party".

Now turn to the *vote-maximizing politician*. Every "yes" counts one vote; every "no" does not count, as measured by the function $\mu(\cdot)$

$$\mu(\omega^h + s^h) = \begin{cases} 1 & \text{if } \omega^h + s^h \geq 0 \\ 0 & \text{if } \omega^h + s^h < 0 \end{cases}. \tag{3}$$

Every voter, of course, knows the exact values of his ω^h and s^h. The politician, however, is incompletely informed of the individual voters' behavior. Let us assume he knows exactly the economic consequences of his pricing policy, as expressed by the utility differences ω^h. He does not know exactly whether some particular person likes or dislikes him. He only knows that there is some distribution of sympathy and antipathy among the voters. For the politician, therefore, s is a random variable, $\tilde{s}$. Let him assume, without limitation of generality, $\tilde{s}$ is normally distributed with density function $\psi(s^h)$, expectation of zero and variance σ^2

$$\psi(s^h) = \frac{1}{\sigma\sqrt{2\pi}} \exp\left[-\frac{1}{2}\left(\frac{s^h}{\sigma}\right)^2\right]. \tag{4}$$

For any single individual the incompletely informed politician assumes sympathy s^h to be distributed with $\psi(s^h)$.

Not being informed about the exact values of s^h, but only knowing $\tilde{s}$ is a normally distributed random variable, the politician can only rely upon the expectation of any single vote. Replacing $\omega^h + s^h =: t^h$, we obtain

$$\Phi_h(\omega^h) = \int_{-\infty}^{+\infty} \mu(\omega^h + s^h)\psi(s^h)ds^h = \int_{-\infty}^{+\infty} \mu(t^h)\psi(t^h - \omega^h)dt^h \tag{5}$$

as shown in figure 16.

Figure 16 shows how an individual with utility difference w^h can be expected to vote. For $\sigma^2 \to 0$ the voters would be expected to be pure homines oeconomici, deciding according to their utility difference only

$$\Phi_h(w^h) = \mu(w^h) = \begin{cases} 1 & \text{if } w^h \geq 0 \\ 0 & \text{if } w^h < 0 \end{cases}. \tag{6}$$

The higher σ^2, on the other hand, the more sympathy and antipathy will count, as shown in figure 16 for $\sigma = 0,2$ and $\sigma = 1$.

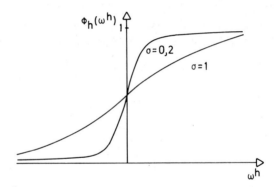

Figure 16

The objective function of the vote-maximizing politician results from aggregating the expectation of votes

$$\Phi(p) = \sum_{h=1}^{H} \Lambda(r^h)\Phi_h(w^h(p, r^h)). \tag{7}$$

where $\Lambda(r^h)$ measures the relative frequency of the expectation Φ_h in the population [4], the population being subdivided into $h = 1, \ldots, H$ groups of identical people, $\sum_h \Lambda(r^h) = 1$.

Differentiating this objective function leads to

$$\frac{\partial \Phi}{\partial p_e} = \sum_{h=1}^{H} \Lambda(r^h) \int_{-\infty}^{+\infty} \mu(t^h) \frac{\partial}{\partial p_e} \psi(t^h - \omega^h) dt^h. \tag{8}$$

Excluding all ranges where $\mu(t^h) = 0$ we obtain

$$\frac{\partial \Phi}{\partial p_e} = \sum_{h=1}^{H} \Lambda(r^h) \int_{o}^{\infty} \frac{\partial}{\partial p_e} \psi(t^h - \omega^h) dt^h$$
$$= -\sum_{h=1}^{H} \Lambda(r^h) \int_{o}^{\infty} \psi'(t^h - \omega^h) \frac{\partial \omega^h}{\partial p_e} dt^h. \tag{9}$$

Hence

$$\frac{\partial \Phi}{\partial p_e} = -\sum_{h=1}^{H} \Lambda(r^h) \frac{\partial v^h}{\partial p_e} [\psi(t^h - \omega^h)]_o^{\infty}$$
$$= \sum_{h=1}^{H} \Lambda(r^h) \frac{\partial v^h}{\partial p_e} \psi(\omega^h). \tag{10}$$

For voters who follow economic reasoning only, $\sigma^2 = 0$, the differentiation (10) will degenerate. All $\omega^h \neq 0$ do not contribute to the sum. Therefore $\partial \Phi / \partial p_e \neq 0$ can only occur if there happen to be individuals whose income r^* leads to $\omega^h(r^*) = 0$. Then the whole weight of $\psi(\omega^h)$ is attached to those individuals whence $\partial \Phi / \partial p_e = \infty$. Hence $\partial \Phi / \partial p_e$ varies erratically between 0 and ∞, depending not only on the incomes but also on the price vector p. For $\sigma^2 = 0$ it is therefore impossible to employ the usual

---

[4] Any bracket $\Lambda(r^h)$ consists of many people, which allows us to concentrate on the expectation alone, ignoring the variance.

optimization approach. Only if we assume a continuum of consumers, does everything work nicely (Bös-Zimmermann (1983)). Assuming this continuum to be an approximation to $n \to \infty$, we can treat the case of $\sigma^2 = 0$ as equally important as the case of $\sigma^2 > 0$ in the following pricing rules.

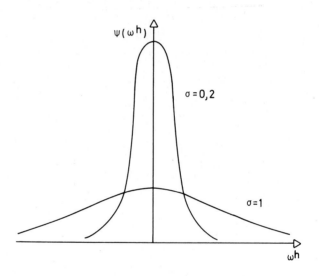

Figure 17

The influence of changing price p_e on the objective function according to (10) depends on the individual utility effects $\partial v^h / \partial p_e$ weighted by the number of individuals with the respective utility and on the politician's attention paid to the individual utility difference $\psi(\omega^h)$ as shown in figure 17. Note that originally we introduced $\psi(s^h)$ as the density function of the individual "sympathy" variable s^h. In the course of the above differentiation we obtained $\psi(\omega^h)$ which can best be interpreted as the politician's attention.

For any pair of p and p^* the politician must pay most attention to utility differences in a close neighborhood of $\omega^h = 0$. This includes the "sympathizers" with small negative ω^h and the "just converted" with small positive ω^h. The sympathy of the first group may represent the votes of tomorrow; the votes of the second can be lost easily. Both groups may be floating voters at the next election. Less attention is paid to the "political opponents" with large negative ω^h and the "permanent followers" with large positive ω^h. The sympathy of the first can be won only at disproportionate effort; the votes of the second seem almost certain.

Which price structure will a politician employ who follows the political strategy of maximizing $\Phi(p)$? As a special case of our general rule (4-14) we obtain

$$\sum_{i=o}^{n} (p_i - \widetilde{C}_i) \frac{\partial z_i^D}{\partial p_e} = -(1 - POL_e) z_e \qquad e \in E, \qquad (11)$$

where (after inserting Roy's identity) POL_e equals

$$POL_e = \frac{1}{\beta_o} \sum_{h=1}^{H} \Lambda(r^h) \psi(\omega^h(p, r^h)) \frac{\partial v^h}{\partial r^h} \cdot \frac{x_e^h}{x_e} \qquad e \in E. \qquad (12)$$

There is a striking formal similarity between distributionally oriented pricing (10-1) and political pricing (11). This raises the question whether democratic maximization of political sympathy and votes is a good vehicle towards distributionally desirable results.

Remember first that F_e in (10-1) weighted the individual consumption shares by $\lambda^h(\partial v^h/\partial r^h)$ which is always assumed to be a decreasing function of individual incomes. Weighting by such a decreasing function can be found also in POL_e. However, in POL_e only the individual marginal utilities $(\partial v^h/\partial r^h)$ are of relevance, which excludes many of the typical features of distribution policy as represented by λ^h, for instance Rawlsian policy.

Can we argue that $\Lambda(\cdot)\psi$ replace the social valuation λ^h? $\Lambda(r^h)$ is an approximation to a density function of the income distribution. From empirical estimations we know that such a function increases for lower and decreases for higher incomes. Hence weighting with $\Lambda(r^h)$ will typically not imply particular emphasis on the *poor*. However, as usually there are more lower-income than higher-income earners, the $\Lambda(r^h)$-values accentuate policies in favor of lower-income earners.

Finally, we have to emphasize the role of ψ. It stresses the importance of fishing for political sympathy and of being afraid of losing "uncertain" voters. In other words, it stresses the interests of floating voters. Needless to say, this criterion has nothing to do with distribution policy. Moreover, in our general model we lack specific information as to which income earners are the floating voters and which publicly supplied goods are bought primarily by floating voters.

Summarizing, there are some plausible arguments which suggest that distributionally "desirable" results may follow from political pricing. However, no general conclusions can be established [5].

---

[5] If we assume a continuum of consumers we can perform the transition $\sigma^2 \to 0$ in our results. Then POL_e depends only on those individuals whose utility difference is just equal to zero. The vote-maximizing politician will therefore reduce the price of those goods that are mainly demanded by the floating voters. No particular distributional components remain in POL_e.

CHAPTER 17   MAXIMIZING BUDGETS

An investigation of the political determination of public prices must not be restricted to vote maximization. It may be even more realistic to assume a principal-agent relationship where the majority-seeking politician does not set the prices himself, but delegates this task to the bureaucracy of a ministry or of a public utility. The government becomes the "sponsor", the price setting board becomes the "bureaucracy".

If a bureaucrat wants to maximize his influence, his prestige, his income, he can do so most successfully by maximizing the number of his subordinates, the amount of money he can decide upon, in short: by maximizing his budget (Niskanen (1971)). However, the sponsor who has to grant the bureaucrat's budget will not appropriate just any amount the bureaucrat applies for. The budget BUD the sponsor is willing to grant will depend on the output the bureau is offering

$$BUD = BUD(z_{m+1}, \ldots, z_n) \qquad \begin{aligned} BUD_e &= \partial BUD/\partial z_e > 0; \\ \partial^2 BUD/\partial z_e^2 &< 0. \end{aligned} \qquad (1)$$

where $z_e \geq 0$, $e = m+1, \ldots, n$, are the outputs of the bureau. For the one-service bureau with which he deals almost exclusively, Niskanen specifies BUD as a quadratic function of output, thus assuming a linearily decreasing marginal valuation of the bureau's service. This political valuation may be rooted in arguments about political sustainability. Needless to say, there exist many other possible explanations we do not need to consider as in this section we are interested mainly in bureaucrat's behavior.

Consider a bureaucrat whose budget comes from two sources: the revenue from selling his services to his customers and from a grant BUD. This is Niskanen's "mixed bureau" (1971, 87-105) where the bureaucrat faces "two separate demands" for any particular good: a market demand $x_e(p)$ and a "sponsor demand" BUD_e. However, there is a great difference between these "demand" functions: the sponsor does not consume any quantity of good z_e, but only pays for it. Hence, we shall characterize BUD_e as a political valuation function rather than as a demand function.

The mixed bureau can be interpreted as a public enterprise which sells its goods or services at prices which do not cover costs and expects some ministry to cover its deficit.

The most interesting economic feature of such a bureau is the particular demand-cost balance. In extreme situations the mixed bureau may be constrained by demand only: customers and sponsor are willing to grant a budget that altogether exceeds the costs. (Assume that a unique optimum exists in such a case because of the satiation properties of customers' and sponsor's demand.) Usually, however, we expect the mixed bureau to be constrained by the deficit limit (or profit prescription) Π:

$$\sum_{i=o}^{n} p_i z_i + BUD(z_{m+1}, \ldots, z_n) = \Pi(z, \rho). \qquad (2)$$

This revenue-cost constraint implies an interesting twofold political influence on the bureau. On the one hand the sponsor is willing to appropriate grants BUD, depending on the quantities produced. On the other hand, the bureau is expected to break even, or to avoid too high deficits or to achieve a profit ($\Pi \gtreqless 0$ respectively).

Given the revenue-cost constraint, the market equilibrium conditions and its technology, the mixed bureau will maximize its budget, consisting of revenue plus grant

$$\Phi(p, z) = \sum_{i=m+1}^{n} p_i z_i + BUD(z_{m+1}, \ldots, z_n). \qquad (3)$$

Note that in applying (4-14) we have not only to consider $\partial\Phi/\partial z_i$ and $\partial\Phi/\partial p_e$, but also to replace $\widetilde{C}_i$ with $\widetilde{C}_i - \gamma BUD_i$ because of the unusual revenue-cost constraint (2). The resulting price structure can be written as

$$\sum_{i=o}^{n}\left[p_i - \left(\frac{\beta_o}{1+\beta_o}\right)\widetilde{C}_i + \left(\frac{1+\beta_o\gamma}{1+\beta_o}\right)BUD_i\right]\frac{\partial z_i^D}{\partial p_e} = -z_e \qquad e \in E. \qquad (4)$$

The mixed bureau behaves as if it were a perfect monopolist who acts on a modified marginal-cost function

$$C_i = \delta_1 \widetilde{C}_i - \delta_2 BUD_i \qquad\qquad i \in E \qquad\qquad 0 < \delta_1 , \ \delta_2 < 1 \qquad (5)$$

instead of the usual marginal-cost function $\widetilde{C}_i$. The exact meaning of δ_1 and δ_2 can be seen in (4).

The "social cost function" in (5) shows that the bureaucrat adopts a cost-benefit attitude, taking the political marginal valuation of output as a sort of external social benefit which reduces the marginal production costs. This may even imply negative social costs C_i !

How production economics and political economics are integrated depends on the coefficients δ_1 and δ_2. *Production cost consideration* is determined by production-side problems only as we could well expect. (δ_1 depends on β_o only.) The more sensitively the achievable budget reacts to additional endowments of labor, the larger the influence of production costs on public pricing. (δ_1 is increasing in β_o). The *political considerations*, on the other hand, depend on the demand-cost balance of the bureau. Heuristically speaking the percentage δ_2 is lower, the more the bureaucrat converges to the demand-constrained case ($\gamma \to 0$). The more customers and sponsor are willing to pay, the less the necessity for the bureaucrat to concentrate on the political valuation of its outputs. How far the political valuation is taken into account in the limiting, demand- constrained, case depends on production-side arguments only. If, on the other hand, the bureaucrat converges to the budget-constrained case ($\gamma \to 1$), the political valuation of its outputs has to be considered increasingly. This structure of public pricing reveals the sponsor's political dilemma: he loses influence on public pricing the more money he is willing to pay for it.

B   MANAGERS OF PUBLIC ENTERPRISES AND UNIONS [1]

CHAPTER 18   MAXIMIZING OUTPUT OR REVENUE, MINIMIZING ENERGY INPUTS

Proving managerial success with reference to output or revenue data is of particular interest for public enterprises. The latter are often prevented from seeking maximum profits and therefore their managers' success cannot be appraised with reference to profit data. An interesting example of the practical application of *output maximization* by a public enterprise is the maximization of passenger miles pursued by London Transport some years ago (Glaister-Collings (1978), Bös (1978b)).

Although economists would argue that adding quantities of different goods does not make any sense, in practice such targets can often be found. For example consider patients of hospitals who receive first class (z_1) and second class (z_2) treatment, respectively, or rail passengers travelling first class (z_1) or second class (z_2). It can be seen that, under certain circumstances, the maximization of a sum of different quantities makes sense.

The board's objective function is as follows

$$\Phi(z) = \sum_{i=m+1}^{n} z_i \tag{1}$$

and leads to a pricing structure

---

[1] In most of part B we use linear objective functions. Thus, there may arise particular problems in the case of constant returns to scale and with respect to corner solutions, but these will be ignored.

$$\sum_{i=o}^{n} (p_i - (\widetilde{C}_i - \frac{1}{\beta_o})) \frac{\partial z_i^D}{\partial p_e} = -z_e \qquad\qquad e \in E. \qquad (2)$$

The board behaves as if it were a monopolist but underestimates margi nal costs ($\widetilde{C}_i - 1/\beta_o$ instead of $\widetilde{C}_i$). As each marginal cost term is reduced by the same absolute amount, high-cost goods will be favored relatively less than low-cost goods with the expected result of increasing the sales of the latter. The maximum output will therefore consist of too much low-cost output as compared with the welfare-optimal mix.

Let us now turn to *revenue maximization*. Revenue is a somewhat superficial indicator of economic success. Management is often inclined to use such an objective mainly because in the recent past of rapid growth these figures were growing impressively. Attempting to show managerial success with reference to revenue data is also of interest in private enter- prises. Baumol (1959, 47-48) has pointed out that in practical business any "program which explicitly proposes any cut in sales volume, whatever the profit considerations, is likely to meet a cold reception". Let us now investigate the economic consequences of revenue maximization as another possible objective of our board

$$\Phi(p, z) = \sum_{i=m+1}^{n} p_i z_i. \qquad (3)$$

We obtain the following pricing structure

$$\sum_{i=o}^{n} \left[p_i - \frac{\beta_o}{1 + \beta_o} \widetilde{C}_i \right] \frac{\partial z_i^D}{\partial p_e} = -z_e \qquad\qquad e \in E \qquad (4)$$

which, as might be expected, equals the budget maximizing result, except for the sponsor demand BUD_e. The board behaves as if it were a monopolist, but underestimates marginal costs, $[\beta_o/(1 + \beta_o)] < 1$. As every marginal cost term is reduced by the same relative amount, there is no inherent tendency to mass production of low-cost goods, in contrast to the case of output maximization.

Another simple managerial objective of recent interest is *energy saving.* Let good k be energy, supplied by private firms, $j \in K$. The board is interested in minimizing energy inputs. Hence it maximizes

$$\Phi = z_k - \sum_h x_k^h(\cdot) + \sum_{j \notin K} y_k^j(\cdot) \qquad k \in \{1, \ldots, m\}. \tag{5}$$

The energy saving pricing structure is as follows

$$\sum_{i=o}^{n} (p_i - \widetilde{C}_i) \frac{\partial z_i^D}{\partial p_e} - \frac{1}{\beta_o} \sum_{j \in K} \frac{\partial y_k^j}{\partial p_e} = -z_e \qquad e \in E = \{m+1, \ldots, n\}. \tag{6}$$

The economic meaning of this pricing structure can be seen best if we neglect cross-price elasticities among outputs, whence

$$\left[p_e - \left(\widetilde{C}_e + \frac{1}{\beta_o} \frac{\sum_{j \in K} \partial y_k^j / \partial p_e}{\partial z_e^D / \partial p_e} \right) \right] \frac{\partial z_e^D}{\partial p_e} = -z_e \qquad e \in E. \tag{7}$$

Assume normal reaction of demand, $\partial z_e^D / \partial p_e < 0$, and complementarity of energy and other goods, $\partial y_k^j / \partial p_e < 0, j \in K$ [2]. The more energy-intensive the production of some good, the higher in absolute value $\sum_{j \in K} \partial y_k^j / \partial p_e$.

Therefore a board that follows pricing rule (7) behaves as if it adhered to monopolistic pricing but overestimates the marginal costs. The more energy-intensive the production, the more the respective marginal

---

[2] Recall footnote 3 of table 1, chapter 4.

costs must be overestimated which leads to higher prices of energy-intensive goods.

The same results can be obtained if the only supplier of energy is the public sector. The objective of minimizing energy inputs, then, is as follows:

$$\Phi = -\sum_h x_k^h(\cdot) + \sum_j y_k^j(\cdot) \qquad\qquad k \in \{1,\ldots,m\}. \tag{8}$$

The resulting price structure

$$\sum_{i \varepsilon F}(p_i - \tilde{C}_i)\frac{\partial z_i^D}{\partial p_e} - \frac{1}{\beta_o}\frac{\partial z_k^D}{\partial p_e} = -z_e \qquad e \in F = \{k, m+1, \ldots, n\} \tag{9}$$

can be interpreted analogously to the above case of private energy supply. (The complementarity of energy and other outputs implies $\partial z_k^D/\partial p_e < 0$ $k \neq e$; normally reacting demand implies $\partial z_e^D/\partial p_e < 0, e \in F$ [3]).

Moreover, the equations (9) imply a particular energy pricing rule. If, for explanatory clearness, cross-price effects are once again suppressed, the following holds

$$\left[p_k - \left(\tilde{C}_k + \frac{1}{\beta_o}\right)\right]\frac{\partial z_k^D}{\partial p_k} = -z_k. \tag{10}$$

We obtain the expected tendency of increasing energy prices because of "overestimated" marginal costs. As could be expected, the input minimizing pricing rule is just the reverse of the output maximizing rule as can easily be seen by comparing eqs. (2) and (10).

---

[3] Recall, once again, footnote 3 of table 1, chapter 4.

CHAPTER 19   MINIMIZING PRICE INDICES

In countries with large public enterprise sectors attempts are sometimes made to reduce the rate of inflation through the pricing policies of those enterprises (Bös (1978a)). Great Britain or Austria provide appropriate examples. In other countries public pricing is more likely to be aimed at the target of index minimization the higher the inflation rate and the larger the sector of "indexation" in an economy.

The simplest attempt to reduce a price index drastically is by setting public prices of zero. However, such a policy is usually excluded in our general approach, since we explicitly consider a revenue-cost constraint. In our case the enterprise's board will consider one of the statistical price indices, as computed and published by some statistical office. Such indices compare quantities of money that can purchase a constant basket of commodities at changed prices. Thus substitution by consumers is ignored in the analysis (which leads to an overestimation of effective price changes when Laspeyres indices are used and an under-estimation when Paasche indices are used). The most common index follows Laspeyres and takes as fixed some base period's basket of consumer goods. We denote variables of the base period by the superscript "^{o}" and define the board's objective function as follows

$$\Phi(p) = - \sum_{i=m+1}^{n} p_i x_i^o / \sum_{i=m+1}^{n} p_i^o x_i^o. \tag{1}$$

The resulting price structure equals

$$\sum_{i=o}^{n} (p_i - \widetilde{C}_i) \frac{\partial z_i^D}{\partial p_e} = -(1 - L_e) z_e \qquad e \in E, \tag{2}$$

where

$$L_e = \frac{x_e^o}{x_e} \cdot \frac{1}{\sum p_i^o x_i^o} \cdot \frac{1}{\beta_o} \qquad e \in E. \qquad (3)$$

According to the common practice of statistical offices x_e^o is always of the order of magnitude of individual demand, whereas $z_e(= x_e)$ is total supply. This problem can be taken into account by transforming (3) into

$$L_e = \frac{x_e^o}{\bar{z}_e} \cdot \frac{1}{H \sum p_i^o x_i^o} \cdot \frac{1}{\beta_o} \qquad e \in E \qquad (4)$$

where $\bar{z}_e = z_e/H$, H being the number of consumers.

The periodical index revisions for developed countries have shown a shifting of consumption from necessities towards non-necessities. Hence, L_e is high for such goods where lower-income groups account for large shares of total consumption.

Therefore, the economic interpretation of eqs. (2) is analogous to the interpretation of eqs. (10-1). Qualitatively, minimizing a Laspeyres price index has the same distributional effects as maximizing a welfare function of a board with distributional aims! This result is due to the fact that, in minimizing a Laspeyres index account is taken of the weights of the base period in which necessities bought by lower-income groups get higher weights than those which would correspond to present consumption. This is a "desirable" distributional consequence of the "politician's error", i.e. of acting on the basis of past consumption patterns which ought, perhaps, to induce second thoughts regarding the frequent 'a priori' rejection of an index minimization strategy for public pricing.

Furthermore, we have to bear in mind that, with a constant basket of commodities, the distributionally "desirable" effects increase quantitatively with the passage of time, because deviations of actual consumption from the corresponding proportions of the basket of the base period increase with time. Therefore, after some years minimizing a Laspeyres index may not only imply qualitatively equal, but also quantitatively similar, results as maximizing a distributionally weighted welfare function [1].

---

[1] For details see Bös (1978a). Minimizing a true cost of living index leads to welfare optimal, i.e. Ramsey pricing.

CHAPTER 20   THE INFLUENCE OF UNIONS

The influence of employees' pressure groups on the management of nationalized enterprises or public utilities differs widely from country to country.

A first extreme are labor managed firms, like in Yugoslavia, the pressure groups being the workers' councils. They typically try to maximize value added per employee and the disincentive effects of such a policy are well-known from both practice and theory. Labor unions, starting from a wider horizon, will oppose the job restrictions that do often result from such a firm's policy.

The other extreme are nationalized firms which behave in the same way as private firms without any special influence of labor unions. Hence, in these cases there is no particular difference between the objectives of the managers of nationalized and of private firms.

Typically, however, nationalized enterprises or public utilities will follow a middle course. Their objectives will be some compromise between those of management and the union. Such a result need not only follow from close contacts between managers of public enterprises and unionists although such contacts will often be found. Unions will be interested in public firms in any case, as they are usually large firms whose management policy has a great influence on the whole economy.

We formulate the compromise between the management of a public enterprise and the representatives of some labor union in the following simple way.

Management may be thought of as aiming to maximize output, while the union's utility may be assumed to depend on the number of working hours and on the real wage rate (Gravelle (1984), Rees (1982)).

Hence, we impute to the public sector the following objective:

$$\Phi(p, z) = \sum_{i=m+1}^{n} z_i + \rho U(p_o, z_o) \tag{1}$$

where the first part describes manager's interest in output, the second part describes the union's interest in wage rate and working hours. The partial derivatives of the union's utility function are $U_p > 0$ and $U_z < 0$ (additional plausible assumptions are that $U_{pp} < 0$ and $U_{zz} > 0$.)[1] $\rho > 0$ is a parameter measuring the strength of the union's influence, which depends on its bargaining power (Rees (1982)).

As usual, we treat public inputs and outputs $\{z_i\}$ and public prices $\{p_e\}$ as instruments. Additionally, the board has to fix the wage rate p_o [2]. This instrument choice makes it necessary to differentiate between different kinds of labor, p_o referring to the labor force used in the public sector only, whereas some other kind of labor is used in the private sector only, its wage rate determined by demand and supply in that sector [3].

We apply (4-14) to obtain the following price structure

$$\sum_{i=o}^{n} \left(p_i - \left(\tilde{C}_i - \frac{1}{\beta_o} \frac{\partial \Phi}{\partial z_i} \right) \right) \frac{\partial z_i^D}{\partial p_e} = -z_e - \frac{1}{\beta_o} \frac{\partial \Phi}{\partial p_e} \qquad e = o, m+1, \ldots, n, \tag{2}$$

where

$$\frac{\partial \Phi}{\partial z_i} = \begin{cases} \rho U_z & \text{for } i = 0 \\ 0 & \text{for } i = 1, \ldots, m \\ 1 & \text{for } i = m+1, \ldots, n \end{cases} \quad ; \quad \frac{\partial \Phi}{\partial p_e} = \begin{cases} \rho U_p & \text{for } e = 0 \\ 0 & \text{for } \end{cases}.$$

---

[1] U_p is short-hand for $\partial U / \partial p_o$; similar interpretations hold for U_z, U_{pp}, U_{zz}.

[2] As p_o is an instrument variable, some other price must be taken as numeraire.

[3] Assumption b), presented in chapter 4, implies that "goods with publicly controlled prices are neither supplied nor demanded by private firms". If z_o and only z_o were labor, and p_o regulated, the above assumption would exclude labor inputs of private firms. Hence these labor inputs must explicitly be introduced into the analysis as a separate input good.

The economic interpretation of this pricing structure is a little complicated. How regulated output prices deviate from marginal costs can be seen best if (2) is transformed as follows

$$
p_e - \widetilde{C}_e = -\frac{z_e}{\partial z_e^D/\partial p_e} - \sum_{\substack{i=o \\ i\neq e}}^{n}(p_i - \widetilde{C}_i)\frac{\partial z_i^D/\partial p_e}{\partial z_e^D/\partial p_e} - \sum_{i=m+1}^{n}\frac{1}{\beta_o}\cdot\frac{\partial z_i^D/\partial p_e}{\partial z_e^D/\partial p_e} -
$$
$$
-\frac{\rho U_z}{\beta_o}\cdot\frac{\partial z_o^D/\partial p_e}{\partial z_e^D/\partial p_e} \qquad e = m+1,\ldots,n.
$$

$$(3)$$

The first two terms on the right hand side can be interpreted similarly to the corresponding terms in eq. (11-3) above. There is, first, a *monopolistic tendency* for p_e to exceed $\widetilde{C}_e$ if demand reacts normally $(\partial z_e^D/\partial p_e < 0)$. There is, second, a *reallocation effect* towards p_e above $\widetilde{C}_e$ if all prices exceed the respective marginal costs and if good e is a "substitute" for all other goods in the sense $\partial z_i^D/\partial p_e > 0 \ \forall i \neq e$.

The third term reflects the manager's *interest in output maximization*, again implying a tendency for p_e to be above $\widetilde{C}_e$ if good e is a "substitute" for all other goods in the sense mentioned above.

The fourth term reflects the *union's interests*. It implies a tendency for lower p_e if decreasing p_e increases total public labor input $(\partial z_o^D/\partial p_e > 0)$. This, in turn, implies a tendency towards lower prices of relatively labor-intensive goods. The economic plausibility for these effects is as follows: let p_e be a labor-intensive good and let its price decrease. If demand reacts normally, z_e^D increases. Hence the use of inputs in the public sector will be shifted to a higher percentage of labor inputs. This tendency will be intensified if we think of the demand for other goods which will also be influenced by changing p_e.

The typical influence of a union's policy, summarized in the fourth term, will be stronger the greater the union's bargaining power (ρ) and the more interested the union is in securing jobs (U_z). The influence will be counterbalanced by production-side effects of labor inputs (β_o) [4].

---

[4] It may be noted that one cannot deduce unambigously whether the union's influence leads to wage increases or decreases. Transforming (2) for e $= 0$ in a similar way as (3) shows that the influence of the union on the wage level p_o is reflected by $\frac{\rho}{\beta_o} \cdot \frac{1}{\partial z_o^D/\partial p_o} \cdot$ $[\frac{\partial U}{\partial z_o} \cdot \frac{\partial z_o^D}{\partial p_o} + \frac{\partial U}{\partial p_o}]$ which can be rewritten simply as $\frac{\rho}{\beta_o \partial z_o^D/\partial p_o} \frac{\partial U^*}{\partial p_o}$, taking into account that our definition of $z_o^D(p_o)$ together with $z_o = z_o^D$ implies $U^* = U^*(z_o^D(p_o), p_o)$ at the optimum. But $\partial U^*/\partial p_o$ can, of course, be either positive or negative.

CHAPTER 21 QUALITY IN POSITIVE THEORY MODELS

The previous chapters have described optimal positive theory pricing when quality levels are held constant. Let us now consider how optimal quality levels are determined in the positive approach. How does optimal quality depend on the objective chosen? Will a vote maximizer choose a higher quality level than an output maximizer? Answers to such questions can be given by applying the general results of chapter 4, above all eq. (4-15)

$$\sum_{i=o}^{n}\left(p_i - \tilde{C}_i + \frac{1}{\beta_o}\frac{\partial \Phi}{\partial z_i}\right)\frac{\partial z_i^D}{\partial q_e} = c_{qe} - \frac{1}{\beta_o}\frac{\partial \Phi}{\partial q_e} \qquad e \in E. \qquad (4-15)$$

Let us compare this public firm quality choice with the corresponding marginal condition of a profit maximizing monopolist

$$\sum_{i=o}^{n}(p_i - c_i)\frac{\partial z_i^D}{\partial q_e} = c_{qe} \qquad e \in E. \qquad (1)$$

There is a formal identity of both pricing rules if we impute to the public firm the following modified marginal costs

$$c_i^* = \tilde{C}_i - \frac{1}{\beta_o}\frac{\partial \Phi}{\partial z_i} \qquad \text{quantity marginal costs} \qquad (2)$$

$$c_{qe}^* = c_{qe} - \frac{1}{\beta_o}\frac{\partial \Phi}{\partial q_e} \qquad \text{quality marginal costs.} \qquad (3)$$

Hence we are once again left with the result that the public firm behaves as if it were a profit maximizing monopolist who misestimates costs. The direction of miscalculation depends on $\partial\Phi/\partial z_i$ and $\partial\Phi/\partial q_e$ respectively [1] and varies from one objective function to the other as can be seen in table 3. The miscalculation of marginal costs will, most probably, influence prices and qualities in the following way:

$$\frac{\partial\Phi}{\partial z_i} < 0 \Rightarrow c_i^* > \widetilde{C}_i \text{ (higher quantity marginal costs)} \Rightarrow \text{higher price} \quad (4)$$

$$\frac{\partial\Phi}{\partial q_e} < 0 \Rightarrow c_{qe}^* > c_{qe} \text{ (higher quality marginal costs)} \Rightarrow \text{lower quality} \quad (5)$$

where "higher" and "lower" refers to the price and quality choice of a profit maximizing monopolist (neglecting the difference between c_i and $\widetilde{C}_i$).

Applying table 3 to our plausibility (5) we conclude as follows: there is a tendency towards higher quality in political models of vote-maximizers, there is a tendency towards lower quality in case of energy minimization [2]. The other positive theory objectives are neutral.

Therefore, the answer to one of the introductory questions is as expected: tendencially, a vote maximizer will choose a higher quality level than an output maximizer.

---

[1] $\partial\Phi/\partial p_e$ influences the quality choice because both prices and qualities result from the system of equations (4-14) and (4-15).

[2] In the energy minimizing case, the signs of $\partial\Phi/\partial q_e$ rest on the assumptions of normal reaction of demand with respect to its own price, and of complementarity between energy and all other goods $e \neq k$.

TABLE 3 [1]

objective	objective function to be maximized	$\frac{\partial \Phi}{\partial q_e}$
votes	$f(v^1,...,v^H)$	$\sum_h \frac{\partial f}{\partial v^h}\frac{\partial v^h}{\partial q_e}>0$
"discretionary" budget	$\sum_{m+1}^n p_i z_i + BUD(z_{m+1},...,z_n)$	0
output	$\sum_{m+1}^n z_i$	0
revenue	$\sum_{m+1}^n p_i z_i$	0
energy (supplied by private firms $j \in K$)	$z_k - \sum_h x_k^h(\cdot) + \sum_{j \notin K} y_k^j(\cdot)$	$-(\frac{\partial z_k^D}{\partial q_e} + \sum_{j \in K}\frac{\partial y_k^j}{\partial q_e})<0$
energy (publicly supplied)	$-\sum_h x_k^h(\cdot) + \sum_j y_k^j(\cdot)$	$-\frac{\partial z_k^D}{\partial q_e}<0$
Laspeyres price index	$-\sum_{m+1}^n p_i x_i^o / \sum_{m+1}^n p_i^o x_i^o$	0
combined manager and trade union interests	$U^1(z_{m+1},...,z_n) + U^2(p_o,z_o)$	0

---

[1] For $\partial \Phi/\partial z_i$ and $\partial \Phi/\partial p_e$ see table 1, chapter 4.

CHAPTER 22 A SET OF AXIOMS FOR PRICES TO ACHIEVE A FAIR ALLOCATION OF COSTS

This chapter is devoted to a recent approach to public pricing that differs conceptually from all the other approaches outlined in this book. The approach to be outlined now does not rest on the principles of optimizing some objective function subject to production feasibility and a revenue-cost constraint, and the conditions for market equilibria. Rather it proceeds by formulating some basic axioms to which prices should correspond and seeks those pricing rules that are uniquely determined by these axioms. The (game-) theoretical background is rather advanced, yet the basic ideas of the approach as presented below, are nevertheless easily understandable. Moreover, the approach is not purely theoretical exercise of l'art pour l'art, but has actually been applied in practice.

Some economists at Cornell University were asked to compute fair internal telephone billing rates for their university (Billera-Heath-Raanan (1978)). Problems arose because costs for long distance calls follow different schedules, consisting of different basic fees and variable charges the university has to pay to the telephone company (direct distance dialing – DDD – , foreign exchange lines – FX – , wide area telecommunications service – WATS). Thus two people calling Chicago at the same time may cause different costs for the university, if one uses the FX-line, the other DDD, because the computer routes the first call to the cheaper FX-line and the second, which comes in some seconds later, to DDD, as FX and all WATS-lines are occupied. Is it fair to charge different internal billing rates in such a case?

The authors solved the problem by applying the Shapley-value of non-atomic games (Aumann-Shapley (1974)). Billera-Heath (1979), Mirman-Tauman (1982) and Samet-Tauman (1982) then redefined the game-theoretic axioms as axioms on the relation between prices and cost functions. They succeeded in finding a nice set of axioms that is understandable on its own even by readers who are not familiar with sophisticated game theory. Thus they created a new, generally applicable, theory of pricing which meanwhile has been further developed in Mirman-Samet-Tauman (1983), Bös-Tillmann (1983) and Samet-Tauman-Zang (1981).

The most striking feature of cost-axiomatic pricing is that it starts from axioms on the relation between prices and cost functions and hence needs no information on consumer tastes. However, there is not a priori guaranteed that the application of such price schedules will always imply a general equilibrium. And if an equilibrium under cost-axiomatic prices is to obtain, the estimation of private tastes enters again.

Consider a producer who has to produce particular quantities of consumption goods $\varsigma = (\varsigma_1, \ldots, \varsigma_n); \varsigma_i > 0$. Total costs of producing ς are given by $C(\varsigma)$, a continuously differentiable long-run cost function (all inputs are treated as variable: $C(0) = 0$). Input prices are fixed. Increasing returns to scale are included. The quantities ς shall be sold at prices $p = (p_1(C, \varsigma), \ldots, p_n(C, \varsigma))$ that fulfill the following four axioms (Samet-Tauman (1982)):

Axiom 1 (Rescaling): The price should be independent of the unit's measurement. Let G and C be two cost functions and

$$G(z_1, \ldots, z_n) = C(s_1 z_1, \ldots, s_n z_n) \qquad s_i > 0 \quad \forall i. \tag{1}$$

Then for each ς and each $i = 1, \ldots, n$

$$p_i(G, \varsigma) = s_i p_i(C, (s_1 \varsigma_1, \ldots, s_n \varsigma_n)). \tag{2}$$

The rationale for this axiom is trivial: the price of ς_i if measured in tons, has to be 1000 times the price of ς_i if measured in kilos.

Axiom 2 (Consistency): The same price shall be charged for goods which have the same influence on costs in the following sense: if G is a one variable cost function and if for every z

$$C(z_1, \ldots, z_n) = G\left(\sum_i z_i\right), \tag{3}$$

then for every i and every ς

$$p_i(\overset{i}{C}, \varsigma) = p\left(G, \sum_i \varsigma_i\right). \tag{4}$$

Typical examples are red and blue cars which should be sold at the same price. Objections to this axiom stress different situations of demand: if, at the same prices, red cars can and blue cars cannot be sold, it makes sense to sell blue cars at a lower price.

Axiom 3 (Additivity): If the cost function can be broken into subcosts, the prices can be found by adding the prices determined by the subcosts.

If C, G^1 and G^2 are cost functions and for each z

$$C(z_1, \ldots, z_n) = G^1(z_1, \ldots, z_n) + G^2(z_1, \ldots, z_n), \tag{5}$$

then for each ς

$$p(C, \varsigma) = p(G^1, \varsigma) + p(G^2, \varsigma). \tag{6}$$

Axiom 3 refers only to cases where the cost function is separable. Then there are no interdependencies between subcosts and the additivity of pricing makes sense.

Axiom 4 (Positivity): The price of a commodity the production of which requires investment, is not negative.
Let ς be given. If C is not decreasing at any $z \leq \varsigma$, then $p(C, \varsigma) \geq 0$. (7)

The reasoning is straightforward.

Samet-Tauman (1982) prove that prices which correspond to these four axioms are of the form

$$p_i(C,\varsigma) = \int_0^1 C_i(s\varsigma)d\mu(s) \qquad i = 1,\ldots,n \qquad \varsigma \neq 0. \qquad (8)$$

This rather complicated mathematical formulation can be grasped most easily if one interprets the prices p as "some average" of the marginal costs C_i where the measure $\mu(s)$ denotes how "the average" is to be computed. We can clarify this further if we show how, by changing μ, we can generate, as polar cases of the same pricing formula, the "pure" marginal-cost prices as well as the "Aumann-Shapley" break-even prices:

a) Marginal-cost pricing

Axiom 4 is strengthened in order to obtain Axiom 4*.

Axiom 4* (Positivity)

Let ς be given.
If C is nondecreasing in a neighborhood of ς, then $(C,\varsigma) \geq 0$.   (9)

This requires that prices be non-negative at ς even if C is nondecreasing in a neighborhood of ς only.

If axioms 1 to 3 and 4* are fulfilled [1], the price mechanism reduces to

$$p_i(C,\varsigma) = C_i(\varsigma) \qquad (10)$$

which is the marginal-cost pricing rule as a special case of the above general pricing rule.

b) Aumann-Shapley pricing

We add a break-even axiom.

---

[1] Some additional normalization is necessary as shown in Samet-Tauman (1982, 905).

Axiom 5 (Break even)

$$\sum_i p_i(C, \varsigma)\varsigma_i = C(\varsigma) \qquad \text{for each } \varsigma > 0. \qquad (11)$$

If axioms 1 to 5 (including 4, not 4*) are fulfilled, the pricing rule is

$$p_i(C, \varsigma) = \int_0^1 C_i(s\varsigma)ds. \qquad (12)$$

The reader should be aware that (12) does not mean the usual kind of average-cost pricing. As we are dealing with a more-than-one-good approach the average is found by proportionate variations s of all quantities ς along a ray going from 0 to ς.

Thus cost-axiomatic prices include marginal-cost prices and cost-covering prices as special cases. We recall that welfare maximizing prices also include marginal-cost and cost-covering prices as special cases. What, then, is the *difference between pricing according to these two approaches*?

First, *marginal costs* enter the pricing rules in different ways. All kinds of welfare maximizing pricing, following our general rules (3-21) or (3-24) depend on the marginal costs $\widetilde{C}_i$ at the optimum - and only at the optimum. Cost axiomatic pricing, following eqs. (8) also depends on alternative production possibilities, on the values of the respective marginal costs for any quantity along a ray between 0 and ς. This difference is interesting with respect to the whole philosophy of the meaning of pricing rules. Perhaps one should think of pricing rules as depending also on further alternative production possibilities, e.g. the production of higher quantities $(C_i(s\varsigma)$ for $s > 1)$.

Only in the case of pure marginal-cost pricing does this particular difference between the welfare approach and the cost-axiomatic approach disappear.

Second, the *demand side* is treated differently. The welfare approach typically assumes an equilibrium between quantities demanded and supplied (the only exception in this book being the peak-load model). No such constraint enters the cost-axiomatic approach. However, will prices that are determined only by cost axioms always be "demand compatible"? Or will demand at given prices exceed or fall short of supply? Mirman and Tauman (1982) have already shown that Aumann-Shapley prices are demand compatible and Bös-Tillmann (1983) have shown that *all* cost-axiomatic prices are demand compatible if the financing of deficits of public utilities is explicitly included in an equilibrium approach.

The proof has, of course, extended the applicability of cost-axiomatic pricing to a considerable extent. Only after this general proof of the demand compatibility of cost-axiomatic pricing can these price schedules be treated as an equivalent and perhaps superior alternative to welfare- maximizing price schedules.

Generally, it will be complicated to decide which approach is superior. Compare, for example, Ramsey and Aumann-Shapley prices. Both are cost-covering. However, one cannot expect these prices to coincide. If there are different price elasticities of demand for two goods that have the same influence on costs (in the sense of axiom 2 above), Ramsey prices of these two goods will differ, Aumann-Shapley prices will be equal. In such a case, somebody who adheres to the welfare approach will stress the welfare losses caused by Aumann-Shapley prices. Somebody who adheres to the above axioms on costs will stress the weaknesses of the social welfare function. There is no generally accepted result concerning the superiority of one of these two approaches.

PART FOUR: APPLICATION OF THE THEORETICAL RESULTS: THE EXAMPLE OF LONDON TRANSPORT

CHAPTER 23   ECONOMIC THEORY AND EMPIRICAL ANALYSIS (I): SPECIFYING DEMAND

This chapter deals with the demand for outputs. Inputs, including labor, are not treated explicitly. Hence it is convenient to use the goods' index $i = 1, \ldots, n$ for outputs only. $x = (x_1, \ldots, x_n) >> 0$ is a vector of consumed quantities, $p = (p_1, \ldots, p_n)$ is a vector of the respective prices which are given to the consumers.

23.1   MICROECONOMICS OF THE REPRESENTATIVE CONSUMER

The theoretical chapters of this book can deal satisfactorily with utility functions which differ across individuals. This is impossible for the empirical chapters because there is no information on the individual consumer decisions, only on total demand. Hence, the empirical chapters must be based on the concept of a representative consumer [1].

The representative consumer acts according to the usual microeconomic theory as shown in figure 18. We distinguish between primal and dual approaches.

The primal approach starts from the direct utility function u(x) which the representative consumer is assumed to maximize subject to the budget

---

[1] Sometimes we must switch to a sort of "disaggregated representative consumer", for example for the treatment of public pricing with distributional objectives.

constraint $\sum_i p_i x_i = r$, where r is an average labor and non-labor income, imputed to the representative consumer. This utility maximization yields the Marshallian demand functions $x(p,r)$ and the maximum achievable value of utility, u^*. The indirect utility function $V(p,r)$ combines these results and represents optimal utility u^* as depending on the Marshallian demand functions. For explanatory reasons we present the basic approach on estimating demand without reference to quality.

$$max_x u(x) \qquad\qquad min_x r(x) = p^T x$$
$$s.t. p^T x = r \qquad\qquad s.t. u(x) \;=\; \hat{u}$$
$$\Downarrow \qquad\qquad\qquad\qquad \Downarrow$$
$$x = x(p,r); u* \quad \Longleftarrow \quad (c) \quad \Longrightarrow \quad \hat{x} \;=\; \hat{x}(p,\hat{u}); r*$$
$$\Downarrow \qquad\qquad\qquad\qquad \Downarrow$$
$$(a.1) \qquad\qquad\qquad (a.2)$$
$$\Downarrow \qquad\qquad\qquad\qquad \Downarrow$$
$$V = V(p,r) \quad \Longleftarrow \quad (b) \quad \Longrightarrow \quad R \;=\; R(p,\hat{u})$$

Figure 18

Source: Deaton-Muellbauer (1980a, 38).

The dual approach imputes to the representative consumer the objective of minimizing expenditures, given a fixed utility level. As primal and dual approaches are only different ways to describe the achievement of the same consumer optimum, the fixed level $\hat{u}$ of the dual approach must be assumed to be identical with that level which results from the primal approach, $\hat{u} = u^*$. Therefore $\hat{u}$ is the present utility level of the consumer, not some utility level of a base period. The result of consumer's expenditure minimization are the Hicksian or compensated [2] demand functions $\hat{x}(p, \hat{u})$ and the minimum possible expenditures r^*. The expenditure function $R(p, \hat{u})$ combines these results and represents minimal expenditures $r^* = R(\cdot)$ as depending on the Hicksian demand functions.

The different functions of the primal and the dual approach are closely connected as noted by (a) to (c) in figure 18. Let us briefly mention these connections:

a.1) differentiating the indirect utility function with respect to any price yields Roy's identity

$$\frac{\partial V}{\partial p_i} = -x_i \frac{\partial V}{\partial r} \qquad i = 1, \ldots, n; \qquad (1)$$

a.2) differentiating the expenditure function with respect to any price yields the Hicksian or compensated demand functions

$$\frac{\partial R}{\partial p_i} = \hat{x}_i \qquad i = 1, \ldots, n. \qquad (2)$$

Equations (1) and (2) show the basic difference between Marshallian and Hicksian demand. In the first case income effects matter $(\partial V / \partial r)$, in the second case they do not.

b) for fixed prices the expenditure function is inverse to the indirect utility function [3]

$$R = V^{-1}(p, \hat{u}); \qquad (3)$$

---

[2] The compensation in case of "compensated" demand refers to the present utility level $\hat{u}$ whereas the compensation in case of the "compensated variation" refers to some base utility level u^0.

[3] In many cases this inversion is not well-defined analytically.

c)   The Hicksian is equal to the Marshallian demand function if we specify the income in the Marshallian function by $r^* = R(p, u^*) = R(p, \hat{u})$:

$$\hat{x}_i(p, \hat{u}) = x_i(p, R(p, \hat{u})) \qquad i = 1, \ldots, n. \tag{4}$$

The reason is simple. For both Hicksian and Marshallian demand the adding-up condition of demand systems must be valid:

$$\text{Income (expenditures)} = \sum_i p_i x_i(p, r) \tag{5a}$$

$$\text{Income (expenditures)} = \sum_i p_i \hat{x}_i(p, \hat{u}). \tag{5a}$$

Therefore x_i must equal $\hat{x}_i$ if income and prices are equal. Hicksian and Marshallian demand always intersect, equation (4) being the equation of the point of intersection. We assume this point to be unique. The most interesting consequence of this intersection can be seen by differentiating equation (4) with respect to any price. The result of this differentiation is the well-known Slutsky equation

$$\frac{\partial \hat{x}_i}{\partial p_k} = \frac{\partial x_i}{\partial p_k} + \frac{\partial x_i}{\partial r} \cdot \frac{\partial R}{\partial p_k} = \frac{\partial x_i}{\partial p_k} + \frac{\partial x_i}{\partial r} \cdot x_k \qquad i, k, \ldots, n \tag{6}$$

where we made use of $\partial R/\partial p_k = \hat{x}_k$ from equation (2), and $\hat{x}_k = x_k$ from equation (4).

The Slutsky substitution matrix with elements $\partial \hat{x}_i/\partial p_k$ is symmetric and negative semidefinite. The last property implies that the compensated own price effects are nonpositive, $\partial \hat{x}_k/\partial p_k \leq 0$.

Our empirical analysis would be simple if we could restrict ourselves to estimating only Marshallian demand functions $x(p, r)$. However, some important pricing rules, for instance Ramsey pricing, depend on Hicksian rather than Marshallian demand functions. Our empirical analysis must therefore be extended to include the computation of Hicksian demand functions $\hat{x}(p, \hat{u})$. Furthermore, the indirect utility function of the representative consumer $V(p, r)$ is the natural candidate for an empirical index of social welfare losses or gains resulting from changes of public prices. However, if $x(\cdot), \hat{x}(\cdot)$, and $V(\cdot)$ are to be determined empirically, the empirical estimates of $u(\cdot)$ and $R(\cdot)$ follow directly. To sum up it can be said that we have to compute all functions of figure 18.

23.2 SOME BASIC PRINCIPLES FOR ESTIMATING SYSTEMS OF DEMAND FUNCTIONS

When estimating systems of demand functions, three different starting positions can be chosen (Lau (1977)):

a) Specify the *direct utility function* of the representative consumer, and maximize this function given the budget constraint. The main deficiency of this approach is a possible inability to solve the resulting optimum conditions explicitly for the quantities demanded. However, if the functional form of the demand functions remains unknown, the functional form of the indirect utility function and of the expenditure function also remain unknown.

A functional form which hase been widely used is the Stone-Geary specification (extensively treated in Phlips (1983, 119-132))

$$u(x) = \sum_i b_i ln(x_i - d_i)$$
$$0 < b_i; \ \sum_i b_i = 1; \ x_i - d_i > 0^{4)}.$$

(7)

---

[4] The imposition of these restrictions guarantees adding-up, homogeneity of degree

Maximizing utility under the usual budget constraint leads to the linear expenditure system

$$p_i x_i = d_i p_i + b_i (r - \sum_k d_k p_k). \qquad (8)$$

Expenditures for any good i consist of a minimum expenditure $d_i p_i$ which is necessary to attain a minimum subsistence level. The "supernumerary" income $r - \sum_k d_k p_k$ is then spent on consumption in the proportions b_i.

The resulting expenditure function equals

$$R = \sum_i d_i p_i + \Pi_i (p_i / b_i)^{b_i} \cdot exp\ u \qquad (9)$$

(Deaton-Muellbauer (1980a, 42)).

b) Specify the *Marshallian demand functions*. Only those functional relationships of demand, prices and income must be chosen which are compatible with a utility maximizing representative consumer. The latter property usually is called "integrability". However, those functions which can be estimated easily, like simple linear relations between quantities, prices and income, or their logarithms, often lack the integrability property. Demand functions which can be estimated easily and have the integrability property usually belong to utility functions with restrictive economic background, like constant budget shares etc. Even the linear expenditure system starts from restrictive economic assumptions [5] (Deaton (1974, 1978), Phlips (1983, 119-132)) [6].

---

zero, Slutsky symmetry and Slutsky negativity of the resulting demand system.

[5] For instance the assumption that all goods are substitutes in the Hicksian sense.

[6] For examples of other simple and integrable demand and expenditure functions see Lau (1977).

c) Specify the *indirect utility function* of the representative consumer. In that case one does not have to bother about the utility maximization as it is included in the definition of the indirect utility function. Moreover, by applying Roy's identity, the demand functions can be obtained by simple differentiation whence their functional form is explicitly determined as long as the indirect utility function is differentiable.

A well-known example [7] is the translog specification (Christensen, Jorgensen, Lau (1975)). This specification approximates utility by a Taylor series expansion

$$lnV = a_o + \sum_i a_i ln(p_i/r) + \frac{1}{2}\sum_i\sum_k d_{ik} ln(p_i/r) ln(p_k/r) \qquad (10)$$

which leads to budget shares of the following type

$$w_i = \frac{p_i x_i}{r} = \frac{a_i + \sum_k d_{ik} ln(p_k/r)}{\sum_k a_k + \sum_g\sum_k d_{gk} ln(p_k/r)}. \qquad (11))$$

It can be seen directly from the budget shares that the underlying demand system fulfills the adding-up and homogeneity conditions. Slutsky symmetry requires $d_{ik} = d_{ki}$. However, as the translog function is a Taylor series expansion, this property follows directly from the symmetry of the second derivatives of the utility function. The reader might explicitly perform the Taylor series expansion to see that $d_{ik} := \partial^2 V(\bar{p}/\bar{r})/\partial(p_i/r)\partial(p_k/r)$, where $\bar{p}/\bar{r}$ denotes the point about which the Taylor series is expanded.

In this book we are going to specify the indirect utility of an "almost ideal demand system", which in part is based on the translog approach. We will estimate Marshallian demand by means of the budget share functions

---

[7] For further examples see Lau (1977), and Howe-Pollak-Wales (1979).

derived from indirect utility. The chosen specification allows the analytical computation of Hicksian from Marshallian demand. (For details see section 23.4 below.)

23.3   DESIRABLE PROPERTIES OF A DEMAND SYSTEM

Any estimation of demand systems starts from some given data and is required to hold at least in a neighborhood of the actual data. We do not postulate the global validity of an estimated demand system for all conceivable price-income situations.

Lack of data prevents us from applying non-parametric estimations of demand. We restrict ourselves to demand which depends on prices and on income in a particular specified functional relation. This system of demand functions is assumed to be at least once continuously differentiable in the parameters. As Lau (1977) stresses this assumption is not too grave as it is never possible to falsify it with a finite body of data.

The demand functions must relate to the given data in describing non-negative prices, quantities, income, and adding-up budget shares. As these properties are given by construction of the data, they cannot be tested empirically.

In the following we present some desirable properties of systems of demand functions, as postulated in many of the relevant papers on the topic. Every paper has its own catalogue; one of the best is due to Lau (1977). The desirable properties refer to the compatibility of theory and empirical tests and to the empirical implementation.

23.3.1   COMPATIBILITY OF THEORY AND EMPIRICAL TESTS

(a) Integrability
We postulate that the demand system to be tested shall be capable of describing actual demand as resulting from utility maximization of the representative consumer. This postulate imposes certain observable restrictions on the behavior of the representative consumer.

(a.1) Homogeneity.   The demand functions $x(p, r)$ must be homogeneous of degree zero in p and r. This property can be implemented in the system of demand functions by a priori imposing particular restrictions on the parameters. If no restrictions are chosen, the empirical estimation can be used to test the hypothesis of homogeneity.

(a.2) Slutsky symmetry.   The matrix of the Slutsky substitution effects must be symmetric. Once again, this property can be implemented by a priori given restrictions on the parameters. Otherwise, the empirical estimation can be used to test the symmetry hypothesis.

(a.3) Slutsky negativity.   The matrix of the Slutsky substitution effects must be negative semidefinite. In flexible approaches like translog, this property cannot be imposed a priori by assumptions on the parameters. It must always be tested a posteriori. Cobb-Douglas or Stone-Geary utility functions, on the other hand, a priori impose Slutsky negativity on the demand systems.

(b) Incorporation of additional nonprice variables
We postulated that the demand system depends on additional nonprice variables which in case of our book are the quality indicators q [8]. Demand does not depend on prices and income alone, but also on the quality of the good,

---

[8]   The introduction of explicit quality indicators does not prevent us from additionally distinguishing qualities by distinguishing different goods. If, for example, x_1 is demand for first class railway transportation, and x_2 second class, both may depend on prices and on waiting time. See subsection 1.6.1 and section 15.1 above.

like waiting or travelling time in case of transportation demand, congestion time in case of telephone demand, reliability of supply in case of electricity demand. The usual omission of such explanatory non-price variables may be one of the reasons why empirical tests so often reject homogeneity or Slutsky conditions. Omitting the relevant non-price variables, these models are wrongly specified and, hence, cannot exhibit the relation between demand, prices and income correctly [9].

Additional variables can be incorporated more easily if the indirect utility function is specified. In that case we obtain a "conditional indirect utility function" (Lau (1977)), $V(p, q, r)$, and can easily find the analogue to Roy's identity for the additional variables as we did in subsection 3.5.1. The direct utility approach, on the other hand, might become even more complicated than usual if the additional variables constitute further constraints on the utility maximization. The obvious example refers to transportation problems where a direct utility function is to be maximized given a money income constraint and a constraint on the time to be spent travelling.

---

[9] Deaton-Muellbauer (1980b, 312, 322) come to a similar conclusion on the basis of their estimation of British consumption patterns. Comparing their estimations of demand systems with and without imposed homogeneity they observe that the imposition of homogeneity generates positive serial correlation in the errors. Hence they believe that the rejection of homogeneity is "due to insufficient attention to the dynamic aspects of consumer behavior" (p. 316), and suggest the "introduction of (arbitrary) time trends" (p. 322). We believe the introduction of well-specified quality indicators is better than the introduction of arbitrary time trends.

23.3.2   EMPIRICAL IMPLEMENTATION

(a) Flexibility [10]

Given some arbitrary data set, the specification of utility or demand functions should be chosen in such a way that all possible reactions of the representative consumer can be described adequately. For any given set of data, all possible price and income and quality elasticities should be achievable through an appropriate set of parameter values.

We postulate second-order flexibility of the indirect utility function so as to guarantee first-order flexibility of the resulting demand functions. Second-order flexibility means that the parameters of the estimated function can represent the actual utility and all first- and second-order derivatives of the actual utility function at the given point.

The straightforward way to achieve the necessary number of parameters for second-order flexibility is to start from a second-order Taylor approximation to any arbitrary utility function, which is just what translog and other flexible approaches do. For a homogeneous indirect utility function depending on the normalized prices $p_1/r, \ldots, p_n/r$ we need $n^2 + n + 1$ parameters to represent n^2 derivatives of the second order, the n derivatives of the first order, and the utility itself. The translog function, for instance, has exactly $n^2 + n + 1$ parameters.

Other usual utility functions lack second-order flexibility and thus impose a priori restrictions on consumer behavior. The best-known functions which are not flexible are the indirect addilog function (Houthakker (1960)), the CES – indirect function for more than two goods, and the Stone-Geary function for more than two goods [11].

---

[10] The term "flexibility" is used by Caves-Christensen (1980a). Others speak of "interpolation properties" (Lau (1977)).

[11] As long as the basic restrictions (7) are fulfilled and as long as base consumption t_i is always smaller than total demand x_i for all i.

(b) Uniformity

This property is fulfilled if any single demand function has the same algebraic form. Uniformity is not only a matter of aesthetics, based on a sort of anonymity principle which a priori allows any consumption good to be denoted by any arbitrary index. Uniformity also implies that no a priori information on the demand for particular goods is used when specifying demand functions.

There is no theoretical necessity for such a procedure. One could easily think of consumers whose demand for necessities follows a different pattern to their demand for luxuries. Different algebraic forms of demand functions would then be a natural choice. However, as long as we have no particular information on such differences of the algebraic form of demand, it is best to start from uniform specification.

23.4   THE ALMOST IDEAL DEMAND SYSTEM

According to the last subsection, we should specify demand systems in such a way that they are compatible with economic theory and are flexible enough so as to reflect all possible reactions of the representative consumer. The best-known specifications of demand, however, do not fulfill both postulates.

Cobb-Douglas, Stone-Geary and CES utility functions are compatible with consumer theory, but lack second-order flexibility, at least for the case of more than two goods. Starting from one of those utility functions allows the analytical computation of all functions of figure 18, the indirect utility function as well as the expenditure function, the compensated demand function as well as the non-compensated. This desired property is obtained at the expense of flexibility. It is no longer possible to describe all conceivable activities of the consumer by the specified demand system, rather the specification imposes severe restrictions on his behavior. The assumption of constant budget shares, as implied by Cobb-Douglas utility functions, provides the best example.

Translog utility functions, on the other hand, are second-order flexible and therefore do not restrict consumer's behavior a priori. However. it is impossible to invert the translog indirect utility function analytically in order to obtain the corresponding expenditure function. The restriction to numerical solutions implies a great loss of elegance of the analysis.

The "almost ideal demand system" (AIDS) which has recently been proposed by Deaton and Muellbauer (1980b) is the first specification which is both compatible with theory and flexible. This demand system can be applied to describe properties of demand when fairly short time series are available as is the case with our investigation of London Transport. (Deaton-Muellbauer applied AIDS to annual data of British consumer expenditures, 1954 - 1974.) Therefore, we are going to apply AIDS to estimate the demand for London bus and underground services and to estimate the representative Londoner's indirect utility and expenditure function.

The basic idea of AIDS is the explicit distinction between two types of *expenditure functions*: subsistence expenditures $R_S(p)$ and bliss expenditures $R_B(p)$. As there is no a priori information on substistence expenditures, Deaton and Muellbauer use a translog specification:

$$lnR_S(p) = a_o + \sum_i a_i lnp_i + \frac{1}{2}\sum_i\sum_k d_{ik}^* lnp_i lnp_k. \tag{12}$$

Bliss expenditures, $R_B(p) > R_S(p)$ reflect a sort of Stone-Geary behavior. After spending money for subsistence expenditures which by definition must be bought in any case, the consumer plans to spend the supernumerary income according to a Cobb-Douglas type of behavior [12]:

$$lnR_B(p) = lnR_S(p) + b_o\Pi_i p_i^{b_i}. \tag{13}$$

---

[12] The reader might compare (13) and (8) and consider that in (8) exp u can be replaced by b_o.

Note, however, that the left-hand side of (13) is the logarithm of the expenditure function and not the expenditure function itself as in the Stone-Geary
case (8).

We postulate that utility is at its lowest possible level if the representative consumer is so poor as to be restricted to subsistence consumption

$$r = R_S(p) \rightarrow V(p,r) = 0. \tag{14}$$

If his actual expenditures are equal to the bliss level, the highest possible utility level is achieved. We normalize this level to unity and obtain

$$r = R_B(p) \rightarrow V(p,r) = 1. \tag{15}$$

Utility thus is normalized between 0 and 1, depending on where the
actual expenditures lie between subsistence and bliss [13].

There are of course many conceivable *utility functions* which correspond
to the above normalization. Most convenient is the following specification:

$$V = \frac{ln(r/R_S(p))}{ln(R_B(p)/R_S(p))} = \frac{ln\ r - lnR_S(p)}{lnR_B(p) - lnR_S(p)}. \tag{16}$$

The representative consumer thus compares the ratio of actual and subsistence expenditures with the ratio of bliss and subsistence expenditures.
The utility function V is monotonically increasing and concave in r.

This specification implies the following *expenditure function.* By regarding imcome r as the minimal expenditures $R(p,V)$, necessary to keep
utility constant, the above indirect utility function can be inverted easily
to obtain the expenditure function. In fact, the inversion is reduced to a

---

[13] In spite of this interpretation, empirical estimations of AIDS might, under special
circumstances, lead to values of V which do not lie between 0 and 1. See Deaton-
Muellbauer (1980b, 324).

simple tautological transformation. Solving (16) explicitly for $r = R(p, V)$ we obtain

$$lnR(p,V) = (1 - V)lnR_S(p) + VlnR_B(p). \qquad (17)$$

Note that both the subsistence and the bliss expenditure function depend on prices only. The income enters expenditure via the utility function V only.

Substituting the specification of $R_S(\cdot)$ and $R_B(\cdot)$, (12) and (13), we obtain

$$lnR(p,V) = a_o + \sum_i a_i lnp_i + \frac{1}{2}\sum_i\sum_k d_{ik}^* lnp_i lnp_k + Vb_o\Pi_i p_i^{b_i}. \qquad (18)$$

For n prices and income, the above specification of the expenditure function exhibits $n^2 + 2n + 2$ parameters for $n^2 + 2n + 3$ degrees of freedom (utility itself plus all first- and second-order derivatives). Hence, one of the derivatives must be normalized [14].

We proceed by differentiating the expenditure function with respect to prices to obtain the *Hicksian demand functions* in budget share form

$$\hat{w}_i = \frac{p_i\hat{x}_i}{R} = a_i + \sum_k d_{ik} lnp_k + b_i Vb_o\Pi_k p_k^{b_k} \quad i = 1,\ldots,n \qquad (19)$$

where $d_{ik} = 1/2(d_{ik}^* + d_{ki}^*)$.

Substituting the indirect utility function V (16) into the Hicksian demand functions yields the *Marshallian demand functions* in budget share form

---

[14] Deaton-Muellbauer (1980b), investigating the second-order flexibility of the expenditure function, propose $\partial^2 lnR/\partial V^2 = 0$.

$$w_i = \frac{p_i x_i}{R} = a_i + \sum_k d_{ik} ln p_k + b_i ln(r/P) \qquad i = 1, \ldots, n. \qquad (20)$$

The variable P, defined as a price index in Deaton-Muellbauer (1980b), is identical with the subsistence expenditures R_S [15]. The reader should not be surprised at this identity. The theory of true cost of living indices shows how close expenditure functions and price indices are [16].

To understand the above demand system (20), consider two extreme cases:

(a)   choose $a_i = d_{ik} = 0, i = 1, \ldots, n$. Then the subsistence consumption is constant, $ln R_S = a_o$, and the supernumerary consumption follows the bliss specification. In that case the budget shares depend on the "real income" r/a_o only, the influence being measured by the coefficients b_i,

(b)   choose $b_i \to 0$. Then $ln R_B(p) \to ln R_S(p)$ and $ln R(p, V) \to ln R_S(p)$. Total consumption follows the subsistence specification. The budget shares depend on prices alone, price changes working through the coefficients d_{ik}.

AIDS provides a useful framework for the analysis of demand in public pricing models because it presents explicit algebraic specifications

–   of the representative consumer's indirect utility function which can be used to estimate welfare gains and losses of different pricing policies;

---

[15]   For transforming $ln R_S$ into $ln P$ recall the definition $d_{ik} = 1/2(d_{ik}^* + d_{ki}^*)$.

[16]   For econometric purposes it can sometimes be appropiate to approximate $ln P$ by some known index, for example by $ln P^* = \sum_k w_k ln p_k$. For details see Deaton-Muellbauer (1980b, 316-322).

- of the Hicksian demand functions whose derivatives we need for computing marginal-cost prices, Ramsey prices and other prices which explicitly depend on compensated demand;

- of the Marshallian demand functions whose derivatives we need for computing distributionally modified prices and pricing rules based on the positive theory.

The reader may be reminded that in most other cases of flexible indirect utility functions only Marshallian demand will be specified algebraically whereas Hicksian demand will have to be computed numerically by inverting the indirect utility function [17].

The compatibility of AIDS and the theoretical concept of a utility maximizing representative consumer leads to the following restrictions on the parameters of the system:

$$\text{(Adding-up) } \sum_i a_i = 1; \sum_i d_{ik} = 0; \sum_i b_i = 0 \tag{21}$$

$$\text{(Homogeneity) } \sum_k d_{ik} = 0 \tag{22}$$

$$\text{(Slutsky symmetry)} d_{ik} = d_{ki}. \tag{23}$$

As already mentioned, Slutsky negativity can never be imposed a priori, but always has to be tested a posteriori.

Finally we substitute the price index $P = R_S$ into equation (20) to obtain the AIDS Marshallian demand in the following form

---

[17] For recent papers on the estimation of compensated demand functions see Hausman (1981) and Vartia (1983).

$$w_i = (a_i - b_i a_o) + \sum_k d_{ik} lnp_k$$

$$+ b_i (ln \ r - \sum_k a_k lnp_k - \frac{1}{2} \sum_g \sum_k d_{gk} lnp_g lnp_k). \tag{24}$$

After explicitly introducing qualities, this function will be the basis of our estimations.

CHAPTER 24   ECONOMIC THEORY AND EMPIRICAL ANALYSIS (II): SPECIFYING TECHNOLOGY

London Transport data allow separate consideration of the production of bus and of underground transport services because joint inputs are comparatively low compared with the specific inputs. Moreover, the production functions of the other goods we shall consider in our analysis can also be separated totally from bus and underground production. Hence, we can restrict ourselves to technologies $z_i = z_i(\ell_i, \kappa_i)$, where z_i is output of good i, to be produced by two specific inputs, labor ℓ_i and capital κ_i. All quantities are positive. The wage rate p_o and the rate of interest p_κ are given exogenously. As the analysis is restricted to technologies with one output and two specific inputs, it is possible to suppress the goods' indices in the following sections.

It may be noted that the analyses below can be extended to technologies with one output and more than two specific inputs. The restriction to labor and capital has been chosen only for expositional clarity.

24.1   DUALITY

The duality of one output – many input – technologies is formally identical with the duality of consumer demand, see for instance Diewert (1982). This formal identity results from replacing the one-dimensional objective "utility" with the one-dimensional objective "output".

In the primal approach we consider the firm as maximizing output, as defined by the direct production function $z(\ell, \kappa)$, subject to its input budget. This output maximization yields the factor demand functions and the maximum obtainable output, z^*. The indirect production function $Z(p_o, p_\kappa, c)$

combines these results and represents maximum output z^* as depending on the factor demand functions. (c is the input budget.) The treatment of quality is postponed to a subsequent section.

$$
\begin{array}{ll}
max_{\ell,\kappa}\ z = z(\ell,\kappa) & min_{\ell,\kappa}\ c(\ell,\kappa) = p_o\ell + p_\kappa\kappa \\
\text{s.t. } p_o\ell + p_\kappa\kappa = c & \text{s.t.}\quad z(\ell,\kappa) \quad = \quad \hat{z} \\
\Downarrow & \Downarrow \\
\ell = \ell(p_o, p_\kappa, c); z^* & \hat{\ell} \ = \ \hat{\ell}(p_o, p_\kappa, \hat{z}); c^* \\
\kappa = \kappa(p_o, p_\kappa, c); z^* & \hat{\kappa} \ = \ \hat{\kappa}(p_o, p_\kappa, \hat{z}); c^* \\
\Downarrow & \Downarrow \\
(a.1) & (a.2) \\
\Downarrow & \Downarrow \\
Z = Z(p_o, p_\kappa, c) & C \ = \ C(p_o, p_\kappa, \hat{z})
\end{array}
$$

$$\ell = \ell(p_o,p_\kappa,c); z^* \quad\Longleftarrow\quad (c) \quad\Longrightarrow\quad \hat{\ell} = \hat{\ell}(p_o,p_\kappa,\hat{z}); c^*$$

$$Z = Z(p_o, p_\kappa, c) \quad\Longleftarrow\quad (b) \quad\Longrightarrow\quad C = C(p_o, p_\kappa, \hat{z})$$

Figure 19

In the dual approach we consider the firm as minimizing the cost of producing at least the level $\hat{z}$. As primal and dual approach describe the same producer behavior, the fixed quantity $\hat{z}$ of the dual approach must be assumed to be identical with that level which results from the primal approach, $\hat{z} = z^*$. The result of producer's cost minimization are "output compensated" factor demand functions $\hat{\ell}(\cdot)$ and $\hat{\kappa}(\cdot)$ and the minimum possible costs $c^* = C(\cdot)$ depending on the output compensated factor demand functions.

The different functions of the primal and of the dual approach are closely related, similar to the primal and dual approach of utility theory [1].

---

[1] The interpretations of the relations (a) to (c) in figure 19 are exactly analogous to those of figure 18.

For details see Diewert (1982) [2].

24.2   SOME BASIC PRINCIPLES OF ESTIMATING TECHNOLOGY

When estimating technology, three different starting positions can be chosen (Intriligator (1978, 251–302)):

a)   Specify the direct production function of the firm. As all variables of this function are empirically observable, it can be estimated directly whereas the direct utility function could only be estimated indirectly by estimating the corresponding Marshallian demand functions. Hence, the empirical implementation of the primal approach of technology is not restricted to particular special cases, as is the case with the primal approach of demand systems.

Nevertheless, most empirical studies dealt with Cobb-Douglas or CES-production functions, and some extensions of those functions.

b)   Specify the factor demand functions $\ell(\cdot)$ and $\kappa(\cdot)$. In that case the same "integrability" problems arise as in the case of specifying Marshallian consumer demand functions. Usually, once again Cobb-Douglas specifications of factor demand were chosen in empirical studies.

c)   Specify the cost function. The most usual specifications apply Cobb-Douglas, (generalized) Leontief, or translog functions. It is not usual to start from a specification of the indirect production function al-

---

[2]   The production function $z(\cdot)$ must be continuous and monotonically increasing in ℓ and κ. Moreover, z must be a strictly quasiconcave function, which means that the isoquants must be strictly convex. The latter property does not exclude increasing returns to scale.

though its nice analytical properties would strongly suggest doing that.

In this book we are going to estimate the factor demand functions $\hat{\kappa} = \hat{\kappa}(p_o, p_\kappa, \hat{z})$ and $\hat{\ell} = \hat{\ell}(p_o, p_\kappa, \hat{z})$ because they provide a good basis for the computation of empirical equivalents to the Boiteux marginal costs

$$c = p_o \frac{\partial \hat{\ell}}{\partial \hat{z}} \ (= -p_o \frac{\partial g/\partial \hat{z}}{\partial g/\partial \hat{\ell}}). \tag{1}$$

The wage rate p_o is not equal to unity in the empirical chapters whereas it had been normalized to unity in the theoretical chapters. The negative sign in the brackets comes from $\hat{\ell} > 0$, whereas in the theoretical chapters we had assumed $z_o < 0$.

The reader should not be confused by our taking the "compensated" factor demand as the basis of estimation. First, it depends on observable variables only, unlike the compensated demand which is derived from expenditure minimization given utility. Secondly, it expresses the cost-minimizing factor demand given the output quantity, and hence is a natural candidate for an estimator of a Boiteux equivalent to marginal costs. Thirdly, we always consider changing labor input as caused by changing outputs, whence we follow the most ususal description of producer behavior. Hence, for simplicity, we will drop the "hat" in the following, switching to the notation $\kappa = \kappa(p_o, p_\kappa, z)$ and $\ell = \ell(p_o, p_\kappa, z)$.

24.3 DESIRABLE PROPERTIES OF THE FIRM'S TECHNOLOGY REPRESENTATION

We use the term "technology representation" for any kind of empirical description of a firm's technology, regardless of whether we deal with the direct production function, the system of factor demand functions, or the cost function.

We consider the following subset of all possible technology representations:

a) the technology is described by specified functional relations (the approach is parametric);

b) production (or cost) functions are at least twice continuously differentiable in the relevant variables;

c) the estimates relate to given data and are assumed to hold at least in a neighborhood of these data;

d) the relevant functions relate to the data in describing nonnegative prices, quantities, budget input, and adding-up factor-cost shares.

The description of the technology must be compatible with theory and must have particular desirable properties with respect to the empirical implementation.

24.3.1 COMPATIBILITY OF THEORY AND EMPIRICAL TESTS

(a) Integrability

The system of factor demand which either is estimated directly or derived from the estimated production or cost function must be homogeneous of degree zero in factor prices and input budget. The properties of the "compensated" factor demand functions must be analogous to those of the compensated demand functions: symmetric cross-price effects and negative semidefinite matrix of the "substitution effects". For details see our treatment of the corresponding problems on the demand side.

(b) Incorporation of additional nonprice variables

The chosen description of the technology should include the quality indicators q. These variables can be introduced easily into the cost function and into the indirect production function. However, contrary to the demand side, their inclusion in the direct production function is not difficult because we can estimate this function directly without bothering about the functional specification of factor demand. Complications arise if a direct production function shall be used as a basis for the explicit derivation of a factor demand system.

24.3.2 EMPIRICAL IMPLEMENTATION

(a) Flexibility

As in the case of demand we postulate second-order flexibility of the production (or cost) functions we are going to estimate. This postulate leads to the rejection of Cobb-Douglas specifications and of many CES-type specifications [3] and recommends some sort of second-order Taylor approximation like translog.

(b) Uniformity

Postulating uniformity is usual, but can be given up if a priori information suggests specific differences in the production of the investigated goods.

24.4   LONG–RUN VERSUS SHORT–RUN MARGINAL COSTS

In long-run cost functions every factor of production is variable whereas in short-run cost functions some factors of production are fixed within the length of the period for which the function is taken to be valid.

---

[3] The CES-production function is not flexible of the second-order if more than two inputs are considered.

Owing to the type of cost function, the public enterprise is required to consider either short-run or long-run marginal costs. Both requirements are equivalent if optimal short-run marginal costs are determined for a given optimal amount of fixed factors of production (optimal size of the firm).

This can be shown easily (Varian 1978, 27). Consider some output z whose production depends on aggregate capital inputs κ_F which are fixed in the short run, but variable in the long run. Without restriction of generality we suppress all inputs which are variable both in the short and in the long run.

The short-run cost function is as follows

$$C = C(z, \kappa_F). \tag{2}$$

The long-run cost function, on the other hand, equals

$$C = C(z, \kappa_F(z)) \tag{3}$$

where $\kappa_F(z)$ is the cost minimizing demand for capital inputs. Let z^* be some level of output. Then $\kappa_F^* = \kappa_F(z^*)$ is the associated demand for capital inputs.

Hence long-run marginal cost is

$$\frac{\partial C(z^*, \kappa_F(z^*))}{\partial z} = \frac{\partial C(z^*, \kappa_F^*)}{\partial z} + \frac{\partial C(z^*, \kappa_F^*)}{\partial \kappa_F} \cdot \frac{\partial \kappa_F}{\partial z}. \tag{4}$$

Since κ_F^* is the cost minimizing choice of the capital inputs, given z^*, we must have

$$\frac{\partial C(z^*, \kappa_F^*)}{\partial \kappa_F} = 0. \tag{5}$$

Hence, long-run marginal costs at z^* are equal to short-run marginal costs at (z^*, κ_F^*).

The theoretical identity of long-run and short-run marginal costs is at variance with the opinion of many empirical studies that long-run costs are always higher than short-run costs because the former include operating costs and capacity costs, the latter only operating costs. As this is the source of many misunderstandings, we should confront this practicioners' view with the theoreticians'.

We start from the annual reports of a public enterprise where the production costs of the last year are published, subdivided into different cost components

$$C(t) = C^1(t) + C^2(t) + \ldots + C^N(t) \tag{6}$$

where t refers to the year under consideration.

Best known is the subdivision of costs into

- operating costs, C^{OP}, which are regarded as directly dependent on the output quantities, and

- capacity costs, C^{CAP}, which are regarded as directly dependent on the required plant capacity.

The salary of a London bus driver is part of the operating costs, the investment in building the new Bond Street station is part of the capacity costs. Ex post, of course, in the annual report, costs can always be split as follows

$$C(t) = C^{CAP}(t) + C^{OP}(t). \tag{7}$$

However, if we look at the changes of capacity and of operating costs which took place in some period t, there are the following two alternatives:

(i)   The enterprise changed its capacity within the time interval that is relevant for our measurement ($C^{CAP}(t) \neq 0$). Both capacity and operating inputs contributed to the total costs, they were combined in an optimal or suboptimal way to produce output. Hence we have no empirical figures on how much operating costs would have occured if capacity had remained constant. Therefore, any empirical investigation must consider both parts of the costs simultaneously. C(t) is an approximation to the long-run costs.

(ii)   The enterprise did not change its capacity within the relevant time interval $(C^{CAP}(t) = 0)$. Total costs in period t consisted of operating costs only. $C^{OP}(t)$ is an approximation to the short-run costs.

By means of empirical analysis it is impossible to investigate long-run and short-run costs simultaneously because the only conceivable situations are (i) or (ii). Therefore it is wrong to pick up operating costs alone, calling them "short-run costs", in cases in which both components of costs changed. It would be equally wrong to measure short-run costs by out-of-pocket costs which are only a part of total costs and of operating costs. They can only be an approximation to short-run costs if all other parts of costs remained unchanged within the relevant period.

Usually, the cost estimations are based on a time interval which is comparatively long (e.g. one year). Thus we can assume that in most cases capacity will have changed within this interval. Accordingly, public enterprises will not be informed about their short-run costs, and it will be operational to instruct public enterprises to apply long-run cost functions in their pricing rules [4].

In actual empirical analyses a further problem arises. Typically the enterprise in question will not combine capacity and operating costs in that cost-minimizing way which has been postulated by microeconomic theory. Hence, whatever we do, we will only obtain approximations to the theoretical concepts. For details see section 26.2 below.

---

[4]   This may have been one of the reasons why the British White Paper (1967) instructed nationalized industries to apply long-run marginal-cost pricing. However, this White Paper failed, as clearly revealed in NEDO (1976), and was replaced with a new White Paper (1978) which intentionally avoided any explicit pricing rules. But the White Paper (1978) has not been very influential, which perhaps might have been expected because of the inconsistencies of the 1978-paper as for instance discussed in Heald (1980).

CHAPTER 25   BUS AND UNDERGROUND SERVICES IN LONDON

25.1   RECENT ORGANIZATIONAL AND POLITICAL HISTORY

The modern history of public passenger transportation in London [1] began in 1933 when Herbert Morrison's proposals for a unified organization of all public passenger transportation modes in the London area became law. The London Passenger Transport Act instituted a comprehensive public control of London buses, tramways, and the underground. Moreover, a close coordination with the mainline railway companies was established, with respect to their commuter services in the London area. This coordination included a revenue pooling arrangement and the creation of a Standing Joint Committee to ensure co-operation. The pool ended with the war and the mainline railways' part in the coordinated system was not reestablished after both London Transport and the railway companies were nationalized (effective from 1 January, 1948) as part of the Labour Party nationalization program.

As a nationalized industry London Transport was responsible to the central government, with its degree of autonomy varying over time. In 1970, however, the overall financial and policy control shifted to local government, i.e. to the Greater London Council (GLC). A London Transport Executive (LTE) became responsible for the day-to-day operation of the London (red) buses and the underground [2]. The years to follow were characterized by

---

[1] As a standard reference, not only for the recent, but also for the earlier stages of London Transport see Barker–Robbins (1963, 1974).

[2] Transport (London) Act 1969; the changes came into effect on 1 January, 1970. The former London Transport Board's country bus services and green line coaches were transferred to London Country Bus Services Limited, now a subsidiary of the National

intense political influence on London Transport fares policies.

Starting in 1970, the LTE planned to "conduct its affairs on a commercial basis" [3]. Traffic receipts covered all working expenditures in 1970. However, this line of fares policy lasted for the next two years only. Then a period of "fare freeze" began, starting from the central government's macroeconomic target of fighting inflation by resisting price increases.

The local authority, the GLC, accepted this policy, financing the LT deficits which resulted from keeping output prices constant in spite of increasing input prices. GLC grants eventually amounted to 38% of the working expenditures in 1975 [4]. Thereafter the financial situation was improved by fares increases, reducing GLC grants to 20-25 % of the working expenses during 1977 – 1980. The LTE, during that period, aimed at maximizing passenger miles given the permitted deficit before grants.

The situation changed abruptly when in 1981 the Conservative administration of the GLC was defeated in the local elections and the newly appointed Labour administration started its "Fares Fair" policy. In November 1981 London Transport fares were cut by a third and local rates (i.e. property taxes) increased to finance both the increased LT deficit and the forfeit of £ 50 m of rate support grant from the central government which would have resulted from GLC's policy. The opponents to this policy argued that it was outside the power of GLC under the 1969 Transport Act, and the House of Lords, in Bromley Borough Council v. Greater London Council, declared the "Fares Fair" policy as unlawful [5]. GLC's statutory duty to promote 'integrated, efficient and economic' transport services and LTE's statutory duty to guarantee 'efficiency, economy and safety of operation' were interpreted as obligation to run LT 'on ordinary business principles'.

Bus Company.

[3] London Transport: Annual Report and Accounts 1970, p. 4.

[4] "Fares relief" (revenue support) and "renewal of infrastructure" grants; not included capital grants.

[5] [1982] 1 All E.R. 129. For an extensive discussion see Gravelle (1983).

Most Lords interpreted the words 'economic' and 'economy' in the above quotations in the narrow and constraining sense of not making a loss and required LT to apply the break-even policy it had started from in 1970. Moreover, it was held that the forfeit of central government grants was a failure of GLC's fiduciary duty to the ratepayers, distorting the proper balance of duties to passengers and to ratepayers.

As a consequence of the decision of the House of Lords, LT fares were doubled in March 1982. Then, however, the GLC prepared a proposal which would restore, in nominal terms, the level of fares before the "Fares Fair" experiment, and a declaration by the Divisional Court [6] declared that this fares cut was a lawful exercise of GLC's powers. The Court accentuated the qualification 'so far as practicable' to the break-even requirement in the London Transport Act and argued that the Bromley decision must be interpreted as permitting LT losses provided the general duties (on integrated, efficient and economic transport services ...) were fulfilled [7]. This interpretation actually reverses the Bromley decision and we must conclude that these decisions did not greatly contribute to clarifying the economic meaning of the London Transport Act.

Following this decision, London Transport reduced its fares by 25 % in May 1983, introduced simplified zonal underground fares and a system of travelcards to be used on both bus and underground.

The failure of judicial processes to restrain local public transport losses effectively led to statutory action: in 1983 the control of losses of public transportation was shifted to a considerable degree from the Labour dom-

---

[6] R.v. London Transport Executive, Ex parte Greater London Council [1983] 2 W.L.R. 702. See, once again, Gravelle (1983). There was no appeal against this dicision because the ratepayers were not represented in the case and LTE was in favor of the fares cut.

[7] As distinct from the 1982–situation, the fares cut would not have resulted in a loss of central government grant. The GLC was no longer entitled to the relevant grant because of other, non–transport, overspending.

inated local governments to the Conservative central government [8]. And finally, in 1984 the control of bus and underground services in London was withdrawn totally from the local administration by the establishment of a new corporation, London Regional Transport (LRT), which is responsible to the Secretary of State for Transport [9]. LRT is a planning authority. It controls its subsidiaries, London Bus Ltd. and London Underground Ltd. [10], which companies actually provide the relevant passenger transportation. It has to co-operate with British Rail and other relevant bodies with respect to public passenger traffic in and around Greater London. The introduction of "Capitalcards" in early 1985 to be used on BR and LRT transportation modes has been the first result of such co-operation.

LRT is responsible for the development of market strategies, including fares structures, to bring about maximum use of the services provided within the given financial limits. The Secretary of State for Transport decides how much grant is to be paid and then is allowed to levy a maximum of two thirds from the local authority, GLC, in the form of property taxes.

The central government in 1984 declared its intention to de-regulate all bus services [11]. London is excluded from this proposal "for the time being", but it will clearly have some effect. Following a requirement of the London Regional Transport Act, LRT has already invited other operators to bid for the operation of some of London's bus services under contract.

---

[8] Transport Act 1983.

[9] London Regional Transport Act 1984 chapter 32, following the proposals of a White Paper (1983).

[10] Further subsidiaries are LRT Bus Engineering Ltd. and LRT International.

[11] White Paper (1984).

25.2 RECENT ECONOMIC HISTORY

25.2.1 DEMAND

The demand for London bus and underground services has declined over the last 25 years as can be seen from figure 20. It is reasonable to assume that the increase in private cars is the reason for the decrease in the demand for public transport. An international comparison,however, shows that passenger travel by bus and rail in the recent past has increased in nearly all European countries [12] although the trend towards private transportation also prevails in these countries.

The House of Commons' Transport Committee argued that the decline of public transport in London has been caused mainly by inadequate coordination of the main operators, comparatively high fares and comparatively low service levels [13].

a) Inadequate coordination of the main operators

Public transport in the Greater London is produced by three main operators, namely London Regional Transport (LRT), British Rail (BR) and London Country Bus Services (LCBS). Their failure to achieve better coordination refers to services, timetables, fares structures, interchange facilities as well as to general investment planning. The most surprising example of the lack of coordination was the non-existence of any through tickets allowing interchange from London buses to the underground and vice versa. Even the simple idea of a "travelcard", valid on both buses and the underground, which gives freedom to interchange freely without financial penalty was introduced only in 1983.

---

[12] For details see: Transport Committee (1982, xliii), Transport Statistics, Great Britain, 197. - 198., chapter on international comparisons.

[13] Transport Committee (1982).

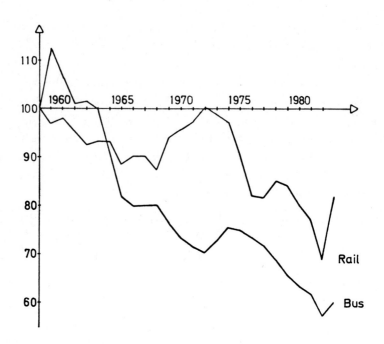

Figure 20: Passenger miles (1958 = 100)

Source: London Transport in 19.., published annually 1958-1962 ;
London Transport Executive, Annual report and accounts, since 1970.

Notes: Bus data from 1958-1962 have been adjusted in two ways, first
to exclude coaches and country buses 1958-1962 and second to switch from
"miles travelled" (indicated in the sources until 1964) to "miles paid for"
(indicated from 1965 on). For details see Bös (1985b).

For the single ride it is still not possible to buy through-tickets if both LRT modes must be used to reach the destination.

There have been many sophisticated proposals to bring about a new unified administration of all different public transportation modes in the Greater London area [14], the latest by the House of Commons' Transport Committee [15]. The actual reorganization by the London Regional Transport Act (1984) was much less ambitious and did not create joint LRT and BR bodies [16]. However, some responsibilities for *coordination* between bus, underground and British Rail transportation have been created by the new legislation. Moreover, part II of the London Regional Transport Act contains reserve powers to bring BR's London services under LRT's *control*. The provision will only be brought into effect if a special order is made by the Secretary of State (who is said to hope not to have to make such an order).

b) Comparatively high fares

1980 comparisons with public transportation systems in major European cities contrast the 78 % "farebox ratio" [17] of London bus and underground services with the lower 60 % of Munich, 50 % of Vienna, 30 % of Brussels and 23 % of Milan. But, after the failure of GLC's attempt to join the low fares league ("fares fair" policy), the trend has been to maintain at least a 75 to 80 % farebox ratio.

---

[14] See Glaister (1982a, 163–165) for an overview.

[15] Transport Committee (1982, lxvii–lxxiii).

[16] With the exception of the London Regional Passengers' Committee which is a users' consultative body without too great an influence.

[17] Transport Committee (1982, xlvi). The farebox ratio is defined as the proportion of fare income paid by the travelling public to expenditure incurred on operating, maintaining and administering the undertaking. The definition excludes interest payments, depreciation and renewal provisions and concession payments made by the authorities for the aged and handicapped.

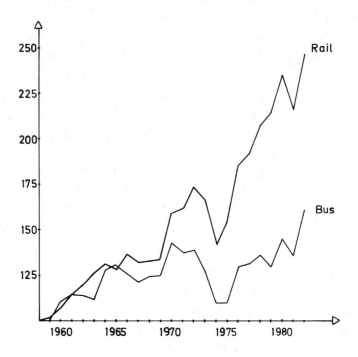

Figure 21: Real average fares per passenger mile (1958 = 100)

Source: London Transport in 19.., published annually 1958–1962; Passenger Transport in Great Britain 1969 (Ministry of Transport, HMSO,
London); London Transport Executive, Annual report and accounts, since
1970; Annual Abstracts of Statistics 1984, CSO.

Notes: There were two adjustments of the time series 1958–1964, first
to exclude coaches and second to switch from "miles travelled" to "miles
paid for". Real terms were obtained by dividing by the Retail price index,
1970=100. For details see Bös (1985b).

Figure 21 shows that London bus and rail fares have been increasing in real terms during the last 25 years, interrupted only by the "fare freeze" policy of the early seventies and the "fares fair" policy of 1981/82. This development typically has led to bus and underground prices which exceed British Rail prices for comparably short distances [18].

The average fares of figure 21 are the ratios of annual traffic revenues (fare incomes) and the annual passenger miles. The high level of aggregation will be employed throughout our analysis and all price elasticities will refer to the aggregate average fares. This approach is usually adopted in most investigations on London Bus and underground demand and the data are easily available from LT's annual reports.

The aggregation implies skipping over many problems of fares policy. In fact, London bus and underground fares follow a graduated scale, starting from basic flat fares for travelling within London's central zones and stepwise increasing fares for longer trips. The flat fares for central London journeys were introduced as a part of the fares fair policy and maintained afterwards because they were successful in increasing use of the services.

The advantages and disadvantages of flat versus graduated fares were intensively discussed after the "Harrow experiment" in 1981 [19]. This experiment replaced a graduated scale (10p, 16p, 24p, 32p, 40p) with a 20p flat fare on a number of routes in the Harrow area. The arguments against graduated fares were

-   graduated fares inhibit trip length. Hence, the increase of longer-distance trips might cushion the loss of shorter-distance trips if fares are simplified.

---

[18] Transport Committee (1982, xliv).

[19] See LT's report R 244 (Fairhurst (1981)).

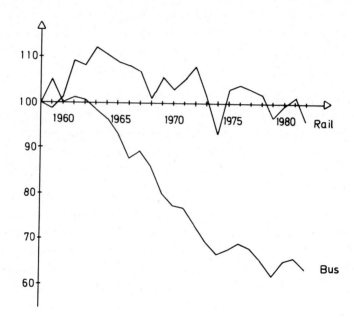

Figure 22: Car miles per route miles (1958=100)

Source: London Transport in 19.., published annually 1958-1962; Passenger Transport in Great Britain 1969; London Transport Executive, Annual report and accounts, since 1970.

Notes: Bus data from 1958-1962 were adjusted to exclude coaches. For details see Bös (1985b).

- graduated fares create incentives for fraud and overriding. As this sort of dishonest behavior is eliminated by flat fares, they can be set at a lower level than the average graduated fare.

- graduated fares inhibit the transition to one-person operated buses because they are complicated to administer.

On the other hand, a flat fare system deters short-distance trips and as a great part of LRT fares income results from short trips, a one-flat-fare system for all distances would considerably decrease revenues. Hence, the above mentioned mixed system was chosen, with flat fares in central London zones only.

It should be mentioned that most arguments in favor of flat fares hold also for a system of Passes or Travelcards. In fact, the introduction of Travelcards in 1983 was a very successful innovation in LT's fares structure: according to recent estimates it has increased the use of services by 15 per cent (10 per cent on the buses and 20 per cent on the underground).

c) Comparatively low service quality

We must first decide upon the best indicator of bus und underground quality levels. Assuming passengers respond most to the total journey time, waiting times and in-vehicle-times suggest themselves as the natural choice of quality indicators. However, this time aspect neglects other quality factors, for instance decaying, old and dirty stations or rolling stock [20].

As our time series consists of the annual data 1958-1982 only and we are using the complicated AIDS system, there are not enough degrees of freedom to introduce many quality indicators into our estimation. Moreover, we want to follow the theoretical approach of this book in concentrating on that facet of quality which is dominant with respect to individual evaluations. In case of transportation waiting time is the dominant facet of quality.

However, for the long time span of our investigation, direct data on

---

[20] For details see Transport Committee (1982, xxxv - xxxix).

waiting times are not available. Hence, we had to use a proxy: the number of vehicle miles per route mile probably is the best indicator. Figure 22 shows that this indicator exhibits a decline of bus quality of 36,3 % and of underground quality of 3,7 % from 1958 to 1982. It may be noted that both indicators of bus and of underground quality are very low in the early seventies, especially 1974. These low qualities are due to staff shortages.

Waiting time is quite significant in explaining bus demand, but not in underground demand where the overall level of supply, i.e. vehicle miles, is a more significant indicator of quality (see chapter 26 below). This different response of bus and of underground demand indicates that the public significantly responds to waiting times where they actually are considered as causing trouble, as is the case with bus supply. As underground waiting times are satisfactorily low, demand responds to overall supply which is not only determined by the vehicle miles run at a given route mileage but also by the opening of new lines (especially the Victoria line) and the extension of old ones (especially the Heathrow extension).

25.2.2   COSTS

The period of our investigation was a period of increasing (real) wages and prices of capital and other input goods, including the oil price shocks of the seventies. It was a period of intensive technical progress although the impression is strong that this does not appear to have influenced London bus and underground services greatly. In the following we present some details of labor and capital inputs in the provision of public passenger transport services in London.

Staff related costs represent about 70 % of the "total costs of operations" of London bus and underground [21]. Staff related costs in 1983

---

[21]   See e.g. London Transport: Annual Report and Accounts 1983, p.30.

amounted to £ 600m. This high labor intensity of production is not only due to the particular character of the services involved, but decisively depends on "considerable dilatoriness" [22] in dealing with overmanning, and on the wage levels brought about by the influence of the Transport and General Workers' Union.

The central manning problems are: too many crew-operated services and an antiquated labor intensive system of ticket sales and control.

During the recent twenty years more than 50 % of crew-operated buses have been replaced by one-person operated buses, which led to a considerable reduction in bus staff numbers (figures 23, 24). The percentage of one-person operated services is eventually expected to approach 100 % [23]. This development is made possible by the growth of off-bus sales of tickets (mainly travelcard and capitalcard), by simpler fare structures and simpler ways of on-bus ticketing. Moreover, recently the maintenance and fuel costs of the new generation of one-person operated buses have been lowered considerably.

With the exception of the Victoria line most underground rolling stock originally was designed for two-person operation although tickets have always been sold off-board. After a recent agreement with unions on one-person operation, however, the investment to convert rolling stock is going on [24]. Even driverless train operation is possible from the technological point of view although the psychological disadvantages of such a system seem to outweigh the cost advantages.

---

[22] Transport Committee (1982, xxxv).

[23] See Monopolies and Mergers Commission (1984, 96-97).

[24] One-person operation is possible if sliding-door stock is available which can be operated by the driver.

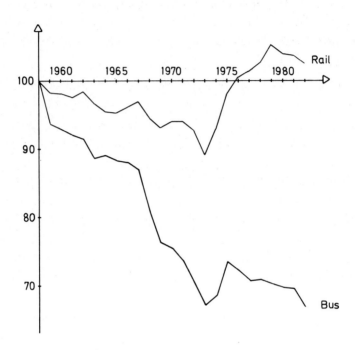

Figure 23: Staff (1958=100)

Source: London Transport in 19.., published annually 1958-1962; London Transport Executive, Annual report and accounts, since 1970.

Notes: Coaches have been excluded in data from 1958-1962. The Central Administration staff has been partitioned 60 : 40 (Bus - Rail). For details see Bös (1985b).

Further transition to one-person operations depends on capital investment funds for the modernization of rolling stock and on the co-operation of the trade unions, whose minimal requirement is the protection of the livelihoods of the present labor force.

Similar problems prevent any quick changes in fare collection and ticket inspection, although international comparisons give good examples of how to achieve faster fare collection by off-bus and off-train ticket sales and by "honor" systems combined with occasional intensive controls at individual stations and trains. Recent advances in fare collection, however, have been the introduction of zonal fares in central London (1982), of travelcards for use on both bus and the underground (1983) and of capitalcards for use on bus, underground and British Rail (1985). Note that the introduction of the travelcard and the capitalcard are of no relevance for our empirical study as we use 1958–1982 data only.

Non-staff operating costs are less important. Fuel and power amount to £ 50 m in 1983, other materials and services to £ 64 m, depreciation of rolling stock, plant and machinery to £ 85,1 m. The oil price shock led to a rise of costs of fuel and power from 3.7 % of the operating costs in 1973 to 6.3 % in 1974. Since 1974, however, they have remained within the 6.5 to 7.5 % bracket.

Investment expenditures (figure 25) reflect a rapid increase in bus investment in spite of the construction of several new underground lines and extensions. The peaks in bus investment in the early and mid-seventies resulted from the purchases of one-person operated buses which replaced one third of the crew-operated ones. Subsequently, however, disadvantages of the one-person operated buses became clear (mechanically lower reliability, loss of passengers because of the automatically closing doors etc.) [25]. After solving these problems, a new generation of one-person operated buses was introduced in the end-seventies and early eighties.

---

[25] For details see Monopolies and Mergers Commission (1984, 45-47, 108).

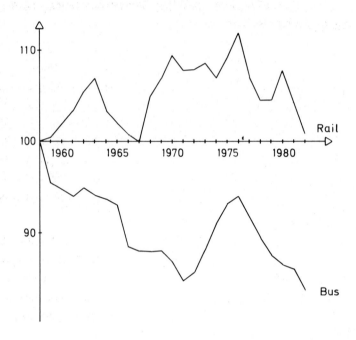

Figure 24a: Passenger rolling stock (1958=100)

Source: London Transport in 19.., published annually 1958-1962; London
Transport Executive, Annual report and accounts, since 1970.

Notes: Coaches have been excluded in data from 1958-1962. For details
see Bös (1985b).

The underground investment program also concentrated on the replacement of rolling stock, and lately on the renewal of stations. Most spectacular were the new underground lines, and extensions, built since 1962: the Victoria line [26] 1962–1971 (including the Brixton extension), the Piccadilly line extension to Heathrow (1970–1977, now to be extended to terminal 4), and the Jubilee line (1971–1979). Although these investment programs were spectacular, the reader should not overestimate their financial importance compared with the investment in rolling stock and other LT expenditures. If we consider the five years where investment in the Jubilee line and the Piccadilly line extension to Heathrow were at their peak (1972–1976), we obtain the following average expenditures:

Operating costs (Ø 1972 – 1976)

Staff related costs	£ 184,9 m
Power and fuel	£ 13,1 m

Investment expenditures (Ø 1972 – 1976)

Jubilee line	£ 13,0 m
Piccadilly line extension	£ 4,9 m
Railway rolling stock	£ 11,4 m
Buses	£ 8,7 m
Other investments (e.g. stations, signalling and construction)	£ 13,8 m

---

[26] To cost-benefit analysts the Victoria line has become well-known because of Foster and Beesley's (1963) study.

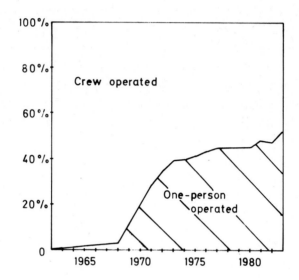

Figure 24b: One-person operated buses

Source: London Transport Executive, Annual report and accounts, since
1970.

Notes: For details see Bös (1985b).

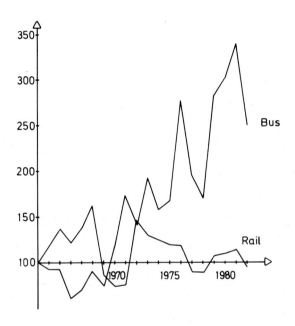

Figure 25a: Investments (real) (1958=100)

Source: London Transport Executive, Annual report and accounts, since 1970.

Notes: For details see Bös (1985b).

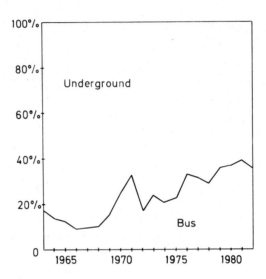

Figure 25b: Bus versus underground investments

Source: London Transport Executive, Annual report and accounts, since 1970; London Transport in 19.., published annually 1958-1962.

Notes: For details see Bös (1985b).

25.3   EMPIRICAL STUDIES ON BUS AND UNDERGROUND DEMAND

25.3.1   LONDON TRANSPORT'S ECONOMIC RESEARCH REPORTS

After many earlier attemps [27] the most successful demand estimation by LT's staff is presented in the research report R 248 (1981) [28]. This investigation is based on weekly data of the period 1970 – 1980 and applies the following specification to bus (i = 1) and underground (i = 2) demand:

$$z_i = a_o \; exp(a_1 t) \; p_i^{b_1} \; exp(b_2 \frac{p_i - p_k}{p_i + p_k}) \; exp(b_3 \frac{p_i - p_{BR}}{p_i + p_{BR}}) \cdot$$
$$r^{b_4} \; q_i^{d_i} \; q_k^{d_k} \; exp(\ldots) \tag{1}$$

where we have suppressed the goods indices, i = 1,2, of the coefficients a_o to d_k. This demand function shows precisely those functional relationships with which we deal in the theoretical parts of this book, demand being explained by the own price, the price of substitutes (p_k referring to the other mode, p_{BR} referring to British Rail), income r, and quality levels q_1, q_2. The variables are measured by the following indicators:

z_i – receipts at constant fares, i.e. traffic receipts for the relevant period divided by an index of the level of fares in that period, $z_i = (p_i z_i)/(p_i/p_i^o)$. Hence the regression analysis explicitly refers to $p_i^o z_i$. As p_i^o, the price of a base period, is constant, all results refer to z_i as well;

p_i, p_k – an index of fares based on the gross yields of fares revisions, divided by the index of retail prices; a similar transformation holds for p_{BR};

---

[27] For instance report R 201 (Fairhurst (1973)), report R 210 (Fairhurst–Morris (1975)) and report R 235 (Rendle–Mack–Fairhurst (1978)).

[28] Frerk–Lindsay–Fairhurst (1981).

$r-$ level of real retail sales; as a proxy for the income of the representative consumer;

q_i, q_k- level of bus and train car miles operated (exponentially smoothed for some models) as proxies for the quality levels.

The term $exp(\dots)$ refers to further variables which improve the statistical fit, such as weather, extent of tourism, level of car stock in the UK and dummy variables for main fares revisions and for the opening of Heathrow Central. $Exp(a_1 t)$ is a simple time trend.

The above specification of demand and choice of indicators avoid multicollinearities between prices. Autoregression of variables was avoided by applying the usual transformation of all variables.

a) Fares elasticities

The demand functions (1) imply the following *fares elasticities*

$$\varepsilon(z_i, p_i) = b_1 + b_2 \frac{2p_i p_k}{(p_i + p_k)^2} + b_3 \frac{2p_i p_{BR}}{(p_i + p_{BR})^2} \qquad (2)$$

$$\varepsilon(z_i, p_k) = -b_2 \frac{2p_i p_k}{(p_i + p_k)^2}. \qquad (3)$$

Surprisingly, the price elasticities turn out to be nearly constant over the investigated period [29] (table 4).

---

[29] $2(p_i p_k)/(p_i + p_k)^2$ is always of the order of 0.5, and so is $2(p_i p_{BR})/(p_i + p_{BR})^2$.

TABLE 4: SUMMARY OF ELASTICITY FINDINGS, R 248[1]

Fares elasticities (1 – bus, 2 – rail)

	Weekday	Weekend (off–peak)
ε_{11}	−0.52	−0.57
ε_{12}	+0.17	+0.17
ε_{22}	−0.40	−0.48
ε_{21}	+0.15	+0.15

Service elasticities (1 – bus, 2 – rail)

	Weekday	Weekend (off–peak)
$\varepsilon(z_1, q_1)$	+0.66	+0.54
$\varepsilon(z_1, q_2)$	−0.10	−0.24
$\varepsilon(z_2, q_2)$	+0.20	+0.30
$\varepsilon(z_2, q_1)$	−0.33	−0.19

Income elasticities (1 – bus, 2 – rail) [2]

	Weekday	Weekend (off–peak)
$\varepsilon(z_1, r)$	+0.20	not sign.
$\varepsilon(z_2, r)$	+0.45	+0.50

---

[1] The above elasticities are taken from the summary pages of LT's report although the off-peak elasticities result from a combination of significant off-peak coefficients and significant peak coefficients which are substituted where the off-peak coefficients are not significant.

[2] Estimated as retail sales elasticities.

The results indicate that bus and underground demand respond inelastically to fares changes; all absolute values of fares elasticities are smaller than unity. Underground fall below bus elasticities, peak below off-peak elasticities. The latter difference is small because R 248 identified peak with weekday traffic, off-peak with weekend traffic. In an earlier report, R 218 (1975) [30], the peak was taken to cover the periods 07.30 – 09.30 and 16.00 – 18.30 and the off-peak 09.30 – 16.00 and 18.30 – 21.00, all data referring to Monday – Friday only, other data not included. This investigation led to the tentative conclusion that off-peak traffic is approximately twice as elastic as peak traffic [31].

The cross-price elasticities indicate that bus and underground are substitutes ($\varepsilon_{ik} > 0$). Bus demand is more elastic than underground demand . Weekend demand is more elastic then weekday demand.

The constancy of the direct elasticities has recently been challenged in report R 252 (1982) [32] which postulates fares elasticities which increase with increasing fares. This hypothesis has not yet been put to an extended empirical test comparable to R 248. In a worked example, however, Fairhurst used the specification [33]

$$z_i = a_o exp(-bp_i). \tag{4}$$

Empirical tests of this hypothesis are to be expected.

---

[30] Fairhurst–Lindsay–Morris (1975).

[31] Fairhurst–Lindsay–Morris (1975, 18).

[32] Fairhurst (1982).

[33] The same specification has been used in Bös–Tillmann–Zimmermann (1984).

b) Income and service elasticities

Let us now turn to the *income* and *service* elasticities of report R 248 which are represented in table 4.

The *income elasticities* are less than unity for both bus and underground. Hence, following the most usual definition, both bus and underground are "necessities", bus even more than underground. We will see in the next subsection that the percentage of higher-income earners in underground consumption is significantly larger than in bus consumption [34].

Finally, the *service elasticities* reflect the great influence of quality on bus demand in contrast to underground demand. The reason may be the awareness of the population of the continuous decrease of bus quality whereas underground quality fluctuates around the same level (see figure 22 above).

25.3.2   FURTHER EMPIRICAL EVIDENCE

The response of bus and underground demand to fares, incomes and service qualities has been estimated in a variety of books, papers and research reports of other official or non-official UK institutions.

a) Fares elasticities

Let us begin with Glaister's (1976b) unpublished paper whose main advance in estimating *fares elasticities* was to consider the autoregression of residuals which had been neglected in the earlier LT economic research reports. Most interesting are the high underground fares elasticities obtained in his study.

---

[34] See Grey (1975), chapter 6.

TABLE 5:   SUMMARY OF ELASTICITY FINDINGS
Glaister (1976b), Glaister–Lewis (1978)

Fares elasticities $(1 - \text{bus}, 2 - \text{rail})$

Uncompensated (Glaister (1976b))	Compensated (Glaister–Lewis (1978))	

Weekday		Peak		Off–peak[1]
ε_{11}	-0.56	η_{11}	-0.35	-0.87
ε_{12}	$+0.30$	η_{12}	$+0.14$	not sign.
ε_{22}	-1.00	η_{22}	-0.30	-0.75
ε_{21}	$+1.11$	η_{21}	not sign.	not sign.

Income elasticities $(1 - \text{bus}, 2 - \text{rail})$

(Glaister–Lewis (1978))

	Peak	Off–peak
$\varepsilon(z_1, r)$	0.40	0.40
$\varepsilon(z_2, r)$	0.80	0.80

---

[1] "We took an estimate of roundly 2.5 in drawing peak and off–peak values from 5–day 24–hour relationship." (Glaister–Lewis (1978, 348)).

TABLE 6: SUMMARY OF INCOME ELASTICITY FINDINGS
Grey (1975) [1]

Elasticities of bus trips and bus fares with respect to gross household income

Gross household income per year (£)

	400	875	1,375	1,750	2,600	6,000
number of trips	0.79	0.41	0.19	0.08	–0.12	–0.52
fare per trip	0.23	0.12	0.08	0.07	0.05	0.03

Elasticities of rail [2] trips and rail fares with respect to gross household income

Gross household income per year (£)

	400	875	1,375	1,750	2,600	6,000
number of trips, all ticket types	1.21	0.55	0.35	0.28	0.19	0.08
fare per trip, ordinary single tickets only	0.17	0.26	0.31	0.32	0.32	0.25

[1] Source: Grey (1975, 115, 119).
[2] Rail includes both London underground and British Rail suburban services.

However, the next paper (Glaister–Lewis (1978)) presents lower estimates. Moreover, by simply inserting uncompensated elasticities and income elasticities into the Slutsky equations, the authors compute compensated elasticities which are shown in table 5. However, as most cross-price elasticities are not significant [35], the Slutsky symmetry hypothesis cannot be tested by the given material.

b) Income elasticities

Most impressive are Grey's (1975) estimates of income elasticities because they explicitly differentiate between household income groups (table 6). He computed income elasticities of the number of trips and of the trip length, the latter measured by the average fare per trip. The sample refers to 1971–1972 figures where the median income of all households in the "Greater London Transportation Survey" is £ 1750 per annum. The elasticities are computed for both bus and rail where rail includes both London underground and British Rail suburban services.

Grey's results may be interpreted by concentrating on three characteristic household groups.

(i)   Low-income earners (£ 400), when given more income, increase both bus and rail trips to a remarkable extent: underground even is treated as a luxury! They also increase the average trip lengths, especially when using the bus. However, their main response is to use bus or rail much more often; increasing the trip length is only a secondary response.

(ii)   The median-income household's (£ 1750) number and length of bus trips remains nearly unchanged; however, it increases both number and length of rail trips.

---

[35] Off-peak η_{12} = off-peak η_{21} = 0.28($\pm$ 0.74) (!).

(iii)   High-income earners ($£$ 6000) treat bus trips as an inferior good and
if they go by bus, leave the length of their trips unchanged. Rail
trips, too, do not change very much as a result of income increases,
but trip length increases, for instance because people can afford to
live further away from where they work.

Further estimates of income elasticities have been published by Glaister
and Lewis (1978). Their income elasticities (table 5) are comparatively high
as compared with R 248 (table 4) and Grey (table 6). Moreover, they assume
identical peak and off-peak income elasticities, which is not very plausible
because they follow the R 218 differentiation between peak and off-peak
periods according to the hours of the day. Identical peak and off-peak
income elasticities are only plausible on the basis of the R 248 differentiation
according to weekday versus weekend. In fact, the hypothesis of different
peak and off-peak income elasticities cannot be falsified on the basis of LT's
R 248 estimates.

c) Service elasticities

Using a model developed by Glaister, the trade-off between fares and
quality levels recently has been challenged in the Department of Transport's (1982) report on urban public transport subsidies in the main English conurbations. Let us concentrate on the application of the model to
London. The report starts from low direct price elasticities (-0.3) for bus
and underground) and from the cross price elasticities of R 248. The service
quality, measured by "waiting time equivalents", takes account of waiting
time, load factor and in-vehicle-time as most appropriate quality indicators.
The model covers the whole transport system, which implies consideration
of private-public transport interrelationships [36], including the mutual congestion effects. As a result, the report concludes that fares and service
levels on London bus and underground are out of balance in benefit-cost
terms. A balanced position would be achieved by reducing bus fares and

---

[36]   For particular investigations on London taxis see Beesley (1979), and Beesley–
Glaister (1983).

bus services up to 30 % while on the underground reducing fare by about 10 % and increasing the underground services (miles) by nearly 20 %. The welfare-improving effect of the underground quality increase is based on its low costs. The additional costs to London Transport are low, and there is no effect on road congestion.

25.4   EMPIRICAL STUDIES ON BUS AND UNDERGROUND COSTS

An interesting estimate of bus and underground costs was provided by the economic research report R 252 (1982) [37]. The estimation started from two basic assumptions:

(i)   that LT in 1982 was "operating at broadly minimum marginal costs given the present infrastructure [38]. Both cutting and expanding output would increase marginal costs although the marginal-cost functions of bus and underground were thought of as being rather flat. As expected, the underground MC-function is flatter than that of bus transport, mainly because of the higher percentage of staff costs in expanding bus services and the need to pay higher wages to attract the necessary employees. It would, however, have been better to test for minimum marginal costs at 1982 outputs instead of assuming it.

(ii)   that the area under the MC-curves at 1982 output levels be equal to 1982 total costs. This second assumption, by including total costs, characterizes the relevant functions as long-run marginal-cost functions.

The best fit was obtained by choosing quadratic marginal-cost functions

$$MC_1 = 29.2 - 15.2z_1 + 3.45z_1^2 \quad (bus) \tag{5}$$

---

[37] R 252 (Fairhurst (1982)); especially the appendix (Lindsay (1982)).
[38] Fairhurst (1982, 7).

$$MC_2 = 32.9 - 20.5z_2 + 3.93z_2^2 \quad (underground) \tag{6}$$

where z_1 and z_2 are measured in billion passenger miles.

By construction, the marginal cost functions (5) and (6) have their minimum at the 1982 values, namely,

- 13.3 p per bus passenger mile at an estimated output of 2.7 billion passenger miles;

- 6.2 p per underground passenger mile at 2.6 billion miles.

However, the quadratic functions turned out to underestimate marginal costs and linear cost functions were therefore used in the London submodel of METS (1984) [39]. The recommended functions are of the type

Total costs = Fixed costs plus marginal cost times passenger miles[40].

$$\tag{7}$$

By substituting the actual 1982 figures [41] we obtain marginal costs of 17 p per bus passenger mile and 8 p per underground passenger mile.

The constant marginal-cost assumption can also be found in the simulation analyses of Glaister–Lewis (1978) and Glaister-Collings (1978), as shown in table 7. Bus data were obtained from LT's bus scheduling model, peak data always including the allowance of 5 p per passenger mile for congestion costs caused by buses. The underground data are based on information from LT. The differences between peak and off-peak, and between short-run and long-run, marginal costs are somewhat tentative and "need to

---

[39] Model for evaluating transport subsidies (METS), Department of Transport and M.J.N. Consulting Limited.

[40] The same type of cost function could be formulated with respect to car miles.

[41] METS (1984), user manual, p. 37, splits bus costs in 1982 into £ 362 m variable and £ 76 m fixed costs; underground into £ 186 m variable and £ 186 m fixed costs.

be revised as further evidence becomes available" [42]. Glaister-Lewis even challenge the hypothesis that the large off-peak capacities must imply much lower off-peak marginal cost. As a large proportion of maintenance work is done during the off-peak, the number of trains available in the off-peak time is significantly reduced.

Finally we should mention Glaister-Lewis' (1978) tentative estimation of marginal social costs of private vehicle use. They consider two alternatives: social marginal costs of a peak passenger mile (a) decline linearly from 21 p at current traffic levels to 7 p at half that level; (b) decline linearly from 15 p to 11 p. Case (b) in their opinion is more appropriate for London.

---

[42] Glaister–Lewis (1978, 350).

TABLE 7: SUMMARY OF CONSTANT MARGINAL COST STUDIES
(pence per passenger mile)

Glaister-Lewis (1978); nominal values of 1975

Cases	Bus		Rail	
	Peak	Off-peak	Peak	Off-peak
1(short-run)	11	6	2	1
2(long-run)	14	6	30	1
3(long-run)	14	6	10	1

Glaister–Collings (1978); nominal values of 1975

Bus	Rail
7	2

Department of Transport (1984); nominal values of 1982

new cost function [1] (total costs = fixed costs plus marginal cost times passenger miles)

Bus	Rail
17	8

---

[1] Using the data of METS (1984, 37).

CHAPTER 26 ESTIMATING NORMATIVE AND POSITIVE PRICES FOR BUS AND UNDERGROUND IN LONDON

26.1 THE AIDS SPECIFICATION OF DEMAND

26.1.1 ANALYTICAL OUTLINE OF THE SPECIFICATION

Let us specify a demand system which is capable of investigating the interdependencies between public transport, as supplied by London Regional Transport (LRT), private transport, and the aggregate consumption of all other goods. Such an investigation requires a four good demand system, referring to LRT bus services (i = 1), LRT underground services (i = 2), private transport in private cars as well as in taxis (i = 3), and the aggregate "good" which represents all other goods (i = 4). The demanded quantities x_i, i = 1,2, are measured in passenger miles.

Recall the AIDS–specification of Marshallian demand as defined in chapter 23

$$
w_i = (a_i - b_i a_0) + \sum_k d_{ik} ln \ p_k
$$
$$
+ b_i (ln \ r - \sum_k a_k ln \ p_k - \frac{1}{2} \sum_g \sum_k d_{gk} ln \ p_g ln \ p_k) \quad i = 1, \ldots, 4. \tag{1}
$$

Adding up, homogeneity and Slutsky symmetry are taken into account by imposing the following restrictions

$$\sum_i a_i = 1, \sum_i b_i = 0, \sum_g d_{gk} = 0, d_{gk} = d_{kg}. \qquad (2)$$

The negativity of the matrix of substitution effects cannot be imposed by restrictions of the parameters and must be tested a posteriori [1].

Imposing the above restrictions on the AIDS system (1) leads to the specification

$$w_i(p,r) = (a_i - b_i a_o) + b_i ln\ r + \sum_{\substack{k=1 \\ k\neq i}}^{4} (d_{ik}^S - b_i a_k) ln\ p_k$$

$$- (\sum_{\substack{k=1 \\ k\neq i}}^{4} d_{ik}^S + b_i a_i) ln\ p_i \qquad (3a)$$

$$+ \frac{1}{2} \sum_{\substack{g,k=1 \\ g<k}}^{4} b_i d_{gk}^S ln^2(p_g/p_k) \quad i = 1,2,3$$

where a_4 is short-hand notation for $1 - \sum_{k=1}^{3} a_k$, and d_{ij}^S denotes the symmetric coefficients of the non-linear AIDS terms, $d_{ij}^S = d_{ij}$ if $i < j$, and $d_{ij}^S = d_{ji}$ if $i > j$. The above specification implies that the empirical estimation of the budget share equations for w_1, w_2, and w_3 is sufficient to implement the whole demand system because the budget share equation w_4 can be computed residually by applying the conditions (2) and considering

$$w_4(p,r) = 1 - \sum_{k=1}^{3} w_k(p,r). \qquad (3b)$$

After estimating Marshallian demand we can proceed to compute Hick-

---

[1] For details see subsection 26.1.2 below.

sian demand functions. Recall the specification in chapter 23 above:

$$\hat{w}_i = \frac{p_i \hat{x}_i}{R} = a_i + \sum_k d_{ik} ln\ p_k + b_i V b_o \Pi_k p_k^{b_k} \quad i = 1, \ldots, 4. \qquad (23 - 19)$$

Knowing all coefficients a_o, a_i, b_i, d_{ik}, we only have to determine b_o and V to obtain $\hat{w}_i$. The coefficient b_o cannot be estimated empirically but must be determined according to a plausible empirical implementation of

$$ln\ R_B(p) = ln\ R_S(p) + b_o \Pi_i p_i^{b_i}. \qquad (23 - 13)$$

Since b_o can be interpreted as the logarithm of the ratio of bliss and of subsistence expenditures when prices are unity (i.e. in the base year [2)]), choosing a plausible value is not difficult.

After finding a plausible value of b_o we can compute the value of V for every subsequent year of our investigation, t = 1958,..., 1982:

$$V(p_t, r_t) = \frac{ln(r_t/R_S(p_t))}{ln(R_B(p_t)/R_S(p_t))}$$

where the expenditure functions R_B and R_S are determined by the estimated coefficients and the given information on prices and income.

Given b_o and V we have the information which is needed to compute the Hicksian demand functions. As b_o and V enter the Hicksian demand functions in a multiplicative way, fixing b_o means a normalization of V. The coefficients of the estimated demand functions, therefore, are not very sensitive to the chosen value of b_o. The ordinal ranking of different price systems according to welfare V is independent of the choice of b_o.

As a next step we introduce *quality* into our demand system, measured by the bus and underground quality indicators q_1 and q_2. We do not introduce quality indicators of private transport and of aggregate consumption.

[2)] See the following subsection.

The qualities q_1 and q_2 are implemented like prices, but without restriction on the parameters, as there are no particular adding-up or Slutsky requirements. Straightforward extension of the AIDS demand system would imply the introduction of so many second-order terms that empirical estimations on the basis of our annual data would become impossible. Hence the analysis was restricted to a loglinear expansion of the Marshallian demand system

$$ln \; R(p,q,V) = ln \; R(p,V) + \sum_{k=1}^{2} d_k^q ln \; q_k \tag{4}$$

which implies the following budget share equations

$$w_i(p,q,r) = w_i(p,r) - \sum_{k=1}^{2} b_i d_k^q ln \; q_k \qquad i = 1,2,3 \tag{5a}$$

$$w_4(p,q,r) = 1 - \sum_{i=1}^{3} w_i(p,q,r). \tag{5b}$$

We estimated (5a) as a non-linear system of equations in the original coefficients $a_i, i = 1,2,3$; $b_i, i = 1,2,3$; $d_{ik}^S, i = 1,2,3, k = 1,\ldots,4, i \neq k$; d_1^q, d_2^q [3]. The summation conditions (2) were then used to obtain the remaining coefficients $a_4, b_4, d_{ik}, i = 4, \; k = 1,\ldots,4$.

---

[3] Numerical identification of a_o typically is problematical when estimating the AIDS system. Hence we will have to use a priori information on a_o as explained in the following subsection.

26.1.2   THE EMPIRICAL IMPLEMENTATION

We estimated the non-linear system of equations (5a) by *maximum likelihood* [4], based on annual data from 1958 to 1982.

As AIDS basically is a Taylor series expansion, we *normalized* the 1970– values of all prices and income to unity and transformed the other values correspondingly. By this procedure price and income logarithms became small figures whence the Taylor approximation worked much better than with the original, not transformed, figures.

Our normalization is compatible with the representative consumer's budget constraint. We divide

$$\sum_i p_i x_i = r \tag{6}$$

by the 1970 income of the representative consumer $r(70)$ and expand the left-hand side by multiplying every price by $1 = p_i(70)/p_i(70)$:

$$\sum_i \frac{p_i}{p_i(70)} \cdot \frac{p_i(70)x_i}{r(70)} = \frac{r}{r(70)}. \tag{7}$$

This equation can be rewritten as

$$\sum_i p_i^n x_i^n = r^n, \tag{8}$$

using suitably defined normalized variables. The time series p_i^n and r^n fluctuate around 1. It can be shown that the price and income elasticities of demand are invariant under this transformation.

As Deaton and Muellbauer (1980b, 316) pointed out, the *practical identification of a_o* is likely to be problematical, but this can be overcome by

---

[4] We use an implementation of a full information maximum likelihood estimator (FIML), see Weihs (1984).

assigning a value to a_o a priori. For that purpose consider the subsistence expenditure function

$$ln\ R_S(p,q) = a_o + \sum_i a_i ln\ p_i + \frac{1}{2}\sum_i\sum_k d_{ik}^* ln\ p_i ln\ p_k + \sum_{k=1}^{2} d_k^q ln\ q_k \quad (9)$$

for the basic year 1970. In this year all prices and qualities are normalized to unity and therefore their logarithms vanish. Hence, in our estimation, a_o must be the logarithm of the subsistence expenditures of the "representative Londoner" in 1970. We assume these subsistence expenditures to be 25 % of our 1970 normalized income of unity and therefore $a_o = -1.4$.

A similar procedure is necessary to find a meaningful value of the *coefficient* b_o which is needed to compute the Hicksian demand. As all 1970 prices are unity, $(23 - 13)$ yields

$$b_o = ln\frac{R_B(70)}{R_S(70)}. \quad (10)$$

If bliss expenditures are eight times the subsistence expenditures, we obtain $b_o = 2.1$ which value was chosen in our analysis. Some alternative computations on the basis of $b_o = 1.4$ $(R_B = 4 \cdot R_S)$ showed that the quantitative results on demand and the qualitative results on welfare are quite robust with respect to changing b_o, just as we had expected.

In estimating demand we had to cope with multicollinearity of prices and with autoregression of residuals.

The two main *multicollinearities* resulted from the following economic problems. First, the general price level and the other prices, mainly our indicator of the private traffic price, are highly correlated. Hence, we ran a linear OLS regression $p_3 = B_o + B_1 p_4$ and divided all prices and the income by the resulting $B_o + B_1 p_4$ to obtain prices p_i'. As could be expected, however, there remains a high correlation between the time series p_1' and p_2' as fares of bus and of the underground were always changed simultaneously in the same direction, albeit at a different scale. Hence, we ran another OLS linear regression $p'_2 = D_o + D_1 p'_1$ and divided all prices p'_i and the income by the resulting $D_o + D_1 p'_1$ to obtain prices $p"_i$. These prices, and this income, then were normalized to unity in 1970.

This treatment of multicollinearity made it possible to start from prices and income in nominal terms,' but actually to estimate demand depending on prices and income in real terms.

Autoregression of residuals was corrected as usual, assuming an autoregressive scheme of the first order. Consider any of the simultaneously estimated equations for $w_i, i = 1, 2, 3$. Assume the maximum likelihood residuals of any year t and year t–1 to be linearly dependent, as measured by a coefficient G. There remains an unexplained part of the residuals which is taken to be independently distributed with zero mean and constant variance. The coefficient G therefore is used to form a transformed regressand $w_i(t) - G w_i(t-1)$ and transformed regressors, $ln\ r(t) - G \cdot ln\ r(t-1)$; $ln\ p(t) - G \cdot ln\ p(t-1)$; $ln^2[p_g(t)/p_k(t)] - G \cdot ln^2[p_g(t-1)/p_k(t-1)]$. Then maximum likelihood is applied to estimate the relation between the transformed regressand and the transformed regressors. The value of G was chosen so as to find a satisfactory combination of significance of the AIDS coefficients and of the Durbin–Watson values. $G = 1$ (stationarity) did not lead to the best results in terms of t–values, R^2 and DW.

As a last step of the empirical implementation we proved that the *Slutsky matrix is negative semidefinite* in all years of the computation. Hence the demand situation in any of the years 1958–1982 can actually be described as if it resulted from rational behavior of a representative consumer.

The estimated underground demand function is less significant than both bus and private traffic demand functions, as can be seen in table 8. This lower significance most probably results from our reducing the AIDS flexibility by imposing homogeneity and Slutsky symmetry. We tried to improve the statistical fit by adding political variables like the LT deficit or particular underground dummy variables, for instance for the opening of the Victoria line (0 till 1970, 1 from 1971). However, in our AIDS system, these variables did not help to improve the fit of the $x_2(\cdot)$ estimation.

26.1.3   DATA

The information on London Transport demand has been taken from the LT's Annual Report and Accounts; the information on the other two goods from the Transport Statistics and the CSO's Annual Abstracts of Statistics. Details of the data basis are presented in Bös (1985b) which will be sent to the reader on request.

The *quantity variables* in the estimations refer to passenger miles of bus and underground and to expenditures for private traffic and general consumption expenditures divided by appropriate price indices. The *price variables* are the average fares per passenger mile, the traffic price index and the retail price index. Income is measured by a time series of disposable income. For income, private traffic and general consumption expenditures we had to be content with UK data instead of Greater London data. *Qualities* are measured by bus miles per route miles and by underground car miles.

26.1.4   THE RESULTING ELASTICITIES OF DEMAND

The Marshallian elasticities ε which result from our estimation are presented in table 9.

Most striking are the high *direct price elasticities* of bus and of underground demand, on average –0.80 and –0.98. Only Glaister (1976b) obtained similar estimates. The high elasticities result from applying annual rather than weekly data, contrary to London Transport's own demand estimations. By using annual data we take account of long-term adjustments of bus and underground demand. It has been well-known in the literature that long-run elasticities are higher because they include the adaptation of travel habits, for instance consumer decisions on whether to buy a new car or not. Moreover, the long-run adjustment includes the reaction of the demand for season tickets which is excluded in the short-run. (Season tickets were issued for 1 month's, 3 month's or 1 year's time.) Glaister (1976b) split the demand into normal demand and season ticket demand and showed the latter to be much more price elastic. Finally we should assume weekly data to include a lot of noise in spite of London Transport's corrections of the weekly data. On the basis of the less noisy annual data we must expect higher elasticities.

Much less striking are the bus and underground *cross-price elasticities* with values of +0.25 each. Bus and underground therefore are substitutes as we could well expect. The response to the price of the other mode is not very strong which fits to the conventional knowledge of the different fields of activity of bus and underground: of all passenger journeys by bus, 80 percent are in the suburbs, whereas radial services into and out of the center of London are the domain of the underground.

Next, the estimations indicate that bus has become an inferior good, its *income elasticity* decreasing from +0.34 in 1958 to –0.10 in 1982. Since bus is the lower-income earner's transportation mode (Grey (1975)), its services cannot be replaced easily by private transportation which explains the low $\varepsilon_{13} = 0.02$ (on average) [5]. Bus services and total consumption are substitutes ($\varepsilon_{14} = 0.45$ on average). The underground, on the other hand, is a luxury, because its income elasticity exceeds unity, and is a strong complement to total consumption. These results can be explained by referring to the many shopping and entertainment underground trips to the center of London, for instance trips to first class shops in the West End, to theaters, cinemas, restaurants etc. Moreover, the underground demand is particularly

---

[5] This low value depends on our setting $d^S_{13}=0$. However, even if d^S_{13} is not deleted but left as an insignificant coefficient, ε_{13} is only 0.2 on average. Moreover, if d^S_{13} is not equated to zero, two further coefficients are insignificant (t-value <1).

sensitive to changes in the costs of private transportation.

Underground has the higher own price elasticity *and* the higher income elasticity which is a very plausible result. It has always puzzled me [6] that the earlier empirical studies on London Transport obtained an implausible combination of high income and low own price elasticity for the underground and vice versa for bus [7]. The present result corroborates the most usual assumptions on necessities versus luxuries as treated in section 10.3 on distributional pricing.

Due to the ever increasing road congestion bus demand became particularly sensitive to changes in *qualities*: the response to the own quality $\varepsilon(x_1, q_1)$ increased from 0.68 in 1958 to 1.14 in 1982, the response to the underground quality $\varepsilon(x_1, q_2)$ from –0.20 in 1958 to –0.34 in 1982. The underground, on the other hand, is characterized by very low quality elasticities.

On the basis of the Marshallian demand functions the Hicksian demand functions can be computed. The 1982 Marshallian and Hicksian price elasticities are presented in table 9.5. The connection between Marshallian and Hicksian price elasticities can be understood easily if the Slutsky equation $\eta_{ik} = \varepsilon_{ik} + w_k \, \varepsilon(x_i, y)$ is considered. Those Hicksian elasticities which result from changing prices $k = 1, 2$ do not differ very much from the Marshallian elasticities because the budget shares w_1 and w_2 are very small [8]. There is more difference in the elasticities if p_3 changes. Moreover, the Hicksian elasticities with respect to price p_4 differ significantly from the respective Marshallian elasticities because of the high budget share w_4. Most striking is the response of underground demand to changes of price p_4, the retail price index. Underground and "total other consumption" are Marshallian complements ($\varepsilon_{24} < 0$) but Hicksian substitutes ($\eta_{24} > 0$).

Finally, we are interested in the response of price elasticities to price

---

[6] See Bös (1981, 94).

[7] See table 4 and table 5 above.

[8] The 1982 values are: $w_1 = 0.009$; $w_2 = 0.010$; $w_3 = 0.104$; $w_4 = 0.877$.

changes. For this purpose we investigate different [9] prices p_1 and p_2 and compute the corresponding price elasticities. We concentrate on Hicksian elasticities [9a]. However, the qualitative results can also be obtained from studying Marshallian elasticities.

p_1	p_2	η_{11}	η_{12}	η_{22}	η_{21}	η_{14}	η_{24}
10.9	12.2	−0.76	0.26	−0.97	0.24	0.48	0.06
11.9	11.2	−0.76	0.27	−0.97	0.24	0.48	0.08
18.2	15.3	−0.79	0.23	−0.97	0.22	0.53	0.14

It can be seen that the price elasticities are comparatively robust with respect to price changes whence London Transport's constant elasticity demand function seems to be a better approximation to the actual behavior of demand than the exponential demand functions (25-4). In the case of an exponential demand function $x_i = A_o \exp(-3.3p_i)$, as proposed in LT report R 252, the bus price elasticity would increase by 64 % if the price p_1 changes from 10.9p to 18.2p whereas, in our example, the AIDS elasticity increases by only 4 %. And the simultaneous change of p_2 from 12.2p to 15.3p implies an almost constant price elasticity η_{22}.

---

[9] We chose the actual 1982 prices, Ramsey prices, and marginal cost prices for the MTC-specification of costs, as computed in section 26.3 below.

[9a] There are small differences to the Hicksian elasticities in table 9.5 because of rounding errors in table 9.5.

TABLE 8: AIDS OF LONDON TRANSPORT DEMAND 1958 – 1982
(Autoregression coefficient G = 0.65)

Coefficients	t-value	Coefficients	t-value
$a_o=-1.4^{1)}$	–	$d_{12}^S=0.0025$	1.80
$a_1=0.0261$	6.70	$d_{13}^S=0^{2)}$	–
$a_2=0.0083$	4.85	$d_{14}^S=-0.0045$	4.17
$a_3=0.0210$	1.12	$d_{23}^S=0.0060$	1.00
$b_o=ln8^{1)}$	–	$d_{24}^S=-0.0086$	1.44
$b_1=-0.0103$	3.74	$d_{34}^S=-0.0098$	1.77
$b_2=0.0010$	0.82	$d_1^q=1.0349$	2.45
$b_3=0.0462$	3.51	$d_2^q=-0.3068$	1.25

Fit of demand equations for goods 1 to 3 (bus, underground, private traffic)

Bus	$R^2=0.96$	;	$DW=1.69$
Underground	$R^2=0.55$	;	$DW=1.48$
Private Traffic	$R^2=0.97$	;	$DW=1.76$

---

[1] A priori fixed as described in subsection 26.1.2 .

[2] d_{13}^S turned out to be not significantly different from zero, with a t-value of 0.32, and was therefore equated to zero.

TABLE 9:   DEMAND ELASTICITIES

$(1$ – bus, 2 – underground, 3 – private traffic, 4 – consumption$)$

9.1   Bus demand

year	ε_{11}	ε_{12}	ε_{13}	ε_{14}	$\varepsilon(x_1,r)$	$\varepsilon(x_1,q_1)$	$\varepsilon(x_1,q_2)$
1958	−0.86	0.16	0.01	0.34	0.34	0.68	−0.20
1959	−0.85	0.17	0.01	0.36	0.30	0.73	−0.22
1960'	−0.85	0.17	0.01	0.36	0.30	0.72	−0.21
1961	−0.85	0.16	0.01	0.34	0.34	0.69	−0.20
1962	−0.85	0.17	0.01	0.35	0.31	0.71	−0.21
1963	−0.84	0.18	0.01	0.38	0.27	0.76	−0.23
1964	−0.84	0.18	0.01	0.37	0.27	0.76	−0.22
1965	−0.84	0.18	0.01	0.37	0.27	0.76	−0.22
1966	−0.82	0.20	0.02	0.41	0.19	0.84	−0.25
1967	−0.82	0.21	0.02	0.43	0.16	0.87	−0.26
1968	−0.80	0.22	0.02	0.46	0.10	0.94	−0.28
1969	−0.79	0.24	0.02	0.49	0.04	0.99	−0.29
1970	−0.80	0.22	0.02	0.45	0.11	0.92	−0.27
1971	−0.80	0.22	0.02	0.46	0.11	0.92	−0.27
1972	−0.77	0.25	0.02	0.53	−0.03	1.07	−0.32
1973	−0.74	0.29	0.02	0.60	−0.18	1.22	−0.36
1974	−0.71	0.32	0.03	0.68	−0.31	1.36	−0.40
1975	−0.72	0.32	0.03	0.66	−0.28	1.33	−0.39
1976	−0.77	0.25	0.02	0.53	−0.03	1.07	−0.32
1977	−0.77	0.25	0.02	0.52	−0.02	1.05	−0.31
1978	−0.76	0.27	0.02	0.55	−0.09	1.12	−0.33
1979	−0.73	0.30	0.03	0.63	−0.23	1.27	−0.38
1980	−0.75	0.27	0.03	0.56	−0.11	1.15	−0.34
1981	−0.74	0.29	0.03	0.59	−0.16	1.20	−0.36
1982	−0.75	0.27	0.03	0.56	−0.10	1.14	−0.34

9.2   Underground demand

year	ε_{21}	ε_{22}	ε_{23}	ε_{24}	$\varepsilon(x_2,r)$	$\varepsilon(x_2,q_1)$	$\varepsilon(x_2,q_2)$
1958	0.27	−0.98	0.67	−1.07	1.11	−0.11	0.03
1959	0.27	−0.98	0.65	−1.05	1.11	−0.11	0.03
1960	0.27	−0.98	0.66	−1.05	1.11	−0.11	0.03
1961	0.28	−0.98	0.68	−1.09	1.11	−0.12	0.03
1962	0.28	−0.98	0.67	−1.08	1.11	−0.11	0.03
1963	0.27	−0.98	0.67	−1.07	1.11	−0.11	0.03
1964	0.25	−0.98	0.61	−0.98	1.10	−0.10	0.03
1965	0.27	−0.98	0.65	−1.05	1.11	−0.11	0.03
1966	0.28	−0.98	0.67	−1.08	1.11	−0.11	0.03
1967	0.27	−0.98	0.65	−1.04	1.11	−0.11	0.03
1968	0.27	−0.98	0.66	−1.06	1.11	−0.11	0.03
1969	0.29	−0.98	0.71	−1.14	1.12	−0.12	0.04
1970	0.26	−0.98	0.64	−1.02	1.10	−0.11	0.03
1971	0.24	−0.98	0.59	−0.94	1.10	−0.10	0.03
1972	0.23	−0.98	0.57	−0.91	1.09	−0.10	0.03
1973	0.24	−0.98	0.58	−0.93	1.10	−0.10	0.03
1974	0.26	−0.98	0.64	−1.03	1.11	−0.11	0.03
1975	0.27	−0.98	0.67	−1.07	1.11	−0.11	0.03
1976	0.27	−0.98	0.66	−1.05	1.11	−0.11	0.03
1977	0.26	−0.98	0.62	−1.00	1.10	−0.11	0.03
1978	0.24	−0.98	0.58	−0.93	1.09	−0.10	0.03
1979	0.23	−0.98	0.56	−0.89	1.09	−0.09	0.03
1980	0.23	−0.98	0.56	−0.90	1.09	−0.09	0.03
1981	0.23	−0.98	0.57	−0.91	1.09	−0.10	0.03
1982	0.23	−0.98	0.57	−0.91	1.09	−0.10	0.03

9.3   Private traffic

year	ε_{31}	ε_{32}	ε_{33}	ε_{34}	$\varepsilon(x_3,r)$	$\varepsilon(x_3,q_1)$	$\varepsilon(x_3,q_2)$
1958	-0.03	0.13	-0.93	-1.22	2.05	-1.09	0.32
1959	-0.03	0.13	-0.93	-1.26	2.08	-1.12	0.33
1960	-0.02	0.11	-0.94	-1.02	1.88	-0.91	0.27
1961	-0.02	0.10	-0.94	-0.99	1.86	-0.89	0.26
1962	-0.02	0.10	-0.94	-1.00	1.86	-0.89	0.26
1963	-0.02	0.09	-0.95	-0.90	1.78	-0.80	0.24
1964	-0.02	0.08	-0.96	-0.80	1.69	-0.72	0.21
1965	-0.02	0.08	-0.96	-0.75	1.64	-0.67	0.20
1966	-0.02	0.08	-0.96	-0.73	1.63	-0.65	0.19
1967	-0.02	0.08	-0.96	-0.73	1.63	-0.65	0.19
1968	-0.01	0.07	-0.96	-0.68	1.59	-0.61	0.18
1969	-0.01	0.07	-0.97	-0.62	1.54	-0.56	0.17
1970	-0.01	0.06	-0.97	-0.62	1.53	-0.55	0.16
1971	-0.01	0.07	-0.97	-0.63	1.54	-0.56	0.17
1972	-0.01	0.06	-0.97	-0.55	1.48	-0.49	0.15
1973	-0.01	0.06	-0.97	-0.54	1.46	-0.48	0.14
1974	-0.01	0.06	-0.97	-0.58	1.50	-0.51	0.15
1975	-0.01	0.06	-0.97	-0.58	1.50	-0.51	0.15
1976	-0.01	0.06	-0.97	-0.57	1.49	-0.51	0.15
1977	-0.01	0.06	-0.97	-0.57	1.49	-0.51	0.15
1978	-0.01	0.06	-0.97	-0.55	1.47	-0.49	0.15
1979	-0.01	0.05	-0.97	-0.52	1.45	-0.47	0.14
1980	-0.01	0.05	-0.97	-0.51	1.44	-0.46	0.14
1981	-0.01	0.05	-0.97	-0.53	1.46	-0.47	0.14
1982	-0.01	0.05	-0.97	-0.50	1.43	-0.45	0.13

9.4 Aggregate consumption

year	ε_{41}	ε_{42}	ε_{43}	ε_{44}	$\varepsilon(x_4,r)$	$\varepsilon(x_4,q_1)$	$\varepsilon(x_4,q_2)$
1958	-0.00[1]	-0.01	-0.01	-0.94	0.96	0.04	-0.01
1959	-0.00	-0.01	-0.01	-0.94	0.96	0.04	-0.01
1960	-0.00	-0.01	-0.01	-0.94	0.96	0.04	-0.01
1961	-0.00	-0.01	-0.01	-0.94	0.96	0.04	-0.01
1962	-0.00	-0.01	-0.01	-0.94	0.96	0.04	-0.01
1963	-0.00	-0.01	-0.01	-0.94	0.96	0.04	-0.01
1964	-0.00	-0.01	-0.01	-0.94	0.96	0.04	-0.01
1965	-0.00	-0.01	-0.01	-0.94	0.96	0.04	-0.01
1966	-0.00	-0.01	-0.01	-0.94	0.96	0.04	-0.01
1967	-0.00	-0.01	-0.01	-0.94	0.96	0.04	-0.01
1968	-0.00	-0.01	-0.01	-0.94	0.96	0.04	-0.01
1969	-0.00	-0.01	-0.01	-0.94	0.96	0.04	-0.01
1970	-0.00	-0.01	-0.01	-0.94	0.96	0.04	-0.01
1971	-0.00	-0.01	-0.01	-0.94	0.96	0.04	-0.01
1972	-0.00	-0.01	-0.01	-0.93	0.96	0.04	-0.01
1973	-0.00	-0.01	-0.01	-0.93	0.96	0.04	-0.01
1974	-0.00	-0.01	-0.01	-0.94	0.96	0.04	-0.01
1975	-0.00	-0.01	-0.01	-0.94	0.96	0.04	-0.01
1976	-0.00	-0.01	-0.01	-0.93	0.96	0.04	-0.01
1977	-0.00	-0.01	-0.01	-0.93	0.96	0.04	-0.01
1978	-0.00	-0.01	-0.01	-0.93	0.96	0.04	-0.01
1979	-0.00	-0.01	-0.01	-0.93	0.96	0.04	-0.01
1980	-0.00	-0.01	-0.01	-0.93	0.96	0.04	-0.01
1981	-0.00	-0.01	-0.01	-0.93	0.96	0.04	-0.01
1982	-0.00	-0.01	-0.01	-0.93	0.96	0.04	-0.01

---

[1] small, but negative.

9.5   Marshallian and Hicksian price elasticities of demand (1982)

ε_{11}	ε_{12}	ε_{13}	ε_{14}
-0.75	0.27	0.03	0.56

η_{11}	η_{12}	η_{13}	η_{14}
-0.75	0.27	0.02	0.47

ε_{21}	ε_{22}	ε_{23}	ε_{24}
0.23	-0.98	0.57	-0.91

η_{21}	η_{22}	η_{23}	η_{24}
0.24	-0.97	0.68	$+0.05$

Note: The Hicksian elasticities were derived from the figures of tables 9.1 to 9.4, using the Slutsky equation.

26.2   THE TRANSLOG SPECIFICATION OF FACTOR DEMAND FUNCTIONS

26.2.1   ANALYTICAL OUTLINE OF THE SPECIFICATION

We use a translog specification of the factor demand $\ell_i(p_{oi}, p_{\kappa i}, z_i)$ and $\kappa_i(p_{oi}, p_{\kappa i}, z_i)$, i = 1 (bus), 2 (underground). The supplied quantities z_i are measured in place miles. Given the restriction to 25 annual data we have to reduce the number of quadratic terms without losing too much information about the influence on marginal costs of output quantities, prices and qualities. Hence we specify [10]

---

[10] For ease of exposition we suppress the further indices of the coefficients a_1 to a_9.

$$ln\ l_i = a_o + a_1 ln\ z_i + a_2 ln\ p_{oi} + a_3 ln\ p_{\kappa i} + a_4 ln\ q_i +$$
$$+ (1/2)a_5(ln\ z_i)^2 + a_6 ln\ z_i ln\ p_{oi} + a_7 ln\ z_i ln\ p_{\kappa i} + \qquad (11)$$
$$+ a_8 ln\ z_i ln\ q_i + a_9 \Phi_i \qquad i = 1, 2$$

where Φ_i stands for further variables which improve the statistical fit, such as the ratio of one-person / crew-operated buses in the bus factor demand and particular investment figures in the underground factor demand [11]. The demand for capital inputs is specified analogously.

According to (11) the marginal labor response $\partial l_i / \partial z_i$ depends on output, prices and quality in an additively separable way, that is

$$\frac{\partial \ell_i}{\partial z_i} = \frac{\ell_i(z_i)}{z_i} \left[a_1 + a_5 ln\ z_i + a_6 ln\ p_{oi} + a_7 ln\ p_{\kappa i} + a_8 ln\ q_i \right] \qquad (12)$$

and analogously for $\partial \kappa_i / \partial z_i$.

We estimated the translog specification (11) as depending on *place miles* z_i, which is a meaningful concept given the fact that the actually produced quantities are place miles and not passenger miles. This specification, however, does not immediately fit into a framework where optimal prices per passenger mile shall be computed from demand and cost side functions. Hence, we have to compute labor and capital inputs per passenger mile on the basis of the estimated labor and capital inputs per place mile.

The number of place miles per passenger mile is the load factor. We would expect the load factor to be endogenously determined by demand and cost side influences. If that were correct we would need a model of the load factor to close the gap between the demand and the production side

---

[11] We did not succeed in improving the statistical fit of the underground factor demand functions by adding particular investment figures. Hence $a_9 = 0$ for both input functions which are published in tables 10.3 and 10.4 below.

of our model. Fortunately we do not need such a model. It can be shown
that the load factor significantly is determined by the rate of unemployment
which is exogenous to our model. This can be seen by the following linear
regressions, using 1958 - 1982 data:

$$LF_1 = 4.832 + 0.111RU \qquad R^2 = 0.87; \; DW = 1.87$$
$$(\pm 0.827) \quad (\pm 0.051) \tag{13a}$$

$$LF_2 = 6.978 + 0.460RU \qquad R^2 = 0.90; \; DW = 2.01$$
$$(\pm 1.431) \quad (\pm 0.089) \tag{13b}$$

where LF_1 is the load factor and RU is the rate of unemployment. Autoregression of residuals was corrected by choosing G = 0.95. The figures in
brackets are standard deviations. The rate of unemployment is exogenously
given to our model and so are the load factors according to (13). Hence,
the load factor can be treated as an exogenous variable. Factor inputs per
passenger mile are given by factor inputs per place mile times load factor.
For 1982 the respective load factors were $LF_1 = 5.31$ and $LF_2 = 10.78$.

26.2.2   ON COMPUTING MARGINAL COSTS

We recall the Boiteux definition of marginal costs, $c_i = -p_o(\partial z_o/\partial z_i)$.
Hence it seems to be the straightforward procedure to estimate marginal
costs by marginal labor costs (MLC), based on the empirical factor demand
function $\ell_i(\cdot)$:

$$MLC_i := p_{oi}\frac{\partial \ell_i}{\partial z_i}. \tag{14}$$

We remember from subsection 2.4.5 that c_i is identical to marginal
costs C_i only if all inputs have been combined in a cost-minimizing way. It
must be assumed that London Transport did not meet the requirements of

cost efficiency. Hence MLC_i is not equal to marginal costs C_i. However, it can be used as an approximation.

Moreover, if $p_{oi}(\partial \ell_i / \partial z_i)$ is computed on the basis of an empirical labor demand function, it can only be considered as an approximation to the Boiteux marginal costs c_i of the theoretical chapters in spite of the formal identity. The theoretical concept assumed $g_i(z_i) = 0$ even if the public enterprise did not minimize costs but chose some marginal rates of transformation deviating from input price ratios. It must be assumed that London Transport did not meet the requirements of production efficiency. Hence the empirical $p_{oi}(\partial \ell_i / \partial z_i)$ is not equal to the theoretical $p_{oi}(\partial g_i / \partial z_i)/(\partial g_i / \partial z_o)$. However, it can be used as an approximation.

Furthermore we must recall that both labor and capital inputs changed in every year of the investigation. Therefore the empirical figures cannot be taken as representing short-run costs, but a total cost function

$$TC_i = p_{oi}\ell_i + p_{\kappa i}\kappa_i \tag{15}$$

can reflect long-run costs, or at least an approximation to them.

Therefore we can use marginal total costs (MTC)

$$MTC_i := p_{oi}\frac{\partial \ell_i}{\partial z_i} + p_{\kappa_i}\frac{\partial \kappa_i}{\partial z_i} \tag{16}$$

as another approximation to marginal costs C_i. But then these empirical computations of marginal total costs can also be taken as an approximation to the theoretical Boiteux marginal costs c_i.

Regardless of whether we use the empirical factor demand functions to compute marginal labor costs $MLC_i(\cdot)$ or marginal total costs $MTC_i(\cdot)$, we always obtain an approximation of the Boiteux theoretical marginal costs only. We cannot say which is the better approximation. Hence all further computations use both concepts, to give a lower and an upper limit of the marginal costs of our theoretical model.

Applied economists, who prefer to do so, are free to identify MLC with short-run marginal costs and MTC with long-run marginal costs. Note, however, that our reasoning is quite different from the usual practical terminology. We introduce MLC and MTC as two approximations to our theoretical concept, not as two economically different concepts based on operating versus capacity costs.

26.2.3   THE EMPIRICAL IMPLEMENTATION

We estimated the factor demand equations (11) by maximum likelihood, based on annual data from 1958 to 1982.

Translog, as AIDS, is a Taylor series approximation. Hence, it works better for small values of the relevant variables. Accordingly we normalized to unity the 1970 values of the time series of prices and qualities. The other variables were transformed correspondingly.

Moreover, we normalized the quantities $z_i = LF_i x_i$ in a way which is compatible with the demand side of the model, that is

$$z_i^n = \frac{z_i p_i(70)}{r(70)} = LF_i x_i^n. \tag{17}$$

Additionally, the input quantities were normalized to

$$\ell_i^n = \frac{\ell_i p_o(70)}{r(70)} \; ; \; \kappa_i^n = \frac{\kappa_i p_\kappa(70)}{r(70)}. \tag{18}$$

Then

$$\frac{\partial \ell_i}{\partial z_i} = p_i(70)\frac{\partial \ell_i^n}{\partial z_i^n} \; ; \; \frac{\partial \kappa_i}{\partial z_i} = p_i(70)\frac{\partial \kappa_i^n}{\partial z_i^n} \tag{19}$$

which allows to go back to the actual effects $\partial\ell/\partial z$, $\partial\kappa/\partial z$ on the basis of the estimated normalized effects.

As a next step we proceeded from marginal inputs per place mile z_i to marginal inputs per passenger mile x_i

$$\frac{\partial\ell_i}{\partial x_i} = LF_i\frac{\partial\ell_i}{\partial z_i} \; ; \; \frac{\partial\kappa_i}{\partial x_i} = LF_i\frac{\partial\kappa_i}{\partial z_i}. \tag{20}$$

The marginal input requirements $\partial\ell/\partial x$ and $\partial\kappa/\partial x$ are the basis of computing approximations to the marginal costs per passenger mile.

We applied the usual transformations to deal with autoregression of residuals. Moreover, there were many problems of multicollinearity which we solved in the following way:

a.   we divided both wage rate and interest rate by the retail price index;

b.   if two regressors were too highly correlated, we excluded one of them from the estimation. For instance, we excluded either $ln\ z_i$ or $(ln\ z_i)^2$ which series are highly correlated. Unfortunately, in one case the quality indicator had to be excluded because the frequency data were highly correlated with place miles.

The estimated labor input functions are less significant than the capital input functions, as can be seen in table 10. This lower significance can be explained by the influence of labor unions and other political bodies which is not specified explicitly in our factor demand functions. However, we did not succeed in improving the statistical fit of the labor demand functions by introducing political variables like the amount of the LT deficit or dummy variables for changes in the GLC governing party (0–Tory, 1–Labour). The estimation of capital inputs does not depend on similar political influences because of the exclusion of depreciation.

26.2.4   DATA

The data are taken from LT's Annual Report and Accounts and from the CSO's Annual Abstracts of Statistics. Details of the data basis are presented in Bös (1985b).

The LT reports give detailed statistics of annual bus costs and annual underground costs. On the basis of these cost figures it was possible to compute the annual expenditures for labor and for capital for both bus and underground. We divided these expenditures by p_{oi} and $p_{\kappa i}$, respectively, to obtain proxies for the labor and capital inputs ℓ_i and κ_i. The provision for depreciation was excluded from the estimation of κ_i-functions, because it depends on general entrepreneurial decisions and not on place miles.

The average price of capital inputs $p_{\kappa i}$ was computed on the basis of CSO's table on gross domestic fixed capital formation, comparing the figures at current price and at the given price of some basic year [12]. Average earnings of LT staff were published in CSO's annual abstracts of statistics from 1963 to 1978, for both bus and underground. These time series could be taken as a basis for the computation of p_{oi}, extending the series to the time span 1958 to 1982. For this purpose we used control series of p_{oi} for bus and for underground obtained by dividing the respective labor costs by the appropriate staff figures.

Place miles data were taken from the LT annual reports. The load factor LF_i was computed as passenger miles per place mile [13].

---

[12] For bus services we considered the figures on 'buses and coaches'; for underground services the figures on 'railway rolling stock, ships and aircrafts', 'plant and machinery' and 'other new buildings and works'.

[13] The LT reports publish another load factor, namely passenger miles per seat mile.

26.2.5   THE RESULTING MARGINAL COSTS

Table 11 presents the marginal costs which result from our translog estimation. The results are in accordance with the previous studies on LT costs. For the year 1975 we obtain marginal labor costs of 5p per bus passenger mile and of 3p per underground passenger mile. The corresponding marginal total costs are 7p and 5p. The underground marginal costs are significantly higher than in Glaister-Collings (1978) who assumed 7p per bus passenger mile and 2p per underground passenger mile. However, in Glaister-Lewis (1978) the authors provide for higher marginal costs if peak traffic is taken into account [14]. As our study includes both peak and off-peak traffic our estimates seem to be roughly in accordance with the estimates of the Glaister group. For the year 1982 our results fit to the METS marginal cost functions which assume short-run marginal costs of 17p and 8p per passenger mile. These values correspond to our marginal labor costs of 15p and 9p.

The actual costs of London Transport are well approximated by the translog factor input functions. Comparing the translog costs for the AIDS quantities at actual prices and the actual costs in 1982 we obtain

| | Labor costs 1982 (£ mill) | | Capital costs 1982[15] (£ mill) | |
	bus	underground	bus	underground
Actual costs	340.0	227.4	49.1	87.1
Translog	343.6	224.8	43.0	79.0

Note: for details of the computation of actual 1982 labor and capital costs see Bös (1985b).

---

[14]   See table 7 above.

[15]   Excluding depreciation, but including renewal for infrastructure.

Finally, we are interested in the response of MLC and MTC to changes in place miles. Marginal costs which decrease in place miles indicate increasing returns to scale. We first investigated $\partial MLC_i/\partial z_i$ and $\partial MTC_i/\partial z_i$ [16] at the actual 1982 place miles (bus: 12.38 billions, underground 24.53 billions). Moreover, we also computed these first derivatives at those place miles which would result from the application of any optimal prices which will be presented in the following section. In all cases the marginal labor costs are decreasing, whereas the marginal total costs are increasing. However, all marginal cost curves are relatively flat. An increase in bus place miles from 12 to 13 billions leads to a decrease of MLC per passenger mile from 14.30p to 13.93p and to an increase of MTC from 19.82p to 20.42p. An increase in underground place miles from 24 to 25 billions reduces MLC from 8.21p to 8.06p and increases MTC from 15.86p to 16.17p.

It is interesting to note that due to decreasing returns to scale there is no welfare economic justification of a London Transport deficit if the "long-run" cost function MTC is applied. However, the opposite holds if the "short-run" function MLC is chosen. We shall see in subsection 26.3.3 below that, given the deficit at the actual 1982 prices, Ramsey prices are below marginal costs for MTC, but above marginal costs for MLC.

---

[16] The actual computation of $\partial MLC_i/\partial z_i$ and $\partial MTC_i/\partial z_i$ has to consider the fact that we compute factor demand functions which depend on normalized place miles z_i^n. Hence we apply some transformations to express the marginal-cost changes depending on non-normalized place miles z_i. The place miles z_i were chosen according to $z_i = LF_i \cdot x_i$ where x_i are AIDS-demand quantities given the actual 1982 prices.

TABLE 10:

LONDON TRANSPORT FACTOR INPUT FUNCTIONS, 1958 – 1982

10.1 Bus, labor inputs

Coefficients (eq. (11))	t-value	
$a_o = -3.3555$	7.87	$R^2 = 0.96$
$a_2 = -0.1629$	1.41	$DW = 1.52$
$a_4 = -0.3869$	1.41	$G = 0.20$
$a_5 = -0.3362$	3.37	
$a_9 = +0.0033$	2.23	
$a_1 = a_3 = a_6 = a_7 = a_8 = 0$		

a_9 refers to Φ_1 : one-person operated buses / crew-operated buses.

10.2 Bus, capital inputs

Coefficients (eq. (11))	t-value	
$a_o = -1.5473$	1.82	$R^2 = 0.90$
$a_2 = -0.2503$	1.29	$DW = 2.15$
$a_3 = +1.6548$	2.45	$G = 0.75$
$a_4 = -1.4095$	2.84	
$a_5 = -1.1174$	5.75	
$a_1 = a_6 = a_7 = a_8 = a_9 = 0$		

10.3   Underground, labor inputs

Coefficients (eq. (11))	t-value	
$a_o = -4.1214$	7.64	$R^2 = 0.81$
$a_2 = +1.4422$	1.09	$DW = 1.49$
$a_5 = -0.2889$	1.67	$G = 0.75$
$a_6 = +0.5425$	1.05	
$a_8 = +0.3034$	1.80	
$a_1 = a_3 = a_4 = a_7 = a_9 = 0$		

10.4   Underground, capital inputs

Coefficients (eq. (11))	t-value	
$a_1 = +2.4274$	70.08	$R^2 = 0.87$
$a_2 = +0.8300$	2.84	$DW = 1.94$
$a_3 = -1.3055$	5.07	$G = 0.80$
$a_4 = -2.3502$	5.56	
$a_o = a_5 = a_6 = a_7 = a_8 = a_9 = 0$		

TABLE 11:

LONDON TRANSPORT MARGINAL COSTS PER PASSENGER MILE

(pence, at current prices)

year	MLC Bus	MTC Bus	MLC Underground	MTC Underground
1958	0.68	1.30	0.25	0.78
1959	0.67	1.24	0.26	0.79
1960	0.72	1.35	0.31	0.88
1961	0.81	1.50	0.33	0.90
1962	0.82	1.54	0.37	1.07
1963	0.90	1.57	0.38	1.03
1964	1.05	1.72	0.43	1.15
1965	1.31	2.11	0.52	1.29
1966	1.39	2.19	0.56	1.35
1967	1.49	2.31	0.61	1.42
1968	1.59	2.47	0.67	1.53
1969	1.71	2.59	0.72	1.60
1970	1.87	2.75	0.81	1.69
1971	2.13	3.18	0.96	1.95
1972	2.44	3.61	1.10	2.23
1973	2.69	3.80	1.33	2.43
1974	3.22	4.53	1.67	3.03
1975	4.63	6.70	2.85	4.99
1976	5.74	8.14	3.68	6.73
1977	6.44	9.36	3.78	7.42
1978	7.19	10.45	3.90	7.53
1979	8.74	12.74	4.43	8.44
1980	11.08	16.50	5.95	11.02
1981	12.62	18.99	7.05	13.59
1982	14.83	21.02	8.75	18.08

26.3   OPTIMAL PRICES FOR LONDON BUS
AND UNDERGROUND SERVICES

26.3.1   INTRODUCTION

In the following we present the estimates of selected public pricing rules for the year 1982. Each estimation is based on a system of equations, consisting of two marginal conditions and the revenue-cost constraint, to be solved for bus fare p_1, underground fare p_2 and a third variable which typically is a Lagrangean parameter. The sole exception is marginal-cost pricing where no revenue-cost constraint is considered.

The marginal conditions are taken from the theoretical chapters of the book. They alternatively depend on Marshallian and Hicksian *demand functions*. Ramsey prices, for instance, are defined on the basis of Hicksian demand, Feldstein prices on the basis of Marshallian demand. The AIDS specification fits to the theoretical dichotomy because it presents analytical estimates for both Marshallian and Hicksian demand.

However, there is an information problem when substituting the AIDS specification into the theoretical marginal conditions. The marginal conditions require knowledge of $\partial z_i / \partial p_e$, alternatively Marshallian and Hicksian. Sometimes they also require knowledge of $\partial y_i / \partial p_e$. However, from our demand estimations we only know $\partial x_i / \partial p_e$, both Marshallian and Hicksian. A similar problem arises in the revenue-cost constraint. The theoretical constraint refers to $z_e(\cdot)$ only, our empirical estimations to $x_e(\cdot)$. The empirical knowledge is only sufficient for the estimations if we assume publicly and privately supplied goods to be strictly separated, whence

$$y_1 = y_2 = 0; \quad z_3 = z_4 = 0. \tag{21}$$

These assumptions imply both trivialities and non-trivialities. It is trivial that the private economy does not supply public transportation and that London Transport does neither supply private transportation nor total other consumption x_4. It is not trivial that private firms are assumed not to use LT outputs as inputs of their production and that LT is assumed not to use privately supplied outputs as inputs of bus and underground production. However, only the separability of public and private supply enables us to substitute the empirical demand functions and their derivatives into the theoretical system of equations.

Let us next turn to the empirical implementation of the *cost side* of the theoretical system of equations. We use two different concepts. First the translog estimation of factor demand which has been described in section 26.2. Second the linear cost functions which were proposed by London Transport and used in the London submodel of METS (1984). These functions are available for 1982 only. They specify bus costs CB and underground costs CU at 1982 prices

$$CB = \pounds 76\text{mill fixed costs} \quad \text{plus} \quad \pounds 362\text{mill variable costs} \qquad (22)$$

$$CU = \pounds 186\text{mill fixed costs} \quad \text{plus} \quad \pounds 186\text{mill variable costs.} \qquad (23)$$

If we compute the AIDS demand at the actual 1982 prices we obtain 2452 mill bus passenger miles and 2422 mill underground passenger miles whence the METS-cost functions in our model are [17]

$$CB = 76 + 0.1476\, x_1 \qquad (24)$$

$$CU = 186 + 0.0768\, x_2 \qquad (25)$$

where CB and CU are measured in million pounds and x_i in million passenger miles.

---

[17] METS (1984) started from a 1982 demand of 2132 mill bus passenger miles and 2361 mill underground passenger miles. Then the marginal costs .re 17p and 8p, as mentioned on p. 375. By the way: the actual 1982 figures, according to the LT Annual report and accounts were 2332 mill bus passenger miles and 2275 mill underground passenger miles

Let us finally deal with the empirical implementation of the *revenue–cost constraint* Π. We apply the fixed constraint

$$p_1 x_1 + p_2 x_2 - \sum_{i=1}^{2} \left(p_{oi} \ell_i + p_{\kappa i} \kappa_i \right) = \Pi^o \qquad (26)$$

or in the case of the METS–specification

$$p_1 x_1 + p_2 x_2 - CB - CU = \Pi^o. \qquad (27)$$

The deficit Π^o has been chosen in such a way that it is fully compatible with our empirical demand and cost functions at the given prices and income in 1982. Therefore Π^o is different in (26) and (27). However, both hypothetical values of Π^o do not differ too much from the actual deficit of London Transport. The actual LT deficit in 1982 was £ 246.8 mill whereas the deficits which underlie our computations are £ 247.1 mill in the METS case and £ 217.1 mill in the translog case [18].

After computing Π^o as described above it is held constant for the different pricing rules. The only exception, of course, is marginal-cost pricing where no revenue-cost constraint enters.

Given the empirical implementation we solve the marginal conditions and the revenue-cost constraint to obtain a tuple of fares plus the third variable (Lagrangean parameter). The result must then be shown to be consistent and optimal.

Consistency refers to the representative consumer model. It is not sufficient that we have shown the AIDS Slutsky matrix to be negative semidefinite for all actual prices from 1958 to 1982. The same property must hold for any computed prices. If the AIDS Slutsky matrix is not negative semidefinite for some particular prices, the result cannot be taken as if it came from a representative consumer's utility maximization. Those prices, therefore,

---

[18]   £ 127.6 mill plus £ 89.5 mill depreciation.

would be inconsistent with the model we have described in figure 18 and specified in the almost ideal demand system. Fortunately, we succeeded in proving the Slutsky negativity in all cases treated below.

We have not proved the *optimality* of any resulting couple of fares from the second-order conditions because their computation implies unsurmountable difficulties. However, we computed welfare measures which indicate whether the results go in the right direction. The same procedure was applied for positive theory objectives.

The measurement of welfare optimality is different for Marshallian and Hicksian demand. If Marshallian demand is applied, we measure the optimality of alternative price systems by the value of the indirect utility function of the representative consumer. The higher this value, the better. In the case of pricing with distributional objectives the optimality is measured by the value of a social welfare function which aggregates the indirect utility functions of ten "representative consumers". The aggregation applies the distributional weights which are imputed to the board.

If Hicksian demand is applied, utility is fixed for every single year on the basis of the given prices and the given income of the representative consumer. We measure the optimality of alternative price systems by the expenditures which are necessary to achieve the fixed utility:

$$r^* = R(p^*, \bar{V}) \quad \text{with} \quad \bar{V} = V(\bar{p}, \bar{r}, \bar{q}). \tag{28}$$

The bars refer to the actual prices, income and qualities in the respective year for which the optimal prices p^* are computed. The lower the expenditures r^*, the better off the representative consumer.

26.3.2   MARGINAL–COST PRICES

The determination of marginal-cost prices differs according to the chosen cost function. If the METS cost functions are applied, we obtain short-run marginal-cost prices by simple differentiation $\partial CB/\partial x_1$ and $\partial CU/\partial x_2$. If we start from factor demand equations we either obtain a system for the determination of marginal labor costs (MLC)

$$p_i = \bar{p}_{oi} \frac{\partial \ell_i}{\partial x_i} (z_i(p_1, p_2, \bar{p}_3, \bar{p}_4, \bar{r}, \bar{q}), \bar{p}_{oi}, \bar{p}_{\kappa i}, \bar{q}) \quad i = 1, 2 \qquad (29)$$

or of marginal total costs (MTC)

$$p_i = \bar{p}_{oi} \frac{\partial \ell_i}{\partial x_i} (\cdot) + \bar{p}_{\kappa i} \frac{\partial \kappa_i}{\partial x_i} (\cdot) \quad i = 1, 2. \qquad (30)$$

Bars refer to the realizations of variables in the respective year.

The resulting marginal-cost prices are [19] (in pence per passenger mile):

	Marginal cost prices			For comparison:
	METS	$\widetilde{\text{MLC}}$	MTC	actual prices
$p_1(82)$	14.8	15.8	18.2	10.9
$p_2(82)$	7.7	7.7	15.3	12.2

---

[19] In table 11 above, MLC and MTC were computed for the actual place miles of 1982. When computing optimal prices we started from the AIDS quantities given the actual 1982 prices. This, and the transition to $\widetilde{\text{MLC}}$, explains the difference between the marginal-cost prices and the marginal-cost values in table 11.

The "short-run" marginal-cost prices (METS and $M\widetilde{L}C$ [20])) of bus services are twice the underground fares whereas the "long-run" concept MTC leads to prices which do not differ so much from each other. The simple reason is the inclusion of the high underground capital inputs in the "long-run" concept.

Replacing the actual 1982 average fares by marginal-cost prices would have implied a considerable price increase for bus services, regardless of the definition of marginal costs. The underground fares would have been lower than the actual prices if "short-run" definitions like METS or $M\widetilde{L}C$ had been applied, but higher in the case of "long-run marginal costs" MTC.

26.3.3   RAMSEY PRICES

We compute Ramsey prices from the system of equations

$$\sum_{i=1}^{2} (p_i - c_i) \frac{\partial \hat{x}_i}{\partial p_e} = -\gamma \hat{x}_e \qquad\qquad e = 1, 2 \qquad\qquad (8-1)$$

$$\text{Revenue} - \text{costs} = \Pi^o \qquad\qquad (31)$$

This is a system of three equations to be solved for p_1, p_2 and γ. The resulting Ramsey prices (in pence per passenger mile) are presented in a table on the next page.

---

[20] We used the approximation $M\widetilde{L}C_i$ to guarantee that the numerical solutions converge to prices which are meaningful from the economic point of view. $M\widetilde{L}C_i$ is a homotopy with parameter 0.1, $M\widetilde{L}C_i = p_o(\partial \ell/\partial x_i) + 0.1 p_\kappa(\partial \kappa/\partial x_i)$. If the homotopy parameter converges to zero, the underground fare converges to zero, too. However, the AIDS underground demand at zero price is so high that this situation cannot be described adequately by the factor input functions we have estimated. – $M\widetilde{L}C_i$ was applied for the computation of marginal-cost prices, Ramsey prices and prices which adjust to monopolistic structures in the private economy. The other prices were computed by using the original $MLC_i = p_o(\partial \ell/\partial x_i)$.

	Ramsey prices			For comparison:
	METS	$\widetilde{MLC}$	MTC	actual prices
$p_1(82)$	15.2	15.8	11.9	10.9
$p_2(82)$	7.9	7.7	11.2	12.2

The "short-run" concepts METS and $\widetilde{MLC}$ lead to Ramsey prices above marginal costs [21]. Compared with marginal-costs, underground fares are increased less than bus fares ($\Theta_1 = 0.03$; $\Theta_2 = 0.02$ for the METS cost function). This result is due to the more elastic underground demand.

The "long-run" concept MTC leads to Ramsey prices below marginal costs and the bus fares are reduced to a higher extent than the underground fares ($\Theta_1 = -0.64$; $\Theta_2 = -0.52$). This result is also as expected, because it is well-known that Ramsey prices below marginal costs favor the price-inelastic good [22].

26.3.4   PRICING WITH DISTRIBUTIONAL OBJECTIVES

In this case we compute the prices from the following system of equations:

$$\sum_{i=1}^{2}(p_i - c_i)\frac{\partial x_i}{\partial p_e} = -(1 - F_e)x_e \qquad e = 1, 2 \qquad (10-1)$$

$$\text{Revenue} - \text{costs} = \Pi^o \qquad (31)$$

---

[21] For the $\widetilde{MLC}$ specification we obtain Ramsey prices of $p_1=15.842$ and $p_2=7.730$ whereas the marginal costs are $\widetilde{MLC}_1=15.801$ and $\widetilde{MLC}_2=7.714$.

[22] See pp. 191-192 above.

This is a system of three equations in three unknowns, the Feldstein prices p_1, p_2 and a parameter λ which is part of the distributional characteristics F_e.

To compute the distributional characteristics we assumed that there are ten representative consumers with identical AIDS–utility function but different disposable incomes. The incomes are assumed to follow a lognormal distribution which was computed on the basis of UK Gini-coefficients of incomes after taxes [23].

The distributional characteristics are specified as follows:

$$F_e(p) = \frac{\lambda}{x_e(p,r)} \sum_{h=1}^{10} (r^h)^{-\delta} f(r^h) x_e^h(p,r^h) \frac{\partial v^h}{\partial r^h}(p,r^h) \quad \delta = 0,1; e = 1,2$$

$$(32)$$

where $f(r^h)$ is the relative frequency of individual incomes.

This formula incorporates two alternative distributional value judgements of the board, namely,

$$\frac{\partial W}{\partial v^h} \equiv \lambda \qquad \text{if } \delta = 0, \tag{33a}$$

$$\frac{\partial W}{\partial v^h} \equiv \frac{\lambda}{r^h} \qquad \text{if } \delta = 1. \tag{33b}$$

The first specification is utilitarian. The interests of lower-income earners are stressed in F_e because the individual marginal utility of income $\partial v^h / \partial r^h$ decreases in income. The second specification describes a more egalitarian board because the social marginal welfare of individual utility also decreases in income.

---

[23] The help of A.B. Atkinson is gratefully acknowledged. The data come from: Royal Comission, report No 1, tables 65 and 67, report No 5, table 5, report No 7, table 2.3; National Income and Expenditure (1980, 113; 1981, 110); Economic Trends, Aug 1984, table A.

λ replaces γ which was the third variable in the Ramsey case. Both parameters measure marginal welfare changes which result from changes in other variables. In the Feldstein case λ accentuates the distribution problem as expressed by the marginal welfare of individual utilities. In the Ramsey case γ accentuates the allocation problem as expressed by the marginal welfare of relaxing the revenue-cost constraint.

a) $\partial W/\partial v^h \equiv \lambda$

	Feldstein prices			For comparison:
	METS	MLC	MTC	actual prices
$p_1(82)$	12.9	14.4	10.87	10.90
$p_2(82)$	9.3	8.0	12.25	12.20

b) $\partial W/\partial v^h \equiv \lambda/r^h$

	Feldstein prices			For comparison:
	METS	MLC	MTC	actual prices
$p_1(82)$	12.2	12.8	10.5	10.9
$p_2(82)$	9.9	9.3	12.8	12.2

The resulting Feldstein prices favor the bus services at the expense of the underground. The bus fare is lower, the more the distributional objective is accentuated as can be seen by comparing the two alternative systems of Feldstein prices we have computed. This result is not surprising because in 1982 bus services are an inferior good and underground services are a luxury. It is interesting that Feldstein prices are almost identical with the actual prices if the MTC specification of costs and the $\partial W/\partial v^h \equiv \lambda$ specification of the distributional objective are applied. However, this coincidence must not be taken as an evidence of LT's distributional pricing policy based on long-run cost functions. When asked by the department of transport, LT recommended the METS specification instead of any long-run cost concept.

Given the METS-specification we could approximate the actual prices by increasing the relative distributional weights of the lower-income people, that is, by choosing some adequate value of $\delta > 1$. However, that result would be a coincidence, too. The distributional objectives of the Fares Fair policy centered on favoring public transportation at the expense of local rate payers. The difference between bus and underground fares in 1982 can as well be explained by the objective of passenger-miles (or revenue) maximization, given a short-run cost function: the lower marginal costs of underground services coupled with the high underground price elasticity lead to the same tendency of lower underground and higher bus fares as result from Feldstein pricing. However, we can conclude that LT's actual pricing policy in 1982 implies distributional results which favor lower-income earners at the expense of higher-income earners although most probably this has not been the primary objective of the fares policy for London bus and underground services.

26.3.5   ADJUSTMENT TO MONOPOLISTIC PRICING

The adjustment to private monopolistic structures is based on the marginal conditions [24]

$$\sum_i (p_i - c_i) \frac{1}{LF_e} \frac{\partial \hat{z}_i}{\partial p_e} = -\gamma \frac{1}{LF_e} z_e - (1-\gamma) \sum_i \sum_j (p_i - c_i^j) \frac{\partial y_i^j}{\partial p_e} \quad e \in E.$$

(34)

Let us condense the private sector into two representative firms

---

[24] Equation (34) is identical with (11-2) but explicitly takes account of the fact that chapter 26 measures supply z_i in place miles, but demand x_i in passenger miles.

$$\sum_j (p_i - c_i^j) \frac{\partial y_i^j}{\partial p_e} = (p_i - c_i) \frac{\partial y_i}{\partial p_e} \qquad i = 3, 4. \tag{35}$$

Since we assume separability of public and private supply we obtain

$$\frac{1}{LF_e} z_e(\cdot) = \hat{x}_e(\cdot); \quad e = 1, 2. \tag{36a}$$

$$\frac{1}{LF_e} \frac{\partial \hat{z}_i}{\partial p_e} = \frac{\partial \hat{x}_i}{\partial p_e}; \quad e, i = 1, 2 \tag{36b}$$

Moreover, we assume that good 3 and good 4 are supplied by monopolists whose supply behavior follows their subjective demand functions. As a proxy for these subjective demand functions we use our AIDS demand for goods 3 and 4. We obtain

$$\frac{\partial y_i}{\partial p_e} = \frac{\partial \hat{x}_i}{\partial p_e}; \quad e = 1, 2; \quad i = 3, 4. \tag{36c}$$

The Hicksian derivatives $\partial \hat{x}_i / \partial p_e$ and the demand $\hat{x}_e(\cdot)$ can be computed using the AIDS specifications.

A particular information problem refers to the monopolistic price-cost margins of the private economy. It is beyond the scope of this study to estimate the degree of monopoly of the UK private economy. Therefore we treat the monopolistic price-cost margins as exogenous variables and compute the adjustment of public prices for some empirically meaningful values of Θ_3 and Θ_4, namely, 10 and 20 per cent.

The reader should be aware that the independent determination of the price elasticities and the price-cost margins is an empirical ad-hoc assumption. However, this assumption could only be given up in a more general model on the UK producer behavior which is beyond the scope of this book.

For separable public and private supply and for exogenous Θ_3, Θ_4, the adjustment to private monopolistic structures is characterized by the system of equations

$$\sum_{i=1}^{2} (p_i - c_i) \frac{\partial \hat{x}_i}{\partial p_e} = -\gamma \hat{x}_e - (1 - \gamma) \sum_{i=3}^{4} \Theta_i p_i \frac{\partial \hat{x}_i}{\partial p_e} =$$

$$= -\gamma \hat{x}_e - (1 - \gamma) \frac{r}{p_e} \sum_{i=3}^{4} w_i \, \Theta_i \, \eta_{ie} \quad e = 1, 2 \tag{37}$$

$$\text{Revenue} - \text{costs} = \Pi^o \tag{31}$$

The notation is as usual: r denotes the income of the representative consumer, w_i are the budget shares.

All prices which result from the adjustment to private monopolistic pricing should be compared with Ramsey prices. The latter represent the case of $\Theta_3 = \Theta_4 = 0$, given the same deficit Π^o.

First we assumed monopolistic structures in the non-transportation market x_4 (budget share $w_4 = 0.877$) whereas private transportation x_3 was assumed to remain competitively. Bus and underground fares do not respond very sensitively to an increase of Θ_4. A transition from private competitive pricing to a price-cost margin of 20 % implies an increase of the bus fare by 3.9 % (METS) and by 2.4 % (MTC) and a reduction of the underground fare by -3.0 % (METS) and by -2.0 % (MTC).

Case a) $\Theta_3 = 0$; $\Theta_4 = 0.1$

	Monopoly-adjusted prices			For comparison: Ramsey		
	METS	$M\widetilde{L}C$	MTC	METS	$M\widetilde{L}C$	MTC
$p_1(82)$	15.5	16.2	12.0	15.2	15.8	11.9
$p_2(82)$	7.7	7.6	11.1	7.9	7.7	11.2

Case b) $\Theta_3 = 0$; $\Theta_4 = 0.2$

	Monopoly-adjusted prices			For comparison: Ramsey		
	METS	$M\widetilde{L}C$	MTC	METS	$M\widetilde{L}C$	MTC
$p_1(82)$	15.8	16.6	12.1	15.2	15.8	11.9
$p_2(82)$	7.6	7.5	10.9	7.9	7.7	11.2

It is easy to explain why the bus fare increases and the underground fare decreases. In chapter 11 we showed that a tendency for higher prices holds if a good is a net substitute for all privately supplied goods with positive price-cost margins. In our numerical example both bus and underground services are substitutes for x_4. However, bus services are a stronger substitute for x_4 than underground services ($\eta_{14} = 0.48$; $\eta_{24} = 0.08$). And the constant deficit implies that only one price increases.

However, we have also computed other examples where the results are more surprising and cannot be interpreted as easily as the cases a) and b). Consider, for instance, cases where both x_3 and x_4 are sold at monopolistic prices, $\Theta_3 = \Theta_4 = 0.1$ and 0.2, respectively. In these cases c) and d) the

Case c) $\Theta_3 = \Theta_4 = 0.1$

	Monopoly-adjusted prices			For comparison: Ramsey		
	METS	$M\widetilde{L}C$	MTC	METS	$M\widetilde{L}C$	MTC
$p_1(82)$	15.0	15.6	11.8	15.2	15.8	11.9
$p_2(82)$	8.0	7.8	11.2	7.9	7.7	11.2

Case d) $\Theta_3 = \Theta_4 = 0.2$

	Monopoly-adjusted prices			For comparison: Ramsey		
	METS	$M\widetilde{L}C$	MTC	METS	$M\widetilde{L}C$	MTC
$p_1(82)$	14.8	15.3	11.7	15.2	15.8	11.9
$p_2(82)$	8.1	8.0	11.3	7.9	7.7	11.2

transition from private competitive pricing to price cost margins of 10 % or of 20 % implies a *reduction* of the average bus fare and an *increase* of the average underground fare. The result is surprising. Although underground is the stronger substitute for private transportation ($\eta_{23} = 0.66$; $\eta_{13} = 0.017$) we would not have expected η_{23} to be very important because the budget share of x_3 is not very high ($w_3 = 0.104$). Hence we still would have expected increasing bus fares because of the strong substitute relation η_{14} given the high budget share $w_4 = 0.877$.

The surprising results of cases c) and d) can be explained best by showing the analytical and numerical structure which underlies the movement of p_1 and p_2 depending on changes in Θ_3 and Θ_4. Given constant marginal costs (METS) or marginal costs which do not change too intensively (MTC in our example), we may also consider the movement of Θ_1 and Θ_2 depending on changes in Θ_3 and Θ_4. Transforming (37) we obtain

$$\begin{pmatrix} \Theta_1 \\ \Theta_2 \end{pmatrix}^T \begin{pmatrix} \eta_{11} & \eta_{12} \\ \eta_{21} & \eta_{22} \end{pmatrix} = -\gamma(1,1) - (1-\gamma)\begin{pmatrix} \Theta_3 \\ \Theta_4 \end{pmatrix}^T \begin{pmatrix} \eta_{13} & \eta_{23} \\ \eta_{14} & \eta_{24} \end{pmatrix}. \tag{38}$$

The empirical computations show that all price elasticities are almost constant for the small price changes of cases a) to d). However, the changes in monopolistic private pricing significantly influence the welfare effects of the public deficit, as measured by γ. The following analysis will therefore assume constant elasticities but a Lagrangean parameter $\gamma = \gamma(\Theta_3, \Theta_4)$. We denote $\gamma_i := \partial\gamma/\partial\Theta_i$; $i = 3, 4$.

Starting from Ramsey prices ($\Theta_3 = \Theta_4 = 0$), total differentation of (38) yields [25]

$$\begin{pmatrix} d\Theta_1 \\ d\Theta_2 \end{pmatrix} = \frac{1}{D} \begin{pmatrix} \eta_{22} & -\eta_{12} \\ -\eta_{21} & \eta_{11} \end{pmatrix} \left[-(1-\gamma)\begin{pmatrix} \eta_{13} & \eta_{14} \\ \eta_{23} & \eta_{24} \end{pmatrix} - \begin{pmatrix} \gamma_3 & \gamma_4 \\ \gamma_3 & \gamma_4 \end{pmatrix} \right] \begin{pmatrix} d\Theta_3 \\ d\Theta_4 \end{pmatrix} \tag{39}$$

[25] Note that all terms which are multiplied by Θ_3 or Θ_4 do not appear in (39) because $\Theta_3 = \Theta_4 = 0$.

where the determinant $D = \eta_{11}\,\eta_{22} - \eta_{12}\,\eta_{21} > 0$. This formula shows that $d\Theta_1$ and $d\Theta_2$ respond to $d\Theta_3$ and $d\Theta_4$ according to a very complex pattern, including all price elasticities and the impact of Θ_3 and Θ_4 on the welfare valuation of the public deficit.

On the basis of equation (39) the surprising results of the numerical examples c) and d) become much less surprising. Given the interdependence of all η_{ik}, γ and γ_i we may always have to expect surprising results.

It is interesting to investigate the implications of (39) after substituting numerical values for η_{ik}, γ and γ_i. We choose case c) and consider a change from Ramsey prices, $\Theta_3 = \Theta_4 = 0$, to monopoly-adjusted prices, $\Theta_3 = \Theta_4 = 0.1$. The costs are specified according to MTC. The Lagrangean multiplier is $\gamma = -0.350$ in the Ramsey case and $\gamma = -0.437$ in the monopoly-adjusted case. As proxies for γ_i we use $\gamma_3 = -0.455$ and $\gamma_4 = -0.413$ [26]. Then we obtain

$$
\begin{pmatrix} d\Theta_1 \\ d\Theta_2 \end{pmatrix} = \frac{1}{D}\begin{bmatrix} -0.972 & -0.266 \\ -0.235 & -0.761 \end{bmatrix}\left[\begin{pmatrix} -0.023 & -0.645 \\ -0.893 & -0.102 \end{pmatrix} + \right.
$$
$$
\left. + \begin{pmatrix} 0.455 & 0.413 \\ 0.455 & 0.413 \end{pmatrix}\right]\begin{pmatrix} d\Theta_3 \\ d\Theta_4 \end{pmatrix} = \frac{1}{D}\begin{bmatrix} -0.303 & 0.143 \\ 0.232 & -0.183 \end{bmatrix}\begin{pmatrix} d\Theta_3 \\ d\Theta_4 \end{pmatrix}. \tag{40}
$$

Substituting $d\Theta_3 = d\Theta_4 = 0.1$ into (40) yields

$$
\begin{pmatrix} d\Theta_1 \\ d\Theta_2 \end{pmatrix} = \frac{1}{D}\begin{pmatrix} -0.0161 \\ +0.0049 \end{pmatrix} = \begin{pmatrix} -0.0238 \\ +0.0072 \end{pmatrix} \tag{41}
$$

which is just the surprising result of a decreasing bus fare and an increasing underground fare we have obtained in cases c) and d).

---

[26] Our computations yield the following multipliers: $\gamma(R) := \gamma(\Theta_3=0; \Theta_4=0) = -0.350$; $\gamma(M1) := \gamma(\Theta_3=0; \Theta_4=0.1) = -0.392$; $\gamma(M2) := \gamma(\Theta_3=\Theta_4=0.1) = -0.437$. Then $\tilde{\gamma}_4 = \gamma(M1) - \gamma(R) = -0.0413$, whence $\gamma_4 = \tilde{\gamma}_4/\Delta\Theta_i = -0.413$. Moreover $\tilde{\gamma}_{3,4} = \gamma(M2) - \gamma(R) = -0.087$, whence $\tilde{\gamma}_3 = \tilde{\gamma}_{3,4} - \tilde{\gamma}_4 = -0.045$ and $\gamma_3 = \tilde{\gamma}_3/\Delta\Theta_i = -0.455$.

On the other hand, substituting $d\Theta_3 = 0$ and $d\Theta_4 = 0.1$ into (40) yields

$$
\begin{pmatrix} d\Theta_1 \\ d\Theta_2 \end{pmatrix} = \frac{1}{D} \begin{pmatrix} +0.0143 \\ -0.0183 \end{pmatrix} = \begin{pmatrix} +0.0211 \\ -0.0270 \end{pmatrix} \tag{42}
$$

which is just that expected and by no means surprising result we have obtained in cases a) and b).

26.3.6 REVENUE MAXIMIZATION

The computation is based on the system of marginal conditions

$$
\sum_{i=1}^{2} \left(p_i - \frac{\beta_o}{1 + \beta_o} c_i \right) \frac{\partial x_i}{\partial p_e} = -x_e \qquad e = 1, 2 \tag{18 - 4}
$$

$$
\text{Revenue} - \text{costs} = \Pi^o \tag{31}
$$

where $\beta_o = \beta(\partial g / \partial z_o)$. Once again we have a system of three equations in three unknowns, the prices p_1, p_2 and the parameter β_o. This parameter measures infinitesimal changes of the objective function which result from changes in the initial endowments of labor.

Unfortunately, we did not succeed in finding a revenue maximum [27]. Regardless of the specification of the cost function we always obtained prices which implied a revenue lower than the revenue at actual prices. Hence

---

[27] Even greater problems arose for the output optimization according to (18-2). For the linear cost function the numerical solution procedure did not converge at all, although the interative process seemed to hint at deterrent bus prices (approximately £ 3000. -) which would imply closing down the bus services and concentrating on the underground services. For the MTC-specification the numerical solution procedure converges, but not to a maximum. Total output at the resulting prices of $p_1(82)=8.9$ and $p_2(82)=26.4$ would be lower than total output at the actual prices.

the marginal conditions and the revenue-cost constraint are fulfilled at a minimum or at a saddle point.

| | Prices according to (18-4) | | | For comparison: |
	METS	MLC	MTC	actual prices
$p_1(82)$	11.6	11.5	10.3	10.9
$p_2(82)$	10.8	11.0	13.3	12.2

26.3.7   PRICE INDEX MINIMIZATION

We start from the system of equations

$$\sum_{i=1}^{2}(p_i - c_i)\frac{\partial x_i}{\partial p_e} = -(1 - L_e)x_e \qquad e = 1, 2 \qquad (19-2)$$

$$\text{Revenue} - \text{costs} = \Pi^o \qquad\qquad (31)$$

which can be solved for the three unknowns p_1, p_2 and the parameter β_o which is a part of L_e.

The Laspeyres characteristics L_e are defined as

$$L_e = \frac{x_e^o}{x_e} \cdot \frac{1}{\sum p_i^o x_i^o} \cdot \frac{1}{\beta_o} \qquad e = 1, 2 \qquad (19-3)$$

$\sum_{i=1}^{4} p_i^o x_i^o$ are the total expenditures of the base period 1970, x_e^o is the consumption of good e in 1970.

As expected, price-index minimization has the same distributional effects as maximizing a welfare function of a board with distributional aims.

	Index-minimizing prices			For comparison: Feldstein prices ($\partial W/\partial v^h = \lambda/r^h$)		
	METS	MLC	MTC	METS	MLC	MTC
$p_1(82)$	11.5	11.4	10.62	12.2	12.8	10.56
$p_2(82)$	11.0	11.2	12.65	9.9	9.3	12.77

This distributional distortion of prices matters qualitatively as well as quantitatively. In the case of the MTC-specification of costs, index-minimization leads to prices which resemble Feldstein prices for $\partial W/\partial v^h = \lambda/r^h$. If the METS-specification is chosen, the distributional distortion of prices becomes even more important: index-minimizing bus fares are lower, and underground fares higher, than Feldstein prices for $\partial W/\partial v^h = \lambda/r^h$.

APPENDICES[1]

APPENDIX 1   THE SIZE OF THE PUBLIC ENTERPRISE SECTOR IN EUROPE

The following tables are based on

- data of the Centre Européen de l'Entreprise Publique (CEEP) for Germany, France, and Italy and

- data of the National Economic Development Office (NEDO) for the United Kingdom.

Difficulties in presenting data on the importance of public enterprises in different countries are caused by differences in the relevant definitions. The following problems arise with respect to the above mentioned sources of our tables:

(a) The CEEP-data for *France* are defined following the strict majority of shares or ownership rule unless otherwise stated; see the definition of the law concerning the democratisation of the public sector of 1983 (CEEP 1984, 51-52). Interpreting the French data, one should always consider the extended nationalization activities of 1982.

(b) The CEEP-data for *Germany* also follow the majority of shares or ownership rule. Traditional exceptions are VEBA AG and Volkswagenwerk AG of which German federal and state governments hold only a minority, but which are nevertheless regarded as public enterprises (CEEP 1984, 85).

---

[1] I gratefully acknowledge the help of R. Frensch, I. Vogelsang, CEEP, ICC, NEDO, and the US Department of Commerce, Bureau of Economic Analysis.

(c) The CEEP-data for *Italy* are calculated only

    – for non-agricultural and non-financial sectors,

    – where there is both a public and private sector presence.

The first restriction excludes national banks or local savings-banks. The second excludes, for instance, Italian rail and mail services, but includes air transport (Alitalia) and telecommunications. When computing the public sector shares of national GNP, investment or employment, the national data are reduced analogously (CEEP 1984, 190, 192).

(d) The NEDO-data for the *United Kingdom* cover only public corporations, mainly the nationalized industries. As compared to the wider concept of public enterprises, the former exclude public trading bodies other than public corporations as well as limited companies, mainly subsidiaries of the National Enterprise Board.

TABLE A1:   FRANCE

	gross value added[1]	employees[2]	gross plant investmen
	of public enterprises (billion F[3]); in brackets: in percent of all enterprises	of public enterprises (thousands); in brackets: in percent of total employees	of public enterprises (billion F[3]); in brackets: in percent of all enterprises
1972	90.7 (11.6)		30.0 (22.8)
1973	100.1 (11.7)	1439 (9.3)	33.0 (22.4)
1974	117.7 (11.6)		36.2 (21.3)
1975	137.0 (11.9)		45.6 (25.6)
1976	158.0 (12.0)	1582 (10.0)	53.0 (28.1)
1977	178.0 (12.0)		63.0 (30.7)
1978	204.0 (12.2)		70.0 (30.7)
1979	227.0 (13.0)	1633 (10.3)	78.0 (27.1)
1980	260.0 (13.2)		93.0 (27.3)
1981	290.0 (13.3)		99.0 (27.2)
1982[4]	410.0 (16.5)	2280 (14.6)	129.0 (31.7)

Source: CEEP-reports 1978, 1981, 1984.

---

[1] Excluding the financial sector, but including the agricultural sector.

[2] Including the financial sector, but excluding the agricultural sector.

[3] In current prices.

[4] The increase of the 1982 figures is due to the new nationalization measures.

TABLE A2:   GERMANY (FRG)

	value added[1]				employees[2]	gross plant investments
	of public enter-prises (billion DM[3]); in brackets: in percent of all economic areas				of public enter-prises (thousands); in brackets: in percent of all employees of all economic areas	of public enter-prises (billion DM[3]); in brackets: in percent of all economic areas
	gross	net	(gross	net)		
1972		64.1	(-	9.6)	2003 (7.5)	30.1 (14.0)
1973		72.9	(-	9.8)	2021 (7.6)	32.1 (14.3)
1974		79.4	(-	9.9)	1990 (7.6)	34.1 (15.8)
1975[4]		84.0	(-	10.1)	1931 (7.6)	32.6 (15.2)
1976	122.2	91.0[4]	(10.7	10.0[4])	1983 (7.9)	32.8 (14.1)
1977	125.8		(10.3	-)	1973 (7.9)	30.2 (12.1)
1978[4]	135.4		(10.4	-)	1973 (7.8)	32.8 (11.9)
1979	140.5		(10.5	-)	1952 (7.5)	36.2 (11.9)
1980	145.1		(10.2	-)	1984 (7.6)	43.0 (12.7)
1981[4]	155.1		(10.4	-)	2002 (7.7)	46.4 (13.7)
1982[4]	167.2		(10.7	-)	1989 (7.8)	48.4 (14.7)

Source: CEEP-reports 1978, 1981, 1984.

---

[1] Before reduction of assumed payments for bank services.

[2] Persons employed in Germany, annual average.

[3] In current prices.

[4] Provisional data (1975 and 1978 remain provisional, as there is no two year over-lapping in the data of the different reports).

Footnotes, table A3 (Italy), continued

[4] This approximate percentage refers public enterprises to *all* non-financial and non-agricultural undertakings, without the restriction to those sectors where there is both a public and private sector presence. This approximation is suited best for international comparisons, as other countries typically refer public enterprise data to total national reference figures, not to those sectors only where both public and private enterprises operate.

[5] This approximate percentage refers public enterprises to *all* non-agricultural undertakings (including finance) without the restriction to those sectors where there is both a public and private sector presence. This approximation is suited best for international comparisons, as substantiated in footnote 4) above.

Footnotes, table A4 (United Kingdom)

[1] At factor cost, before providing for depreciation but after providing for stock depreciation.

[2] At June each year. Two part-timers counted as one full-timer.

[3] GDFCF.

[4] For list of public corporations and their dates of entry and exit into the public corporations sector of the economy see National Income and Expenditure, HMSO, annually.

[5] At current prices.

TABLE A3:   ITALY [1]

	gross value added	employees	gross plant investment
	of public enter- prises (billion L[2]); in brackets: in percent of total gross value added	of public enter- prises (thousands); in brackets: in percent of all employees	of public enter- prises (billion L [2]); in brackets: in percent of total gross plant investment
1972	5404.3 (13.8)	1091.9 (13.2)	3256.0 (40.0)
1973	6747.3 (14.7)	1157.3 (14.1)	3540.9 (35.0)
1974[3]	8240.2 (23.0)	1213.6 (22.8)	4097.6 (43.6)
1975	9914.4 (24.3)	1265.3 (23.7)	4702.4 (47.4)
1976	12271.9 (23.8)	1283.4 (24.6)	5426.0 (46.7)
1977	14535.3 (24.0)	1291.6 (25.0)	6190.7 (49.0)
1978	16741.2 (24.7)	1278.8 (25.4)	6792.7 (47.1)
1979	20288.5 (24.6)	1284.1 (25.5)	7631.0 (46.2)
1980	24557.2 (24.5)	1294.6 (25.9)	9977.4 (47.8)
1981	29395.3 (25.1)	1301.4 (26.8)	12316.3 (49.7)
1982	((14.0))[4]	((15.0))[5]	((30.0))[4]

Source: CEEP-reports 1973, 1975, 1978, 1981, 1984.

---

[1] Non-agricultural and non-financial sectors where there is both a public and private sector presence.

[2] In current prices.

[3] The 1974-jump in the figures does not result from nationalization measures, but from deliberate economic policy favoring public enterprises, as explained in the 1975 CEEP-report.

TABLE A4:   UNITED KINGDOM

	output[1] (value added)	employment[2]	fixed investment[3]
	of public corporations[4] (billion £ [5]); in brackets: in percent of GDP	of public corporations[4] (thousands); in brackets: in percent of total employed labor force	of public corporations[4] (billion £ [5]); in brackets: in percent of total fixed investment
1972	5.6 (10.2)	1902 (7.8)	1.8 (15.2)
1973	6.4 (9.6)	1890 (7.5)	2.1 (14.0)
1974	8.0 (10.6)	1985 (7.9)	2.9 (16.5)
1975	10.6 (11.1)	2035 (8.1)	3.9 (18.4)
1976	13.0 (11.7)	1980 (8.0)	4.7 (19.0)
1977	14.5 (11.3)	2089 (8.4)	4.8 (17.7)
1978	16.5 (11.1)	2061 (8.2)	4.9 (15.9)
1979	18.0 (10.5)	2065 (8.1)	5.6 (15.2)
1980	21.3 (10.7)	2038 (8.1)	6.6 (16.0)
1981	23.9 (11.0)	1867 (7.7)	6.8 (16.3)
1982	26.5 (11.1)	1756 (7.3)	7.2 (15.6)
1983	27.7 (10.7)	1663 (7.0)	8.0 (16.2)

Source: I gratefully acknowledge the help of A. Kilpatrick (NEDO) who updated the NEDO (1976) figures as presented in the above table.

Footnotes see p. 428

APPENDIX 2   THE SIZE OF THE GOVERNMENT
AND REGULATED ENTERPRISE SECTOR IN THE
UNITED STATES

The following tables are based on the U.S. Department of Commerce's monthly survey of current business.

Government enterprises, according to these surveys are defined as
"... the activities of government whose operating costs are at least to a substantial extent covered by the sale of goods and services to the public. Interest paid and interest received are excluded from costs and sales, respectively, in judging whether the activity qualifies as a government enterprise."[1]

More complicated is the delimitation of the *regulated sector*. There are no comprehensive data sources which give separate information for US regulated and non-regulated industries. Hence we have selected figures for US sectors where the most intensive regulation takes place. However, it should be kept in mind that recent deregulation activities make any delimitation based on these data a little superficial.

---

[1] Survey of current business, March 1980, p. 33, footnote 3.

TABLE A5:   GOVERNMENT AND REGULATED ENTERPRISES' SHARE OF US GNP

	Government enterprises	Transportation	Communication	Public utilities (electricity, gas, sanitary services)	Finance and insurance[1]	GNP (billion $ [2]
	%	%	%	%	%	
1972	1.49	3.95	2.51	2.39	3.79	1171.1
1973	1.33	3.93	2.50	2.33	3.22	1306.6
1974	1.44	3.98	2.50	2.21	3.08	1413.2
1975	1.45	3.64	2.60	2.54	3.34	1528.8
1976	1.50	3.68	2.63	2.58	3.73	1718.0
1977	1.40	3.73	2.58	2.60	4.02	1918.3
1978	1.38	3.79	2.58	2.56	4.32	2163.9
1979	1.33	3.78	2.50	2.38	4.34	2417.8
1980	1.33	3.74	2.55	2.52	4.31	2631.7
1981	1.31	3.59	2.59	2.65	4.20	2957.8
1982	1.30	3.47	2.80	2.88	4.23	3069.3
1983	1.30	3.48	2.80	3.01	4.52	3304.8

Source: Survey of current business, July 1976, July 1979, July 1983, July 1984.

---

[1] Excluding real estate.

[2] In current prices.

TABLE A6: FULL TIME EQUIVALENT EMPLOYEES IN US GOVERNMENT AND REGULATED ENTERPRISES

	Govern-ment enter-prises	Transpor-tation	Communi-cation	Public utilities (electricity, gas, sanitary services)	Finance and insurance[1]	Total full time equivalent employees
	%	%	%	%	%	(millions)
1972	1.90	3.54	1.51	0.96	4.12	72.3
1973	1.85	3.49	1.48	0.94	4.12	75.5
1974	1.90	3.50	1.48	0.94	4.21	76.4
1975	2.00	3.37	1.49	0.97	4.37	74.4
1976	1.90	3.34	1.45	0.92	4.35	76.7
1977	1.84	3.34	1.42	0.91	4.38	79.3
1978	1.80	3.33	1.41	0.90	4.40	83.2
1979	1.77	3.36	1.44	0.90	4.49	85.9
1980	1.81	3.29	1.49	0.93	4.68	85.9
1981	1.79	3.22	1.52	0.95	4.80	86.7
1982	1.79	3.11	1.57	0.99	4.99	84.8
1983	1.79	3.06	1.52	0.99	5.08	85.2

Source: Survey of current business, July 1976, July 1979, July 1983, July 1984.

---

[1] Excluding real estate.

TABLE A7: EXPENDITURES FOR NEW PLANT AND EQUIPMENT BY US REGULATED [1] ENTERPRISES

	Transpor- tation	Communi- cation	Public utilities (electricity, gas, sanitary services)	Finance, insurance, and real estate[2]	Total nonfarm business
	%	%	%	%	(billion $ [3])
1972	5.60	10.21	13.55	11.32	119.9
1973	5.40	9.90	12.97	11.64	132.2
1974	5.23	10.14	12.38	10.47	135.2
1975	5.42	9.35	11.90	11.31	119.7
1976	5.00	9.09	12.07	10.24	123.1
1977	4.65	9.82	12.49	10.22	134.9
1978	4.51	10.44	12.02	11.83	146.0
1979	4.34	10.64	11.62	11.96	157.3
1980	3.87	10.79	11.02	11.91	158.5
1981	3.54	11.27	10.82	12.32	159.0
1982	3.60	10.73	11.91	12.79	150.3
1983	3.50	9.73	12.25	[4]	145.3

Source: Survey of current business, September 1981 (revised computation 1947 – 1980), December 1984.

---

[1] The above source does not contain figures of government enterprises.

[2] Distinction between (i) finance and insurance, and (ii) real estate is impossible on the basis of the survey of current business tables.

[3] At 1972 prices.

[4] Not available on the basis of the December 1984 survey.

LIST OF SYMBOLS

a	parameters of empirical estimations of demand systems
b	parameters of empirical estimations of demand systems
c	marginal costs (with respect to quantity as defined in section 3.3: $c_i := (\partial g/\partial z_i)/(\partial g/\partial z_o)$; with respect to quality as defined in section 3.5: $c_{qe} := (\partial g/\partial q_e)/(\partial g/\partial z_o)$)
d	parameters of empirical estimations of demand systems
e	– index of regulated prices and qualities ($e \in E$)
	– expenditure function
f	– function
	– (second) index of regulated prices (chapter 11)
$f_e(\tau)$	– density function of time-dependent demand (chapter 14)
g	production function (public firm $g(\cdot)$; private firms $g^j(\cdot)$)
h	index of consumers ($h = 1, \ldots, H$)
i	index of commodities ($i = o, \ldots, n$)
j	index of private producers ($j = 1, \ldots, J$)
k	– (second) index of commodities ($k = o, \ldots, n$),
	– number of regulated prices ($e = 1, \ldots, k$) (chapter 7)
ℓ	labor input ($\ell := -z_o$)
m	– index of private monopoly prices (chapter 11)
	– index of minimal supply (chapter 14)

$m+1$ number of public inputs $\left(i = o, \ldots, m \text{ in chs. } 4, 6,16\text{-}22\right)$

$n+1$ number of commodities $\left(i = o, \ldots, n\right)$

p price

q quality

r lump-sum income

s – factor of proportional variation of different variables

   – political sympathy variable *(chapter 16)*

t – index of time

   – price-marginal cost difference $\left(t_i := p_i - c_i\right)$

   – transformed variable $t^h := \omega^h + s^h$ *(chapter 16)*

u direct individual utility function *(defined in 2.1.1)*

v indirect individual utility function *(defined in 2.1.1)*

w weights which add up to unity, for instance the budget shares in the empirical chapters or the weights in 11.2

x consumer net demand *(if positive)*,

   consumer net supply *(if negative)*

y net output of private producers *(if positive)*,

   net input of private producers *(if negative)*

z net output of the public enterprise *(if positive)*,

z net input of the public enterprise *(if negative)*

A matrix, general notation (chapter 5)

B coefficients of empirical estimations

BUD budget (chapter 17)

C cost function

$\widetilde{C}_i$ modified marginal costs (defined in subsection 3.3.2:

$$\widetilde{C}_i = c_i + \gamma(\partial\Pi/\partial z_i))$$

CAP capacity (chapter 12)

CB linear cost function, bus (chapter 26)

CU linear cost function, underground (chapter 26)

D coefficients of empirical estimations

DV dummy variable (chapters 5, 6)

E – set of regulated prices (and qualities), $E \subset I$,

            – excess demand (chapter 14)

F distributional characteristic à la Feldstein (defined in subsection 3.3.1: $F_e := \Sigma_h \lambda^h (\partial v^h/\partial r^h)(x_e^h/x_e))$

$F_e(\tau)$ distribution function of time-dependent demand (ch.14)

G – coefficients of empirical estimations

            – cost function (chapter 22)

H number of consumers $(h = 1, \ldots, H)$

I – set of all commodities, $I = \{o, \ldots, n\}$

            – indifference curve

J number of private producers $(j = 1, \ldots, J)$

L   – total employment (chapter 12)

          – length of period (chapter 14)

          – weights (ch. 19: minimization of a Laspeyres price index)

M   set of prices, fixed by the private firm (chapter 11)

METS   linear cost function (chapter 26)

MLC   marginal labor costs (chapter 26)

MTC   marginal total costs (chapter 26)

N   number of coalitions (subsection 8.1.2)

P   price index

POL   political weights (chapter 16)

Q   quality characteristic (defined in subsection 3.5.2:

$$Q_e := \Sigma_h \lambda^h (\partial v^h / \partial r^h)(\partial e^h / \partial q_e))$$

R   expenditure function (empirical chapters)

RAP   regulatory adjustment process (chapter 8)

RU   rate of unemployment

S   – Slutsky substitution effect

          – quantity sold at any point of time (chapter 14)

SUB   subsidy (chapter 7)

T   – index which indicates transposed vectors or matrices

          – index of time (chapter 7)

TV   traffic volume (chapter 12)

U – individual utility function, Leibenstein type (2.4.2)

         – union's utility function (chapter 20)

V indirect utility function of the representative consumer (empirical chapters)

W welfare function (defined in section 2.1)

Y individual income (subsection 2.4.2)

Z indirect production function (chapter 24)

α Lagrangean parameters (market clearing conditions)

β Lagrangean parameter (public enterprise's technology)

β_o $:= \beta(\partial g/\partial z_o)$

γ Lagrangean parameter (public budget constraint)

Γ rationing function (chapter 14)

Δ – difference

         – finite changes of variables

δ – Lagrangean parameter (section 9.3)

         – weights (chapters 17, 26)

ε uncompensated elasticity of demand

ς public output (chapter 22)

η compensated elasticity of demand

Θ price-cost margin $(\Theta_i := (p_i - c_i)/p_i)$

κ *capital input*

λ *social valuation of individual utility (defined in section 3.3:* $\lambda^h :=$ $(\partial W/\partial v^h)/\beta(\partial g/\partial z_o))$

Λ *– distribution of incomes* r^h *(chapter 16)*

       – social valuation of individual utility

       (defined in subsection 2.1.2: $\Lambda^h := \partial W/\partial v^h$*)*

$\mu(\cdot)$ *voter's decision function (chapter 16)*

μ *measure (chapter 22)*

ν *– shadow price of quality (section 3.5)*

       – Lagrangean parameter

ξ *vectors of price changes* (dp_e) *(chapter 5)*

π *private firm's profit*

Π *public revenue-cost constraint*

ρ *– exogenous variables of the public revenue-cost constraint*

       (defined in subsection 2.5.1: $\Pi := \Pi(p, q, z, \rho)$*)*

       – parameter measuring union's influence (chapter 20)

σ *variance of the political sympathy variable* s^h *(chapter 16)*

τ *time dependent demand (chapter 14)*

Φ *objective function, positive theory*

χ *vectors in Farkas' and Motzkin's theorem (chapter 5)*

Ψ *– set of all moments of excess demand (chapter 14)*

       – density function of the sympathy variable s^h *(ch. 16)*

ω *individual voter's utility difference (chapter 16)*

REFERENCES

ALCHIAN, A.A., 1961, Some economics of property, RAND Corporation Study P-2316 *(RAND Corporation, Santa Monica, CA)*.

AMTRAK REORGANIZATION ACT, 1979, Public Law 96-73, *September 29.*

ATKINSON, A.B., 1970, On the measurement of inequality, *Journal of Economic Theory 2, 244-263.*

ATKINSON, A.B. and J.E. STIGLITZ, 1980, Lectures on public economics *(McGraw Hill, London.*

ATTALI, J., 1978, Towards socialist planning, in: S.Holland, ed., Beyond capitalist planning *(Basil Blackwell, Oxford), 34-46.*

AUMANN, R.J. and L.S. SHAPLEY, 1974, Values of non-atomic games *(Princeton University Press, Princeton, NJ).*

AVERCH, H. and L.L. JOHNSON, 1962, Behavior of the firm under regulatory constraint, *American Economic Review 52, 1052-1069.*

BACKHAUS, J., 1979, Ökonomik der partizipativen Unternehmung I *(Mohr, Tübingen).*

BAILEY, E.E., 1973, Economic theory of regulatory constraint *(Heath, Lexington, MA).*

BAILEY, E.E. and J.C. MALONE, 1970, Resource allocation and the regulated firm, *Bell Journal of Economics and Management Science 1, 129-142.*

BARKER, T.C. and M. ROBBINS, 1963, 1974, A history of London Transport, Vol. I: *The nineteenth century, Vol. II: The twentieth century to 1970 (Allen & Unwin, London).*

BARON, D.P. and R.R. DE BONDT, 1979, Fuel adjustment mechanisms and economic efficiency, *Journal of Industrial Economics 27, 243-261.*

BARON, D.P. and R.R. DE BONDT, 1981, On the design of regulatory price adjustment mechanisms, *Journal of Economic Theory 24, 70-94.*

BAUMOL, W.J., 1959, Business behavior, value and growth *(Harcourt, Brace & World, New York)*.

BAUMOL, W.J., 1976, Scale economies, average cost, and the profitability of marginal cost pricing, in: R.E. Grieson, ed., *Public and urban economics, Essays in honor of William S. Vickrey (Heath, Lexington, MA)* 43-57.

BAUMOL, W.J., 1977, On the proper cost tests for natural monopoly in a multiproduct industry, *American Economic Review 67, 809-822.*

BAUMOL, W.J., E.E. BAILEY and R.D. WILLIG, 1977, Weak invisible hand theorems on the sustainability of multiproduct natural monopoly, *American Economic Review 67, 350-365.*

BAUMOL, W.J. and D.F. BRADFORD, 1970, Optimal departures from marginal cost pricing, *American Economic Review 60, 265-283.*

BAUMOL, W.J. and D. FISCHER, 1978, Cost-minimizing number of firms and determination of industry structure, *Quarterly Journal of Economics 92, 439-467.*

BEATO, P., 1982, The existence of marginal cost pricing equilibria with increasing returns, *Quarterly Journal of Economics 97, 669-688.*

BEATO, P. and A. MAS-COLELL, 1984, The marginal cost pricing rule as a regulation mechanism in mixed markets, in: M. Marchand, P. Pestieau and H. Tulkens, eds., The performance of public enterprises *(North-Holland, Amsterdam) 81-100.*

BEESLEY, M.E., 1979, Competition and supply in London taxis, *Journal of Transport Economics and Policy 13, 10-131.*

BEESLEY, M.E., 1981, Liberalisation of the use of British telecommunications network, *Report to the Secretary of State, Department of Industry (Her Majesty's Stationery Office, London).*

BEESLEY, M.E. and S. GLAISTER, 1983, Information for regulating: the case of taxis, *Economic Journal 93, 594-615.*

BERGSON, A., 1972, Optimal pricing for a public enterprise, *Quarterly Journal of Economics 86, 519-544*.

BERGSON, A., 1973, On monopoly welfare losses, *American Economic Review 63, 853-870*.

BILLERA, L.J. and D.C. HEATH, 1979, Allocation of shared costs: A set of axioms yielding a unique procedure, *Technical Report (Cornell University, Ithaca, NY)*.

BILLERA, L.J., D.C. HEATH and J. RAANAN, 1978, Internal telephone billing rates - A novel application of non-atomic game theory, *Operations Research 26, 956-965*.

BOADWAY, R.W., 1974, The welfare foundations of cost-benefit analysis, *Economic Journal 84, 926-939*.

BÖS, D., 1978a, Cost of living indices and public pricing, *Economica 45, 59-69*.

BÖS, D., 1978b, Distributional effects of maximisation of passenger miles, *Journal of Transport Economics and Policy 12, 322-329*.

BÖS, D., 1978c, Effizienz des öffentlichen Sektors aus volkswirtschaftlicher Sicht, *Schweizerische Zeitschrift für Volkswirtschaft und Statistik 114, 287-313*.

BÖS, D., 1980, Öffentliche Unternehmungen, *in: F. Neumark, H. Haller, and N. Andel, eds., Handbuch der Finanzwissenschaft, third edition, vol. II (Mohr, Tübingen), 3-60*.

BÖS, D., 1981, Economic theory of public enterprise, *Lecture Notes in Economics and Mathematical Systems 188 (Springer, Berlin)*.

BÖS, D., 1983, Public pricing with distributional objectives, in: J. Finsinger, ed., *Public sector economics (Macmillan, London) 171-188*.

BÖS, D., 1984, Income taxation, public sector pricing and redistribution, *Scandinavian Journal of Economics 86, 166-183*.

BÖS, D., 1985a, Public sector pricing, in: A. Auerbach, and M. Feldstein, eds.,

Handbook of public economics, Vol. I (North-Holland, Amsterdam), 129-211.

BÖS, D., 1985b, Public enterprise economics: theory and application, appendix 3, data basis of London Transport estimations, *Mimeo (Institute of Economics, University of Bonn).*

BÖS, D., B. GENSER and R. HOLZMANN, 1982, On the quality of publicly supplied goods, *Economica 49, 289-296.*

BÖS, D. and G. TILLMANN, 1982, Public enterprise deficits, lump-sum taxation and path dependent consumer surplus, *Mimeo (Institute of Economics, University of Bonn).*

BÖS, D. and G. TILLMANN, 1983, Cost-axiomatic regulatory pricing, *Journal of Public Economics 22, 243-256.*

BÖS, D., G. TILLMANN and H.-G. ZIMMERMANN, 1984, Bureaucratic public enterprises, in: D. Bös, A. Bergson and J.R. Meyer, eds., Entrepreneurship, *Zeitschrift für Nationalökonomie, Supplementum 4 (Springer, Vienna), 127-176.*

BÖS, D. and H.-G. ZIMMERMANN, 1983, Winning votes and political sympathy, *Mimeo (Institute of Economics, University of Bonn).*

BOITEUX, M., 1956, 1971, Sur la gestion des monopoles publics astreints à l'équilibre budgétaire, *Econometrica 24, 22-40. English edition: On the management of public monopolies subject to budgetary constraints: Journal of Economic Theory 3, 219-240.*

BORCHERDING, T.E., 1980, Toward a positive theory of public sector supply arrangements, *Mimeo (Simon Frazer University, Burnaby, B.C., Canada)*

BORCHERDING, T.E., W.W. POMMEREHNE and F. SCHNEIDER, 1982, Comparing the efficiency of private and public production: The evidence from five countries, in: D. Bös, R.A. Musgrave and J. Wiseman, eds., Public Production, *Zeitschrift für Nationalökonomie, Supplementum 2 (Springer, Vienna) 127-156.*

BROWN, D.J. and G. HEAL, 1979, Equity, efficiency and increasing returns, *Review of Economic Studies 46, 571-585.*

BROWN, D.J. and G. HEAL, 1980a, Two-part tariffs, marginal cost pricing and increasing returns in a general equilibrium model, *Journal of Public Economics 13, 25-49.*

BROWN, D.J. and G. HEAL, 1980b, Marginal cost pricing revisited, *Mimeo (Econometric Society World Congress, Aix-en-Provence).*

BROWN, G., Jr. and M.B. JOHNSON, 1969, Public utiliy pricing and output under risk, *American Economic Review 59, 119-128.*

BURNS, M.E., 1973, A note on the concept and measure of consumer's surplus, *American Economic Review 63, 335-344.*

CARLTON, D.W., 1977, Peak load pricing with stochastic demand, *American Economic Review 67, 1006-1010.*

CAVES, D.W. and L.R. CHRISTENSEN, 1980a, Global properties of flexible functional forms, *American Economic Review 70, 422-432.*

CAVES, D.W. and L.R. CHRISTENSEN, 1980b, The relative efficiency of public and private firms in a competitive environment: The case of Canadian railroads, *Journal of Political Economy 88, 958-976.*

CEEP (Centre Europeen de l'Entreprise Publique), 1984, Public enterprise in the European Economic Community: English version of the CEEP review 1984 *(C.E.E.P., Brussels).*

CHARZAT, M.M., 1981, Rapport N° 456, assemblée Nationale 1981-1982, au nom de la commission spéciale changée d'examiner le project de loi de nationalisation $(n^o$ 384), *tome I, présentation génerale.*

CHIPMAN, J.S. and J.C. MOORE, 1976, The scope of consumer's surplus arguments, in: A. Tang, F. Westfield and J. Worley, eds., Evolution, welfare and time in economics *(Heath, Lexington, MA) 69-124.*

CHRISTENSEN, L.R., D.W. JORGENSON and L.J. LAU, 1975, Transcendental logarithmic utility functions, *American Economic Review 65, 367-383.*

CORNET, B., 1982, Existence of equilibria in economies with increasing returns, *Working Paper (University of California, Berkeley, CA).*

COWLING, K. and D.C. MUELLER, 1978, The social costs of monopoly power, *Economic Journal 88, 727-748.*

CREW, M.A. and P.R. KLEINDORFER, 1979, Public utility economics *(Macmillan, London).*

DANSBY, R.E., 1975, Welfare optimal peak-load pricing and capacity decisions with intraperiod time varying demand, *Economic Discussion Paper 39 (Bell Laboratories, Holmdel, NJ).*

DAVIES, D.G., 1980, Property rights and economic behavior in private and government enterprises, The case of Australia's banking system, *Research in Law and Economics, forthcoming.*

DEATON, A., 1974, A reconsideration of the empirical implications of additive preferences, *Economic Journal 84, 338-348.*

DEATON, A., 1978, Specification and testing in applied demand analysis, *Economic Journal 88, 524-536.*

DEATON, A. and J. MUELLBAUER, 1980a, Economics and consumer behavior *(Cambridge University Press, Cambridge UK).*

DEATON, A. and J. MUELLBAUER, 1980b, An almost ideal demand system, *American Economic Review 70, 312-326.*

DELORS, J., 1978, The decline of French planning, in: S. Holland, ed., Beyond capitalist planning *(Basil Blackwell, Oxford), 9-33.*

DEPARTMENT OF TRANSPORT, 1982, Urban public transport subsidies: An economic assessment of value for money, *Technical Report and Summary Report (London).*

DIAMOND, P.A., 1975, The many-person Ramsey tax rule, *Journal of Public Economics 4, 335-342.*

DIAMOND, P.A. and D.L. MCFADDEN, 1974, Some uses of the expenditure function in public finance, *Journal of Public Economics 3, 3-21.*

DIEWERT, W.E., 1978, Optimal tax perturbations, *Journal of Public Economics 10, 139-177.*

DIEWERT, W.E., 1982, Duality approaches to microeconomic theory, in: K.J. Arrow and M.D. Intriligator, eds., *Handbook of Mathematical Economics, vol II (North-Holland, Amsterdam), 535-599.*

DIXIT, A., 1975, Welfare effects of tax and price changes, *Journal of Public Economics 4, 103-123.*

DRÈZE, J.H., 1964, Some postwar contributions of French economists to theory and public policy with special emphasis on problems of resource allocation, *American Economic Review 54, No. 4, Part 2 (Supplement), 1-64.*

DRÈZE, J.H., 1984, Second-best analysis with markets in disequilibrium: Public sector pricing in a Keynesian regime, in: M. Marchand, P. Pestieau and H. Tulkens, eds., The performance of public enterprises *(North-Holland, Amsterdam) 45-79.*

DRÈZE, J.H. and M. MARCHAND, 1976, Pricing, spending, and gambling rules for non-profit organizations, in: R.E. Grieson, ed., Public and urban economics, *Essays in honor of William S. Vickrey (Heath, Lexington, MA) 59-89.*

FAIRHURST, M.H., 1973, An analysis of factors affecting bus and rail receipts (1970-72), *Economic Research Report R 201 (London Transport Executive, London).*

FAIRHURST, M.H., 1981, Why simplify? A case for simplified fares, *Economic Research Report R 244 (London Transport Executive, London).*

FAIRHURST, M.H, 1982, Public transport subsidies and value for money - some indicative results, *Economic Research Report R 252 (London Transport Executive, London).*

FAIRHURST, M.H., J.F. LINDSAY and P.J. MORRIS, 1975, An analysis of the fares revision introduced on 23 March 1975, *Economic Research Report R 218 (London Transport Executive, London)*.

FAIRHURST, M.H. and P.J. MORRIS, 1975, Variations in the demand for bus and rail travel up to 1974, *Economic Research Report R 210 (London Transport Executive, London)*.

FAULHABER, G.R. 1975, Cross-subsidization: Pricing in public enterprises, *American Economic Review 65, 966-977*.

FAULHABER, G.R. and S.B. LEVINSON, 1981, Subsidy-free prices and anonymous equity, *American Economic Review 71, 1083-1091*.

FAULHABER, G.R. and J.C. PANZAR, 1977, Optimal two-part tariffs with self-selection, *Economic Discussion Paper 74 (Bell Laboratories, Holmdel, NJ)*.

FELDSTEIN, M.S., 1972a, Distributional equity and the optimal structure of public prices, *American Economic Review 62, 32-36. (Corrected version of p. 33, footnote 7: American Economic Review 62, 763)*.

FELDSTEIN, M.S., 1972b, Equity and efficiency in public sector pricing: The optimal two-part tariff, *Quarterly Journal of Economics 86, 175-187*.

FELDSTEIN, M.S., 1972c, The pricing of public intermediate goods, *Journal of Public Economics 1, 45-72*.

FELDSTEIN, M.S., 1974, Financing in the evaluation of public expenditure, in: W.L. Smith and J.M. Culbertson, eds., Public finance and stabilization policy, *Essays in honor of Richard A. Musgrave (North-Holland, Amsterdam), 13-36*.

FINSINGER, J. and I. VOGELSANG, 1981, Alternative institutional frameworks for price incentive mechanisms, *Kyklos 34, 388-404*.

FOSTER, C.D., 1976, The public corporation: Allocative and X-efficiency, in: J.A.G. Griffith, ed., From policy to administration, *Essays in honour of W.A. Robson (London) 139-173*.

FOSTER, C.D. and M.E. BEESLEY, 1963, Estimating the social benefit of constructing an underground railway in London, *Journal of the Royal Statistical Society 126 sec. A, 46-78.*

FOSTER, C.D. and H. NEUBURGER, 1974, The ambiguity of the consumer's surplus measure of welfare change, *Oxford Economic Papers 26, 66-77.*

FRERK, M., I. LINDSAY and M.H. FAIRHURST, 1981, Traffic trends in the seventies, *Economic Research Report R 248 (London Transport Executive, London).*

GARNER, M.R., 1983, Outline of course Gv 220 - Public enterprise, Mimeo *(London School of Economics and Political Science).*

GEORGESCU-ROEGEN, N., 1968-69, Revisiting Marshall's constancy of marginal utility of money, *Southern Economic Journal 35, 176-181.*

GLAISTER, S., 1974, Generalised consumer surplus and public transport pricing, *Economic Journal 84, 849-867.*

GLAISTER, S., 1976a, Peak load-pricing and the Channel tunnel: A case study, *Journal of Transport Economics and Policy 10, 89-112.*

GLAISTER, S., 1976b, Variations in the demand for bus and rail travel in London, 1970 to 1975, *Mimeo, The London School of Economics.*

GLAISTER, S., 1982a, Some proposals on the de-regulation of transport services in London, in: D. Bös, R.A. Musgrave and J. Wiseman, eds., *Public Production, Zeitschrift für Nationalökonomie, Supplementum 2 (Springer, Vienna), 157-182.*

GLAISTER, S., 1982b, Urban public transport subsidies: An economic assessment of value for money, *Technical Report and Summary Report (Department of Transport, London).*

GLAISTER, S. and J.J. COLLINGS, 1978, Maximisation of passenger miles in theory and practice, *Journal of Transport Economics and Policy 12, 304-321.*

GLAISTER, S. and D. LEWIS, 1978, An integrated fares policy for transport in

London, *Journal of Public Economics 9, 341-355.*

GRAVELLE, H.S.E, 1981, Public enterprise management incentive mechanisms: Some difficulties, *Discussion Paper 75 (Queen Mary College, London).*

GRAVELLE, H.S.E., 1982a, Incentives, efficiency and control in public firms, in: D. Bös, R.A. Musgrave and J. Wiseman, eds., Public production, *Zeitschrift für Nationalökonomie, Supplementum 2 (Springer, Vienna), 79-104.*

GRAVELLE, H.S.E., 1982b, Reward structures in a planned economy: Comment, *Discussion Paper 83 (Queen Mary College, London).*

GRAVELLE, H.S.E., 1983, Judicial Review and public firms, *International Review of Law and Economics 3, 187-205.*

GRAVELLE, H.S.E., 1984, Bargaining and efficiency in public and private sector firms, in: M. Marchand, P. Pestieau and H. Tulkens, eds., The performance of public enterprises *(North-Holland, Amsterdam) 193-220.*

GREEN, H.A.J., 1962, The social optimum in the presence of monopoly and taxation, *Review of Economics Studies 29, 66-78.*

GREEN, H.A.J., 1975, Two models of optimal pricing and taxation, *Oxford Economic Papers 27, 352-382.*

GREY, A., 1975, Urban fares policy *(Saxon House, Westmead, Farnborough, Hants; Heath, Lexington).*

GUESNERIE, R., 1975, Pareto optimality in non-convex economies, *Econometrica 43, 1-29.*

GUESNERIE, R., 1980, Second-best pricing rules in the Boiteux tradition: Derivation, review and dicussion, *Journal of Public Economics 13, 51-80.*

HAGEN, K.P., 1979, Optimal pricing in public firms in an imperfect market economy, *Scandinavian Journal of Economics 81, 475-493.*

HAMMOND, P.J., 1977, Dual interpersonal comparisons of utility and the welfare economics of income distribution, *Journal of Public Economics 7, 51-*

71.

HAMMOND, P.J., 1984, Approximate measures of social welfare and the size of tax reform, in: D. Bös, M. Rose and C. Seidl, eds., *Beiträge zur neueren Steuertheorie (Springer, Berlin), 95-115.*

HANSON, A.H., 1965, Public enterprise and economic development, *2nd edition (Routledge & Kegan Paul, London).*

HARBERGER, A.C., 1954, Monopoly and resource allocation, *American Economic Review 44, Papers and Proceedings, 77-87.*

HATTA, T., 1977, A theory of piecemeal policy recommendations, *Review of Economic Studies 44, 1-21.*

HAUSE, J.C., 1975, The theory of welfare cost measurement, *Journal of Political Economy 83, 1145-1182.*

HAUSMAN, J.A., 1981, Exact consumer's surplus and deadweight loss, *American Economic Review 71, 662-676.*

HAYEK, F.v., 1960, The constitution of liberty *(Routledge & Kegan Paul, London).*

HEALD, D., 1980, The economic and financial control of U.K. nationalised industries, *Economic Journal 90, 243-265.*

HEALD, D. and D. STEEL, 1981, The privatisation of UK public enterprises, *Annals of Public and Co-operative Economy 52, 351-367.*

HOLLAND, S., 1975, The socialist challenge *(Quartet Books, London).*

HOLLAND, S., 1978, Planning disagreements, in: S. Holland, ed., Beyond capitalist planning *(Basil Blackwell, Oxford), 137-161.*

HOTELLING, H., 1932, Edgeworth's taxation paradox and the nature of demand and supply functions, *Journal of Political Economy 40, 577-616.*

HOTELLING, H., 1935, Demand functions with limited budgets, *Econometrica 3, 66-78.*

HOTELLING, H., 1938, The general welfare in relation to problems of taxation and of railway and utility rates, *Econometrica 6, 242-269.*

HOUTHAKKER, H.S., 1960, Additive preferences, *Econometrica 28, 244-257.*

HOWE, H., R.A. POLLAK and T.J. WALES, 1979, Theory and time series estimation of the quadratic expenditure system, *Econometrica 47, 1231-1247.*

HOWELL, D., 1981, Freedom and capital: prospects for the property-owning democracy *(Basil Blackwell, Oxford).*

INTRILIGATOR, M.D., 1971, Mathematical optimization and economic theory *(Prentice-Hall, Englewood Cliffs, NJ).*

INTRILIGATOR, M.D., 1978, Econometric models, techniques and applications, *Advanced textbooks in economics, vol. 9 (North-Holland, Amsterdam).*

JOSKOW, P. and R. NOLL, 1980, Theory and practice in public regulation: A current overview, *Conference Paper 64 (National Bureau of Economic Research, Cambridge, MA).*

KAHN, A.E., 1970, 1971, The economics of regulation: Principles and institutions, *2 Volumes (Wiley, New York).*

KAMERSCHEN. D.R., 1966, An estimation of the "welfare losses" from monopoly in the American economy, *Western Economic Journal 4, 221-236.*

KAWAMATA, K., 1974, Price distortion and potential welfare, *Econometrica 42, 435-460.*

KAWAMATA, K., 1977, Price distortion and the second best optimum, *Review of Economic Studies 44, 23-29.*

KENDRICK, J.W., 1975, Efficiency incentives and cost factors in public utility automatic revenue adjustment clauses, *Bell Journal of Economics 6, 299-313.*

KEYSER, W. and R. WINDLE, eds., 1978, Public enterprise in the EEC, 7 Volumes *(Sijthoff & Noordhoff, Alphen aan den Rijn).*

KLAPPHOLZ, K., 1972, Equality of opportunity, fairness and efficiency, in: M. Peston and B. Corry, eds., *Essays in honour of Lord Robbins (Weidenfeld and Nicolson, London), 246-289.*

KLEVORICK, A.K., 1966, The graduated fair return: A regulatory proposal, *American Economic Review 56, 477-484.*

KOREN, S., 1964, Sozialisierungsideologie und Verstaatlichungsrealität in Österreich, in: W. Weber, ed., Die Verstaatlichung in Österreich *(Duncker & Humblot, Berlin) 9-339.*

KRELLE, W., 1976, Preistheorie, Vol. I: Monopol- und Oligopoltheorie, Vol. II: Theorie des Polypols, des bilateralen Monopols (Aushandlungstheorie), Theorie mehrstufiger Märkte, gesamtwirtschaftliche Optimalitätsbedingungen (including pricing by public enterprises), *Spieltheoretischer Anhang, 2nd edition (Mohr, Tübingen).*

LANGOHR, H. and C. VIALLET, 1982, Nationalization, compensation and wealth transfer: An empirical note about the French experience 1981-1982, *Mimeo (CIRIEC-Conference on the Concept and Measurement of the Performance of Public Enterprises, Liège).*

LAU, L.J., 1977, Complete systems of consumer demand functions through duality, in: M.D. Intriligator, ed., Frontiers of quantitative economics, *Vol. IIIA (North-Holland, Amsterdam) 59-85.*

LE GRAND, J. and R. ROBINSON, eds., 1984, Privatisation and the welfare state, *(Allen & Unwin, London).*

LEIBENSTEIN, H., 1966, Allocative efficiency vs. "X-efficiency", *American Economic Review 56, 392-415.*

LEIBENSTEIN, H., 1969, Organizational or frictional equilibria, X-efficiency, and the rate of innovation, *Quarterly Journal of Economics 83, 600-623.*

LEIBENSTEIN, H., 1976, Beyond economic man *(Harvard Univ. Press, Cambridge, MA).*

LELAND, H.E. and R.A. MEYER, 1976, Monopoly pricing structures with imperfect discrimination, *Bell Journal of Economics 7, 449-462.*

LINDSAY, I., 1982, Cost and demand functions, appendix to report R 252 *(London Transport Executive, London).*

LIPSEY, R.G. and K. LANCASTER, 1956-57, The general theory of second best, *Review of Economic Studies 24, 11-32.*

LITTLECHILD, S.C., 1970, A game theoretic approach to public utility pricing, *Western Economic Journal 8, 162-166.*

LITTLECHILD, S.C., 1979, Controlling the nationalised industries: quis custodiet ipsos custodes ?, *Series B Discussion Paper No. 56 (University of Birmingham).*

LONDON REGIONAL TRANSPORT ACT 1984 chapter 32 *(Her Majesty's Stationery Office, London).*

LONDON TRANSPORT EXECUTIVE,   Annual report and accounts, *London, annually.*

LUENBERGER, D.C., 1973, Introduction to linear and nonlinear programming *(Addison-Wesley, Reading, MA).*

MALINVAUD, E., 1977, The theory of unemployment reconsidered *(Basil Blackwell, Oxford).*

MANGASARIAN, O.L., 1969, Nonlinear programming *(McGraw-Hill, New York).*

MARCHAND, M., P. PESTIEAU and J.A. WEYMARK, 1982, Discount rates for public enterprises in the presence of alternative financial constraints, in: D. Bös, R.A. Musgrave and J. Wiseman, eds., Public production, *Zeitschrift für Nationalökonomie, Supplementum 2 (Springer, Vienna) 27-50.*

MARCHAND, M., P. PESTIEAU and J.A. WEYMARK, 1984, Discount rates for public enterprises in the presence of alternative constraints: a correction, *Zeitschrift für Nationalökonomie 44, 289-291.*

MARCHAND, M., P. PESTIEAU and H. TULKENS, 1984, The performance of public enterprises: normative, positive and empirical issues, in: M. Marchand,

P. Pestieau and H. Tulkens, eds., The performance of public enterprises *(North-Holland, Amsterdam)*, 3-42.

McCAIN, R.A. 1980, A theory of codetermination, *Zeitschrift für Nationalökonomie* 40, 65-90.

McKENZIE, G. and D. ULPH, 1983, An exact welfare measure, Mimeo, Revised version *(Annual Meeting of the Econometric Society, New York, 1982)*.

METS (Model for evaluating transport subsidies) user manual, 1984, Department of Transport and M.J.N. *Consulting Limited, London.*

MEYER, R.A., 1975, Monopoly pricing and capacity choice under uncertainty, *American Economic Review* 65, 326-337.

MILLWARD, R. and D.M. PARKER, 1983, Public and private enterprise: comparative behaviour and relative efficiency, in: R. Millward - D. Parker - L. Rosenthal - M.T. Sumner - N. Topham, *Public Sector Economics (Longman, London).*

MINASIAN, J.R., 1964, Television pricing and the theory of public goods, *Journal of Law and Economics* 7, 71-80.

MIRMAN, L.J., D. SAMET and Y. TAUMAN, 1983, An axiomatic approach to the allocation of a fixed cost through prices, *Bell Journal of Economics* 14, 139-151.

MIRMAN, L.J. and Y. TAUMAN, 1982, Demand compatible equitable cost sharing prices, *Mathematics of Operations Research* 7,40-56.

MIRRLEES, J.A., 1975, Optimal commodity taxation in a two-class economy, *Journal of Public Economics* 4, 27-33.

MISHAN, E.J., 1976, The use of compensating and equivalent variations in cost-benefit analysis, *Economica* 43, 185-197.

MISHAN, E.J., 1977, The plain truth about consumer surplus, *Zeitschrift für Nationalökonomie* 37, 1-24.

MITCHELL, B.M., W.G. MANNING, Jr. and J.P. ACTON, 1977, Electricity pricing and load management, Foreign experience and California opportunities, *RAND Corporation, Study R-2106 (RAND Corporation, Santa Monica, CA).*

MONOPOLIES AND MERGERS COMMISSION, 1984, London Transport Executive, A report on the arrangements made by the Executive for the maintenance of buses and coaches, *Cmnd 9133 (Her Majesty's Stationery Office, London).*

MUSGRAVE, R.A., 1959, The theory of public finance *(McGraw-Hill, New York).*

NEDO (National Economic Development Office), 1976, A study of U.K. nationalised industries *(Report, appendix volume and several background papers) (Her Majesty's Stationery Office, London).*

NELSON, J.R., ed., 1964, Marginal cost pricing in practice *(Prentice-Hall, Englewood Cliffs, NJ).*

NG, Y.-K., 1979, 1983, Welfare economics, first and second edition *(Macmillan, London).*

NG, Y.-K., 1982, A dollar is a dollar: Efficiency, equality, and third-best policy, *Mimeo (Monash University, Clayton, Vic.).*

NG, Y.-K., 1984, Quasi-pareto social improvements, *American Economic Review 74, 1033-1050.*

NG, Y.-K. and M. WEISSER, 1974, Optimal pricing with a budget constraint - The case of the two-part tariff, *Review of Economic Studies 41, 337-345.*

NISKANEN, W.A., 1971, Bureaucracy and representative government *(Aldine, Chicago, IL).*

NISKANEN, W.A., 1975, Bureaucrats and politicians, *Journal of Law and Economics 18, 617-643.*

OI, W.Y., 1971, A Disneyland dilemma: Two-part tariffs for a Mickey Mouse monopoly, *Quarterly Journal of Economics 85, 77-96.*

OLSEN, M., 1974, On the priority of public problems, in: R. Marris, ed., The corporate society *(Macmillan, London)*, 327-331.

PANZAR. J.C., 1976, A neoclassical approach to peak load pricing, *Bell Journal of Economics 7, 521-530.*

PANZAR, J.C. and R.D. WILLIG, 1977a, Economies of scale in multi-output production, *Quarterly Journal of Economics 91, 481-493.*

PANZAR, J.C. and R.D. WILLIG, 1977b, Free entry and the sustainability of natural monopoly, *Bell Journal of Economics 8, 1-22.*

PAUWELS, W., 1978, The possible perverse behavior of the compensating variation as a welfare ranking, *Zeitschrift für Nationalökonomie 38, 369-378.*

PETERS, W., 1985a, Can inefficient production promote welfare ?, *Zeitschrift für Nationalökonomie, forthcoming.*

PETERS, W., 1985b, The weak dominance of cost inefficient public production for reaching the welfare optimum, *Mimeo (Institute of Economics, University of Bonn).*

PHLIPS, L., 1983, Applied consumption analysis, *Advanced textbooks in economics, vol. 5, second edition (North-Holland, Amsterdam).*

PIGOU, A.C., 1937, Socialism versus capitalism *(Macmillan, London).*

POSNER, R.A., 1975, The social costs of monopoly and regulation, *Journal of Political Economy 83, 807-827.*

PREST, A.R. and D.J. COPPOCK, eds., 1984, The UK economy, A manual of applied economics, *tenth edition (Weidenfeld and Nicolson, London).*

PRIVATISATION AND AFTER: A SYMPOSIUM, 1984, with contributions by D. Heald, T. Sharpe, P. Forsyth, E. Davis, D. Steel and K. Hartley, *Fiscal Studies 5, 36-105.*

QUOILIN, J., 1976, Marginal cost selling in Électricité de France, *Annals of Public and Co-operative Economy 47, 115-141.*

RAMSEY, F., 1927, A contribution to the theory of taxation, *Economic Journal 37, 47-61.*

REES, R., 1982, Principal-agent theory and public enterprise control, *Mimeo (CIRIEC-Conference on the Concept and Measurement of the Performance of Public Enterprises, Liège)*.

REES, R., 1976, 1984, Public enterprise economics, first and second edition *(Weidenfeld and Nicolson, London)*.

REES, R., 1984, The public enterprise game, *Economic Journal 94, conference papers, 109-123*.

REID, G.L. and K. ALLEN, 1970, Nationalized industries *(Penguin, Harmondsworth)*.

RENDLE, G., T. MACK and M.H. FAIRHURST, 1978, Bus and underground travel in London: an analysis of the years 1966 - 1976, *Economic Research Report R 235 (London Transport Executive, London)*.

ROBERTS, K.W.S., 1979, Welfare considerations of nonlinear pricing, *Economic Journal 89, 66-83*.

ROBERTS, K.W.S., 1980a, Interpersonal comparability and social choice theory, *Review of Economic Studies 47, 421-439*.

ROBERTS, K.W.S., 1980b, Possibility theorems with interpersonally comparable welfare levels, *Review of Economic Studies 47, 409-420*.

ROMER, T. and H. ROSENTHAL, 1979, Bureaucrats versus voters: On the political economy of resource allocation by direct democracy, *Quarterly Journal of Economics 93, 563-587*.

SADKA, E., 1976, Social welfare and income distribution, *Econometrica 44, 1239-1251*.

SAMET, D. and Y. TAUMAN, 1982, The determination of marginal cost prices under a set of axioms, *Econometrica 50, 895-909*.

SAMET, D., Y. TAUMAN and I. ZANG, 1981, An application of the Aumann-Shapley prices for cost allocation in transportation problems, *Working Paper 803 (Faculty of Commerce and Business Administration, The*

University of British Columbia, Vancouver).

SAMUELSON, P.A., 1964, Public goods and subscription TV: Correction of the record, *Journal of Law and Economics 7, 81-83.*

SAPPINGTON, D., 1980, Strategic firm behavior under a dynamic regulatory adjustment process, *Bell Journal of Economics 11, 360-372.*

SCHERER, F.M., 1980, Industrial market structure and economic performance, 2nd edition *(Rand McNally, Chicago, IL).*

SCHMALENSEE, R., 1979, The control of natural monopolies *(Heath, Lexington, MA).*

SCHWARTZMAN, D., 1960, The burden of monopoly, *Journal of Political Economy 68, 627-630.*

SCHWEIZER, U., 1980, Measuring social surplus and the Pareto principle, *Mimeo (Institute of Economics, University of Bonn).*

SEIDL,. C., 1983, Gerechtigkeit und Besteuerung unter besonderer Berücksichtigung der Optimalsteuertheorie,in: D. Pohmer, ed., Zur optimalen Besteuerung, *Schriften des Vereins für Socialpolitik N.F. 128 (Duncker & Humblot, Berlin) 163-259.*

SEN, A.K., 1970, Collective choice and social welfare *(Holden-Day, San Francisco, CA, and Oliver & Boyd, Edinburgh).*

SHESHINSKI, E., 1976, Price, quality and quantity regulation in monopoly situations, *Economica 43, 127-137.*

SMEKAL, C., 1963, Die verstaatlichte Industrie in der Marktwirtschaft. Das österreichische Beispiel *(Carl Heymanns, Cologne).*

SPANN, R.M., 1977, Public versus private provision of governmental services, in: T.E. Borcherding, ed., Budgets and bureaucrats: The sources of government growth *(Duke University Press, Durham, NC) 71-89.*

SPENCE, M., 1975, Monopoly, quality, and regulation, *Bell Journal of Economics 6, 417-429.*

SPENCE, M., 1977, Nonlinear prices and welfare, *Journal of Public Economics 8,* *1-18.*

SPREMANN, K., 1978, On welfare implications and efficiency of entrance fee pricing, *Zeitschrift für Nationalökonomie 38, 231-252.*

STEINER, P.O., 1957, Peak loads and efficient pricing, *Quarterly Journal of Economics 71, 585-610.*

SUDIT, E.F., 1979, Automatic rate adjustments based on total factor productivity performance in public utility regulation, in: M.A. Crew, ed., *Problems in public utility economics and regulation (Heath, Lexington, MA),* *55-71.*

TELSON, M.L., 1975, The economics of alternative levels of reliability for electric power generation systems, *Bell Journal of Economics 6, 679-694.*

THIEMEYER, T., 1964, Grenzkostenpreise bei öffentlichen Unternehmen *(Westdeutscher Verlag, Cologne).*

TILLMANN, G., 1981, Efficiency in economies with increasing returns, *Mimeo (Institute of Economics, University of Bonn).*

TIMMER, C.P., 1981, Is there 'curvature' in the Slutsky matrix ?, *Review of Economics and Statistics 63, 395-402.*

TINBERGEN, J., 1967, Economic policy: Principles and design *(North-Holland, Amsterdam).*

TIVEY, L., 1966, Nationalization in British industry *(Jonathan Cape, London).*

TRANSPORT ACT 1983 (Her Majesty's Stationery Office, London).

TRANSPORT COMMITTEE, HOUSE OF COMMONS, 1982, Fifth Report, Transport in London, volume I, *report, appendices and minutes of proceedings (Her Majesty's Stationery Office, London).*

TRANSPORT (LONDON) ACT 1969 (Her Majesty's Stationery Office, London).

TRANSPORT STATISTICS,   Great Britain, 197. - 198. *(Her Majesty's Stationery Office, London).*

TULLOCK, G., 1967, The welfare costs of tariffs, monopolies, and theft, *Western Economic Journal 5, 224-232.*

TURVEY, R., 1968, Optimal pricing and investment in electricity supply *(Allen & Unwin, London).*

TURVEY, R., 1971, Economic analysis and public enterprises *(Allen & Unwin, London).*

TURVEY, R. and D. ANDERSON, 1977, Electricity economics *(Johns Hopkins University Press, Baltimore, ML).*

USHER, D., 1977, The welfare economics of the socialization of commodities, *Journal of Public Economics 8, 151-168.*

VARIAN, H.R., 1978, Microeconomic analysis *(Norton, New York).*

VARTIA, Y.O., 1983, Efficient methods of measuring welfare change and compensated income in terms of ordinary demand functions, *Econometrica 51, 79-98.*

VISSCHER, M.L., 1973, Welfare-maximizing price and output with stochastic demand: Comment, *American Economic Review 63, 224-229.*

VOGELSANG, I. and J. FINSINGER, 1979, A regulatory adjustment process for optimal pricing by multiproduct monopoly firms, *Bell Journal of Economics 10, 157-171.*

WALSH, A.H., 1978, The public's business *(M.I.T. Press, Cambridge, MA).*

WATZKE, R., 1982, The peak-load problem, *Mimeo (Institute of Economics, University of Bonn).*

WEIHS, C., 1984, IAS-System Bonn, Release 4, Benutzerhandbuch, *Mimeo (Institute of Operations Research, University of Bonn).*

WEYMARK, J.A., 1979, A reconciliation of recent results in optimal taxation theory, *Journal of Public Economics 12, 171-189.*

WHITE PAPER, 1967, Nationalised industries: A review of economic and financial objectives, *Cmnd 3437 (Her Majesty's Stationery Office, London).*

WHITE PAPER, 1978, The nationalised industries, *Cmnd 7131 (Her Majesty's Stationery Office, London).*

WHITE PAPER, 1983, Public Transport in London, *Cmnd 9004 (Her Majesty's Stationery Office, London).*

WHITE PAPER, 1984, Buses, *Cmnd 9300 (Her Majesty's Stationery Office, London).*

WIEGARD, W., 1978, Optimale Schattenpreise und Produktionsprogramme für öffentliche Unternehmen *(Lang, Berne).*

WIEGARD, W., 1979, Optimale Preise für öffentliche Güter bei gegebenen Preisstrukturen in der privaten Wirtschaft, *Finanzarchiv N.F. 37, 270-292.*

WIEGARD, W., 1980, Theoretische Überlegungen zu einer schrittweisen Reform der indirekten Steuern, *Jahrbuch für Sozialwissenschaft 31, 1-20.*

WILLIAMSON, O.E., 1966, Peak load pricing and optimal capacity under indivisibility constraints, *American Economic Review 56, 810-827.*

WILLIG, R.D., 1973a, Consumer's surplus: A rigorous cookbook, Technical Report 98, *Economic Series (Institute for Mathematical Studies in the Social Sciences, Stanford University, Stanford, CA).*

WILLIG, R.D., 1973b, Welfare analysis of policies affecting prices and products, *Memo 153 (Center for Research in Economic Growth, Stanford University, Stanford, CA).*

WILLIG, R.D., 1976, Consumer's surplus without apology, *American Economic Review 66, 589-597.*

WILSON, L.S. and M.L. KATZ, 1983, The socialization of commodities, *Journal of Public Economics 20, 347-356.*

WINCH, D.M., 1965, Consumer's surplus and the compensation principle, *American Economic Review 55, 395-423.*

WORCHESTER, D.A., Jr., 1973, New estimates of the welfare loss to monopoly, United States: 1956-69. *Southern Economic Journal 40, 234-246.*

YOSHITAKE, K., 1973, An introduction to public enterprise in Japan *(Sage, Beverly Hills, CA).*

YOUNG, S. and A.V. LOWE, 1974, Intervention in the mixed economy *(Croom-Helm, London).*

INDEX

Advanced Textbooks in Economics

Edited by C. J. Bliss and
M. D. Intriligator